TAROT
AND
INDIVIDUATION

TAROT
AND
INDIVIDUATION
CORRESPONDENCES WITH
CABALA AND ALCHEMY

DR. IRENE GAD

Nicolas-Hays, Inc.
York Beach, Maine

First published in 1994 by
Nicolas-Hays, Inc.
P. O. Box 612
York Beach, ME 03910

Distributed to the trade by
Samuel Weiser, Inc.
P. O. Box 612
York Beach, ME 03910

Library of Congress Cataloging-in-Publication Data
Gad, Irene
    Tarot and individuation : correspondences with cabala and
    alchemy / by Irene Gad.
        p.   cm.
    Includes bibliographical references and index.
    1. Tarot   2. Cabala.   3. Alchemy.   4. Individuation (Psychology)
    -Miscellanea.   I. Title.
    BF1879.T2G337   1994   93-42844
    133.3'2424--dc20   CIP
ISBN 0-89254-026-5
EB

99 98 97 96 95 94
10 9 8 7 6 5 4 3 2 1

Cover: Painting titled *Kreisläufe* (Circulations) by Heinrich Eichmann.
Copyright © 1994 Estate of Heinrich Eichmann. From a collection
privately owned. The painting is gold and oil on black poliment over
wood plate. Reproduced here from a photograph featured in the
Catalog of the Retrospective Exhibition at "Helmhaus," Zurich, 1974.

Typeset in 11 point Palatino

Printed in the United States of America

The paper used in this publication meets the minimum requirements
of the American National Standard for Permanence of Paper for
Printed Library Materials Z39.48-1984.

To My Father

In Memoriam

TABLE OF CONTENTS

LIST OF ILLUSTRATIONS

TABLES

SPREADS

FOREWORD

Symbols are visible representations of an invisible intangible reality—something from inside is revealed in the world outside, something spiritual in something concrete, something special in something ordinary. To understand their meaning, we must attempt to discover the often-elusive reality that exists behind the tangible, as well as the link between them. At times this hidden reality can portray, for example, our psychic essence, or our dreams for the future, or our longings for change. A primary characteristic of symbols is their transcendent capacity; their meaning is therefore inexhaustible, and we are drawn, again and again, to endeavor their interpretation and to ponder the relationship to life of this specific symbol or that particular image.

Some symbols have more meaning for one person than for another, whereas others are collective; that is, from time immemorial they have accompanied individuals through difficult life situations, helping them to understand themselves better and enabling them, if necessary, to make a new start in a different direction. Such archetypal symbols, images of typical human circumstances or life transitions, are depicted by the tarot cards. These cards are not arbitrarily isolated or randomly placed relative to each other, rather they are linked by an inner cohesive sense that must be thoughtfully uncovered, a task masterfully achieved in this book. The individual archetypal images depicted by the cards have provided a constant challenge that has incited new approaches to their interpretation. *Tarot and Individuation* is motivated by such a thrust.

Irene Gad has chosen an intriguing form of amplification, that is, the procedure whereby a symbol is placed in a wider and greater context. (This is the classic method used by C. G. Jung for the interpretation of collective symbols. However, within this method an author can select the particular system[s] that will provide the necessary amplification.) She looks for the reflection of individual tarot images and their meanings in statements from the cabala, in alchemy, as well as in processes involved in individuation as conceived by C. G. Jung. This is a particularly exciting approach. Furthermore, I found her proposition that the cabalistic Tree of Life can provide a framework for the major arcana to be very appropriate. It seems evident to me that if one sees in the tarot certain stages along the road to individuation, one must also find parallels with the Tree of Life, another major symbol for the essence of the forward struggle of humankind. One's possibilities for understanding are considerably expanded by the addition of this rich philosophical background; however, at no time is her outlook imposed upon the reader. Ultimately, she contends, it is the archetypes themselves and our involvement with them that provide a new orientation, that open up a new level of consciousness, that activate personal images, and with them, a new hope of mastering life's challenges will emerge in the soul of the reader.

Dr. Gad describes, in an easily understandable text, the lawful general transformation processes as mirrored by the tarot cards. How these reflections apply in each person's life is left to the reader.

It is my hope that this original work will find many readers who are open to be challenged anew by the mystery of the tarot and the wisdom contained in the collective symbols that they represent.

Verena Kast
St. Gallen, Switzerland

ACKNOWLEDGMENTS

I wish to acknowledge with gratitude the help I received in the completion of this volume. First of all my thanks to Mary Steiner-Geringer who opened the doors to the magic and mystery of the major arcana. Her encyclopedic knowledge placed the symbols of the Tarot in the archetypal context of the Hindu mythopoetic tradition, the I Ching and the cabala so that from the beginning I was able to see, thanks to her, the multifaceted correspondences of the tarot.

I am indebted to the participants in my workshops who have assisted through discussions and arguments, and to my colleagues who offered challenge and insights into psychodynamic associations and applications.

Lastly I wish to express my profound gratitude for the unstinting generosity of April Barrett, who for the last three years has put energy, time and effort in her creative editing of my text, identifying errors and omissions, offering suggestions and comments and who, with her enthusiastic support, helped me through moments when I was ready to give up.

For permission to use copyright material, I gratefully acknowledge the following publishers and authors.

Cambridge University Press for permission to quote from Jane Harrison's *Themis*;

Camden House for permission to quote from Rainer Maria Rilke's *Sonnets to Orpheus*, translated by L. Norris & A. Keele, 1989;

Chiron Publications for permission to quote from Nathan Schwartz-Salant's *The Borderline Personality*, 1988;

Farrar, Straus & Giroux for permission to quote from Mary Lee Settle's *Charley Bland*, 1989;

Harper Collins Publishers for permission to quote from A. T. Mann's *The Mandala Astrological Tarot*, 1988; from Robert Johnson's *Owning Your Own Shadow*, 1991; and from Rainer-Maria Rilke's *Selected Poems*, cited and translated by Robert Bly, 1981;

Inner City Books for permission to quote from M-L. von Franz, *Alchemy*, 1966, and from Sylvia Perera's *Descent to the Goddess*, 1981;

Keter Publishing House for permission to quote from Gershom Scholem's *Kabbalah*, 1974;

A. Knopf/Pantheon Books/Random House for permission to quote from C. G. Jung's *Memories, Dreams, Reflections*; and A. E. Waite's *The Secret Tradition in Alchemy*, 1926;

Labyrinth Publishing, U. K., for permission to quote from Malcom Godwin's *Angels: An Endangered Species*, 1990;

Llewellyn Publications for permission to quote from Kathleen Burt's *Archetypes of the Zodiac*, 1988;

Newcastle Publishing for permission to quote from *New Thoughts on Tarot*, edited by Greer and Pollack, 1989;

North Atlantic Books for permission to quote from Richard Grossinger's *The Alchemical Tradition in the Late 20th Century*, 1983;

Open Court Publishing Co. for permission to quote from Edward Edinger's *Anatomy of the Psyche*, 1985;

Phanes Press for permission to quote from Adam McLean's *Alchemical Mandala*, 1989; and from his *Commentary on the Mutus Liber*, 1991;

Ferd. Piatnik & Söhne for permission to reproduce cards from their "Tarot de Marseille," formerly known as the "Tarot Rhenan."

Princeton University Press for permission to quote from K. Barnaby; P. d'Acierno *C. G. Jung and the Humanities*, 1990; Rudolf Bernoulli's "Spiritual Development as Reflected in Alchemy and Related Disciplines," in *Spiritual Disciplines*, papers from the Eranos Yearbooks, 1970; M-L. von Franz, *Aurora Consurgens*, 1966; C. G. Jung's *Collected Works*; and Erich Neumann's *The Great Mother*, 1955 and his *Origins and History of Consciousness*, 1973.

Quest Books for permission to quote from Stephan Hoeller's *Royal Road*, 1980; and from Charles Poncé, *The Game of Wizards*, 1975 and *Kabbalah*, 1986;

Schiffer Publishing for permission to quote from Robert Hand's *Horoscope Symbols*, 1981;

Shambhala Publications for permission to quote from Esther Harding's *Woman's Mysteries*, 1971;

Spring Publications for permission to quote from James Hillman's "Salt, a Chapter in Alchemical Psychology," in E. Stroud and G. Thomas: *Images of the Untouched*, 1982; and from Erich Neumann's "On the Moon and Matriarchal Consciousness," *Spring*, 1954;

Thames & Hudson for permission to quote from Z'ev ben Shimon Halevi's *Kabbalah*, 1979 and from Stanislas Klossowski de Rola's *Alchemy*, 1973;

University of California Press for permission to quote from Rainer Maria Rilke's *Selected Poems, Bilingual Edition*, trans. by C. F. MacIntyre, 1956;

U. S. Games Systems for permission to quote from Stuart Kaplan's *Classical Tarot*, 1972, and from his *Encyclopedia of Tarot*, 1988, as well as for permission to reproduce the major arcana cards from the Court de Gébelin and Oswald Wirth decks.

Graphics for the part titles and the tarot spreads in Appendix II are by Beverly Schroeder of Schroeder Graphics.

Readers will discover that there are many decks that can be used to read the archetypal symbols of the tarot. I have used the major arcana from three decks to illustrate this book. The Court de Gébelin trumps appear on pages 28, 38, 45, 51, 58, 64, 75, 83, 91, 98, 206, 214, 226, 236, 244, 256, 266, 274, 285, 298, 303, and 315. The Oswald Wirth tarot trumps are shown on pages 34, 42, 48, 55, 61, 72, 79, 88, 95, 102, 211, 221, 232, 240, 252, 262, 270, 280, 290, 299, 311, and 323. In Appendix II, the Tarot Rhenan trumps lead the discussion for each card (pp. 434-454).

INTRODUCTION

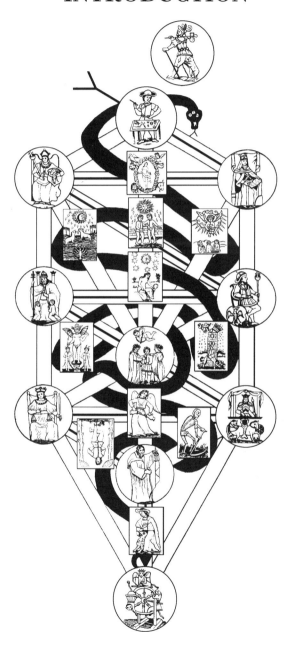

INTRODUCTION

The power of the archetypal structure of the tarot cards never fails to move; one feels lured irresistibly onto its paths, and there one finds what each is prepared to discover. Yet one cannot build on what went on before because, in contrast to alchemy, gnosis, and cabalism, we no longer have any precise knowledge of its history. It may be that we could find, at the very beginning and foundation of the trumps, the idea of correspondences, illustrated by Bernoulli:

> . . . If you strike a match in the dark, you feel the resis-
> tance of the surfaces, you feel the friction, you feel the
> heat that is generated by the rubbing, you hear the
> scratching of the wood, smell the burning sulphur, and
> at the same time see a light flare up. Now, what in real-
> ity is the striking of the match? Is it only the light, only
> the smell, only the scratching, or only the heat? We can-
> not separate these things. The striking of the match is
> precisely the manifestation of an event in different sen-
> sory fields. . . . [O]ur example illustrates an essential
> point: there is no way of proving that a given acoustical
> impression must correspond to a given optical impres-
> sion. These are things that cannot be treated logically.
> (*Spiritual Disciplines*, p. 311).

The method of amplification used in Jungian analysis is based on the idea of correspondences. Its aim is to provide a deeper under-standing of a symbol, to better grasp its content. When images of the collective unconscious appear, one must extend and reinforce their meaning by all the conscious means at our disposal (Jung, CW 7, ¶ 122). The tarot images offer a framework, guides and mileposts on an otherwise uncharted and therefore frightening journey. In a time when belief systems that offer life meaning seem to have failed us, any archetypal imagery that can provide an organizing system could become a container for the psyche in an uncertain world.

All reminiscences from mythology, folklore, "superstitious practices, " have to be recalled insofar as they run in any way parallel to the symbol at hand. In this way we build up a comparative study; we discover the elements out of which the symbol is formed; we ascertain further its original meaning and at the same time become acquainted with the rich world of myth that helps us understand the manifold and profound meanings of our symbol. Through this monographic elaboration, we obtain powerful insight into the marvelously delicate and meaningful network of unconscious imagery (Jung, CW 3, ¶ 330-331). Even the most individual systems are not absolutely unique but offer striking and unmistakable analogies to other systems. From the comparative analysis of many systems, one can discover the typical formations in the background, and this paralleling with other formations will serve to widen the basis upon which the construction rests (Jung, CW 3, ¶ 413). From this vantage point, it doesn't seem unreasonable to look at alchemy and the cabala for amplifications of the meanings of the tarot cards.

TAROT AND CABALA: EARLY CONNECTIONS

Everybody agrees that tarot cards appeared in Western Europe in the 14th century. There is also agreement that, while the usual deck of playing cards continued to be used, the trump cards (the major arcana) practically disappeared from circulation. We are indebted to the French philosopher Antoine Court de Gébelin (1728-1784) for their reemergence. He is quoted as enticing his readers with the following:

> Imagine the surprise which the discovery of an Egyptian book would cause if we learned that a work of the ancient Egyptians still existed in our time. . . . This Egyptian book does exist. . . .[It] is composed of seventy-seven, even seventy-eight sheets or pictures. . . . In a word, this book is the game of tarot (Kaplan, *Encyclopedia of Tarot*, Vol. 1, p. 13).

Surviving the burning of the famous library of Alexandria, reemerging in 1781, and almost 250 years later creating a renewed interest, what message do the major arcana have for us in this time of need? The exploration may be as timely as it might be helpful.

Could it be that the images of the major arcana represented visual prompts connected with an oral tradition and that de Gébelin, born in Provence, may have tapped into its well-kept secret? It is not impossible to imagine that, in a region in which the cabala had flourished during the 11th to the 13th centuries, a region that had also been the scene of a powerful religious movement in the Christian world when the Catharist religious "heresy" spread throughout Languedoc, this region may have preserved the secret esoteric mysteries and may have imparted them to a few initiates by means of the traditional oral transmission.

THE TAROT TRAIL

According to Scholem (*Kabbalah*, p. 45), it is not yet clear to what extent, if any, there was a connection between the new upsurge in Judaism and the profound upheaval in Christianity that found expression in the Catharist movement, for example. There is practically nothing that these two religious movements held in common except, possibly, their view regarding the nature of evil. Nevertheless, it is possible that there were contacts between the different groups, united as they were by a deep and emotional religious awakening, that can no longer be discerned. There is some evidence that the Jews of Provence were well aware of the existence and beliefs of the Cathars as early as the first decades of the 13th century.

Poncé proposes that the particular amalgamation of symbols borrowed from Greek philosophy, alchemy, gnosticism, and cabalism would have found in the intellectual climate of Alexandria an ideal diversity of cultures and philosophical ideas. He further speculates that the Jews alone would have had travel patterns that parallel the appearance of the tarot cards from Spain to France to Italy (*The Game of Wizards*, pp. 156–157). If he is right, it would explain why de Gébelin made reference to Egyptian mysteries and why he would not have needed the Rosetta stone to understand their meaning.

Similarly it does not seem unreasonable to accept the proposition that the tarot cards have some connection to the Gypsies. Whether we accept the idea proposed by Walker (*Secrets of Tarot*, pp. 3–12) that the Gypsies began to migrate westward from India in the ninth century carrying their sacred booklets, the "Bible of Sacred Beliefs," as packs of cards and that they should, therefore, be credited with the dissemination of these occult beliefs, or whether we accept the scientific argument that the Gypsies

appeared in Western Europe only in the 15th century and therefore
cannot be the originators of the cards, one fact remains: the inter-
diction by the Church effectively caused the total disappearance
of the trumps from the cards in circulation after the 15th century.
The south of France, where the cabalists and Cathars found centers of development, also became the traditional gathering places
for Gypsies. To this day, the pilgrimage of Gypsies to Saintes
Maries de-la-Mer is one of the noteworthy regional events in the
Camargue. It may not be unreasonable to accept that the survival
of the alternative religious mystical beliefs that the cards may
illustrate could have been safeguarded by their presentation
under the mask of traditional fortune-telling by the Gypsies.
I cannot help but find this argument plausible, insofar as many
primitive rituals and beliefs have survived around the world
under trivial masks such as children's play (e.g., hopscotch) and
superstitions (e.g., bowing to the new moon). It is also not by
accident that the Fool is the only trump card to survive in common playing cards (as the Joker); the trickster archetype had
insured its own survival!

THE MAJOR ARCANA AS
AN ARCHETYPAL GUIDE

The esoteric teaching of the tarot is a body of knowledge based on
material that was revealed orally because it could not have been
communicated in any other way. It addresses the zone in which
the soul hovers between body and spirit, thus bridging the inner
and outer worlds. I believe that the main theme hidden in the
major arcana is the development, step-by-step, of humankind. It
first depicts our spiritual cosmic background, its condensation
and descent into matter; it then describes what is encountered at
the individual level, as one attempts the journey upward to reconnect body with soul and spirit. Over the centuries the order of
the cards may have shifted, but as in alchemy, it is of no great
importance if one link of the chain sometimes precedes another.

To what use can a Jungian put these cards? It seems to me
that hearing tales about the "homeland" may comfort those who
feel in exile, wherever they are. Knowing about the original harmony and that "as above, so below" may encourage those who are
about to flounder in hopelessness. Moreover, at a very practical
level, the reason for psychic breakdown is often not so much the

invasion of unconscious material, but that the one to whom it happens has too narrow a value system to encompass the experience. One needs sufficient flexibility, either mentally or emotionally, to adopt a broadminded and compassionate attitude toward what comes up from the unconscious without being exploded by it. Jung describes the hoped-for response:

> Analysis should release an experience that grips or falls upon us from above, an experience that has substance and body such as those things which occured to the ancients. If I were to symbolize it I would choose the Annuciation (von Franz, *Alchemy*, p. 269).

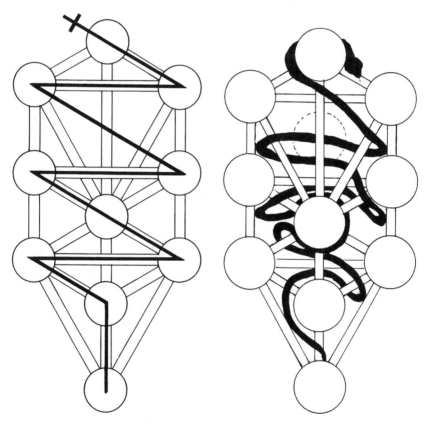

The descending Lightning Flash (*left*) and the ascending Path of the Serpent (*right*), when juxtaposed, may be seen as the archetypal blueprint and its mirror image, the heavenly design and its reflection in human strivings.

Another passage from Jung suggests a profound meaning for two cabalistic representations (see figure on page xxvii) that have never before been connected:

> Accordingly it is with some psychological justification, so it seems to me, that when the Gnostic Nous fell into the power of Physis he assumed the dark chthonic form of the serpent. . . . The dichotomy of God into divinity and humanity and his return to himself in the sacrificial act hold out the comforting doctrine that in man's own darkness there is a hidden light that shall once again return to its source, and that this light actually *wanted* to descend into the darkness in order to deliver the Enchained One who languishes there, and lead him to light everlasting (CW 11, ¶ 380).

THE MAJOR ARCANA AND THE TREE OF LIFE

In Lurianic cabalism (a 16th-century school), it is taught that contemplating the *sephirot* (the ten emanations on the Tree of Life) with faith and hope promotes secret movements from above that evoke the inner lights of each heavenly attribute and turn them toward the supplicating soul below. This perception of the full bliss of the Infinite exerts a beneficial influence, and one becomes conscious of the divine spirit embedded in one's soul. This revelation is represented by the descending Lightning Flash (see figure on page xxvii).

Having had the revelation of the existence of the absolute, impersonal, formless Infinite One, the cabalist strives to restore his or her rightful divinity by slowly redeeming the spirit exiled in matter. This is the slow, painful, upward climb represented by the Path of the Serpent.

Frequently applied to the Path of the Serpent is a statement from a venerable cabalistic work, the "Old Commentary":

> Let the disciple seize hold of the tail of the serpent of wisdom, and having with firmness grasped it, let him follow it into the deepest center of the Hall of Wisdom (Hoeller, 1980, p. 105).

According to Halevi, an "outcrop" of the cabala may be found in the design of the tarot cards:

> The occult feature of the system is the set of major trumps, twenty-two picture cards which relate to the [twenty-two] paths [numbered 11-32, see figure on p. xxxii] on the Tree and the stages of evolution (*Kabbalah*, p. 79).

However, he mentions elsewhere that the most significant fact concerning these twenty-two paths, which connect the ten *sephirot* (figure on p. xxxii), is that some major key must have been lost that may explain the plethora of different interpretations of what these paths represent. Although the *sephirot* are always the same with regard to function, the paths are not constant in the same way. He even says that "they are like chameleons, but with definite colours, only able to assume a certain range of variants" (*Introduction to the Cabala*, p. 97). To connect the minor arcana with the *sephirot* and assign the major arcana to the paths, as some occultists have, has never made sense. I believe, as Halevi seems to (*Introduction to the Cabala* p. 102), that we have reason to speculate that the Tree of Life is the frame of reference needed to complete the impressive graphic symbolism of the major arcana.

I have therefore chosen to amplify, in Part I of this book, the symbolism of the first ten trump cards with the meanings associated with the ten *sephirot* and the first ten letters of the Hebrew alphabet (correspondences between the twenty-two Hebrew letters and the twenty-two tarot cards can be traced to the 19th century). However, instead of assigning the next eleven cards to the paths, as in the occult tradition of the Golden Dawn, I have elected to follow the meandering Path of the Serpent, in which I see a map for the process of individuation. Just as the Jewish mystic following this path was striving to know God with his heart and believed that he could thus unify the physical with the spiritual, the process of individuation guides us through the dark night of the soul to the recognition of the divine spark within, providing thus a bridge between the Self and the Eternal Spirit. The complex figure that emerges (see figure on p. xxx) connects the descent of revelation of the divine (providing the needed spiritual container) with the mileposts for the difficult journey upward.

Major Arcana and the Tree of Life. *Round figures* represent the first ten trumps, placed in the positions occupied by the sephirot on the Tree of Life and connected by the Lightning Flash. *Rectangular figures* represent trumps eleven through twenty-one, placed in ascending order along the Path of the Serpent.

The following passage from Wirth gave me a much needed confirmation of my dual approach:

> Each half of the Tarot must, as a whole, have its general significance, contrasting with that of the other half. . . . The first eleven arcana mark the progress of an essentially active agent, sentient and autonomous. The last eleven, on the contrary, bring to play a passive subject, unaware, sensitive or impulsive, and deprived of initiative (1990, p. 27).

In addition to the appropriate Hebrew letters, cards XI through XXI are amplified (in Part II of this book) with images of alchemy to better grasp the stage in the process of individuation that they depict. The last trump, the Fool (card 0), is placed outside the Tree of Life at the level of *Ain Sof* (see the chapter, "Cabala and Tarot"), the Absolute All, endless and unknowable. This attribution of the Fool reconnects with that of de Gébelin, who assigned the zero trump to *Ain Sof*.

Following the cabalistic tradition, the Lightning Flash traces the principles of creation from *Ain Sof* to the first Divine Emanation in *Kether* (the first *sephira*) to its end in the tenth (last) *sephirot, Malkuth*, the lowest, most condensed point, embedded in the material world. The process of evolution or return to the Light, in contrast, follows the reverse Path of the Serpent. Bias (*The Way Back*) attempted to use the twenty-two paths for the way back. In order to do that he had to proceed in reverse, starting with path thirty-two and ending with path eleven. In the process he associated each path with one of the major arcana images, but these followed no orderly sequence (jumping from card II to XVII to XV, XVIII, IV, XIV, I, XIX, III, VI, XVI, IX, X, VIII, XIII, VII, V, XI, XXI, XX, XII, and 0). Although he also used the image of the Path of the Serpent, I was unable to locate his explanation for the connections he proposed.

Ashcroft-Nowicki (*The Shining Paths*) also presents us with an ascending journey on the Tree of Life, similarly starting with path thirty-two and ending with path eleven. She assigns tarot cards to the paths, following the Golden Dawn tradition, starting with card XXI and ending with card 0; in the process she also reverses the order of cards IV (the Emperor) and XVII (the

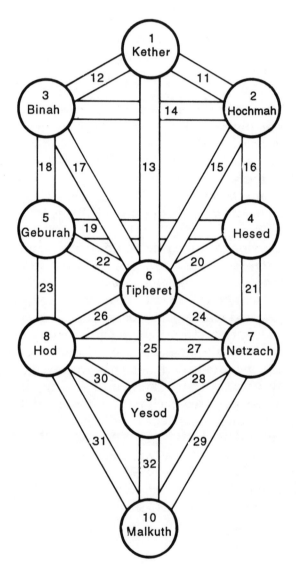

The connecting paths.

Star[s]), just as cards VIII (Justice) and XI (Strength) had been reversed in the Rider deck. Again I found no explanation for the discrepancy between the ascending stages and the descending numbers of the paths and the tarot cards. Given that the twenty-two sephirotic paths start from *Kether* and end in *Malkuth* and thus duplicate the descending direction already indicated by the Lightning Flash, they may be helpful in describing the cabalistic third journey of redescent, the Obligation of Service. Indeed, upon reaching a certain point of ascent, the privilege of just receiving is ended and the third major phase, that of imparting, begins. According to Halevi,

> . . . this not only means assisting those above and helping those below, but direct involvement in the Work of Unification, as the Kabbalah is sometimes called, so as to bring the inner and the outer worlds, and the upper and the lower levels of existence together in consciousness (*Work of the Kabbalist*, p. 15).

While knowledge of the homeland can be comforting in exile as we flounder through darkness in the fear and confusion of our own attempts to return, any markings on the way back are both reassuring and guiding. Caught in our complexes, imprisoned by their archetypal core, we are in need of helpful archetypal energies to assist in our fight for inner freedom.

Persuaded that symbolic amplifications reflect psychic continuity of meaning, von Franz (*Aurora Consurgens*, pp. 154, 191) argues convincingly that we must provide people in danger of being overwhelmed by unconscious contents with as much symbolic knowledge as we can to prepare the ground ahead of time; then when the experience comes, they have a net in which to catch and reexpress it. It seems to me that, in times of transition, when the supporting structures no longer hold either at the individual or at the collective level, we need inner guides to replace the outer signposts that have been lost or destroyed. The richness of our archetypal endowment is slumbering in the depths of our psyche, and just as in astrology planetary transits activate kindred energies of the natal chart, so trigger symbols can miraculously awaken inner archetypal resources. I believe the images of the major arcana to be such trigger symbols, appearing and disappearing throughout history in times of transition and need.

A passage from Greene's *The Outer Planets and Their Cycles* (p. 221ff.) gives historical meaning to the hide-and-seek game that the tarot trumps seem to have been playing. Greene remarks that, in November 1983, Pluto entered Scorpio, a transit through its own sign that will last for about eighteen years and that takes place every 250 years. Deciding to investigate the historical mutations that have occurred during the various times when Pluto has moved through Scorpio in the past, she discovered that both in 1240 and in 1490 new philosophical ideas began to percolate through the Western world. In 1240, this included the flowering of cabalism, of gnosticism, and the Cathar heresy, followed by the crusade to destroy it. In 1490, there was the dawn of the Florentine Renaissance, the rediscovery of the alchemical manuscript *Corpus Hermeticus*, and a renewed interest in the cabala, in gnosticism, and in the tarot. These ideas transformed some of the structures of society that until then had seemed unchanging. Again this revolutionary spirit reemerged 250 years later during the next transit of Pluto and coincided with the socially reforming ideas of the "Encyclopedists," who were instrumental in framing a new social order that found expression in the French Revolution. This was also the time when de Gébelin, in his *Monde Primitif* (published in 1781) intriguingly referred to the tarot cards thus:

> If . . . there survived to this day an ancient Egyptian work, a book that escaped the flames which devoured their superb libraries, and which contained, unsullied, their teachings. . . . [Everyone] . . . would be in a hurry to acquaint themselves with such a precious and remarkable book; . . . people's surprise would . . . reach its highest pitch when, . . . assured that nobody ever imagined it to be Egyptian, that it was held to be nothing, . . . and that the fruits of infinite wisdom were regarded as a collection of fantastic pictures without the least significance in themselves . . . . Nevertheless, it is true: this Egyptian book, sole relic of their superb libraries, survives today (Innes, *The Tarot*, p. 7).

Generally de Gébelin's speculation has been disregarded because of the fact that the Rosetta stone was not discovered until 1799, so that even if he had had such a book, he would not have been able to decipher it. However, given the occult information to which he was most likely privy, this dismissal is unwarranted.

I am aware, upon presenting another book on the tarot, that not only do I presume to connect the images of tarot with alchemy and the Jungian process of individuation, but I also dare enter the old controversial field of the relationships between the cabala and the tarot. Some will find the connections I have proposed difficult to accept. For example, upon confronting this book cabalistic scholars will probably maintain the stance quite clearly expressed by Scholem:

> The many books written on the Kabbalah in the 19th and 20th centuries by various theosophists and mystics lacked any basic knowledge and very rarely contributed to the field. Similarly, the activities of French and English occultists contributed nothing and only served to create considerable confusion between the teachings of the Kabbalah and their own totally unrelated inventions, such as the alleged Kabbalistic origin of the Tarot cards. To this category belong the many and widely read book of Eliphas Levi (actually Alphonse Louis Constant, 1810-1875), Papus (Gerard Encausse, 1868-1916), and Aleister Crowley (1875-1946), all of whom had an infinitesimal knowledge of Kabbalah that did not prevent them from freely drawing on their imagination instead. The comprehensive works of A. E. Waite, on the other hand, were essentially rather confused compilations made from second-hand sources (*Kabbalah*, p. 203).

Moreover, there is little chance that my attributions may be accepted by occult practitioners. One has only to peruse the first part of the second volume of Knight's *Practical Guide to Qabalistic Symbolism* to realize that the basic attitude of occultists is to be "sectarian, exclusive and self-righteous." Knight continues:

> In any case, apart from the validity of Oswald Wirth's remark: "A symbol can always be studied from an infinite number of points of view; and each thinker has the right to discover in the symbol a new meaning corresponding to the logic of his own conceptions, " there is also the chance that we might be all wrong—to judge from A. E. Waite's last pronouncements on the subject

in *The Holy Kabbalah* (1929): "The supposed symbolism of
the Tarot . . . becomes disorganized if there is any doubt
as to the attribution of its Trump Cards to the Hebrew
Alphabet. . . . I may go further and say that the true
nature of Tarot symbolism is perhaps a secret in
the hands of a very few persons, and outside that circle
operators and writers may combine the cards as they
like, but they will never find the right way (p. 231).

At the recent (1989) Newcastle Symposium "New Thoughts on
the Tarot," it became evident that the barriers that had separated
the three major trends in tarot (i.e., exploration of the esoteric tradition, readings and meditation on the images as tools for healing,
and development of new decks) are no longer as precise nor as
insurmountable as in the past. The symposium emphasized that
tarot imagery helps the user to open to new levels of consciousness and stressed the importance of trusting the images themselves, without necessarily adopting the original conceptions of
esoteric tradition (p. 5). Because this new stance comes from
experts who have chosen tarot ". . . as a tool for assisting themselves and others in self-awareness, meeting challenges, discovering purpose and meaning in life's experiences, and creating
change in accordance with a vision of wholeness (p. 7) . . .," I dare
add my own contribution to theirs.

Miraculous statues of the Virgin were often the center of great
gatherings during the Middle Ages. Once, while a pilgrimage to
such was in progress, it is said that a strange event took place:
after a long day with frequent services in the church and a multitude of activities in the country fair just outside it, the pilgrims
and the fair-goers had retired, exhausted. In the dimly lit church,
a friar was snuffing out the last sputtering candles when, all of a
sudden, he was alerted by some unexpected noise coming from
the direction of the miraculous statue. Hiding behind successive
pillars, the friar stealthily advanced toward it and was even more
agitated at seeing long shadows on the wall gesticulating suspi-
ciously. Grabbing a candlestick as a weapon against what seemed
to be a malefactor, he reached the chapel with great trepidation

and faced what, for him, was an outrageous sight. Here, in front of the Most Blessed Virgin, a juggler was standing, almost a beggar, barefoot and shabby, and he was juggling his colored balls just as he had done during the day for all the ordinary people at the fair. For the friar this was the ultimate desecration and too much to tolerate. He seized the sinner by the neck and dragged him then and there to the abbot. But with a mild voice and kind eyes the abbot gently asked, "What were you about, my son?" "Alas," the poor juggler replied, "I was taught no prayers; I have no money. The only thing I have to give is my skill as a juggler. I thought the Blessed Lady might find joy in my offering."

I hope the reader will accept mine.

Part I
THE FLASH OF LIGHTNING

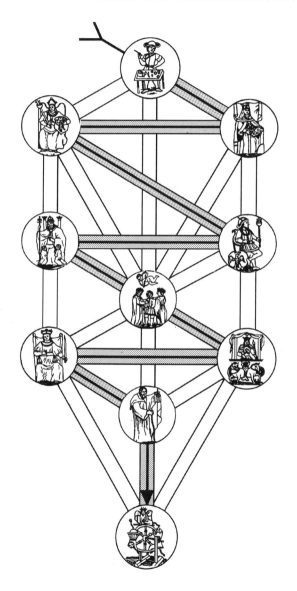

CABALA AND TAROT

> Sometimes even the learned on the subject are more ignorant of its true nature than those who have had a passing contact with it (Halevi, *Kabbalah*, p. 24).

The tarot brings the images of the cabala closer to our own grasp, and at the same time, the cabala amplifies the tarot images. In part, the cabalistic enrichment of the first ten images seems to activate the archetypal backdrop and provides us with a spiritual context. This chapter attempts to present a summary of the most important ideas of the cabala in order to connect it to the tarot imagery and to see where and how they may intersect.

THE EMERGENCE OF THE CABALA

The central tendency of classic Jewish tradition was to focus on the purity of the monotheistic idea of God, worshiped in abstract manner, which was in sharp contrast to the nature religions of the surrounding peoples, and to reject any images or symbols along with the mythical world in which these might have appeared. By the same token, this brought about an "emptying" of the concept of God. Purity was bought at the expense of liveliness and connectedness. What makes God alive to the believer is precisely that which connects the divine with the human soul, and the first casualty of the process that attempts to purify the concept of God is the living religious symbol. It is against this rigid, intellectual "demystification" that the cabalistic movement emerged.

Cabala, meaning tradition (specifically, esoteric tradition), is the term most commonly used for the collection of ideas expressed in Judaism that appeared around the 12th century. The cabala comprises a multiplicity of systems and semisystems of complex and often contradictory and paradoxical aspects and seems to have come to light in the south of France from underground sources originating very probably in the East. The cabalistic movement appeared in the same region and at the same time as a similar reaction against the rigidity of Christian dogma that was expressed in the neo-Manichaeism of the Catharist heresy (Scholem, "Kabbala und Mythus," p. 291).

The cabala contains the knowledge of the Absolute projected upon the realm of creation; it depicts the way in which multiplicity evolves out of unity. It considers the world not as something created but as an emanation visualized as a ray of light or as a lightning flash (see figure 1).

Cabalistic beliefs are expressed in the Tree of Life with its ten *sephirot* (the plural of *sephira*, meaning cipher or number) and the related twenty-two letters of the Hebrew alphabet with their numerical values. The *sephirot* are God's attributes, containers, or tools. They can also be defined in terms of human experience, given that each human is created in God's image. This is not an abstract idea but refers to essential life forms and the substantive wisdom they contain. These spheres (the *sephirot*) are the roots of all polarities; they are also the stages of spiritual ascent. Each was assigned by the Cabalist a Hebrew letter as the key to the contained experiences. Each *sephira* not only reveals certain energies but also influences the direction of their flow, which can turn either upward or downward. Beyond the manifestations that we know, there are many other possible manifestations, and out of the Tree of Life many other Trees of Life can grow.

There are two movements, one focusing on the practical, the other on the theoretical cabala. The theoretical cabala assigns to the letters and numbers the entire knowledge about the hidden forces active in the world. It is a teaching about the divine emanation, which strives to comprehend the relationships between the world and the Absolute. The practical cabala strives for action; it attempts to influence and change circumstances and proposes to achieve this through permutations of God's names; each name is

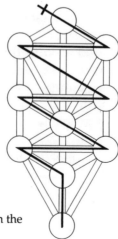

Figure 1. The Lightning Flash on the Tree of Life.

TABLE 1. Hebrew Letters,
Their Significance, and Astrological Attributions.*

Number	Letter	Name	Category	Significance of Name	Element, Planet, Sign
1	א	Aleph	Mother	Ox	Air
2	ב	Beth	Double	House	Mercury
3	ג	Gimel	Double	Camel	Moon
4	ד	Daleth	Double	Door	Venus
5	ה	He	Simple	Window	Aries
6	ו	Vau	Simple	Peg, nail	Taurus
7	ז	Zain	Simple	Weapon, sword	Gemini
8	ח	Cheth	Simple	Enclosure, fence	Cancer
9	ט	Teth	Simple	Serpent	Leo
10	י	Yod	Simple	Hand	Virgo
11	כ	Caph	Double	Palm of the hand	Jupiter
12	ל	Lamed	Simple	Ox goad	Libra
13	מ	Mem	Mother	Water	Water
14	נ	Nun	Simple	Fish	Scorpio
15	ס	Sameck	Simple	Prop, support	Sagittarius
16	ע	Ayin	Simple	Eye	Capricorn
17	פ	Pe	Double	Mouth	Mars
18	צ	Tsade	Simple	Fishing hook	Aquarius
19	ק	Coph	Simple	Back of the head	Pisces
20	ר	Resh	Double	Head	Sun
21	ש	Shin	Mother	Tooth	Fire
22	ת	Tau	Double	Sign of the cross	Saturn

* Modified from Bias, p. xviii, and Knight, Vol. 2, "Index of Paths."

composed of letters, and the letters correspond to numbers. The cabala thus teaches the specific use of the Hebrew letters. Some peculiarities of Hebrew writing allow one to juggle them and obtain from an original text a new form and a new meaning.

The letters have a double meaning, both as numbers and as designations of a mystical being projected upon creation. They are a model for the innumerable, apparently unrelated, phenomena that belong to the "one body" of the divine. The Hebrew alphabet was thus used by the cabalists as a technique for attaining a profound understanding of God, of humankind, and of the world.

Because the old Hebrew language did not have vowels in its written text, all readers of the sacred texts had to introduce vowels where deemed appropriate. This resulted in great confusion, and by about A.D. 600-800, certain signs were introduced in specific places for particular vowels in order to ensure that the sacred texts were uniform. Nevertheless, different methods of inserting the vowels were developed, and some, kept secret by the persons initiated into the esoteric doctrine, were not disclosed to the rest of the population.

The letters, the category, and associated numbers of the Hebrew alphabet are shown in Table 1 on page 5. Also shown are the significance and the astrological attributions of each letter. Note that ancient Hebrew astrology did not use earth. Readers should also note that the recently discovered planets (Uranus, Neptune, Pluto) were not known.

THE LETTERS

In the cabalist tradition, the Hebrew letters have certain correspondences and are assigned certain basic values: *mother, double,* and *simple.* Three letters are designated *mother.* They are said to be derived from the primary letter *yod* (numbered 10). These letters are: *aleph,* the Beginning (numbered 1); *mem,* the Middle (numbered 13); and *shin,* the End (numbered 21 or the all-encompassing 0). See figure 2 on page 7. These three letters permeate all and govern all. (Indeed, the number 3 is contained in the group of three mother letters, in the group of seven [3 + 4] double letters, and in the group of twelve [3 × 4] simple letters; the number 3 can therefore also be designated as *mother).* The *mother letters* are connected with the elements and alchemical symbols. See Table 2.

TABLE 2. MOTHER LETTERS, ELEMENTS, AND ALCHEMICAL SUBSTANCES.*

Number	Letter	Element	Alchemical Substance
1	Aleph	Air	Mercury
13	Mem	Water	Salt
21 or 0	Shin	Fire	Sulphur

* Modified from Kaplan: *Classical Tarot,* p. 55.

Figure 2. Hebrew letters, planets, and the signs of the zodiac.

Seven letters, randomly scattered, are designated *double letters* because of their double (harsh and soft) pronounciation. (See Table 3 on page 8.) They are connected with the seven planets and their corresponding basic metals. (Other systems have connected them to the seven chakras or to the seven days of the week.)

Finally, the remaining twelve letters are designated as *simple*. (See Table 4 on page 8.) They follow a precise sequence that has been connected by some to the zodiac and its twelve signs.

Between the later biblical and post-Temple periods (sixth century B.C. to A.D. sixth century), Jewish mystics drew much influence from the cultures that surrounded them. Out of this came an amalgam of metaphysical systems. In figure 3 (page 8) the name of God and the Hebrew letters are related to Greek and Babylonian concepts of the principles that govern the universe. At the center is the tetragrammaton, YHVH, arranged in the form of the Tetractys of Pythagoras ($1 + 2 + 3 + 4 = 10$) and marked at the corners by the three mother letters, of air, water, and fire. The circles show the remaining nineteen letters of the Hebrew alphabet arranged to correspond to the seven planets and the twelve zodiacal signs (Halevi, *Kabbalah*, p. 66).

TABLE 3. DOUBLE LETTERS AND CORRESPONDENCES.*

Number	Letter	Planet	Metal
2	Beth	Mercury	Mercury
3	Gimel	Moon	Silver
4	Daleth	Venus	Copper
11	Caph	Jupiter	Tin
17	Pe	Mars	Iron
20	Resh	Sun	Gold
22 or 21	Tau	Saturn	Lead

* From Kaplan: *Classical Tarot*, p. 55.

TABLE 4. SIMPLE LETTERS AND CORRESPONDENCES.*

Number	Letter	Sign	Number	Letter	Sign
5	He	Aries	12	Lamed	Libra
6	Vau	Taurus	14	Nun	Scorpio
7	Zain	Gemini	15	Samekh	Sagittarius
8	Cheth	Cancer	16	Ayin	Capricorn
9	Teth	Leo	18	Tsade	Aquarius
10	Yod	Virgo	19	Coph	Pisces

* From Kaplan: *Classical Tarot*, p. 55.

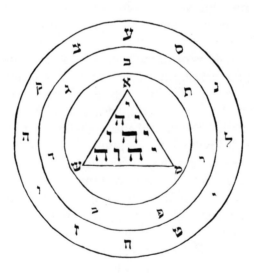

Figure 3. Tetragrammaton as Tetractys and Hebrew letters. From Halevi, *Kabbalah*, p. 66.

The general concept behind these attributions is that each letter represents three categories: a letter, a number, and an idea. Each letter, each word, and as we shall see, each tarot card are thereby endowed with a power connected to the universal forces they represent. If one learns to align these creative forces, one will be able to influence the universe.

THE EMANATION

God has no definite name before He becomes manifest in the *sephirot*. It is only as God emerges from the nameless nothingness that He becomes nameable and so can be spoken of; hence, the name is the carrier of the essential being, and knowledge of the name bestows upon the knower secret, magic powers.

In the cabala the transcendent is called *Ain*. In Hebrew *Ain* means *No Thing* because God is beyond existence. (In *The Power of Myth*, [p. 62], Joseph Campbell points out that God is beyond all categories, even that of existence/nonexistence.) *Ain* is neither above nor below, neither movement nor stillness. The Absolute All is called *Ain Sof*, meaning endlessness, the attribute of God who is everywhere. *Ain Sof* is the totality of what is and is not, the immanent God. It is infinite, without form, and without substance. For the cabalists, *Ain Sof* means *primary cause*, the unlimited and undefinable (see figure 4 on page 10).

The primary will is called *Ain Sof Aur*. This is the absolute wisdom in which thought, thinker, and thinking are one. It remains unchanged even when it becomes the origin of multiplicity, movement, and change.

These three aspects, namely, *Ain, Ain Sof*, and *Ain Sof Aur*, are above the Tree of Life, beyond *Kether*, the crown, through which the creator manifests itself. Here, above the Tree of Life, is the unmanifest of negative existence, the liminal space between God and creation. Void is the still background of all existence. Mirror of mirrors, this noninterfering of negative existence permits the most perfect reflection of creation.

Nearest to our relative universe is the limitless light, or *Ain Sof Aur*, that penetrates everything. The next veil is endlessness, or *Ain Sof*, the first step toward manifestation, the point at which the ultimate void, *Ain*, begins to be focused from the limitless into the limited. Beyond *Ain Sof Aur* there is the Absolute, and beyond that, the Void. These three stages describe the condensation, the

AIN: Void, Absolute Nothing

AIN SOF: Absolute, All Endless

AIN SOF AUR: Limitless, Endless Light

Kether: Crown
Hochmah: Wisdom
Binah: Understanding
Hesed: Mercy
Geburah: Judgement
Tipheret: Beauty
Netzah: Eternity
Hod: Reverberation
Yesod: Foundation
Malkuth: Kingdom

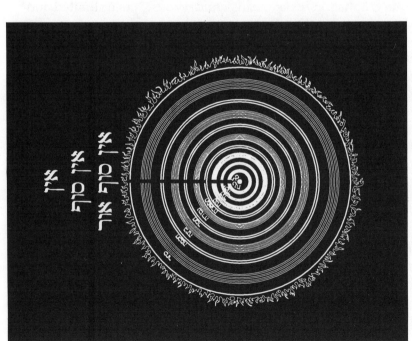

Figure 4. The first manifestation. The *Ain* and *Ain Sof* of Absolute Nothing and All contract to leave a void in which the Divine Will manifests ten Divine Attributes. Will (*Ain Sof Aur*) is visualized as a beam traveling inward from the periphery of Eternal Light to call forth, create form, and make the initial manifestation of the Divine (Halevi, *Kabbalah*, pp. 6, 38).

crystallization of Being that penetrates All, the point at the center of a circumferenceless sphere that is everywhere and nowhere and contains everything. Jung quotes Angelus Silesius who expresses it this way: "God is my centre when I close him in, And my circumference when I melt in him" (Jung, CW 14, ¶ 284).

This inclusive point is called the First Crown, the first name of God, the I AM. All possibilities are included in it. Negative existence is the most difficult to perceive. It is that which is and is not. In it the Absolute is separated from the created, although it is constantly present in it.

THE SEPHIROT AND THE TREE OF LIFE

In contrast to finite things, the Absolute is infinite, beyond time and space, caused and determined by nothing else but itself. Its essence can be defined only by negatives, such as "unrecognizable" or "inconceivable," because humankind cannot conceive of the highest aspect of the Divine.

This highest level of Divinity cannot connect directly with the world. That is why God created the sephirot as tools. These ten sephirot are to be conceived of as active origin, as *logos*. They are mediators through which humanity can see God, up to a point, as through a veil or "through a glass darkly" (I Corinthians 13:12). Our material world can only be a reflection of an original world, infinity.

The ten sephirot are the basic principles of all that is counted, measured, and weighed. From the perspective of the relationship between God and the world, the sephirot present the ten stages on the Tree of Life through which God descends toward humankind and through which humanity ascends toward the divine.

The sephirot have also been presented as concentric circles in another arrangement in which the central emanation is surrounded by ten concentric spheres, with the power of emanation diminishing as it moves farther from the center (see figure 4 on p. 10). They consist of essence, substance, and intelligence; they mediate between creation and the original cause that they depict and contain. They are at the same time finite and infinite: finite with respect to the Absolute, infinite with respect to the created.

The differences between the sephirot reside in the degree to which these attributes are manifested. Depending upon the perspective from which we perceive them, the sephirot are defined as: the ten orders of souls and spirits; the ten names of the ten attributes of God; the ten aspects by which God's essence is revealed, the ten shapes the essence takes, the ten prophetic degrees to which these shapes and this essence are communicated. In contemplative ecstasy, they are the ten ways of glory enjoyed; in cosmology, they, are the ten words through which God has created and animated everything. The ten sephirot are like bodies with a soul that is of divine substance. As principles of created things, they form Adam Kadmon, Primordial Man, the mystical image of God, the symbolic unitary personality.

In order to understand the cabala, one has to contemplate the sephirot thoroughly because, without these keys, one cannot understand the Tree of Life. One must also understand the meaning of each sephira at the human level; the divine image must shine through human concepts. The sephirot are considered emanations and not creations because the emanated cannot be separated from the principle of its origin. The Tree of Life is a schema representing objectively the principles at work in the universe. (See figure 5.) It indicates the flow of forces and the lawful ways of interaction from the divine to the lowliest world. From the human perspective the inaccessible develops in it into definable aspects; from the perspective of *Ain Sof*, it is the outpouring of the flow of life. In the cabala, the reconciliation of opposites into their synthesis, the totality, is projected upon the sphere of the divine in the sephirotic realm and not upon the darkness of matter, as in alchemy.

From the human perspective, development of consciousness out of the unconscious seems automatic. It seems a symbolic mirroring of the development of divine wisdom and knowledge, a simultaneous event in the human and the divine realms. The universe hovers between two poles: the All and the Nothing; both can become entry or exit points for the Absolute. The Absolute has no direct contact with creation; it supports it like the silence behind every sound. Without this negative reality, nothing could exist, just as shadow could not exist without light. The veil of negative existence spans itself between the absolute and the relative universes. The absolute universe is beyond eternity; it is timeless, without form or substance. The relative universe is the manifestation of creation as the unfolding of divine impulse in flower and fruit, only to pass away and return to its origin and be reborn.

The structure of the Tree of Life is based on the emanation of the First Crown. Beyond *Kether* there is no image; it passes into

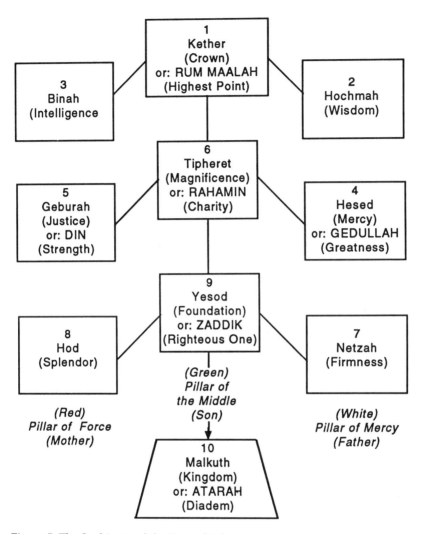

Figure 5. The Sephirot and the Tree of Life.

the infinite and is at times identified with it. After the original impulse of the Creative, a sequence develops that begins with the first sephira, is followed by the next eight sephirot, and converges into the last. This progression is called *Kav*, or the Lightning Flash. Beginning in *Kether* (the Crown) the first sephira, it flows toward *Hochmah* (wisdom), the second sephira; there at the top of the active column, it manifests itself as dynamic potentiality, after which it crosses over to *Binah* (understanding), the third sephira, on the top of the passive column. The active and passive columns are also called the pillars of mercy and severity, respectively.

After having left *Binah* behind, the Lightning Flash touches a point under the crown, *Ruah al Kodesh*, the non-sephira *Daat*. *Daat* is also called the abyss. This is because it is the access and exit point to manifest existence, of that which is above. It is the space through which higher influences can have direct contact with the seven sephirot of construction (as they are known) below, and a place where anything beneath may contact that which is above (Halevi, *Work of the Kabbalist*, p. 9). The flow of emanation now crosses the central pillar of equilibrium and reaches the fourth sephira, *Hesed* (mercy or loving kindness). The force that has thus returned to the active pillar takes over its expansive quality before moving on to the fifth sephira, *Geburah* (judgment). There the force is checked, equalized, and adapted before it reaches *Tipheret* (beauty), the sixth sephira, on the central pillar, a central point of balance, the synthesis of form and energy, existence, creativity, and preservation. *Tipheret* is in direct relation to the Crown through the central pillar. Only the unmanifest sephira *Daat* (knowledge) separates *Tipheret*, the mirror of *Kether* on a lower level, from its object. Next, the emanation reaches the active seventh sephira, *Netzah* (eternity or endurance); at this point the active quality is renewed, thus preserving the level of energy. Again the emanation passes over to the passive eighth sephira, *Hod* (reverberation). From here the flash touches the central pillar in *Yesod* (foundation), the ninth sephira. Directly under *Yesod* on the central pillar is the tenth sephira, *Malkuth* (kingdom). In this sephira all active and passive energies are reunited and condensed. This manifestation of creation, the Lightning Flash (*arrows*), is depicted in figure 6.

The image this evokes is that of a candle flickering in the midst of ten mirrors, set one within the other, each of a different color. The light of the candle is reflected differently in each of the ten mirrors, although it is the same light. The sephirot have been regarded as reflections, as divine powers, or as vessels. Mystics have depicted them as hands, faces, or garments in which God clothes himself to enable humankind to look at his light, which without them, would be blinding. By looking at one garment, the individual can progressively contemplate the next and the next, and in this way the sephirot serve as rungs of the ladder of ascent toward the perception of God. There is general agreement that in

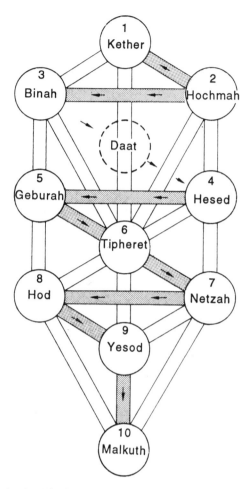

Figure 6. The Lightning Flash and the Sephirot on the Tree of Life.

the sephirot are seen divine attributes, emanations of God's will from the beginning of time until, at the end of time, they will return to the void.

THE FOUR WORLDS

Just as in our physical world there are four elements, namely, fire, air, water, and earth, so there are four corresponding levels in the relative universe. These four levels form a chain of increasing density and are subject to an increasing number of laws and restrictions the farther they are removed from the source of emanation.

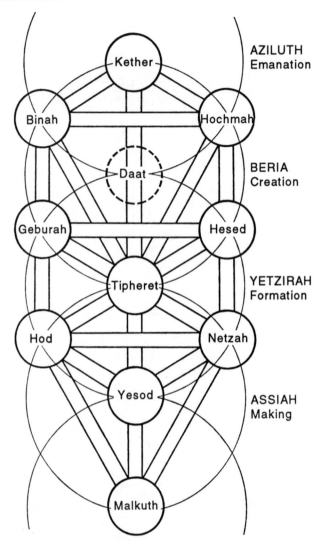

Figure 7. The Four Worlds and the Tree of Life. (Modified from Halevi: *The Way of Kabbalah*, p. 33.)

Each level is a fainter mirror than the preceding one; in our world the image is so dim that we can often only see the surface. Traditionally these four levels are: *Aziluth, Beria, Yetzirah,* and *Assiah.* (See figure 7.) *Aziluth* is the world of first emanation, the archetypal world in its dynamic aspect. The fire conceived in *Aziluth* appears as air in *Beria,* the world of creation, and then as a watery flowing world of form in *Yetzirah,* out of which emerges the fourth, earthy world of action, *Assiah.* On the Tree of Life the four elemental levels are represented by four general horizontal demarcations. *Kether, Hochmah,* and *Binah* form the upper triangle, *Aziluth.* The upper rectangle, *Beria,* is formed by *Hochmah, Binah, Geburah,* and *Hesed;* the lower rectangle, *Yetzirah,* is formed by *Hesed, Geburah, Netzah,* and *Hod; Tipheret* is in the center. The lower triangle *Assiah* is composed of *Netzah, Hod,* and *Malkuth,* with *Yesod* in its center. (See figure 8.)

For the human being, the four worlds correspond to different levels of existence. The lower triangle is the physical body; the

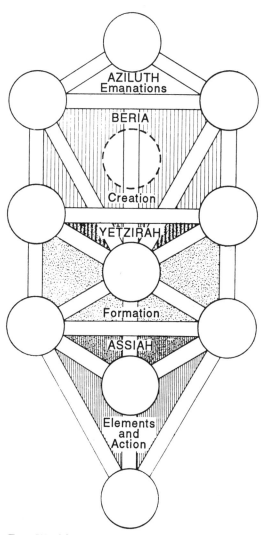

Figure 8. The Four Worlds.

lower rectangle corresponds to the level of feeling; the upper rectangle corresponds to the level of thinking; and the upper triangle corresponds to the level of spirit. Each level contains activities and qualities of the preceding level.

Aziluth is the archetypal world of pure idea and spirit, of pure will, and of the dynamic aspect of the divine attributes, the calling. It is formed by the first three sephirot, namely, *Kether*, *Hochmah*, and *Binah*, which are also known as the supernals.

In *Aziluth* the substance of the divine, the emanation, is inseparable from its original principle. The world of *Beria* follows. It is the world of the divine spheres associated with air as a symbol of divine intellect. It represents the manifestations of divine assignment that put in motion the planned processes. At this level the concepts are not yet visible and numerous possibilities remain open. *Beria*, the world of creation, is manifestation through conception from the union of *Binah*, the mother of mothers, with *Hochmah*, the father of fathers. *Binah*, the throne, the sea, the immovable, original waters bearing the potential of life, is fertilized by pneuma, the spermatic air.

The world of *Yetzirah*, as the kingdom of forms, is closer to our understanding. Here the flowing creative process unfolds. This is the place in which figures come and go, appear and disappear again, and this is the level at which the formless takes shape. *Hesed* and *Geburah* reflect *Hochmah* and *Binah* at a lower level; they govern creation and destruction. They find balance and synthesis in *Tipheret*, the highest level that can be reached by ordinary humans.

The lowest level, *Assiah*, is connected to the earth and is expressed in action, the tool of feeling. *Assiah* is the world we live in. Here the creative impulse of the *Beria* world manifests itself. *Assiah*, the world of substance and action, depicts the same forces on the level of instinct, of the senses, and of passion. *Hod* represents the negative force that expresses itself in reactions and constraints opposed to the natural flow and exchange. *Netzah* is the sphere of expansion, intelligence, and mindfulness associated with earth. It is also the sphere of instinctual cycles and preoccupation with pain and pleasure. *Yesod* is the foundation of the ego, whereas *Malkuth* is seen as the elementary, physical body.

The four worlds penetrate the entire existence. They are depicted in multiple ways—as circles, as halls, as gardens, as Adam Kadmon—but no image can seize their reality. They can be seen as concentric circles in which *Aziluth* is at the periphery and *Assiah* is at the center surrounded by endless light. Behind it are the veils of negative existence contained in the Absolute; inside the concentric circles, the darkness increases.

The cabalists also conceived of a negative-mirror arrangement called *Qliphot*. This is the world of demonic destructive forces created by distortion, imbalance, or atrophy. They have correspondences on all levels of the universe but are out of the line of evolution and development. They become manifest either in hyperactivity or in rigid resistance. In the latter case, their symbol is the shells, which point out through their immobility the hindrance of flow and separation from the living process. Qliphotic situations show stagnation in the developmental process in which the imbalance between opposite poles of energy creates fixation or a regression to primitive dependency. A disturbance of the natural interplay of the sephirot can generate such an imbalance; when permanent, it creates unfortunate situations: on a large scale, world wars; on an individual level, madness or possession. They appear as evil, but their cosmic task is to reveal the area in which the work is incomplete.

SEPHIROT AND TAROT

The tarot may contain the wisdom of the cabala, the secret mystical teachings of the Hebrews. The twenty-two major arcana of the tarot correspond to the twenty-two letters of the Hebrew alphabet and to their respective numbers. (See Table 5 on page 20 for the Hebrew attributions to the major arcana.) These connections become evident when we focus on their practical symbolism. Indeed, both systems refer to the idea of the descent of the creative spirit in progressive stages from emanation to fixation in matter and to the concept that, from an original unity, one reaches—through division and multiplication—the limitless circle containing the All. Both systems are also connected with the teachings contained in alchemy and astrology, including the relationship between planets, signs of the zodiac, numbers, colors, and shapes. They both contain a gnosis, that is, an in-depth knowledge of divine revelation transmitted by tradition.

The relationship between the cabala and tarot is evident not only in the letter-image analogies but also in the idea of the emanation of creative forces descending through the ten sephirot, from spirit to matter into progressively denser levels. The sephirot were also assigned the numbers 1 through 10. If we consider

TABLE 5. HEBREW LETTER ATTRIBUTIONS TO THE MAJOR ARCANA.*

Hebrew		Levi, Papus and Wirth	Waite
Aleph	א	I The Magician or Juggler	0 The Fool
Beth	ב	II The Female Pope	I The Magician
Gimel	ג	III The Empress	II The High Priestess
Daleth	ד	IIII The Emperor	III The Empress
Heh	ה	V The Pope	IIII The Emperor
Vau	ו	VI Vice & Virtue or The Lovers	V The Hierophant
Zain	ז	VII The Chariot	VI The Lovers
Cheth	ח	VIII Justice	VII The Chariot
Teth	ט	VIIII The Hermit	VIII Fortitude or Strength
Yod	י	X The Wheel of Fortune	VIIII The Hermit
Caph	כ	XI Strength	X The Wheel of Fortune
Lamed	ל	XII The Hanged Man	XI Justice
Mem	מ	XIII Death	XII The Hanged Man
Nun	נ	XIIII Temperance	XIII Death
Sameck	ס	XV The Devil	XIIII Temperance
Ayin	ע	XVI The Tower	XV The Devil
Pe	פ	XVII The Star	XVI The Tower
Tsade	צ	XVIII The Moon	XVII The Star
Coph	ק	XVIIII The Sun	XVIII The Moon
Resh	ר	XX Judgment	XVIIII The Sun
Shin	ש	0 The Fool	XX Judgment
Tau	ת	XXI The Universe or The World	XXI The Universe or The World

* Letters of the Hebrew alphabet are shown with their attributions according to Levi, Papus, and Wirth, as compared with those of Waite (Kaplan, *Classical Tarot*, p. 63).

that the ten sephirot and the first ten cards of the major arcana deal with the same concept, then card XI would represent a turning point, much like the surface of a mirror in which one sees the reflection of the sequence of the first ten. Here would be the beginning of the phenomenal world in which creative forces find their expression. The twelfth card would mirror the turning point itself (in reality it does represent a reversal, inasmuch as its image is the Hanged Man). The last card is the Fool (seen from below, it is the first); it would mirror the One, the Beginning.

The twenty-two parts of the created universe are constituted by the primal elements air, water, and fire, plus the seven planets known to the ancients, and the twelve signs of the zodiac. Each of these twenty-two parts is connected to a corresponding letter of the Hebrew alphabet. This makes each letter a powerful symbol related to an already well-established system (element, planet, sign). According to Le Mieux (1985, p.12), the ancient alphabet is certainly the basic key to the tarot.

The divine truths of the Hebrew scriptures expressed in the twenty-two letters were contained both in their phonetic sense as well as in their numerological symbolism. The gradual development of the world out of nothing is shown by the fundamental tetrade and hexade.

> At first there was nothing but the Holy Spirit at the head of all things and represented by the number 1 of the tetrade. Subsequently, the entire universe proceeded in gradual and successive emanations, the air, number 2, emanating from the spirit; water, number 3, proceeded from the air; and ether or fire, number 4, emanated from the water (Kaplan, 1972, p. 53).

The elements of the hexade (which follows the tetrade) represent height, depth, and the four cardinal points. The center of the hexade contains the Holy Temple, which supports the whole. If we were to look at the major arcana in this context, we would recognize the first four forming a *quaternio*, followed by the next six trumps, with Strength in the center appropriately supporting the whole, as shown in figure 9 on page 22.

Kether, the Crown, is the sephira of origin, out of which emerge all others. It comprises past, present, and future. It is first emanation and return, God's name: I AM THAT I AM. All dynamic forces and laws remain motionless in time and space until the unfolding of cosmic cycles begins. The Crown is thus also called *waiting*. With this sephira the revelation of divine mystery begins; however, this light remains at the same time in darkness. We cannot conceive of it because it touches the unlimited. The interchangeable light and darkness is represented by the letter *aleph* as symbol of the physical vehicle. In the tarot it is card I, the Magician, the letter *aleph*, the number 1.

The flash of light that emanates from *Kether* and that can be compared to lightning becomes manifest in the second sephira, *Hochmah*. This is the point beyond all categories of time and space that attracts and discards forms; it is wisdom, active introverted

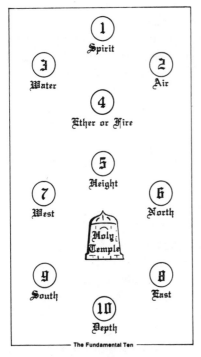
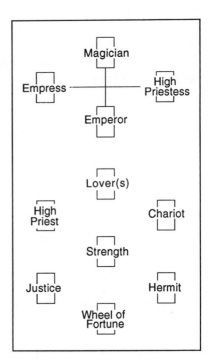

Figure 9. The fundamental ten and the first eleven trumps.

intellect, revelation. It is creative thought, *logos*, the mediator, the word, knowledge, the brain. *Hochmah* shapes the beginning of things and is identified in gnosis with Sophia. In the tarot it is card II, the High Priestess, the letter *beth*, the number 2.

From here on the Divine Will manifests itself in the world. This corresponds to the third sephira, *Binah*, the intellect with its passive, reflecting capacity. It represents discriminating reason, tradition, directed thinking, timely space. It is the emergence of unconscious contents into consciousness, the heart. Binah is the capacity to understand through reflection. It is the recipient of wisdom and also negation as the capacity to differentiate between meaningful and meaningless limitation and shaping. In the tarot it is card III, the Empress, the letter *gimel*, the number 3.

These three supernals form the plan of the universe, creative thought, the upper triad of the Tree of Life, which depicts essential potentials of recognition, the realm of reason. These sephirot belong to the sphere of the divine; one speaks of them only with greatest awe, in fear and in trembling.

The Lightning Flash now touches the fourth sephira, *Hesed*, mercy, active inner feeling, life, love, greatness, power, the male soul. It is the feeling tendency for pity, and forgiveness that tempers the severity and discipline of the next sephira. In the tarot it is card IV, the Emperor, the letter *daleth*, the number 4.

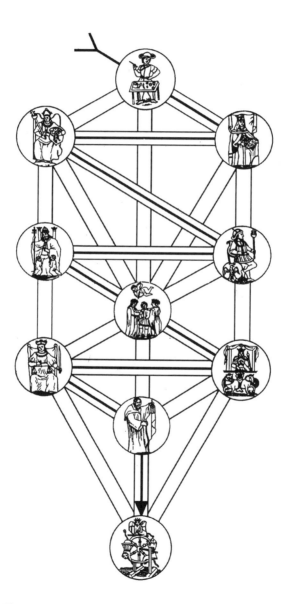

Figure 10. The Lightning Flash, the Tree of Life, and the first ten trumps.

Next the Lightning Flash touches the fifth sephira, *Geburah*, justice. This is the dark passive principle of severe judgment, hardness of decision, punishment, rigor, duty, morality, discipline. When tempered, it can show tolerance and generosity; unrestricted, it may become the origin of evil. In the tarot it is card V, the High Priest, the letter *he*, the number 5.

Now the Light shines in the central sixth sephira, *Tipheret*, the heart of the Tree of Life, beauty in relationship with all the other sephirot. *Tipheret* with *Hesed* and *Geburah* form the triad of the divine soul; with *Hochmah* and *Binah* it forms the triad of the divine spirit. The original forces of the life of the soul, *Hesed* (pity, mercy) and *Geburah* (judgment), to which are subordinated the details of existence, are reconciled by *Tipheret*, the sphere in which love can act without dissolving in itself. In the tarot it is card VI, the Lover (the decision), the letter *vau*, the number 6.

In the second triad, what was formless until now takes form: *Hesed* and *Geburah* reflect *Hochmah* and *Binah* on a lower plane; they govern creation and destruction; they find their synthesis in *Tipheret*. *Tipheret* is the Self that observes All, the angel that watches over the outcome of the conflict between the human and the divine will.

Below *Tipheret* the Lightning Flash manifests itself in two complementary attributes: an active one, expressed in the seventh sephira, *Netzah* (eternity), and a passive one, in the eighth sephira, *Hod* (reverberation). Traditionally they have been called victory and glory; however, eternity and reverberation (or reflection) correspond better to their roots. When related to human beings, they correspond to the vital active processes (*Netzah*) or to passive recognition and control (*Hod*), both coordinating principles that direct movement and progress.

Netzah is the sphere of thinking, intelligence, understanding, of considerate reaction, or of the contrived and the artificial. *Hod* represents negative power that expresses itself in flow and change, in thoughtless reactions, the conflict between the forced and the natural. In the tarot, they are card VII, the Chariot, the letter *zain*, the number 7; and card VIII, Justice, the letter *heth*, the number 8.

On the pillar of equilibrium, the Lightning Flash next encounters the ninth sephira, *Yesod* (foundation), which collects all the preceding energies. The first of its attributes is generation; further Trees of Life evolve from it. In the sephira *Yesod*, collection and flow are united. This is the sphere of the moon, of its constant fluctuations comprised, nevertheless, in a coherent system. If we look at the Tree of Life as a schema of the human body, *Yesod* corresponds to the genitals. *Yesod* is said to be the spout for the "higher waters," the connection between vital energy and the individual; psychologically, it is the sphere of human consciousness. Moreover *Yesod*, placed directly under *Tipheret*, reflects an image in the image, a mirror in the mirror. This mirroring requires purity, and for this reason, the *Zaddik*, the Righteous One, is represented in *Yesod*; thus the idea of sexual abstinence may be traced back to this need for purity. In us this sephira appears as the ego that projects the persona; when purified it can mirror the Self. The majority of our perceptions and willful actions are connected to this sephira, the foundation, background, germinative latent energy. In the tarot it is card IX, the Hermit, the letter *teth*, the number 9.

The third triad is dynamic. It relates to realization and thus to embodiment. It is associated with water as the expression of feeling that manifests itself in changing forms. The triple triad of the Tree of Life is condensed into one sephira, *Malkuth* (the kingdom), the presence of God in matter.

Malkuth is the material world, the body and brain of a human being, but at the same time it is also the "kingdom of God," the synthesis of all the sephirot. Often *Malkuth* is called the *lower Shekina*, the feminine side of God, the Queen of heaven, daughter and bride, banished in matter. The desire and concern of the cabala is to reunite the *Shekina* with God. *Malkuth* is the gate through which the human being begins to climb; here is the first rung of the ladder of spiritual ascent. Just as the Crown contains the germ of the entire tree, the tree appears condensed in the kingdom. In the tarot it is card X, the Wheel of Fortune, the letter *yod*, the number 10. In the manifest world, the higher world becomes visible because *Malkuth* is *Kether*, spirit in matter. It is given to human beings to develop and refine themselves until they see the upper world and the way in which the substances and energies it contains penetrate their bodies.

The Tree of Life is like a germ cell that has divided itself into ten segments. These ten sephirot, through which flows the Divine Emanation, are linked by paths in a complex network connecting each sephira to all the other sephirot. The letters and numbers indicating the paths clarify the quality and the experience of the paths. The fundamental law of the paths attests to their unity, although it appears under manifold aspects. The diverse interpretations of the paths by different cabalistic schools may be due to the fact that some significant key of esoteric knowledge may have been lost. The paths are not as permanent as the sephirot. According to their nature, they depend upon both of the sephirot that they connect. (See figure 11.) They are charged with positive or negative energy from these poles and can also assume the character of the triad. The paths show the flow of forces downward from the divine to the lowest world, with all the lawful interactions. Some esoteric schools have attributed the tarot cards to the paths (Kaplan, 1972, p. 58ff).

The Tree of Life is fourfold: roots, trunk, branches, and fruit; also it is will, spirit, heart, and love of the divine. It is a watered garden when *Yesod* fills it up. In us it is the embodiment, the

Figure 11. The Lightning Flash, the Path of the Serpent, the Tree of Life, and the thirty-two paths. (Modified from Bias, *The Way Back*, p. 28.)

combination of the four elements and their interaction that keeps us alive; it is the quintessence of the elements. The Tree is a microcosm and, in its essence, a true image of the macrocosm. Because of this similarity, we can have insight into the parallel principles of the inner and the outer universes.

The chapters that follow explore the first ten tarot cards and correspondences with the cabala and alchemy, as well as with their astrological attributions. The interpretation that is offered reflects their placement in the downward progression represented by the Lightning Flash.

I
THE MAGICIAN

א

The Hebrew letter *aleph* means breath of life, unity, stability, power. The first sephira on the Tree of Life is *Kether*, the Crown. The human being bears within himself countless possibilities that can be molded by a will striving toward higher developmental levels to reach the ultimate goal: return to the original Unity. In this process the world is changed.

The figure of the Magician reminds us of a hermaphrodite, sufficient unto himself and self-fertilizing. His bearing evokes the letter *aleph* (his arms are positioned in the shape of the letter, which some have interpreted as representing a phallus and two testicles), the Unity, the integration and connection of good and evil, above and below. *Aleph* takes the shape of totality in the Magician, the creative thought of the Most High. It is the principle of emanation, the beginning and the endpoint of the return. His image also represents Adam Kadmon, the primordial man in whom God has insufflated his divine breath. Mediated by him, by the focused pointedness of his thinking, creative forces can become active in the temporal world. His materiality makes dealings on the manifest plane possible. As master of nature, he must recognize and understand God-given laws and see to their application. He has his own world, restricted and narrowed by the limits imposed upon him; yet as image of God, it is his task to see to the development of divine laws. When these laws are followed, both poles of any energy find complementarity and achieve unity in duality. When they are disregarded, conflict ensues and opposition emerges. This opposition constellates the darkness, the origin of all phenomenological experience.

The Magician represents the forces that manifest themselves in the lawful cycle of the world of appearances; that is, unfolding/limitation/regression, life and death. He is the thinking principle, the breath of life that enlivens and directs all powers yet is enclosed by them. In his negative aspect, he represents the destruction brought about by disrespect for universal law.

The Magician is focused purpose; out of the manifold multiplicity comes number one. He is the point in the center: existence that is articulated by this center point, joined and organized. Like the heart, it is the organ of intuitive, penetrating knowledge that transcends and illuminates all other abilities of the soul. Connected to breath, it becomes active; and combined with the spark of spirit, it becomes seed. This seed is the substance immanent in all psychic and intellectual forms. It comprises qualities such as vitality, intelligence, etc., all those spiritual recognitions that are acquired during this lifetime but that outlast death. It contains inborn remnants, readiness for reaction, images, all the real continuity of individuality. The seed is thrown in the universe; the realm of form is activated. Individuals can now experience themselves as centerpoint.

The number 1 emerges out of the numberless, the immaterial point: $1 \times 1 = 1$; $1 \div 1 = 1$. The number 1 stands for the indivisible and, therefore, eternal center, a unity that cannot be grasped by humans because everything perceivable is manifold and therefore divisible. It is the coincidence of absolute freedom and absolute determination in one, the identity of absolute truth with unconditional and undisturbable existence. It is also identity in the unity of intellect and sensitivity, of sluggishness and spontaneity of human knowledge.

Yet, as we have said, Adam Kadmon represents Primordial Man, God's idea of the human being, the model He used when He created humankind, the edge and mediator between microcosm and macrocosm.

THEMES, ASSOCIATIONS, CORRESPONDENCES

The Magician denotes consciousness, breath of life, intuition, attention, the father principle. He signifies the absolute container of all possibilities, the archetypes. He also connotes humanity capable of influencing the natural order. In addition, the Magician stands for unity as a principle of action, the Word. He is the human as the highest being in the relative universe, the relationship between Self and ego.

The ideogram for this card is

Astrological amplification: Traditionally the element air has been attributed to the Magician because air is associated with the Hebrew letter *aleph*. Air was seen as the intermediary between heaven and earth, the soul or warm pneuma, "the very fine substance of God," and caused in man "enthusiasm" (literally, inspiration by the God) (von Franz, *Aurora Consurgens*, p. 291). The general consensus seems to be that the most appropriate connection of the Magician is to the planet Mercury, although other correlations have been made to the element fire, to the Sun, and to Aries or Leo. While both air and Mercury seem to correspond to the energy one senses in this card (air because it is the symbol of divine breath and Mercury because of its connections to both the alchemical *Mercurius* and to the trickster Hermes, messenger of the gods), neither the Sun nor the fire signs Aries or Leo, seem to be as suitable. Even less appropriate are the planets Neptune and Pluto, attributed by some to the sephira *Kether* (Halevi, *Work of the Kabbalist*, p. 138, and Zain, quoted by Knight, *Practical Guide*, p. 229).

Cabalistic amplification:

> When the Concealed of the Concealed wished to reveal himself, he first made a single point: the Infinite was entirely unknown, and diffused no light before this luminous point broke through into vision (Zohar).

The first emanation, *Kether*, is an external aspect of *Ain Sof*. The Infinite became manifest through *zimzum* (contraction) in *Kether*, the first sephira. The cosmic tree grows downward from its root in this first sephira; from here all other sephirot emanate successively, each one revealing an additional stage of the divine process (Scholem, *Kabbalah*, p. 106). Jung quotes the following:

> Of the "crown" (Kether) it is said: "It is the source which makes the tree fruitful and drives the sap through all its arms and branches. For You, Lord of the Worlds . . . You water the tree from that source, which, like the soul in the body, spreads life everywhere" (CW 14, ¶ 159, n. 209).

Psychologically, this mystical "primal nothingness," out of which all the other sephirot emanate, can be interpreted to mean that the collective unconscious is, to begin with, a completely undifferentiated totality that appears in a wealth of archetypal figures and images (Hurwitz, 1968, p.170).

Alchemical amplification: The beginning is One, male and single, and from that one the whole creation proceeded (von Franz, *Aurora Consurgens*, p. 254). The key formula expressing the idea of the unity of the *prima* and *ultima materia*, which pervades the whole of alchemy from the beginning to the end, is: "One is the stone, one the medicine, one the vessel, and one the disposition" (*Unus est lapis, una medicina, unum vas, unum regimen, unaque dispositio*) [Jung, CW 12, ¶ 404, n. 12]. According to Jung (CW 9/1, ¶ 289), in its true apotheosis the *prima materia* is "a light above all lights," a power that contains in itself all the powers of the upper and nether regions. He quotes the ancients:

> The center of nature is "the point originated by God," the "sun point" in the egg. . . . Out of this little point, . . . the wisdom of God made with the creative Word the "huge machine" of the world. . . . [T]his is the bird of Hermes, or the spirit Mercurius. . . . The point symbolizes light and fire, also the Godhead in so far as light is an" image of God" or an "exemplar of the Deity." This spherical light modelled on the point is also the "shining or illuminating body" that dwells in the heart of man (Jung, CW 14, ¶ 41).

The center, a fundamental idea in alchemy, contains the "indivisible point," which is indestructible and eternal; its physical counterpart is gold, a symbol of eternity. From the spiritual perspective,

> . . . nothing is more like God than the centre, for it occupies no space, and cannot be grasped, seen or measured. Such too is the nature of God and the spirits. Therefore the center is an "infinite abyss of mysteries" (Jung, CW 13, ¶ 186).

Psychological interpretation: The Magician personifies the thinking One preceding the unborn idea, that unconscious instant between two conscious moments, that treasure trove of all that is visible and invisible. Around the Magician, a masculine center, extends the feminine generative element within which the creative can become differentiated; without differentiation the Eternal Being remains unmanifest. Recognition becomes possible only when Unity can mirror itself in duality.

The Magician's activity generates movement unperceivable as such. He is the mover of all that moves, stream of consciousness, flow of nourishment. He is energy, sound/light, the carefully focused will, and the paradox. He confronts us with God's dual nature: unity and the syzygy, light and darkness, existence and essence. The Magician is at the same time the transcendent, unchangeable aspect, resting immovable in himself. He is power, expansion, timelessness, but also the beginning stage of the duality of body/soul. In this duality of spirit/matter we can penetrate and go deeper into the creative, changeable aspects of cyclic activity: the soul mediates between spirit and body; it is the locus of intellectual and emotional consciousness, subtle and coarse at the same time; the body is matter, life, consciousness; it represents the creative powers that use time as their tool, expanding and shaping. The Magician gives the first glimpse of the fundamental unity between the individual and the universal, the ephemeral and the eternal, the central point and the infinite circumference, the drop of water containing the ocean.

Jungian interpretation: At the personal level, the Magician represents for Jung a negative father figure, the animus of the Terrible Mother, or the personification of the water of death (CW 5, ¶ 541-543). However, Jung also sees in the Magician an archetypal figure expressing unknown and inhuman feelings and attributes that "are not in any sense applicable to a human personality" (CW 7, ¶ 149). At a deeper level Jung also saw in the Magician the embodiment of a very powerful energy, ambiguous and ambivalent, holding the lost keys of paradise (CW 9/1, ¶ 398).

> The shaman climbs the magic tree in order to find his true self in the upper world. [In this ecstatic journey] he acquires his "mystical organs," which in some sort constitute his true and complete spiritual personality (Jung, CW 13, ¶ 462).

One cannot help but identify Jung's view of the shaman with the energy that the Magician evokes. The released "mana" energizes the "midpoint" of the personality and promotes the next step forward on the road to individuation (CW 7, ¶ 378, 382). Once again

Jung warns against the fatal dangers associated with identification with the archetype and points out that, should the ego lay claim to mana energy, it does so at grave peril to itself. Von Franz saw this danger when she warned:

> In therapy it is not we who connect the individual with God, even that would be a megalomaniac presumption of the psychotherapist. . . . If you are with an analysand the only way you may perhaps help is by always saying: I don't know, but let us ask God. By that you prevent the analysand from drawing rash conscious conclusions or seducing you into making them (*Alchemy*, p. 142).

Even more dangerous may be a seduction into a *folie à deux* in which the analyst is lured into an unconscious identification with the archetypal forces he or she is called upon to invoke. In their profession, psychotherapists are all at risk, as Guggenbuhl-Craig described so well in his *Power in the Helping Professions*, but as Jungians, this danger increases even more due to the archetypal material constellated in the analytic session. The more people seek out Jungians in the hope of finding a guide for their spiritual quest, the greater the need for analysts to become aware of any "uncooked" aspect of their own psyches that might potentially get caught in the lofty heights of their self-ideal. Only when the helper can see her- or himself as a humble channel of redeeming energies can the self- and other-destructiveness of the "mana personality" be averted. Analysts, and Jungian analysts in particular, need to be able to emerge from these powerful experiences in the shamanic world; they need to contain them in the *temenos* of the therapeutic space and to leave them behind as they leave that space. The shamanic garb must be left behind on the analytic armchair, and the pedestrian ego must be reclaimed as the analyst goes out the office door.

SYMBOLIC LANGUAGE OF THE IMAGE

Card I depicts a magician wearing the hat of infinity and holding a staff in his raised hand, while on the table in front of him there is a cup, a sword, and a coin. Out of endlessness appears this one crossing point; out of the innumerable, miraculously, the number 1 springs. Lao-tse names this the most mysterious event: the revelation of the undisclosed. Indeed, it is the very door of revelation that we are facing here: out of the ungraspable, the informal, the first one in human shape is born, and out of this first one all will develop. The building stones of the All are *in potentia* in front of him: the masculine staff; the feminine cup; the sword, which is the union of the two; and the pentacle or coin, which is neither. These objects have also been connected by some to the four worlds, the four elements, and the four functions. See Table 6.

The wand means quintessence, rhythmic swinging, wind, wood. It suggests mastery, activity, goal-oriented active power, communication on equivalent or different levels. It may signify limitation, regulation, time and space, death and resurrection. We are reminded here that God commanded Abraham to sacrifice his son, whom He then replaced with a goat. Through the vertically held staff, the sacrificial fire was lit by the flash of lightning that poured through it. This is not difficult to associate with the Lightning Flash that begins on the Tree of Life in *Kether*, the Crown (with which the Magician is associated), and descends through all the sephirot until it reaches *Malkuth*, the Kingdom, the last and tenth sephira. Here, too, the Magician holds the wand in his left

TABLE 6. THE FOUR SUITS, WORLDS, ELEMENTS, AND FUNCTIONS.

Tarot Card Suit	Playing Card Suit	World	Element	Function
Wand	Club	*Aziluth*	Fire	Intuition
Sword	Spade	*Beria*	Air	Thinking
Cup	Heart	*Yetzirah*	Water	Feeling
Pentacle	Diamond	*Assiah*	Earth	Sensation

hand, which points upward. This gesture also signifies that he knows and has mastered the eternal principles to which all becoming and all vanishing are subjected. He is connected to the heavens and the unmanifest. His staff is a symbol of the power of command, of the masculine principle, of willpower, action, strength, and dignity. The two poles of any staff show that all dualities can be integrated in unity, that opposites have a basic identity, balance, and equivalence. The wand can also be regarded as a lance, spear, or ray. It may be the staff around which the two snakes of Asklepios intertwine. It can itself become a snake, as it did when Moses threw his staff to the ground. As snake, it represents emerging consciousness, transmutation, renewal; it is a symbol of the chthonic world, fiery and cold, conscious and primitive at the same time. Finally the staff connotes using, being active, acting, directed active energy, command, reality as foundation and discipline, lawfulness, matter, space, time, death and new beginning, here and there, connection and separation, protection, concentration.

The cup represents the feminine, form-giving, the containing principle, imagination, love, beauty, wisdom, and justice. The cup is the opening of the mind/spirit. It can be a reminder of the bitter cup of sacrifice and suffering.

The sword, with its cross-shaped hilt, is a symbol of the union of the masculine and feminine principles, the reconciliation of opposites, daring, enthusiasm, passion, and transformation. It is the discriminating stance, analytic thinking, begetting logos, the capacity to cut asunder, to separate, a sunny generative power.

The coin symbolizes matter in which the spiritual values are embedded, outward life, people and the generative power, possession of money, commerce and transaction. The coin points to false and true values that are life annihilating or life promoting. It is gold and earth; it is another symbol of duality comprised in unity, this time with reference to the two faces of the coin. It contributes to adaptation to life conditions and connotes the intellect, which like money, can be used, multiplied, changed, or falsified.

The Magician reminds us also of Hermes and Toth, gods of intelligence and magic, and of Mercury, the patron of merchants and thieves. The table represents an altar, a place of sacrifice. Its three visible legs suggest the three-dimensional world, the three supernal sephirot, while the fourth, sometimes unseen, may

TABLE 7. ALCHEMICAL SUBSTANCES AND FUNDAMENTAL PRINCIPLES.

Substance	Symbol	Principle
sulphur	⚍	(the fiery solar principle)
mercury	☿	(the lunar connecting principle)
salt	⊖	(the solid earth principle)

suggest the invisible sephira *Daat*, knowledge. Psychologically they may also represent the three conscious typological functions, while the fourth (invisible) may evoke the inferior function caught in the unconscious. They can also be seen as representatives of the three basic substances used by alchemists, and shown in Table 7.

The unopened flower at the feet of the Magician denotes the beginning of initiation, body of light, resurrection. It connotes a kept secret, love, intoxication, forgetting, assimilation and transcendence of the four elements. Conceived to be Mercurius and the quintessence itself, the noblest thing that a human meditation can reach, its sap was said to be "mercurial" and incombustible, a sure sign of its incorruptible and eternal nature (Jung, CW 14, ¶ 689). At times it may also represent the figure of the alchemical adept mixed into the "potion" by his own volition (Jung, CW 14, ¶ 702). It directs itself toward the sun in order to absorb the power of its rays in full. It symbolizes playful creativity, transcending consciousness, the totality of the Self, pressure toward self-realization, unity/multiplicity, lawfulness. The feet of the Magician form a right angle, as do the feet of the Lover (card VI), which there symbolize the fateful decision one has to make at the crossroads of life. Here they point out the necessary balance between correct thought and correct action.

The complex figure of the Magician confronts us with his duality. Just as his hands point both upward and downward, he shows us that he is both the one who acts and the one who observes. He has to be aware of his actions and must visualize his images. As artisan, he shows that we must take existence skillfully in our own hands and must provide for ourselves the necessary tools. The Magician is a potter who forms a vessel on his wheel out of a lump of clay. Yet this realization on earth, toward which his right hand points, is not all. Beyond the phenomenological world looms the realization: "as above, so below." The lemniscate, infinity, the brim of his hat, means victory of the eternal spirit, the One, the beginning of the cycles of life, the polarization of the original light.

From the beginning, humanity has intuited that no energy is lost in the All. This recognition is symbolized by the uroboros, a snake biting its own tail. (A Hebrew legend predicts that the world will come to an end when the snake releases it.) In this snake are linked all the material, spiritual, and intellectual elements that are necessary for the building of the cosmos. The four legs with which the uroboros is at times depicted symbolize the four elements with which the Magician works.

In sum, the Magician stands for cosmic life energy, lemniscate, infinity, rounded and closed unity; interpenetration of the four elements, vibration of ether; movement, connection , wind, wood as the fifth element of the totality, constant flow of life and consciousness; the possibility that humankind will reach insight into the planning of the world; action in order to arrive at nonaction; cyclic evolution without beginning or end. The Magician stands for integration of the micro- and macrocosm, the spiral as increment of tension, energetic reserve, the spiritual heaven that the sun pursues in its course, the heavenly heart as the nucleus of meaning, spiritual fire as expressed in light and void. He represents the dual nature of the masculine principle unfolding itself clockwise in the multiplicity of individuality and counterclockwise receding in death (the process of life in regression).

Beth, the second letter of the Hebrew alphabet, is the symbol for house or cave. All initiation begins there or in the desert: it is the *nigredo*, the dark night of the soul, penetration into the darkness in order to better understand its origin. It is the lost and recovered Word.

The sephira that corresponds to the number 2 is *Hochmah*, meaning wisdom, the start and end of initiation. The Word echoes in empty space. *Yin* and *yang* emerge from the Tao. The first emanation, the masculine, is followed by the second, the feminine. In the form represented here, she is Sophia, the discriminating wisdom whom the Gnostics have named *Aion*, or emanation. She is the one who directs our first steps toward understanding reality, which the world of appearances both mirrors and veils. The High Priestess is the counterpart of the Magician; she is the Chosen One. As cosmic principles, they form a couple: they are the primordial pair. The even number 2 implies the other. Whereas the Magician captures and transmits the impulse toward the unfolding of the universe, the High Priestess embodies divine love that fosters and nurtures this impulse. She depicts that impulse of the divine that fertilizes the waters and implants in them the germ of life, thus remaining captive in the body of creation. She is *anima mundi*, female Mercurius, the first separation, polarity, extension as abstract space. She is surface and depth. The High Priestess evokes the temple, whose veil of mystery hangs between the two columns (Jachin and Boaz) seen behind her in some decks. The pillars are the symbol of polarity, of the one point now divided in two, the pull to both right and left.

Her negative aspects are hatred, infertility, death, black magic, bloody religious terror, fatalism, melancholia, and suicide.

THEMES, ASSOCIATIONS, CORRESPONDENCES

The High Priestess pertains to the holy precinct. She denotes breathing, the unconscious, memory, reflection. She is the creating, containing principle that is the basis of all matter. She connotes humanity striving to understand the mysteries of nature. The High Priestess represents consciousness comprising past and future. She also represents duality mirroring unity, and she signifies equivalence of the receptive and generative power.

The ideogram for this card is:

Astrological amplification: Existence in the time before the beginning of time is directly connected to the sources of foreknowledge, so it is no wonder that the High Priestess received her mediumistic qualities from the Moon energy to which she is connected. The Moon represents an attunement from and to the past, a mode of feeling and being to which one needs to pay attention in order to feel inwardly secure and at home in one's life. The Moon spirit shows how to react to all experiences, with what energy one must adjust to the flow of life. The Moon symbolizes specific mental and emotional karmic patterns that may inhibit or help self-expression and adjustment. The primal ocean is the source not only of creation but also of wisdom. Bringing the image of the oceanic realm to birth is part of the creative struggle. Ambiguous and difficult to pin down, the Moon spirit lives in a world in which nothing is quite the same as it was five minutes ago, and yet it is this spirit that must be captured long enough so that it can emerge as a stable image and yield up its wisdom.

Cabalistic amplification: Hochmah is a feminine noun, and there are passages in the cabala in which *Hochmah* is referred to as *she*. However, one must bear in mind that every sephira, except *Kether* and *Malkuth*, stands in a relationship of passive receptivity (feminine) to the preceding sephira and of active transmission (masculine) to the sephira that follows. Only *Kether* is purely masculine, and only *Malkuth* is purely feminine. *Hochmah* is designated as *hyle* and referred to as *homer rishon,* a Hebrew expression that corresponds exactly to the alchemical term *prima materia* (Hurwitz, p. 196). Wisdom, as unconscious thinking and conceiving, according to Hurwitz, is higher than the letters because the letters, as elements of conscious thought, are unable to encompass the unconscious thought of *Hochmah. Hochmah* is

... the *prima materia* which puts on forms and takes them off ... she expends the life-force downward and receives fullness from above, without interruption even for a moment, eternally and beyond comprehension (Hurwitz, 1968, p. 196).

Alchemical amplification: *Aurora Consurgens*, an alchemical text attributed to Thomas Aquinas, contains in the first five chapters the description of a female figure called the Wisdom of God. Considered by the alchemists of the Middle Ages to be identical to the Holy Ghost, she can be seen more accurately, according to von Franz, as representing the sum of all archtypes, the eternal ideas in the mind of God when He created the world (von Franz, 1980, p. 184). Translated into psychological language, it means that the Wisdom of God expresses itself in the collective unconscious. Von Franz also proposes (*Aurora Consurgens*, p. xiii) that Jung's idea of the *unus mundus* is a modern scientific formulation of the archetypal image of *Sapientia Dei* with, however, the difference that *unus mundus* is a concept derived from pure empiricism, whereas that of *Sapientia Dei* is purely metaphysical. At the end of his life, St. Thomas may have bridged this gulf when he experienced how *Sapientia Dei*, the metaphysical concept, suddenly revealed its overwhelming psychic reality.* Von Franz points out that wisdom is conceived not only as illumination from above, but also as a "fount of light in nature" (von Franz, 1980, p. 212). Wisdom emerges from below, from matter, and demands succor through applied, focused human effort, whereby wisdom regains her former sublime status and ultimately ensures the final redemption of humanity (von Franz ,1980, p. 243).

Psychological interpretation. The High Priestess represents the intuition of hidden knowledge, the dawning of wisdom rooted in the dark, the past, the timeless. She is creative inspiration and a bridge between conscious and unconscious layers of the psyche.

---

*It is said that during a sermon Thomas stopped abruptly and retreated to his cell, apparently having had a vision. He isolated himself, speaking to no one, and feverishly wrote what was now being given to him. He had accepted a preaching engagement in a nearby town, and although ailing, he embarked on his way, becoming so ill that he was forced to stop at a monastery where he died. The *Aurora Consurgens* contains his "post-vision" writings which were dutifully recorded by his secretary. These mystical, alchemical writings are, according to von Franz, the outcome and compensation for his lifelong, rigid mysogynistic stance.

Jungian interpretation: Lucidity of consciousness rests upon dark, unconscious seeds out of which grow objective cultural values. It is this unconscious background that is perceived by the mediumistic woman. *Medium* means between, neither this nor that, something intermediate, general, neutral, in the middle, a means, agent, mediator, conveyor. The medial woman is immersed in the psychic atmosphere of her environment and the spirit of her period, but above all, in the collective unconscious. The medial woman is absorbed and molded by it; sometimes she even represents it herself. She then acts "what is in the air," what the environment cannot or will not admit, but what is nevertheless a part of it. It is mostly the dark aspect of a situation or of a predominant idea rejected and condemned like the witches of the Middle Ages, burned because they represented the split-off evil projections and the unacceptable heresies of their times. When the medial woman senses the archetypal foundations of a man's spirit, she then becomes his *femme inspiratrice*. When objective psychic contents in herself and others are not understood or are taken personally, she experiences a destiny not her own and loses herself in ideas that do not belong to her. Instead of being a mediatrix, she becomes the first victim of her own nature. But if she possesses the faculty of discrimination and understands the limits of the personal and the impersonal, the conscious and the unconscious, of what belongs to the ego and what to the environment, then she is able to exert a positive personal and cultural influence (Toni Wolff, *Structural Forms of the Feminine Psyche*, p. 9-10). In Jung's view,

> . . . Sophia, or the *Sapientia Dei*, who is a coeternal and more or less hypostatized pneuma of feminine nature that existed before the creation . . . [and] who already shares certain essential qualities with the Johannine Logos, is . . . closely associated with the Hebrew Chochma (Jung, CW 11, ¶ 609-610).

He quotes (CW 11, ¶ 613) from the *Wisdom of Solomon* that she is "the breath and the power of God" (7:22), "a pure effluence flowing from the power of the Almighty" (7:25), "the brightness of the everlasting light, the unspotted mirror of the power of God" (7:26). She is sent from heaven and from the throne of glory as a "Holy Spirit" (9:10, 17). As a psychopomp she leads the way to God and assures immortality (6:18, 8:13). Sophia signifies God's self-reflection, and for self-reflection wisdom is needed (CW 11, ¶ 617, 727). He points out (CW 11 ¶ 240) that the Holy Ghost and Logos merge in the gnostic idea of Sophia, and again in the *Sapientia* of medieval philosophers who said of her, "The wisdom of the father lies in the lap of the mother." Jung quotes (CW 11, ¶ 610) from *Ecclesiasticus*, written about 600 B.C., in which Wisdom says of herself:

> I came out of the mouth of the most High,
> and covered the earth as a cloud.
>
> I dwelt in high places,
> and my throne is in a cloudy pillar.

SYMBOLIC LANGUAGE OF THE IMAGE

The High Priestess sits on a throne. In alchemy the vessel that had to be sealed with the "clay of wisdom" is the seat of transformation and is, at times, represented by a throne or cathedra (von Franz, *Aurora Consurgens*, p. 227). Behind her a curtain stretches between two columns. This is the "fabric" upon which we project our thoughts; it connects and separates simultaneously. The curtain, itself, is the mystery that should not be lifted. Cabalistic texts describe the curtain *Pargod* hanging before the Throne of Glory into which all souls are woven. The entire past history and future destiny of each single soul is recorded in its mystical fabric. It is the abode of all the souls that have returned from below, but the souls of the wicked have no place in it (Scholem, 1974, p. 159). The two columns represent the pair of opposites: the red column corresponds to fire, the vital power, the sulphur of the alchemists; the blue column is air, vitalizing breath, sensibility, the mercury of the alchemists. The columns also represent stability. In the Christian tradition, they define the narrow gate through which one may step into freedom from spiritual imprisonment.

Some decks show the High Priestess with two keys—logic and intuition—in her left hand. Without their cooperation the book of secret knowledge, held in her right hand, could not become intelligible. They unlock the two doors to the white and black lights, whereby the white light can be found only after the black is known. Truth can be seen only by those to whom the High Priestess entrusts these keys, which in this context stand for equilibrium and equivalence of opposites. At the human level, they may indicate the preponderance of a dogmatic or speculative attitude. Psychologically interpreted, the keys represent the ego and the Self. Alchemically the gold key is the Word, wisdom, and reason; the silver key is intuition, imagination, the capacity to feel and to impress, the potential for enthusiasm, inner stillness. Together they are the duality of opposites confronting each other, the intellectual or speculative order or disorder. They are the absolute reality as revealed by duality. They depict the process of becoming conscious of oneself and of the image one has of oneself and of the world. Often associated with the mysteries, the keys she holds are, like *Aion*'s, the keys to the past and to the future. Ancient mystery cults are always connected with psychopompic deities, some of which are equipped with the keys to the underworld. As guardians of the threshold, they watch over the descent of the initiates into the darkness and guide them through the mysteries. Hecate is one such (Jung, CW 18, ¶ 266).

Her red mantle testifies to her creative power. The two bands that cross her chest symbolize her flashes of intuition. In some decks she holds a scroll on her lap, which represents divine providence, the plan whereby luck and misfortune are assigned their respective places. Her right foot is placed on a pillow. This stance depicts the solidity of knowledge as guide in the world of appearances, and the pillow represents the minute, reliable inklings that can be apprehended from the domain of the unfathomable mystery.

She wears on her head a double diadem crowned by the crescent moon. The two diadems depict exoteric and subtle esoteric teachings. Only a creative imagination—trained in alchemical teachings and gnostic wisdom—allows us to see the archetypal image beyond the perpetually changing fluid forms of reality. The crown or diadem indicates the effects of the spirit as mediator of events in its own realm, awareness and intuition that penetrate form and matter. The moon is the celestial water, spiritual receptivity, fluid motion, formative fantasy, feeling participation, the plowed field that receives the seed. In Egypt, when Isis brings the dismembered Osiris back to life, she does so by shining upon him in her moon aspect. In Greece, Artemis, the virginal hunter and moon goddess, is both chaste and sensual. Both goddesses are accompanied by dogs, the guides of the dead, symbolic of their underworld aspect that is more apparent in Hecate, the dark side of the moon, and in Persephone, the queen of the nether kingdom. Persephone and her mother Demeter, when seen as personifications of nature, are images that urge humankind to cultivate the fields and to await the time of ripeness. Aphrodite is both their opposite and their complement. For man the moon goddess is the recipient of projected light—dazzling and being bedazzled by love. For woman she is reflected light—withdrawal and reflection.

In the cabalistic tradition, Lilith was created simultaneously with Adam, not from his rib as Eve was, but from earth as he was. For this reason she considered herself his equal. They quarreled and Lilith ran away; she became a demon. Lilith is inimical to Eve; she protects illegitimate love and brings misunderstanding into marital relationships. As abandoned or rejected woman, Lilith represents jealousy and envy and the hatred of the familial bond between parents and children. As dark moon and mother of mystery, she sends dreams that arouse all our yearnings and unfulfilled wishes; yet as the archetype of the Old Enchantress, she can also be seen as a spiritually talented being who has liberated herself from the restraint of blind instinct.

Isis, the goddess of the rainbow and bridge between heaven and earth, was depicted as a wisdom figure in mythology. She is the deep feminine understanding that manifests through human nature; she is Sophia; she is the High Priestess (from an interview with Marion Woodman, 1989).

The letter *gimel* is the symbol of the grasping hand. In a wider sense, it symbolizes all containers and channels of nature. The sephira that corresponds to the number 3 is *Binah*, meaning self-aware intelligence, conscious of its aims. It means openness to and assimilation of the sublime, life that can constantly renew itself. Here the triangle shape is completed; the trinity, as represented by the Empress, is an image that emphasizes feminine function; the triangle in her ideogram points to the earth.

The triad of the supernals (ending with *Binah*) represents the three aspects of knowledge. The first sephira, *Kether*, is knowledge; the second, *Hochmah*, is the knower; and the third, *Binah*, "is that of which is known." *Binah* is thus the expression, in full differentiated and substantial form, of what *Hochmah* knows. *Binah* is the supernal mother; she is the receptive aspect of the holy nuptial of the King and Queen; she is the upper *Shekina*, God's presence and dwelling. Mother and container of intelligible form, of images and ideas, she is the subtle aspect of matter, the heavenly water, the sea of all origins, the life force penetrating all things. She is existence, evolution, nature, shape. In her positive active aspects she is the moving, electrifying, exciting power; 1 + 1 + 1 = extension. Her passive aspect is expressed as magnetic, receptive power. In her negative aspect she is intellectualism mistaken for spirituality, lack of sensitivity and flexibility, infertility, alienation from human tasks.

THEMES, ASSOCIATIONS, CORRESPONDENCES

The Empress denotes the onset of breathing, the begetting faculty, fertility of matter entrusted to humankind, wisdom and error, power and efficient knowledge that complete each other. She is animated matter, lawfulness within the cycle of the seasons, zodiacal space, but also aimlessness. Nevertheless, she stands for hope on the spiritual level, , the possibility of spiritual awakening, and the capacity to adapt. In another sense, the Empress represents organic lawfulness applied to action, life as progression, transmutation of matter. She is the capacity of nature to bring forth preexisting ideal forms.

The ideogram for this card is

Astrological amplification: With the exception of a cluster of authors attributing the planet Venus to the Lover(s) (card VI), there seems to be a general consensus connecting the Empress with Venus. Venus is an introverted planet, named after the goddess Venus/Aphrodite, delighting in the beauty of her body, but also a wise judge and counselor. She seeks her fulfillment through stimulation from, and union with, beloved objects. Even quarreling and raging for the sake of a passionate experience of life, which encounter with another brings, is part of Aphrodite's world. For Aphrodite/Venus, the body is sacred. This is, in part, why she is usually portrayed nude; she seems to embody naked, unashamed nature. She also acts as mediator between our world and the world of immortals. Venus is an image of relative sexual equality; she presides over "sunlit sexuality" and embodies conjugal joy and fertility. Procreation, desire and satisfaction, adornment and culture, beauty and erotic arts, all these belong to her. Her lovemaking is civilized art (Greene, 1984, p. 186).

Cabalistic amplification: The third sephira is a river that flows out from the source, welling up from the depths of nothingness (*Hochmah*) and dividing into different streams, following the structure of emanation until all its tributaries flow into the great sea of the last sephira (Scholem, 1974, p. 109). Thus, from the sephira *Binah*, also called "mother of the world," the seven apprehensible and outgoing sephirot are emanated. However, the force of evil in this world (according to some cabalists) is a continuation of the sephira *Binah* that was "substantiated in the destructive potencies corresponding to the seven constructive sephirot of creation" (Scholem, 1974, p. 124).

    Hochmah (the father) and *Binah* (the mother) serve as the supreme archetype for that procreative "coupling," the common root of all intellectual and erotic unions. This coupling is aroused by the reascent of the 288 sparks that had been contained in the broken vessels and returned to the bowels of *Binah* where they animate and quicken the forces within a structure whose function is primarily receptive. Without such assisting forces, which are referred to as "female waters," there can be neither coupling nor unification.

Alchemical amplification: At the upper end of the Empress' scepter is the alchemical symbol for antimony ♁. Antimony bonds with all known metals except gold, and thus is used to purify molten gold. This quality of separating out the gold, allowing it to be free of base metals, is an image of the quality of caring that the Empress energy provides to both partner and children. The Egyptian goddess Isis, who is associated with the Empress, was called by alchemists the feminine transformative aspect of their *prima materia*.

Psychological interpretation: The Empress is the guardian of the generative forces of nature; she is concerned with abundance and harmony on the physical plane, acceptance of the material universe, being embodied, passivity, feeling, emotion, concreteness, grounding. The mother must shape her children, but she must also set them free. The difficulty of her task increases the longer she remains tied to them and carries the burden of their destinies with her. The universal principle of receptivity, which the Empress represents, must be understood as an "inspiring and generating openness to that which is struggling to emerge within as well as without, to the transpersonal and impersonal as well as the personal" (Zabriskie, 1990, p. 275).

Jungian interpretation: *Binah* is seen by Jung as part as the quaternity of *Merkabah* (see definition on p. 77), corresponding to intelligence (CW 9/1, ¶ 576, n. 115) and represented by the eagle (CW 9/1, ¶ 588, n. 136), one of the symbolic angels of Ezekiel's vision.

> And to the woman were given two wings of a great eagle, that she might fly from the presence of the serpent into the wilderness, into her place where she would be nourished for years, and months, and days (*Revelation* 12:14).

In his *Alchemical Studies* (CW 13, ¶ 411), Jung observes that *Binah* is also the place in which the Tree of Life has its roots, and thus life is brought to earth from *Binah*. The Empress symbolizes the cosmic creation forms: matter and energy. She concretizes the world of the archetypes. She is the dynamic principle, denoting the possibility of a limited space becoming a new unity of material or spiritual dimension. She is the intelligence of matter, prototype of forms, shape of abstract concepts, purified soul, experience of the unity of soul and world. God's revelation is embodied in the heart: the shape it takes depends upon the degree of readiness for (and acceptance of) that revelation. She signifies the introjection of the past as the basis for the re-creation of a new unity, acting according to one's own sensibility, earth as furrow that receives the seed from heaven and gives it shape.

Numinous and awe-inspiring divine representations in female form provide feminine models from which to draw sustenance, comfort, and a sense of belonging and worth. Authoritative within, they may be able to fill the gap left by the absence of inspiring female-gender role models and wisdom figures. They may legitimize feminine intelligence and provide release from a constricted ego or a restrictive persona through their archetypal energy.

SYMBOLIC LANGUAGE OF THE IMAGE

The image of the Empress, depicted full-face and in hieratic attitude, conveys the immutability of intelligible forms. The attributes of her rulership are her crown and her world-governing scepter; the moon at her feet denotes her domination over the sublunar world; the twelve stars surrounding her head (of which nine are visible) suggest the twelve signs of the zodiac and point out the importance of the seasonal cycle in regulating the fertility of nature. The following passage from *Revelation* (12:1) comes to mind:

> And a great sign was seen in heaven, a woman clothed
> with the sun, with the moon under her feet and upon
> her head a crown of twelve stars . . .

Her wings denote the wind, indispensible for fecundation, whereas the lily on her left expresses purity, goodness, and beauty. The scepter indicates the shapes in which the invisible unity that underlies the world of forms becomes apparent; it suggests creative intelligence fertilized by imagination. The inverted Venus sign at the top of the scepter (the previously mentioned alchemical symbol for antimony) evokes the sun and the world of the elements that have evolved from it; it stands for physical life.

In Greek mythology, the energy of card III is represented by Hera, queen of heaven, and by her sister Demeter, Goddess of fertility, of the corn, and of the earth. Demeter is the central figure in the Eleusinian mysteries in which the eternal return of death and resurrection leading to spiritual wholeness was celebrated. Her daughter Persephone was abducted by Hades, and Demeter searched for her perseveringly until she found her. Like the corn, Persephone's six months underground is followed by six months above, so the cycle of vegetation is the domain of the Empress. Hera, on the other hand, was not essentially a mother, but a queen, consort, and matriarch. She represents an aspect of the feminine that is related to the male world, the one about which Jung says:

> As a rule her place is on man's intimate side . . . she helps
> the man realize his ends, a needful feminine insight into
> his own psyche which he can achieve alone only at the
> cost of much suffering, if at all (Jung, CW 10, ¶ 240).

Hera, neither an easy nor a very personal mother, was the loyal spouse who lavished vast and effective energy so that her home, the institutions, and the communities she protected should, in truth, be havens for the people and the values she cared for so deeply. She was her own person and presided as queen in her own realm. She provided a kind of steadiness, a steadfast commitment that made her patroness of communities and institutions. When there is no dependable and communal life and when every relationship depends on the feelings of the moment, life itself becomes precarious. Hera's hot temper could not stand for this, as hers was the urge to live a more complete life, the longing for meaning and fulfillment, and the growing disgust with sense-less one-sidedness (CW 10, ¶ 270). When Hera's negative side takes over, impersonality becomes institutional rigidity; jealousy and spite replace warmth; laws and conventions squash spirit and feeling; status and property become more important than persons; and victories become more important than lives.

For the Romans, she is represented by Ceres, Venus, and Juno as symbols of vital power. Their attributes are the dove and the peacock. The dove denotes the process whereby the *prima materia* develops in a child under the influence of the spirit and is wrapped in the substance given by the mother. The peacock symbolizes the wheel of the sun and the one who destroys the snake.

For the Egyptians, she is represented by the cow-headed Hathor, goddess of love and fertility, and by Isis reigning over nature.

IV
THE EMPEROR

ד

The letter *daleth* is the symbol for power, division, the door, the lock. It denotes domination. The sephira that corresponds to the number four is *Hesed,* meaning gentleness, mercy, legitimacy, fate, the part of God's kingdom that corresponds to the quaternity, to the tetragrammaton in its rotation. It indicates multiplicity.

The Emperor governs his empire, visible and invisible, through the lawfulness implicit in all being. He assumes the burden of his office out of love for humankind. With the Empress, he forms a couple harmoniously connected and capable of procreation.

The Emperor reigns over the four regions of the earth and points to the four directions stretching out in space. The number 4 represents the polarity and the balance of activity and passivity. When it results from 3 + 1, it means movement and activity; when it results from 2 + 2, it indicates equilibrium and the preponderance of the concrete (matter, material). The foursome can be viewed as 4 = 2 + 2: spirit and breath of life reign over and animate the four elements, signifying freedom and personal decision. It can also be viewed as 4 = 2 × 2, whereby spirit and breath of life are limited in their expansion by the four elements, signifying compulsion, conventionality, or deference to authority. In contrast to the triangle of card III, the square (the *quaternio*) here can be interpreted as representing integration of the additional element earth to the trinity air, water, fire. Thus the Emperor symbolizes the material, earthly power, the governing, directing, supporting, and protective forces of a personality that has reached freedom on the earthly plane. His negative aspect indicates war, terror, the tyrant.

THEMES, ASSOCIATIONS, CORRESPONDENCES

The Emperor denotes order, reason, action, the material energy that humans need in order to realize their ephemeral creations. With the Emperor, what is virtual becomes actual, and words have magic. He signifies global vision and concepts that can become useful when they are applied at the concrete level. He is also associated with the idea of producing and carrying out; with actions executed at all levels as dictated by truth, fairness, and willpower; and with the four stages of evolution—namely, directed strength, action, word, and meaning.

The ideogram for this card is ⚲

Astrological amplification: There seems to be unanimity in assigning the planet Jupiter to the Emperor. Jupiter/Zeus was the father of gods and men. His name *djeus* means "light of heaven." He is thus the god of lightning and of enlightenment. When he emerges as the victorious king of the gods, overthrowing the rule of the earthy Titans and establishing his own heavenly domain, he reflects the emergence into collective consciousness of a new spiritual principle, for Zeus represents that which belongs to the eternal spirit, in contrast to the doomed and fated life of the body. Zeus escapes from the dominance of the chthonic Great Mother and assumes leadership, and with him arises that bright aspiration that forms the core of all rituals: the promise of the immortal spirit with its benign care, waiting in the embrace of the Good Father (Greene, 1984, p. 235-236).

Cabalistic amplification: The sephira *Hesed* (mercy), also called *Gedullah* (greatness), represents the outgoing power of creation. The flow of Divine Emanation, not diminished in its essential nature, although transformed into another order as it leaves *Binah*, crosses over the pillar of balance and passes into the sephira *Hesed* on the active column.

> This *sephira* in man represents a powerful creative urge, the kind of force that will make a people develop a continent, devote time and money to good works, give loving care to a demanding family, or spend conscientious attention on the practice of an art. It is the emotional

mainspring, the deep-water current that a man draws
on for resource, when ordinary emotions are inadequate.
This is the place where magnanimity originates, and
from where higher feelings rise up (Halevi, 1972, p. 38).

Alchemical amplification: The Emperor represents an archetypal
energy providing growth and expansion, gestation and transformation. His square throne is evocative of the four qualities: dryness (rigidity), coldness (miserliness, barriers against the spirit),
heat (extension, passion), and humidity (dissolution, confusion).
In the center of the natural wisdom, whose circumference, closed
in itself, forms a circle, the alchemist sees the fulfillment of the
mysteries.

> "Here is the number four, within whose bounds the
> number three, together with the number two combined
> into One, fulfills all things, which it does in miraculous
> wise." In these relations between four, three, two and
> one is found . . . the "culmination of all knowledge and
> of the mystic art, and the infallible midpoint of the
> center" (Dorn, quoted by Jung, CW 13, ¶ 187).

To the minds of the alchemists, this meant primarily the God
within that represents and suffers the discord of the elements and
at the same time brings about the union of the four and is identical with the product of that union, the lapis, Primordial Man,
Adam Kadmon (CW 14, ¶ 607).

Psychological interpretation: The Emperor represents the father, a
personification of mind and spirit and of their creative importance. He is the representative of the law, which limits instinctuality. In his positive aspect, he indicates relationship to a good
father, courage, energy, tenacity, orderliness, anticipation of spiritual values, willingness to sacrifice. In his negative aspect, he
shows father fixation, hardness, dogmatism, authoritarianism,
pettiness, aggressivity, and an attitude removed from the world
and reality.

Jungian interpretation: Hesed, the fourth sephira, means mercy,
whereas *Geburah,* the fifth sephira, means judgment. Jung contrasts them using this passage from the *Midrash Rabbah:*

> If I create the world on the basis of mercy alone, its sins
> will be great, but on the basis of justice alone the world
> cannot exist. Hence I will create it on the basis of justice
> and mercy, and may it then stand! . . . If thou desirest
> the world to endure, there can be no absolute justice
> (CW 9/2, ¶ 108 and n. 64).

Indeed, Jung considers that the number 4 signifies conscious totality. It describes the ideal, "spiritual" man and formulates him as a
totality in contrast to the number 5, which is assigned to "natural" man and describes the corporeal human (CW 9/1, ¶ 680).
The *quaternio* points beyond simple antithesis to a double antithesis, the idea of the cross.

> [T]he quaternity as produced by the modern psyche
> points directly not only to the God within, but to the
> identity of God and man. Contrary to the dogma, there
> are not three, but four aspects. . . . The voice of nature
> is clearly audible in all experiences of the quaternity
> (CW 11, ¶ 105).

One cannot help but wonder if the triad of the supernals does not
stop short of the natural balance that the inclusion of the sephira
Hesed would offer. In the *Sefer Yetzirah* (*The Book of Creation*), the
earliest cabalistic text, it is said that at least the first four sephirot
emanate from each other. The first is the spirit of the Living God;
from it comes forth, by way of condensation, the first primal element air, and from air, issuing one after the other as the third and
fourth sephirot—water and fire. The next six sephirot are of a
completely different nature and represent the six dimensions of
space (east, west, north, south, depth, and height) (Scholem,
Kabbalah, p. 24). Indeed the transformation of the triad into a
quaternio seems to create a cross reminiscent of the one Jung presents as the *Anthropos Quaternio* (CW 9/2, ¶ 358ff) or
the archetypal *quaternio* (CW 14, ¶ 612) as shown in the diagram
on page 55.

For Jung the animus and the anima have formed since olden
times the archetypal basis of all masculine and feminine energies.
They represent a supreme pair of opposites making union possible through their mutual attraction. This *coniunctio oppositorum* is
expressed by alchemists in the form of the "Chymical Wedding"
and by cabalists in the form of the union of God and the *Shekina*
(CW 9/2, ¶ 425).

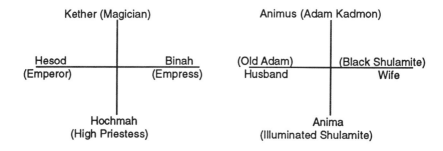

```
        Kether (Magician)                      Animus (Adam Kadmon)
               |                                        |
Hesod                    Binah          (Old Adam)               (Black Shulamite)
(Emperor)               (Empress)        Husband                      Wife
               |                                        |
          Hochmah                                    Anima
      (High Priestess)                       (Illuminated Shulamite)
```

SYMBOLIC LANGUAGE OF THE IMAGE

The Emperor commands: "Incarnate!" He stands for available vital energy, for determination, destiny, fate, love, psyche and consciousness, for the living ego. He is seen in profile; this means that only one aspect of the forces he represents is visible. The worlds veiled and unveiled to our senses are represented by the Emperor's two crowns. His arms form a triangle with his head; his crossed legs repeat the square shape of the throne. In certain decks the arms of the throne end in rams heads (the ram [Aries] is the first sign of the zodiac), indicating the beginning of an organized structure. When this structure changes, so does its function. It also means unity and division of time. The sign of the ram is ruled by Mars, the god of war, the principle of fire energy. As long as the ram remains untamed, this energy brings upheaval, violence, and disruption. Cosmic representation of the animal power of the fire, the male energy shows how glowing, explosive, rebellious, chaotic, and simultaneously creative and destructive it initially is. The Emperor's position as consort of the Empress creates a further connection to Mars (Aphrodite's lover).

The Emperor has to distance himself from inner and outer entanglement when he regulates human social relations; he has to restrain himself and be free of all sympathy and antipathy in order to assign the appropriate position to all things. In Egyptian mythology the Emperor is represented by Osiris brought back to life by Isis.

Although the Emperor is seen wearing armor, he is nevertheless available to human concerns due to his intelligence and his imaginative empathy. Both the black eagle of the escutcheon (the eagle is used by alchemists to refer to the successive volatilizations and sublimations that take place during the work) and the bird of Hermes symbolize the spiritual forces contained by matter and obscured by ego-centeredness. In *Mysterium Coniunctionis* (CW 14), Jung points out that the glowing body, when freed of all corruption and identical to pure water, leaves the bodily dross behind.

At the feet of the Emperor blooms the tulip that was only a bud in card I; it shows that, devoid of arbitrariness, universal law allows the development of all possibilities that people carry within them. The essence of the divine expresses itself in its lawful effect and is shown here by the gold chain and by the Emperor's red robe. The links of the chain around his neck represent immutable, unchangeable contents that are the condensation and aggregate of existence; the chain also suggests that nature must be limited by adaptation through conditioning. The half-moon on his chest denotes inner truth and dominion over unstable and undefined elements. The globe in his left hand is the symbol of his all-encompassing domination; it represents the all-penetrating vital force. The scepter in his right hand represents the unchangeable law that commands all becoming and passing away; the half-moon of the scepter signifies fluctuation; and the heraldic lily on top represents the golden bloom, the unity of living and being. The seven individual shapes that form the scepter may be interpreted as representing the seven lower sephirot "of the Building" in contrast to the preceding upper three supernal sephirot called the sephirot "of the World." They may also stand for the seven ways of being or the seven thoughts revealed to the zaddik in meditation (Hurwitz, p. 176ff).

The throne is square; the stone is cubic. The throne indicates the principle of fixation that organizes an organism at its core. The trinity becomes quaternity. In contrast to the triangle, which is related to spirit, the square is related to the material world that extends in the four cardinal directions. This shape denotes solidity and durability; it manifests the indivisibility of space as its limitation through form. It represents the alchemical philosopher's stone and refers to individuation and the achievement of mastery.

The number 4 also points to the four psychic functions: two perceptual and irrational, namely, intuition and sensation; and two rational, namely, thinking and feeling, the analyzing and synthesizing functions. With our sense organs we can perceive only a three-dimensional space. But space is multidimensional; only the sixth sense can perceive the unmanifest. Four stands for the totality considered in its essence, the all-containing and all-penetrating realization of creative intelligence. It is the number of the first festivals, of nonduality, of the two sexes, of productive love. It stands for the four different states of the four-dimensional creature: unconditional, transcendent, without attribute, and spirit directly connected with material reality.

The letter *he* means breath, religion, incarnated light, individual unity, spirit and matter, authority. The sephira that corresponds to the number 5 is *Geburah*, which stands for strength, power, justice, exterior form. *Geburah* signifies God's stern judgment. His punishment disrupts the stable established order, yet in so doing it creates greater awareness because devastation and destruction of what is are also manifestations of God's radiance (Knapp, 1984, p. 210). Its symbol is the open hand used to show or to apprehend. It is will and intelligence that dominate the four elements.

Five is the middle of the decade. The number 5 appears in all its products and actions, all the potentials of numbers resulting from 5 that end in 5. It has been suggested that the shape of the number 5 can be attributed to the soft spirit resting upon the strong: the strong, severe spirit is God, and the soft spirit is the human being.

The High Priest (the Pope or the Hierophant as this card is usually named) symbolizes the age at which passion has less power to disturb our lives and understanding for human weaknesses increases. Negatively, the High Priest represents dogma and limitation or even total suppression of the capacity to judge due to conventional piety and morality.

THEMES, ASSOCIATIONS, CORRESPONDENCES

The High Priest represents spiritual authority, oral and written teachings, religious knowledge. Humans have a duty to act in accordance with this divine law, and material energy gives their acts reality in the present moment. Universal law is the guiding thread of all activity, and spirituality serves as the link between the absolute and the relative, between the eternal and the temporary. Action thus becomes congruent with knowledge.

The ideogram for this card is ⊗

Astrological amplification: Alternatively assigned the planets Mercury, Mars, and Jupiter, and the zodiacal signs Aries and Virgo, the High Priest stands for strict application of the law, setting bounds and boundaries to the expansiveness and, at times, the indiscriminate mercy that the Emperor represents. I have chosen to associate the High Priest with the planet Mars, which represents courage, initiative, and willpower directed toward what is hopefully a legitimate aim. At times, however, the danger of not sensing the limits and proper use of force is present; this opens the door to overbearing behavior and ultimately to destruction. One has only to think of the destruction that religious wars have brought in their wake, of the cruelty of the Inquisition, and of all the devastation that a thoughtless "law-and-order" stance can bring about to see the connection to Mars, the god of war, the shadow of the High Priest.

Cabalistic amplification: *Geburah* (power), or *Din* (judgment, also rigor), represents the attribute of strict justice. It is defined as "the left hand of the Holy One, blessed be He," and as "a quality whose name is evil," (Scholem, 1974, p. 123) and has many offshoots in the forces of judgment, the constricting and limiting powers in the universe. The source of evil is seen here in the uncontrolled growth in the power of judgment, which was made possible by its separation from its customary union with the quality of loving kindness, represented by *Hesed* (the Emperor). Pure judgment untempered by any mitigating admixture produces from within itself demonic powers, an emanation of the left. This power is active only as long as it receives fresh strength from *Geburah* and, in particular, only as long as humans revive and fortify it through sinful behavior (Scholem, 1974, p. 123).

Alchemical amplification: The paradoxes of the alchemist present us with the ambiguous image of the divine, whose inner polarity is expressed as follows:

. . . the dual aspect of the Cabalistic *Tifereth*, who corresponds to the Son of Man: "To the right he is called the
Sun of righteousness, . . . but to the left [he is called the
Sun] from the heat of the fire of *Geburah*." . . . Of the second day, which is assigned to *Geburah*, it is said: "On
that day Gehenna was created" (*Kabbala denudata* [1677-
1684], pp. 348, 439; quoted in Jung, CW 14, ¶ 633, n. 285).

Psychological interpretation: The High Priest represents inspired
thought, creative intellectual synthesis, and moral law. He is the
forming spirit and the transmitter of traditional wisdom; he is the
guardian of the threshold between human effort and divine grace.

Jungian interpretation: Hesed, the Emperor on his throne, the father
of his people in times of peace, may win our love, but it is *Geburah*,
the High Priest, who commands our respect. We have another
kind of love for the person who can put the fear of God into us, far
more steadfast and permanent, and (curiously enough) far more
emotionally satisfying than the love with which no tinge of awe is
mingled. It is *Geburah* that supplies this element of awe, of the
fear of the Lord that is the beginning of wisdom, and of respect,
which keeps us on the straight path and calls forth our better
nature because we know our sins will find us out.

Whereas the Emperor is the constructive force, the High
Priest, the lord of fear and severity, is the destroyer, the celestial
surgeon, and the dragon slayer. Too much charity is foolish and
may expose the innocent to danger, and too much patience is, at
times, lack of courage. The policy of nonresistance to evil can only
be pursued in a well-organized society governed by moral laws;
it never works in "border" conditions or arbitrary tyranny. What
we need is a just and wise balance, and at times sacrifice is needed
to attain it. *Geburah* is the sacrificial priest of the mysteries.
Sacrifice means deliberate choice of a greater good; it is transmutation of force. Psychic energy is thereby released for use in the
chosen channel. *Geburah* is the courage and resolve that frees from
deadly irresolution and compromise, an astringent cleanser of an
open wound that could otherwise become septic. *Geburah* wields
the pruning knife against the obsolete, against violence used
toward the weak, against dishonesty, sloth, and lack of mercy.
Geburah also comes with its sacred scourge and its restraining
chain, using them for healing, not vengefully, in order to stop

injustice and remove aggression. It is therefore essential to find the right balance and rhythm and the right place because evil can manifest as force applied at the wrong time (too soon or too late) or in the wrong place or in the wrong amount (too much or too little). Numerologically this potential for evil is expressed in the number of this card (V), which reappears in card XV (3×5), the Devil, who represents archetypal evil.

SYMBOLIC LANGUAGE OF THE IMAGE

Card V, the High Priest, is clearly related to card II, the High Priestess. The symbolism of card II, truth and wisdom, is embodied in card V, in the human being. In most number systems, the primordial human is assigned the number 5; the symbol is the pentagram, the five-rayed star with the uppermost tip turned toward God. The two bottom rays, which radiate in two directions, are emphasized by the two clerics, dressed in two different-colored habits. They may also signify two different reactions to the teachings the High Priest seems to impart. The two columns also remind us of card II. In both cards, the columns symbolize the two poles of religious form: adoption of the conventionally acceptable, hypostatizing, divine revelation in accordance with historical, secular, and social points of view and the independent search for the road toward the recognition and integration of one's being.

The High Priest, the two green columns, and the two kneeling students (theology and mysticism) form a pentagram, the divine five-cornered shape, symbol of the human being as mediator between God and the universe. The pentagram is comprised of necessity, knowledge, law, freedom, and action; it represents the fivefold totality of God's image, the integration of the four elements with ether, the spirit. The spirit is generated by the first even number, the feminine 2, and the masculine 3, the first uneven number: $2 + 3 = 5$. Five is also the number of the quintessence, of the indestructible alchemical substance that connects inner to outer life.

For the ancient Egyptians the five-rayed star represented the reunion of humankind with heaven: from crossing ✕ with triunity ∧, it yields ✕. Some Chinese commentators designate 5 as the number of the middle, as *yin* (Eve), the feminine principle that unites with the masculine *yang* (Adam), as the microcosm in which heaven and earth come together. For the Pythagoreans 5 represented the mystical knot, the number of Juno (the goddess of marriage), and the sign of the union of man with woman. In nature it is the will to live and propagate.

Beginning the cycle of generations, this card stands for evolution through life and death, for the polarization of the spirit in vital phenomena, for the dual vital breath.

The High Priest is both the twin and the opponent of the Emperor. God reveals himself as lawgiver through the High Priest and as teacher through the predictions of the prophets. Because the High Priest represents the God who breathed his breath into humankind, in this card individuality can become reality as spirit comes into matter.

Some astrologers have proposed a correspondence to the sign of Taurus, symbol of the union of the Sun and Moon, of the light from above and its mirror image below. The Gnostics, on the other hand, refer to a demiurge that keeps humanity in dependency through morality and religion. But the Pope (another name for this card) is a father figure connected with mother church, which has the authority of the maternal that forms fate by influencing thinking, feeling, and acting. However, in the shadow of Mother Church lurks the Terrible Mother who destroys through rigid holding on to obsolete rulings of the past.

The threefold tiara points to the ruling power of the High Priest over the three worlds: body, soul, and spirit. The tiara is made of three rows with fifteen scallops each ($3 \times 15 = 45$), 45 being the number of humankind as image of God. It signifies enlightened adepts and great teachers.

The scepter of the High Priest indicates his authority in matters of faith as well as over the sacrifices these demand. The white gloves denote that he will not meddle in worldly affairs.

The three folded (hidden) fingers of his right hand signify the mystery of the trinity; the two fingers extended upward signify blessing and the mystery of God's dual nature. The High Priest puts us in the presence of the act of benediction, which is the activation of divine power transcending the individual thought and will of the one who is blessed as well as of the one who pronounces the blessing. In this gesture of blessing, the fingers of the right hand point above and below, a reminder of the Magician's arms. What the Magician (*Kether*) intimates, the High Priest (*Geburah*) strives to bring about: the unity of that which is above with that which is below. The triple cross in his left hand is the cross of the complete and perfect spiritual path; horizontal and vertical, three crossbars divide the vertical into three segments. The three levels of the horizontal path represent love of nature, of one's neighbor, and of higher beings; the three levels of the vertical path represent faith (or purification by divine breath), hope (or illumination by divine light), and love (or mystical union by divine fire).

Cards I through V are read as follows: I indicates the point without dimension; II, the unidimensional line; III, the two-dimensional surface; IV, the three-dimensional cube; and V, the invisible quintessence, the fourth dimension, the potential world, the invisible connection, the attempted trial. Cards IV and V are the raw material of the subtle basis of worldly and spiritual power.

The letter *vau* means freedom, eye, ear, beauty. It means test, but also mutual cooperation and correspondence of the powers of nature. It represents the balance between the visible and the invisible, choice, equilibrium. The sephira that corresponds to the number 6 is *Tipheret* (beauty), or *Rahamin* (compassion). Its symbol is the hook, knot, or point that separates nothingness from being. It represents love as bridge between heaven and earth, God in nature, the idea in the word, light in darkness, the mediator. In its negative sense it stands for black magic, revolt, and destruction.

Other names for this card are decision, crossroads, and choice. This card reveals that reconsideration is still possible, that the directions up or down, right or left, are still open. These dual possibilities are expressed by the number 6 and the two interlaced triangles, the shape of *Anahata*, the heart chakra. See figure 12. The triangle pointing downward symbolizes the divine trinity, God's wisdom that descends from above; the triangle of humanity striving for knowledge points upward, and both are inseparably interwoven. This interweaving means logos and world order, the transition from buildup to destruction, becoming and passing away. It indicates the cycle of *yang* and *yin* wherein light contains the seed of darkness and darkness contains the seed of light.

The number 6 represents balance of powers, oscillation of all phenomena between plus and minus; it stands for creativity, although it is neither its principle nor its driving force. The number 6 signifies perfection because it is composed of 1 plus the first even number, 2, plus the first uneven number, 3: $1 + 2 + 3 = 6$. Six can also be read as $1 + 2 + 1 + 2$. This sequence emphasizes the

Figure 12. The Anahata Chakra.

joint influence of the masculine, active principle and the feminine, passive principle. This card evokes the choice each human being is forced to make; it shows that one must define one's values and that this definition must originate in the depths of one's consciousness; it means self-examination.

THEMES, ASSOCIATIONS, CORRESPONDENCES

The Lover(s) denotes discrimination, mutual relationship, coordination. In case of contradictory experiences, thought forms must be made tangible and intelligible. They must also be brought into harmonious agreement through a caring comprehension. The card shows the yearning of humankind for a harmonious relationship with infinity. The Lover(s) indicates good and evil, love and hate. It also signifies the balance between freedom and necessity. Finally, the card points to the link between cause and effect, destiny.

The ideogram for this card is

Astrological amplification: Traditionally card VI has been associated with the planet Venus, with Sagittarius because of Cupid's bow, and with Taurus, an earth sign ruled by Venus. Although this card seems to present us with an image of ambivalence that may suggest a connection to Gemini (an air sign ruled by Mercury), I believe that the energy is more Taurian. Moreover, Taurus also contains its own duality of earth/spirit. Indeed, this sign is conceived as an expression of the numinous descent of the divine impulse and its amalgamation with the earth, generating an inner conflict between idealism and materialism. Taurus the bull energizes and organizes spirit in matter; preparation, production, and perception are all its domain. The bull is creative, and although he is connected with the fertility of the earth, this is not the same as the fertile creativity of heaven. If the bull is allowed to take over, one may find oneself at the mercy of one's own desires. The underlying theme seems to deal with submission to a greater Self and the realization that the power of the bull is not "mine" but must be directed toward a more transcendent goal (Greene, 1984, pp. 183-189 and Sucher, 1982, pp. 80-82).

Cabalistic amplification: In its root, every soul is a composite of male and female, and only in the course of their decent do they separate into masculine and feminine souls. The descent of the supernal spirit (*Neshamah*) is brought about by the holy union of the king and queen, who are synonymous with *Tipheret* and *Malkuth*. The symbolism used to describe the descent of souls from the world of emanation assigns to each part of the soul a root in the world of the sephirot; the *Ru'ah* (anima) originates in the sephira *Tipheret* (Scholem, *Kabbalah*, p. 157). *Tipheret*, the place of the heart, is (according to Poncé) the place where the individual

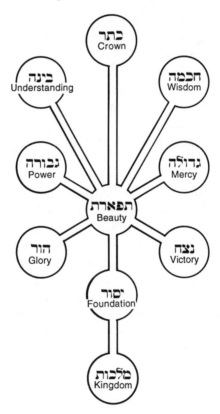

Figure 13. *Tipheret*, the mediating factor, the place of the heart, stands in the center of the Tree of Life. (From Poncé, *Kabbalah*, p. 104.)

becomes conscious of the needs of others. He sees others no longer in the light of his own needs, but in the light of theirs. Located in the center of the middle pillar of equilibrium, *Tipheret* is the sephira that symbolically represents the force needed to unite the opposites and contains the mediating factor, not only between two opposite sides, but also between above and below (Poncé, *Kabbalah*, p. 204).

Tipheret is the fulcrum of the essential nature of humankind; it is our very own, yet it partakes of realms above and below. Here, at the focus of the eight paths, is the synthesis, the watcher in moments of great danger, the observer who sees without eyes, whose awareness marks moments of strange lucidity. Heart of the Tree of Life, *Tipheret/Rahamin* has access to all the sephirot except *Malkuth* (see figure 13). Without *Tipheret*, *Malkuth* would therefore be a soulless automaton devoid of compassion and love.

Alchemical amplification: The play of opposites is characteristic of *coniunctio* symbolism. At times the sun-moon *coniunctio* presents itself not as a resolution of the conflict they represent, that is, the conflict between conscious and unconscious, but finds expression in the alchemical image of the sun with two kinds of rays, an image of the paradoxical duality of all psychological phenomena.

> The sun with two rays is more rightly adapted to influ-
> ence and more able to assimilate the unconscious by
> virtue of an open attitude, just as though there were a
> second consciousness behind consciousness—as if one
> had in the foreground of one's mind the ordinary oper-
> ating consciousness, while at the back something real-
> izes that that is only part of life (von Franz, 1980, p. 149).

This double-rayed conscious attitude (see figure 14) represents the capacity to hold the tension between opposites instead of wavering and being torn by them. This is the inner attitude that

Figure 14. The Sun.

leads to the philosopher's stone, itself an image of the union of opposites in which

> the "flesh" glorified itself in its own way; it would not transform itself into spirit but, on the contrary, "fixed" the spirit in the stone (Jung, CW 13, ¶ 127).

This is a promise that, although heaven was split from earth at the beginning of creation, this split will be healed and they will be rejoined by reconnecting the ego to the Self.

Psychological interpretation: Card VI, the Lover(s), represents both the first decisive choice to separate from regressive bonds and the first opportunity to transcend the tension between the opposites. From this vantage point, one can see that choice between either/or can evolve into the integration of "both/and" or "this and that." Through the conflict created by having to make a choice, one is forced to become aware of contradictory tendencies and to realize that in order to reach integration one has to take a stand at a higher level.

In the process of individuation, very often the same problems come up again and again; they seem to be settled, but after a while, they reappear. Some individuals assimilate a great deal, but feeling is left out, and with it, the moral aspect is omitted.

> They speak of the process of individuation as if they had arrived there and know all about it, which in a way is quite true, for they have assimilated it, let us say in fire, but not yet in earth. So the fire has to change into water and the water into earth, and then the whole thing has to be lived through once more as an ethical problem . . . The *coniunctio* refers to the living spirit and the spiritualization of the body, making the body incorporeal and the spirit concrete, bringing the opposites together in yet another way. In practice that would mean the end of the split between body and spirit (von Franz, *Alchemy*, p. 257-258).

Whenever one is capable of taking oneself out of a situation, it becomes an analogy of something psychological. Thus, all outer events in life can become parables of an inner process of symbolization. When looked at from this point of view, events can be integrated and one would be spiritualizing the physical while at

Figure 15. The six-pointed star, symbol of the alchemical *coniunctio* of water (male triangle, apex up) and fire (female triangle, apex down).

the same time, by applying a psychological realization in the concrete realm, one would be incarnating the spiritual (see figure 15).

Jungian interpretation: The Lover(s) is the only card that traditionally is presented in two entirely different versions. In some decks a young man and woman are being joined in marriage (Visconti-Sforza and Rider-Waite); in others a young man must choose between two women and, by implication, between two roads ahead (Marseilles, Wirth, Court de Gébelin). Instead of rejecting one or the other of these two versions as erroneous, we may see them as attempts to express a difficult concept.

> Because the arcane substance always points to the principal unconscious content, its peculiar nature shows in what relation that content stands to consciousness. If the conscious mind has accepted it, it has a positive form, if not, a negative one. If on the other hand the arcane substance is split into two figures, this means that the content has been partly accepted and partly rejected; it is seen under two different, incompatible aspects and is therefore taken to be two different things (Jung, CW 14, ¶ 195).

The two figures on each side of the young man may represent:

> the attack, first from one side and then from the other, of a dualistic being on the more restricted consciousness of man. The purpose or result of this assault is the widening of consciousness. . . . The one-after-another is a bearable

prelude to the deeper knowledge of the side-by-side, for this is an incomparably more difficult problem. Again, the view that good and evil are spiritual forces outside us, and that man is caught in the conflict between them, is more bearable by far than the insight that the opposites are the ineradicable and indispensable preconditions of all psychic life (Jung, CW 14, ¶ 205-206).

We are reminded here that tears, sorrow, and disappointment are bitter, but wisdom is the comforter in all psychic suffering. Indeed, bitterness and wisdom form a pair of polarities, and the common factor to both is, psychologically, the feeling function (Jung, CW 14, ¶ 330).

The feeling function, the place of listening with the heart, is represented in the cabala, as we have seen, by *Tipheret*, the sixth sephira. The words of the Apostle Paul (I Corinthians 13: 1-3) come to mind:

> I may speak in tongues of men or of angels, but if I am without love, I am a sounding gong or a clanging symbol. I may have the gift of prophecy, and know every hidden truth; I may have faith strong enough to move mountains; but if I have no love, I am nothing. I may dole out all I possess, or even give my body to be burnt, but if I have no love, I am none the better.

These words were the starting point of Jung's reflections on transpersonal love, which he describes in a passage of his *Memories, Dreams, Reflections* (p. 353f). In it, he begins by saying that St. Paul's words might well suggest the first condition of all cognition and the quintessence of divinity itself. He continues:

> Whatever the learned interpretation may be of the sentence "God is Love," the words affirm the *complexio oppositorum* of the Godhead. In my medical experience as well as in my own life I have again and again been faced with the mystery of love, and have never been able to explain what it is. . . . For we are in the deepest sense the victims and the instruments of cosmogonic "love." I put the word in quotation marks to indicate that I do not use it in its connotations of desiring, preferring, favoring, wishing, and similar feelings, but as something

superior to the individual, a unified and undivided whole. Being a part, man cannot grasp the whole. He is at its mercy. He may assent to it, or rebel against it; but he is always caught up by it and enclosed within it. He is dependent upon it and is sustained by it. Love is his light and his darkness, whose end he cannot see. "Love ceases not"—whether he speaks with the "tongues of angels," or with scientific exactitude traces the life of the cell down to its uttermost source. Man can try to name love, showering upon it all the names at his command, and still he will involve himself in endless self-deceptions. If he possesses a grain of wisdom, he will lay down his arms and name the unknown by the more unknown, *ignotum per ignotius*—that is, by the name of God. That is a confession of his subjection, his imperfection, and his dependence; but at the same time a testimony to his freedom to choose between truth and error.

We are reminded that Jung said of the Self:

[T]he self appears as a play of light and shadow, although conceived as a totality and unity in which the opposites are united. Since such a concept is irrepresentable—*tertium non datur*—it is transcendental (Jung, CW 6, ¶ 790).

Indeed, Jung points out that, although the Self expresses the unity of the personality as a whole,

the concept of the self is, in part, only *potentially* empirical . . . it encompasses both the experienceable and the inexperienceable (or the not yet experienced). . . . In so far as psychic totality, consisting of both conscious and unconscious contents, is a postulate, it is a *transcendental* concept, for it presupposes the existence of unconscious factors on empirical grounds and thus characterizes an entity that can be described only in part but, for the other part, remains at present unknowable and illimitable (Jung, CW 6, ¶ 789).

Through a differentiation of the Self, energy is supplied to unconscious contents that it activates and forces to the surface; the act of differentiation involves the detachment of disposable libido from both the outer and the inner object. Thus freed, the libido can energize the transcendent function. The libido retained by the Self is prevented from taking part in the conflict of opposites; it activates creative fantasy, an irrational, instinctive function that has the power to supply a content of such nature that it can unite the opposites.

> [T]he self is our life's goal, for it is the completest expression of the fateful combination we call individuality (Jung, CW 7, ¶ 404).

A crossroad is not only a place of choosing; it is also a place of meeting, of coming together of opposites. It may be that our card reminds us to include the third dimension, a vertical plane that would include the spiritual ascent here at the intersection of the mundane with the heavenly. Halevi presents the sephira *Tipheret* as:

> this self, poised half way between Heaven and Earth. Embedded in the body for a time it partakes of the upper and lower worlds, bringing the divine down into Matter and raising matter up towards spirit. Tipheret is at the juncture of the visible and the invisible (Halevi, *The Tree of Life*, p. 41).

SYMBOLIC LANGUAGE OF THE IMAGE

This card presents a young man standing at a crossroads between two women. He hesitates about the road to take. The woman on the right, dressed in blue, symbolizes sublimated love, wisdom; the one on his left wears an orange dress symbolizing sensuality and instinctual appetites. The motley costume of the young man reveals his ambivalence. In order to reach a decision, he must be strong and bold, as indicated by the tension of the bow in Cupid's hands, which also signifies sexual tension. In certain cards, Cupid is replaced by an angel. In this case, the young man and the angel together represent the involutional and evolutional movement on the earthly and spiritual planes.

The three figures (the young man and the two women) symbolize the Tree of Life with its three columns, representing divine energies and their opposition. The two women represent the problem of conflict as principle of all events. When depicting love and hatred, they symbolize the principle of existence, nature's forces instinctually active. In moral terms they symbolize good and evil; they are two aspects of our own personality. It is not by accident that the symbol of the sephira *Tipheret* is the knot. Indeed, a knot can be a tangle from which one cannot extricate oneself, a symbol of reciprocal paralysis of inner forces emphasizing entanglement with destiny or being caught in a net of one's principles and attitudes. It can also represent the capacity to be bound and committed, dedicated to a cause, or an inability to capture reality and reach the center of the labyrinth. It is therefore a dual symbol of binding and release, a complex image leading to balance and centering.

This card also points out that the initiate must choose between obedience and disobedience, that in order to attain enlightenment, one must submit to God's will , and that to the extent that one persists in self-centeredness, one remains a prisoner. In order to reach the three higher sephirot, one must endure the conflict between the opposites: out of this (being torn apart) one can become strong enough to find a way out, to resolve the drama between one's ideals and one's appetites. This ambivalence connects this card with the astrological sign of Gemini, the twins Castor and Pollux. It also recalls the double-faced Janus, God of beginnings and endings. The Lover(s) points to the necessity of discrimination between reality and whatever false image one may have of oneself or others. The presence of Cupid indicates the centrality of love as fundamental dynamic force, namely, libido.

Some cards show only the two lovers: the sense is then that two can become one, building a common will and a single action. Harmony and unity can also come through recognition that introversion is at the same time extroversion when inner events are experienced externally. The ego loses its position as center and place of refuge. In action and passion, the lost unity is recovered through experienced ecstasy. Paradise is then the present moment. Emptiness becomes apparent. Doors open and fixations to the past are given up. Revelation occurs.

This card also contains the symbol of banishment from paradise. Adam had to choose between obedience and disobedience to God's commands. Through his disobedience, death and separation came into the world. In paradise Adam and Eve felt sheltered, secure in the total harmony. Banished from paradise, the human being who has tasted from the fruit of the tree of knowledge now becomes a self-responsible individual. One must learn through painful experience to conceive and accept the identity of opposites; one must become self-reflective in order to reach the correct solution; one must learn to love and to be capable of self-sacrifice when needed. The choice will determine whether one's life will be self-fulfilling or miserable. The decision determines the direction of the will and has cosmic validity in relation to the fundamental principles of the universe. One's work in the fields allows one to extract sustenance from nature and to expand one's own being toward an all-encompassing love. Eating from the tree of knowledge means becoming conscious and thus aware of one's contradictory nature. It means also the beginning of the capacity to transcend the opposites, striving to attain a higher unity and a more stable balance.

The twelve rays of the cloud that supports Cupid remind us of the twelve stars in card III (the Empress). The fundamental principles of the universe are active here as well as there. However, card VI shows that while love can inspire and exalt, it can also induce loss of grounding and loss of seeing clearly when sight is veiled by love.

The alchemists observed that sexuality is the driving force behind all transformations; it is the libidinal power behind the strivings of humankind and the yearning of nature to bring all its possibilities to fruition from its unlimited richness.

VII
THE CHARIOT

The letter *zain* means triumph, property, arrow, weapon, God's influence. The sephira that corresponds to number 7 is *Netzah*, victory, the world of the angels, of the children of Elohim. The balance among the organized powers of nature that converges upon a common ideal goal is revealed in the essence of number 7. Seven also signifies movement, domination of spirit over matter, mutation, transformation; it reminds us that there are seven principles and seven capital sins. Its negative sense reveals hatred, violence, and destruction.

According to Jung, in the language of initiation the seven stages symbolize transformation (CW 12, ¶ 99). The number also alludes to the seven visible planets and their corresponding metals. The seven metals represent psychologically the collective constituents of personality (von Franz, 1966, p. 273); the uniqueness of the individual is expressed in the specific pattern of their constellation. The spirits of the seven metals are the arcana or the pillars of the *opus*: seven herbs, seven arts, seven stones, seven letters, and seven words. Seven is significant as the number of the days of creation, the seven ages of the world; it is said that in the seventh and last age, the Holy Spirit will appear and the "Great Sabbath" will come upon humankind. The number seven relates to the Holy Spirit because of the seven gifts of grace (von Franz, 1966, p. 215).

The number seven, which is composed of 3 + 4—activity and competence—indicates that freedom is achieved by combining versatility and mastery, exertion and steadfastness. Seven is also a combination of 3 + 3 + 1. The first (material) trinity is represented by the chariot and the two horses; the second (spiritual) trinity is composed of the charioteer, his scepter, and his crown; the sun in midheaven portrays the One. According to Jacob

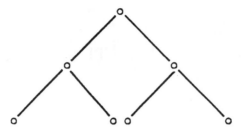

Figure 16. Triad and quaternity.

Boehme, there are in the cosmos seven organizing spirits that actualize eternal wisdom. They consist of an upper triad (desire, motion, rest), a lower, natural triad (love, world, body), and a mediator (lightning or fire) that establishes contact between nature and spirit. In other systems seven stands for the clash between an upper, spiritual triad and a lower, natural quaternity (von Franz, 1966, p. 229). See figure 16.

THEMES, ASSOCIATIONS, CORRESPONDENCES

The Chariot represents receptivity, balance, mastery, and triumph. Pain is necessary to reach insights and gain command over one's passions. Yet psychic mobility triumphs over inertia and fixation. Creative and directive principles are synthesized in this card, and balance exists between intellectual and emotional powers, between endurance and carrying power. The Chariot symbolizes the triumph of exertion over perseverance; conquest, strength, and urgency. Disorientation and/or reorientation may dominate.

The ideogram for this card is ⸬

Astrological amplification: The Chariot has been assigned the planets Neptune, Mars, Venus, as well as the Sun, and the signs Gemini, Sagittarius, and Pisces. I have chosen to associate it with Sagittarius because of its active, expansive, and conquering energy. Indeed, this is not a sign comfortable with the limitations and mundane requirements of life. The primary vision of Sagittarius is the ceaseless quest for spirit that can transcend fate and death. The qualities traditionally associated with Sagittarius create a realm of justice as an alternative to the merciless vengeance of nature and necessity (Nemesis and Moira). Sagittarius is a creature worthy of dignity and honor, part daimon and part god, part beast and part immortal, who turns his eyes to the immortal half of himself and must then pay the price of caring for the suffering body he has so long ignored. Sagittarius can heal and give wise prophetic advice to every man's ills save his own; his soul is wounded by the collision of his benign nature with the darkness and poison of the world. Perhaps because of this rather than despite it, Sagittarius offers hope and optimism to himself and to others (Greene, 1984 p. 235-242).

Cabalistic amplification: After the second century, Merkabah mystics kept hidden the secret of combining and meditating on the letters in order to induce the Lightning Flash. *Merkabah* means not only this technique but also the Divine Vehicle, the Chariot. Gazing into the Chariot meant gazing into the letters of God's name, mentally constructed into the form of a chariot. This was a technique that Abraham Abulafia (1240-1290) used to help his disciples overcome mental obstacles. Human thought was to be transformed into a vehicle for spiritual "enthusiasm," which was the chariot that would draw the disciples closer to the Throne of Glory. Enthusiasm gave material for the imagination and substance for the intellect. Concentrating on the chariot, the disciple felt coursing in his body and through his spine an evoked life force that connected him to God. By probing the apparently random letters that comprise all of nature, he guided the chariot in a perfect display of spiritual horsemanship, completely in control of all his senses. It is conceivable that the sephira *Netzah* (meaning life force) may have contributed to this spiritual horsemanship.

Alchemical amplification: In the alchemical text concerning the "chariot of Aristotle," a serpent is placed "in a chariot of its vessel and is led hither and thither by the fourfold rotation of the natures, but it should be securely enclosed." In Jung's interpretation, the serpent is the *prima materia, Serpens Hermetis*; the fourfold rotation of the natures corresponds to transformation through the four elements, from earth to fire.

> This symbolism describes in abbreviated form the essentials of the opus: the serpent of Hermes . . . the Nous that animates the cold part of nature—that is, the

unconscious—is enclosed in the spherical vessel . . . which in the alchemical view, represents the world and the soul. The psychologist would see it rather as the psychic reflection of the world, namely *consciousness* of the world and the psyche. The transformation corresponds to the psychic process of assimilation and integration by means of the transcendent function (Jung, CW 14, ¶ 261).

Psychological interpretation: The Chariot represents the effect of the alliance of the trained intellect, disciplined body, and practical understanding served by the optimism of youthful energy. It is the victory of balance in action, of successful negotiation of delicate successive adaptations to the necessity of the moment.

Jungian interpretation: The Chariot is, in a sense, the symbol of earthly life (CW 14, ¶ 273); the charioteer is a living spirit who uses the chariot as his body, consisting of the four elements.

The chariot's four posts indicate that

> . . . the four natures or elements are gathered together, . . . i.e., the four aspects or functions are integrated with consciousness, so that the state of totality has almost been attained. Had it really been attained, the opus would be consummated at this point, but the "result" is obtained only by advancing further. The "result" therefore means something more than integration of the four natures (Jung, CW 14, ¶ 265).

Indeed,

> . . . the process of transformation does not come to an end with the production of the quaternity symbol. The continuation of the opus leads to the dangerous crossing . . . signifying death and re-birth. [By the paradox] "running without running, moving without motion" . . . one introduces a coincidence of opposites just at this point (CW 14, ¶ 274) . . . . [T]he union of supreme opposites . . . is the crowning of the opus and the goal of the peregrination (Jung, CW 14, ¶ 276).

The wheels remind us that

... deep inside the psyche the wheels go on turning, performing those cyclic evolutions which bring the mandala of the total personality, the ground-plan of the self, closer to consciousness (Jung, CW 14, ¶ 262).

SYMBOLIC LANGUAGE OF THE IMAGE

In contrast to the Emperor (card IV), installed immobile, rigid, and isolated on his throne, the driver of the Chariot travels through the world filling space with energy, inspiring through spirit, and demonstrating the effort involved in overcoming inertia. His is the victory of movement, of taking in and stepping out, of proceding from the known to the unknown. This card shows that the conflict in the Lover(s) (card VI) is overcome; the charioteer stands above it. Through dynamic liberation from the tension between these opposites, a new level of understanding has been reached. The charioteer's scepter and crown enable us to recognize him as a carrier of two higher principles of personality development, the unfolding and the expanding, which join to lead toward wholeness.

The golden crown, like a halo, connects the charioteer with the illumination and the energy of the sun. The crown is identified with the divine spirit in humankind. Its circular shape expresses its eternal and celestial nature: it is a link between God and humankind, the crown and the crowned, the immortal and the mortal (Knapp, p. 204). Thus, the charioteer may symbolize a mediating function between the human being and God, and a bridge between his or her own material and spiritual natures. The sun overhead represents the impartiality needed to keep the chariot pointed straight ahead. It is the centerpoint of fairness, justice, and focused spiritual energy that urges the individual toward self-development, self-affirmation, and the deliberate assumption of responsibilities.

The charioteer is standing, a position that increases the difficulty of his task because he must both muster his strength and find the delicate balance necessary to steer the horses of instinctual vitality while keeping the chariot steady—perched as it is on two wheels that barely touch the ground at a single point when stationary, but which rapidly change from one moment to the next when moving. He thus illustrates the complex and precarious combination of talents needed to achieve stability by keeping opposites in balance: by offsetting the regressive pull of psychic inertia with the need for change, the security of containment with the curiosity to explore inner and outer space, one can reach detachment from the past and the flexibility to intuitively change direction whenever needed. By combining flexibility and determination, by having the strength to command the horses as well as the delicate sensibility to keep the chariot steady on two wheels, space can be explored, consciousness expanded, and one can achieve a new, transcendent standpoint.

The standing position of the charioteer also represents the connection between the eternal and the human spirit, equanimity and steadfastness under difficult circumstances, the necessity to keep energies in balance and under control in order to be effective. The scepter symbolizes the intrinsic unity inherent in any event, the ability to determine the direction the journey will take, and the possibility of interrupting the movement or repeating it, of accelerating it or slowing it down. The orb on top of the scepter signifies quintessence and represents the innermost center, the kernel. In some decks it displays a triangle in a square, the 3 and the 4, a symbol of embodied spirit. When this symbol is surrounded by a circle, it proclaims that God dwells in his creature through all eternity. The winged globe that emblazons the front panel of the chariot suggests the astral body that provides the frame within which the processes of the material body develop. Its etheric nature guarantees life and is the support and carrier of all vital phenomena. This orb, the *eidolon* of the Greeks, mediator of contact with the earth, suggests cosmic participation in this process.

The charioteer's armor represents defense against the outer world and readiness to do battle. The charioteer is protected against partiality by the masonic square sometimes seen on his breastplate. The two moon crescents on his shoulders signify feminine endurance, his readiness to bear and assume variability. They also signify mastery over the ebb and flow of moods and emotions, over the movements of the heart, over the subtle powers that draw consciousness into ecstatic states. The pole that connects the horses to the chariot denotes strengthening of the will to guide the horses and the vital energy they stand for; it means determination and its practical execution.

Utilizing a chariot signifies action that reveals and expands through advance and retreat. The square shape of the chariot points toward the totality of the occurrence, while its movement allows space to be experienced bodily. Therewith, expansion of consciousness becomes possible and is now able to provide the perspective necessary to see things objectively and to avoid the stultifying monotony of the habitual; it allows change of viewpoint through surprising and fortuitous insight. At another level, the square shape of the chariot may also point to the fine substances directing the dynamic manifestations of the body and mediating between the perceptible and the imperceptible, between the coarse and the subtle.

The four posts indicate the relationship between control and passion, between intellect and instinct. The blue canopy represents the firmament that separates the temporal from the eternal and emphasizes that, despite all our spiritual efforts, we have only a limited capacity for perception. The stars on the canopy, which reiterate the divine guidance, also warn against pettiness. The wheels represent the vital energy that reveals itself in movement; they promote intuitive understanding and expansion of consciousness into unknown territories.

The chariot is pulled by two horses representing creative and destructive forces. It is the function of the inventive intelligence evinced by the charioteer to harness and yoke both the light and the dark horse in innovative service to the task at hand. Left without a guide, they would turn against each other; taken together, the two horses show the balance possible between activity and passivity, intelligence and feeling. In some decks the horses have different colors that can be interpreted as follows. A red or yellow horse indicates fiery temperament, unpredictability, active leadership or, conversely, fearfulness, and sensitivity. A black or blue horse represents passivity, mourning, loss, renunciation. A white horse indicates that instincts are still dormant or are transcended; it may also represent purposeless, naive action. At times one of the horses is depicted rearing; this points to a fear of having to give up a familiar ego stance, a fearful retreat from the abyss. In some tarot decks the two horses are depicted as a single body with two heads. The art of the charioteer is then to harness this creature in such a manner that it does not get entangled in the reins and does not stand in its own way. Symbolically this process is represented by the caduceus, the snake staff of Mercurius. The bridle and reins represent the capacity to stop the train of thought and to be in charge of one's feelings. They depict the process of becoming conscious, of recognizing the road onto which one has to steer. It means the capacity to utilize the skills one has acquired.

Psychologically, becoming conscious of the multiple layers of the ego makes the relativization of the ego and its connection to the Self easier. The possibility of doing so is a given, but there is always the danger that one might abandon the entire process or that, overwhelmed by the unconscious energy of a complex, one might race forward compulsively, out of control, unwilling or unable to rein oneself in.

VIII
JUSTICE

ח

The letter *cheth* is the symbol of justice, distribution, a field, origin and effect, responsibility. The sephira that corresponds to the number 8 is *Hod*, meaning fame, vitality, evolution and involution, the interchangeableness of oscillation and balance. Justice is the sphere of the formulation of forms, taking the natural forces expressed in card VII (the Chariot) and shaping them with authority (card IV, the Emperor) and with sympathy (card VI, the Lover[s]). Neither cold-blooded authority nor mushy sympathy can give shape; the one is too rigid; the other, too incohesive. Form needs the correct amount of cohesion, an optimal mixture of solid and fluid. In its negative sense card VIII reveals the tendency to act impulsively, automatically, or to be too conservative.

The number 8 represents not only the heightened tension and lawful definition of the number 4; seen as two interwoven squares (figure 17), it also suggests a state of balance that is as necessary for Justice as are order and truth. The goddess Maat, the incarnation of truth (symbolized by her diadem of ostrich feathers), accompanied Toth at the weighing of souls in the Egyptian mysteries. Her image is also associated with Justice.

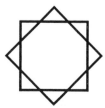

Figure 17. Interlinked squares.

After the seven days of creation, a new cycle begins with card VIII. The first sequence of seven showed the spirit as the principle of movement; card VIII depicts organization of existence, order. Themis (order) brings to mind the Empress (card III), who has now become severe and inexorable; her throne is as immutable as the Emperor's; she has lost her wings.

Compared to card VI, which holds the middle, there is a correspondence across it between cards IV and VIII. (See figure 18.) What would the Emperor be without Justice? His administration would be ineffective if it were not connected to concrete facts. The Emperor (card IV) represents the principle of life; he would radiate it in vain if this principle were not coordinated with Justice. Moreover, nature (card III) also organizes and distributes the powers of life according to the lawful measures of card VIII. And what would Justice be without imaginative sympathy (card VI)?

With the Chariot, the first two trinities are united in the first sequence of seven, corresponding (as suggested above) to the development of spirit. Card VIII begins the second sequence of seven, corresponding to the development of soul. Here the tension inherent in the lawful connections between cause and effect becomes even greater. The third sequence of seven concerns the development of fixation in the body.

Card VIII can also be seen as the second link in the third trinity. From this point of view, Justice takes a passive stance opposite the Chariot. In contrast to the Chariot, representing the spirit as universal mover, Justice depicts creation of life through orderliness and organization. The task of Justice is to lighten, order, and systematize chaos; all creatures can exist thanks to the lawfulness ordained by Justice. Anarchy would otherwise by synonymous with void.

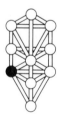

Figure 18. Justice located on the Tree of Life.

THEMES, ASSOCIATIONS, CORRESPONDENCES

Justice denotes balance, action, work. God's justice reveals itself in the universe through oscillation between opposites. The law of reaction comprises the dual movement of the powers of evolution and involution and their union in their results. This card reminds us that human beings must judge their actions and the consequences thereof. Justice also represents the balance between the forces of endurance and dynamism, between emotionality and reason, between absolute and relative truth, between illusion and reality. Justice contributes to maintenance of the social order, responsibility, reward and punishment. It indicates limited human justice.

The Ideogram of this card is

Astrological amplification: To Justice are attributed the planets Saturn, Mercury, and Venus, as well as the signs Capricorn, Libra, and Cancer. Libra, the sign of the balance, is ruled by Venus, goddess of partnership, of reciprocal relationships, communication, communion, beauty, and sympathy. However, Libra is the only sign of the zodiac that is represented by an inanimate object. This suggests that as we arrive at the point of equilibrium reflected in the autumnal equinox, we meet something that is very far removed from the instinctual. Indeed, the faculties of judgment, reflection, discrimination, and sorting out are a basic feature of this sign, the fruit of conscious effort and not a natural development. The goddess of justice has acquired something more refined than the bloody and dark instinct of vengeance; this goddess judges according to human law and morality. Judgment, in the Libran sense, rests upon careful assessment and reflection before any sentence is given (Greene, 1984, p. 221).

Cabalistic amplification: The function of *Hod*, the eighth sephira (meaning splendor, or reverberation), is to pick up and pass on information. *Hod* also controls the vital forces of the body, the voluntary processes. This includes the senses, which can be directed to respond and reverberate to incoming data. Beyond receiving all stimuli from the environment, whether physical, intellectual, or emotional, *Hod* computes the meaning in the sound of words, symbols, and forms and connects inside to outside. Besides responding to the outer world, as does the entire passive column of which *Hod* is the bottom rung, *Hod* also checks *Netzah*, its opposite on the active column. *Hod* is, therefore, the sephira of mental input, of setting limits, of checks and balances (Halevi, *Tree of Life*, p. 32, 34, 42).

Alchemical amplification: Measurement, numbering, weighing, and quantitative consciousness in general belong to the operation of *separatio*. So, likewise, does the setting of boundaries. The golden proportion (a/b = b/c), a *separatio* symbol, expresses the idea that there is a particular way to separate the opposites that creates a third entity (the proportion or mean between them) of great value. The image of the golden mean can be understood psychologically as a symbolic expression of the ego's relation to the Self. The spirit and the letter of the law are also connected with the balance between opposites, and justice can be served only by their reconciliation. The separation of opposites is the original sin committed by becoming conscious, and its redemption is the task of individuation.

Psychological interpretation: In order to give a solid direction to one's life and to estimate correctly one's actions and their consequences, one has to allow the largely ignored aspirations and urges of the unconscious to challenge self-satisfaction with one's successful conscious choices.

Jungian interpretation: Seated between two pillars (will and providence), Justice represents the equilibrium between individual will and universal providence. She holds a sword in her right hand and a balance in her left. In *The Origins and History of Consciousness*, Neumann considers the sword symbolic of an active element of the defense of consciousness against the unconscious. Consciousness cuts unconscious elements into "bite-sized" pieces to make them absorbable. Indeed:

> The assimilative powers of consciousness which enable it to grasp objects first as images and symbols, then as contents and finally as concepts and to absorb and arrange them in a new order, presuppose the analytic function. By its means the destructive tendency of the unconscious becomes a positive function of consciousness . . . . The assimilation of the destructive tendencies of the unconscious is thus closely connected with the "negative" qualities of consciousness (Neumann, 1973, p. 317).

Understanding and digestion of unconscious contents are associated by Jung with

> ... the automatic and instinctive reality of the unconscious, which is aiming all the time at the creation of a new balance and will moreover achieve this aim, provided that the conscious mind is capable of assimilating the contents produced by the unconscious ... (Jung, CW 7, ¶ 253).

The balance that Justice has to maintain weighs individual freedom against universal order, punitive earthy justice against the divine justice of grace, inner against outer standards:

> ... the tragic counterplay between inside and outside ... represents, at bottom, the energetics of the life process, the polar tension that is necessary for self-regulation. However, different ... these opposing forces may be, their fundamental meaning and desire is the life of the individual: they always fluctuate round this centre of balance (Jung, CW 7, ¶ 311).

The threefold nature of the suspended balance pans and the relationship of both pans to their vertical support and to the figure of Justice may be likened to the transcendent function and its relationship to the conflict between opposites. Jung says:

> The shuttling to and fro of arguments and affects represents the transcendent function of opposites. the confrontation of the two positions generates a tension charged with energy and creates a living, third thing ... a movement out of the suspension between opposites, a living birth that leads to a new level of being, a new situation. The transcendent function manifests itself as a quality of conjoined opposites (Jung, CW 8, ¶ 189).

Unlike the sword, the scales of the balance are mobile, a symbol of constant fluid negotiation between the two opposing tendencies it connects; it thus transposes inwardly the exquisite precarious equilibrium that the charioteer in card VII confronted outwardly.

For the narcissistically wounded, caught in the claws of the devouring, destructive parental dragon, the sword of Justice and the courage to use it is the needful gesture. Stuck at the concrete level, Justice's balance could provide them with the capacity to weigh "this" and "that" instead of having to choose between their wrenching "either/or." Most of all, their lost sense of fairness and the despair of ever having the wrongs committed against them recognized—and of being vindicated—could be replaced by a hopeful intimation that change is possible. The painful conflict between opposites that seems insurmountable may find a potential solution in Justice's equanimity and in her commitment to find, in fine-tuned oscillations, the needed equilibrium in the center.

SYMBOLIC LANGUAGE OF THE IMAGE

The dress and bearing of Justice bring to mind the Empress (card III). The figure of Justice holds the balance and the sword and gives a just and measured sentence. She separates right from wrong, authentic from false, detached from personal considerations. Sentences are executed without indulgence in order to reestablish the disrupted balance. She symbolizes both the peaceful and the wrathful faces of God. Justice is represented without wings because here the laws of matter reach their practical application; she cannot rise beyond the material. Her crown bears the sun sign, which means that the principle of higher organization and order assigns to all things their rightful place; it further indicates that recognition of truth frees from doubt and fear and that constructive powers are coordinated. In some decks the circle surrounds a square jewel, symbolizing the role of justice, which encompasses all fundamental manifestation; it may also show the activating power that exists in matter. The sharp indentations of the crown signify severe and sometimes cruel sentences. In other decks Justice wears a triple crown. This may be interpreted as representing the three functions of justice, in turn corresponding to the three degrees of knowledge—instruction, hypothetical (*doxa*); debate, argumentative (*dianoia*); and decision, intuitive (*episteme*). Justice is not possible unless we respect fairness and truth as important ethical principles and unless we allow mercy to balance severity in the judgments we render.

The sword indicates the inexorable manner in which the application of the sentence is executed, for no violation of the law remains unpunished; nevertheless, all persons are judged according to their circumstances and abilities. The sword also means carefulness, precision of differentiation, immediate enforcement of decision. It reminds us that the ruler has the right to pardon and that his discriminations have to be fluid; otherwise, rigidity may take over. Her passive, receptive bearing suggests that the correct results of our actions depend on being in concordance with the basic lawfulness and true nature of things.

The two columns represent life and death determining the domain of activity, time limit. The two ornaments on top of the columns bring to mind the dual aspects of all events. In the human being, this duality represents the capacity to conceive of a point of view opposite to one's own. It stands for complementary aspects, duality, division. When the shape of the ornaments is reminiscent of a pomegranate cut in half, it reminds us that lawfulness has also to be applied in the realm of fertility, of feelings, of life-giving activity. The balance also reminds us that the law of equilibrium is valid in the vital sphere and that any excess of effort must be compensated for by a time of quiet repose. The balance in this context can be seen as representing the highest level of universal lawfulness, the basic condition for endurance and effectiveness, the middle road, the equalization of the polarities of stasis and flow. It indicates that correct attention is the basis for the development of objectivity and that mindfulness must reach throughout all the domains of existence. When everything is in balance, inner stillness provides moments for the call of conscience to be heard and for the truth of existence to be reassessed.

The two balance pans indicate the necessary equalization between activity and passivity, wakefulness and sleep, excitement and depression, expansion and contraction. The indicator needle searches for that which goes beyond the dimensionless point in the middle, the invisible center that remains beyond human perception, the identity of absolute truth and unconditional, undisrupted existence, the point at which the upper and lower worlds meet on their similar journey toward each other. The scale is the instrument of atonement of faults. It is the balance whose one pan is on earth and the other, in heaven; as we are forgiven, so must we forgive. It may also mean sympathy, relationship between Self and ego (either in synthesis or in analysis), the restriction or expansion of space. When the pans are in perfect equipoise, it denotes the integration of conscious and unconscious strivings.

Both the Emperor and Justice carry the sun sign. With respect to the Emperor, it refers chiefly to the heart and all-encompassing love; for Justice, it refers to the connection between understanding and reason. In Egyptian lore, the judge of the dead weighs the soul of the deceased by placing it on one of the balance pans; counterbalanced by a feather on the other, the soul has to be found as light or lighter. The Christian judge of the dead, the Archangel Michael, is the conqueror of the dragon of hell; he is represented in card XIX (the Sun) blowing the trumpet of judgment day.

IX
THE HERMIT ט

The letter *teth* means shrewdness, wisdom roof, shield, everything that protects and isolates. It evokes weaving, an activity that is linked to time. Its symbol is the snake, which has a shape similar to the form of the letter. The sephira that corresponds to the number 9 is *Yesod*, meaning foundation, hierarchy, harmony, order, perfection, potential to become and accomplish, wisdom, prudence, stillness. In a negative sense it means superstition, panic.

The point (card I) shines now: it is the central light of the space extending symmetrically in eight directions. (See figure 19.) Even though the ray of light is not very bright and projects only partially onto the path, it nevertheless reaches into hidden corners.

Nine may be defined as 3 × 3, three triads in one triad—spirit, intellect, and feeling coexisting in the corporeal. It means light, life, love; it means initiation and completion. As 8 + 1, it represents the "novenary foetus," the fulfillment of the mysteries, the culmination of the mystic art. As the quintessence is to the quaternity, so also is the number nine to the *ogdoad* (Jung, CW 13, ¶ 187).

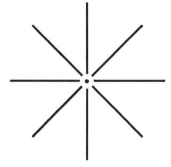

Figure 19. The eight-pointed star and its central light.

THEMES, ASSOCIATIONS, CORRESPONDENCES

The Hermit denotes the courage to face oneself; he connotes wisdom and knowledge. He is will directed by ideals and intelligence, and he represents actions that are determined by prudence, experience, and feeling.

The ideogram for this card is

Astrological amplification: To the Hermit have been attributed the planets Mars, Jupiter, Saturn, and Uranus, as well as the signs Aries and Leo. It seems to me that Aries and Leo, both fire signs, have too much brightness to fit our image. With Scorpio we are forced to conjure up the sagacity needed to handle the primordial darkness and poison that one finds if and when one digs deep enough. Scorpio's daimon drives him into collision with all that is terrifying, shadowy, and destructive in life. Reflection is necessary, as is fire, whether we experience it as the burning of intense emotion contained within or as the light of insight and consciousness. More often than not, the most profound expression of this battle is within the individual, the final goal being transformation rather than riddance and regression. Scorpio sees in this fight, beyond restless groping for power and egotism, the soul's journey through darkness to God. The lofty aspirations of Scorpio can lead to a loathing of life and its temptations, yet both loathing and aspiration spring from the same mysterious core—half sexuality, half spirituality. When they are both embraced, a figure of dignity and redemption emerges (Greene, 1984, p. 234).

Yesod has a phallic aspect: he fills *Malkuth* "and waters her with waters from on high," and signifies the genital region of the Original Man (Jung, CW 14, ¶ 18, n. 120). This sephira is also called *Zaddik*, or the Just One (Jung, CW 14, ¶ 634), the incarnation of the redeemer in each generation, and thus connects with the Scorpio water sign ♏, which presents the image of the triple portal leading to spiritual truth and the experience of transcendence (Sucher, 1982, pp. 94-97).

Cabalistic amplification: *Yesod* (foundation) or *Zaddik* (the Righteous One) is the ninth sephira; it is found at the apex of the lowest triad of the cabalistic tree (figure 20 on page 93). This sephira is considered to be a halfway station through which all souls must pass before entering the "treasure-house of souls," which is located in celestial paradise, where they live in bliss until being called to

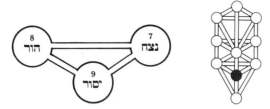

Figure 20. The Hermit located on the Tree of Life. (From Poncé, *Kabbalah*, pp. 128-129.)

descend still further and assume human form (Scholem, 1974, p. 157). On the central column, but on a rung lower than *Tipheret*, *Yesod* is like a mirror/screen, continually reflecting and projecting into ordinary consciousness what is presented by the paths flowing into it. These paths suspend it among the four points *Tipheret, Netzah, Hod,* and *Malkuth,* and through it one can see the inner and the outer worlds. *Yesod* is supplied by data coming from *Hod* (form), *Netzah* (energy), and *Malkuth* (the physical vehicle lived in); ideally *Yesod* is the servant of *Tipheret.*

At times the psychological Yesodic mantle is fashioned here; partly it protects, but partly it imprisons. *Yesod* hovers, a fragile, ephemeral structure held in balance between soul and body consciousness (Halevi, *Tree of Life*, pp. 44-45). *Yesod* belongs both to consciousness and to the unconscious, and so to some extent it forms a bridge between the two realms (Hurwitz, 1968, p. 205). *Yesod* connects *Malkuth*, the earth below, through *Tipheret*, the heart, and soars to *Kether*, the spirit.

Alchemical amplification: *Yesod* has many meanings that are related to Mercurius. In alchemy, Mercurius is the "ligament of the soul," uniting spirit and body. His dual nature enables him to play the role of mediator; he is corporeal and spiritual, and is himself the union of these two principles.

> Correspondingly, in Yesod is accomplished the mystery of the "unitio" of the upper, Tifereth, and the lower, Malchuth. He is also called the "covenant of peace, the . . . firm, reliable, constant" because he leads the emanation of Tifereth down into Malchuth (Jung, CW 14, ¶ 635).

This *unitio* may evoke the blending resulting from the alchemical operation of *liquefactio*, which is one of the ways of first dissolving consciousness and coming closer to the unconscious. One of the initial stages of the alchemical *opus* is very often *liquefactio*, the turning into liquid in order to undo the *prima materia* that is often hardened or solidified and therefore cannot be used to make the philosopher's stone. This is a very apt image for the initial stage of analysis in which one often has to melt down the defensive structures, the scaffolding of the ego indispensable for survival.

Psychological interpretation: When self-examination and isolation replace gregariousness, the resulting introjection activates the unconscious. Although muffled and weak, the spark of eternal light reveals, in the dark night of the soul, dimensions and shapes thus far unattended. The challenge that this search for meaning creates must be met and faced by anyone who reaches beyond conventional values in favor of inner truth.

Jungian interpretation: In volume 14 of his *Collected Works*, Jung places the sephira *Yesod* in context both horizontally and vertically:

> Yesod unites the emanation of the right, masculine side (Nezach, life-force) with the left, feminine side (Hod, beauty). Yesod is as a part to the whole, and the whole is Tifereth, who is named the sun. . . . The earth, Malchuth, is Yesod's "footstool" (¶ 635, 638).

Alchemically and astrologically, Jung has observed:

> Just as Mercurius is the prima materia and the basis of the whole process, so Yesod means "foundation." In natural things Yesod . . . is the basis of the whole art of transmutation.

> As the prima materia is also called lead and Saturn, we should mention that the Sabbath is co-ordinated with Yesod, as is the letter Teth, which stands under the influence of Shabtai (Saturn) (¶ 636, 637).

Jung also warns (CW 11, ¶ 786) that one-sidedness produces very similar forms of monasticism, guaranteeing to the Hermit an unswerving singleness of purpose, a desperate effort to conquer the mere naturalness of life. The Hermit is the assertion of mind over matter, delighting in the use of the most powerful weapon ever devised by nature—the conscious mind. Jung warns of the effects this one-sidedness can have: "despite appearance to the contrary, the spiritual situation of the hermit is one of deficiency after all." What the hermit lacks is the *"actual and immediate experience of spiritual reality"* so that the hunger of his soul can be sated by the vision of numinous images. This experience is in itself, according to Jung, needful "compensation for the emptiness and barrenness of traditional forms of exclusively rational doctrines" (CW 10, ¶ 651).

SYMBOLIC LANGUAGE OF THE IMAGE

The driver of the Chariot (card VII) rashly attempts to force progress, whereas Justice (card VIII) delays decisions through hesitation. These opposites are reconciled in the Hermit: he is neither recklessly active nor stubbornly immobile. He tests the road upon which he treads with his staff, which represents the knowledge he has acquired and gives him the will to stability. The Hermit is the wise old man, the monk, the hunchback. His task is to share his esoteric knowledge and to decide who is mature enough to receive it. The wise old man is able to indicate the germs of future development that are already predicted by the High Priestess (card II). The concentration of spiritual power that he represents expresses the union of the archetypal world with the world of intelligible forms (the Empress, card III) and the universal laws that underlie their representation (the Emperor and Justice, cards IV and VIII).

The Hermit's dark coat indicates that he has turned away from ephemeral things; its blue lining shows that spiritual forces deepen in reclusion. The coat can also be interpreted as denoting introversion of energies, passive activity. His knowledge coordinates and strengthens his will power. The coat deflects any draft of air so that the light will not flicker. The Hermit works in secret, undisturbed by the unexpected; he protects himself from passions that may darken the light of reason. His hidden influence forms the face of the future. The clear sky above shows that he is free from possessiveness and worry. The erect snake signifies the healing powers he commands. The hood emphasizes that he looks neither sideways nor behind, only straight ahead.

The future forms itself in stillness, which is self-reflective. The Hermit shows solitude as a necessity of human existence in order to make contact with oneself in silence. Active solitude puts us in contact with nature. Passive solitude (actually, loneliness) is experienced as fate, as life weariness. As personification of the plastic powers of the universe, the Hermit becomes the craftsman who carefully builds the scaffold of vital structures.

The Hermit represents liberation from superficiality, from diversion, existential anxiety, yearning for security, intense fixation on bodily processes, and from loneliness. The monk's habit shows an adjustment between retreat and helpful activity.

When the snake that winds itself up the staff is interpreted in modern terms as a phallic symbol, the sage becomes connected to Adonis and Attis, who, like the phallus, are both dying and resurrecting gods.

In the hopeless moments of one's "night sea journey," when from the dark side of one's soul there is no end in sight, no flicker of light to guide one, the Hermit could be

> . . . that long-expected friend of his soul, the immortal one, [who] has now really come "to lead captivity captive"; that is, to seize hold of him by whom this immortal had always been confined and held prisoner, and to make his life flow into that greater life (Jung, CW 9/1, ¶ 217).

In the space that extends in all eight directions, the spark of light that has now appeared is the lantern of the Hermit. For the first time a center, an emphasized centerpoint, has emerged in the "World of Action," illuminating a small surface around it. We may be allowed to call this event the birth of consciousness, which according to Bernoulli (1934, p. 407), will now exist for a time, solitary and unrelated.

The Hermit represents the functional third connecting the two opposites: the active Chariot (card VII) and the passive Justice (card VIII). It is the treasure house of images, the sphere of magic, the sphere of the moon. It represents procreative strength, with *Yesod* being called the organ of generation from which new life flows. *Yesod* has also been called the channel of the waters from above, for the spiritual energy that will enliven earth and humankind. Its fluidity is associated with the moon energy transmitting and collecting the emanations of all the other sephirot. Fluidity is expressed as well in the melting and washing away, which is often the alchemical connotation of a dissolution of personality in tears and despair. It is those moments of "loss of soul" that provide

> . . . the highest and most decisive experience of all, which is to be alone with [one's] own self, or whatever else one chooses to call the objectivity of the psyche. The patient must be alone if he is to find out what it is that supports him when he can no longer support himself. Only this experience can give him an indestructible foundation (Jung, CW 12, ¶ 32).

It may be that in these moments it is the visitation of the Hermit that makes all the difference. Indeed, the Hermit (*Yesod* = foundation) is himself this purposeful reflection and concentration of moral and physical forces that come about spontaneously in the psychic space when conscious thought is not yet, or is no longer, possible. The concentration and tension of psychic forces have something about them that always looks like magic: they develop an unexpected power of endurance that is often superior to the conscious effort of will involved (CW 9/1, ¶ 402).

X
THE WHEEL
OF FORTUNE

The letter of *yod* depicts the Wheel of Fortune, the index finger. It is order, extension , time, duration. The image of the Wheel is a symbol of the quest for progress, including resignation and renewed effort, at the individual level.

The sephira corresponding to the number 10 is *Malkuth*, the kingdom, the locus of residence of the exiled *Shekina*. It stands for solidarity among creatures and things linked by the laws of nature. In its negative form it means resistance to Spirit.

Ten is the principle of orderliness of numbers. It means "goal," the interweaving of origin and effect. The number 10 is the symbol of the unreachable oneness into which we may have a glimpse through the ten sephirot that reflect it. It is the oneness as synthesis of all numbers, the sum of the numbers 1 through 4, and key to the mystery of God's names.

The decade is "soul producing," and according to the Pythagoreans, life and light are united in it; it is therefore an image of the world-creating *nous*. The monad is descended from the original pneuma and includes the decade, and the decade, in its turn, includes the monad.

With card X the emanation comes to an end, its possibilities are set, the world has taken shape. Its revolving movement can start, the Wheel turns. When humankind becomes implicated, the Wheel becomes the Wheel of Life—of destiny; human will directs it upward or downward. These two possibilities, suggested in card VI (the Lover[s]), become concretized here. Because these two forces have opposite directions, they create an endless circular movement that can make us run on empty if we don't understand their significance.

THEMES, ASSOCIATIONS, CORRESPONDENCES

The Wheel signifies vital force, becoming, and fate. It is rotation, vortex, change, and periodic repetition. The Wheel also signifies wealth and poverty, showing that what humankind sows will be reaped. It represents corporeality and connotes the capacity of the will to guide. Among its other meanings is the principle of individuality and of individuation; involution or evolution, the spiral, fertilizing energy; orderliness in space and time; the possibility of becoming one with the will of God; and the luck, good or bad, which was dealt us by fate.

The ideogram for this card is

Astrological amplification: To the Wheel of Fortune have been attributed the planets Mercury, Mars, and Uranus, and the signs Scorpio and Virgo, the latter being also the traditional astrological attribution to the corresponding Hebrew letter *yod*, associated with this card. Virgo, an earth sign ruled by Mercury, is a doer and a builder; intellectual liveliness, ambition, and conscientiousness are some of its manifestations. But Virgo is also a stern punisher of crime; she has much in common with the fateful Nemesis. The constellation of the maiden was identified by the Greeks with the goddess Astraea/Dike and was described as

> . . . the way of life of each natural thing, . . . the regular course of the great animal Universe, the way that is made manifest in the seasons, in the life and death of vegetation, and when it comes to be seen that these depend on the heavenly bodies, Dike is manifest in the rising and setting of constellations, in the waxing and waning of the Moon, and in the daily and yearly courses of the Sun (Harrison, 1977, p. 517).

Like Astraea, Virgo does not have a great deal of sympathy for disorder, chaos, or the wastage of time or substance; all earthly things have their time and place within her governance; every natural form in the universe has its appropriate cycle and value. This just virgin is therefore a complex character, fertile and barren at the same time, orderly and righteous, yet with a secret unlived orgiastic side that makes her open to the flow of life and gives her a willingness to trust the natural order and an acceptance of fluidity and change (Greene, 1984, p. 215).

The summer solstice is the place of a great turning point. Day after day, from this point onward, life processes on earth appear reversed. These forces of change might be experienced as evil, but if contained by caringly maintaining a grounded earthly existence, transcendence of the material and its limitation can paradoxically be achieved. Virgo's symbol ♍ may be seen as representing the three gates of revelation, the portals to the mysteries permitting the necessary inner evolution to take place, culminating in a change of orientation toward inner directedness (Sucher, 1982, pp. 82-92).

Cabalistic amplification: Oral law, which gave a detailed interpretation of written law and of its application to life, is embodied in *Malkuth*. The *Shekina*, indicating God's presence, His "dwelling," is the last attribute through which the creator acts on the lower world. It is the "end of thought" whose progressive unfolding demonstrates God's hidden life and is located in the last sephira, a feminine principle, a door or gate through which the individual can begin the ascent up the ladder of perception of the Divine Mystery (Scholem, 1974, p. 112).

In *Malkuth*, the Kingdom, are accumulated all the energies, active and passive, and all the processes received from the sephirot above. Unless the top sephira, *Kether*, is connected with the bottom sephira, *Malkuth*, the Tree of Life is incomplete and heaven cannot reach earth. *Malkuth* is the body, and all the elements contribute equally to its structure: earth in the bones and flesh, water in the blood and lymph, air in the lungs, and fire as the radiant energy, "that property which permeates the whole organism and which so obviously is absent in a corpse" (Halevi, *Tree of Life*, p. 48). *Malkuth* is all that went on before, the whole natural evolution of humankind present in a person's body. It is the lowest of the sephirot, yet it is the most loaded with potential.

Alchemical amplification: The Wheel is a favorite symbol in alchemy for the process of *circulatio*. By this is meant, first, the ascent and the descent, for example, *sublimatio* and *precipitatio*, and second, the rotation of the universe as a model of the work and hence the cycling of the year in which the work takes place. (See figure 21.) Further, the wheel expresses virtues that are important for the work—constancy, obedience, moderation, equality, and humility.

It also conveys the obstacles encountered—being stuck, feeling dismembered. For Jung this

> . . . circulation is not merely movement in a circle, but means, on the one hand, the marking off of the sacred precinct and, on the other, fixation and concentration. The sun-wheel begins to turn . . . . Action is reversed into non-action; everything peripheral is subordinated to the command of the centre . . . . Psychologically, this circulation would be the "movement in a circle around oneself," so that all the sides of the personality become involved (Jung, CW 13, ¶ 38).

Psychological interpretation: The Wheel represents the turning point, a change of direction from extroversion to introversion. It indicates a new beginning: the growing personality changes from confrontation with and relation to the forces outside to attention to and the challenge of the forces it now feels at work inside, which are able to open the way beyond the ego. Accepting change and relinquishing the obsolete facilitates a new orientation and creates inner harmony.

Jungian interpretation: The contemporary moral allegories of the wheel emphasize that the *descensus* and *ascensus* are, among other

Figure 21. *Mercurius* turning the eight-spoked wheel. (From *Speculum Veritatis*, a 17th century ms.)

things, God's descent to the human and the human's ascent to God (Jung, CW 12, ¶ 214). The Wheel of creation takes its rise from the *prima materia*, from which the simple elements evolve. Psychologically, the revolving heavens are reflected in the human unconscious, an *imago mundi* that was projected by the alchemist into his own *prima materia*. The transforming substance is an analogy of the revolving universe or its reflection imprinted in the heart of matter. One is reminded of the vision of Ezekiel, who saw "the wheel within the wheel . . . and the spirit of the living creature that was in the midst of the wheels" (Ezekiel 10:10-17). Jung quotes Jacob Boehme:

> Thus we see that the spiritual life stands turned in upon itself, and that the natural life stands turned out and facing itself . . . (Jung, CW 12, ¶ 214).

Being round, the wheel refers to the Self and to the creative activity in which the Self is manifest. The Wheel thus reveals something of considerable importance: it appears as a concept of wholeness that represents the essence of the individuation process.

SYMBOLIC LANGUAGE OF THE IMAGE

From the outside, the Wheel is turned upward by the good genie Anubis, symbol of expansive force as well as organized and focused intelligence, which is represented by the staff of Mercurius held in its hand. This staff, which also symbolizes constructive active energy, is in certain decks the central vertical pivot of the Wheel. The Wheel is turned downward by Typhon, the winged snake (condensed, materialized power) who carries a trident, symbol of destructive forces. However, the Wheel is turned not only from the outside by gods and demons; well-handled, its spokes (signifying knowledge, willpower, daring, and discretion) contribute to its turning, and thus the individual becomes a cocreator of his or her own destiny. Having eight spokes implies that the Wheel is well balanced and that human destiny will be weighed just as equitably. The eight spokes also indicate a double polarity and suggest that inner and outer problems can be resolved due to the capacity of discernment, represented by the sword of the sphinx.

The double *quaternio* (figure 22) or *ogdoad*, stands for totality—for something that is at the same time heavenly and earthly, spiritual and corporeal, and is found in the unconscious (CW 14, ¶ 8). This is reminiscent of the saying of Bernardus Trevisanus: "The upper has the nature of the lower, and the ascending has the nature of the descending" (CW 14, ¶ 7).

The hub of the Wheel represents stability in the midst of change, a point of reference. It stands for the ability to discriminate and to analyze, for logic, psychic balance, courage, and endurance. Its stability makes the turning of the Wheel possible. It also means equanimity and shows an attitude devoid of focus on petty detail. The vertical axis represents spiritual power, the *Opus Magnus*, Mercurius. The horizontal axis stands for the strength that

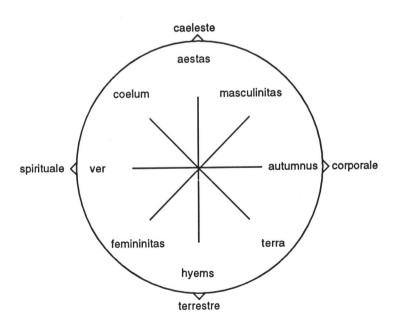

Figure 22. The double *quaternio*.

supports, stimulates, and carries one to the goal; it is sulphur and salt.

The cyclic movement of the Wheel signifies divine providence, karma, becoming, destiny, the limited life of an individual. Each turn actualizes a level or stage of existence. The Wheel also represents willpower at the helm of all forces or the helplessness of a toy in the hand of fate. It shows the flow of time that manifests in change as well as in balance and symmetry, suggesting the underlying law of periodicity. If we focus on the act of turning the wheel, we become aware of the fateful critical moment, the pivotal point. Turning the wheel evokes time that moves in a cycle, circulation, creation of a domain in which human strength and love can manifest. It shows that one can experience and understand the multiple aspects of human activity, that action can be a support for understanding and feeling, but also that we are delivered to our own fate and subjected to revolving repetitions of past patterns.

In Ezekiel's vision the spokes appear decorated with eyes, an image that evokes God's intelligence and activity. The four animals of Ezekiel's vision are also represented in the four corners of this card in some decks. They have become symbols for the four evangelists: Matthew, the angel; Luke, the ox (or steer); Mark, the lion; and John, the eagle.

Above the wheel the sphinx watches motionless. It represents wholeness, balance, stability, diversity in unity. Its human head suggests knowledge, the ox's body denotes power, ability, and activity. The paws hold onto what was won, the wings allow it to soar. Symbol of oneness, the sphinx masters opposing forces and keeps its secret in all eternity. The winged sphinx is a link not only to air and spirit, like the dove, but also to the soul of nature impregnated with animal instinct. The sphinx recalls the angel that guards the entrance to paradise. It suggests the double nature of humankind. The sphinx is both spirit and body; it is discrimination and nondiscrimination; crystallization; universal consciousness and lawfulness; instantaneous knowledge through intuition, perception and concentration; holistic thinking. The complex, enigmatic sphinx and the wheel suggest the cyclic shaping powers alternating darkness and the spiritual fire of light. One must go through this cycle in order to reach true being, vigilantly avoiding entanglement in it. The sphinx is a symbol of quaternity; it has four colors, four elements, and four body parts:

red-fire-head, blue-air-wings, green-water-breast and -forelegs, and black-earth-backside. The sword it holds signifies that it masters the elementary forces of attraction and transforms them into vital energy. Moreover, the Zohar says: "The flaming sword symbolizes the trials with which God overwhelms man, that he may be restored to the way of goodness."

The Wheel of Life is carried upon the water of life by two ships. Their half-moon shape reminds us of the moon crescent adorning the High Priestess' (card II) crown. Here they stand for mobility and sensitivity.

The blue ship indicates extension, existence, impulsivity, the world of appearance and form: *yin*. The red ship indicates depth, intensity, instant, being, spontaneity, structure, life: *yang*. The fact that loaded ships can sail evokes the feeling of trust. Seen as rocking cradles, they are a mother symbol signifying the protective, saving, redeeming, and safekeeping function of the feminine. The embryo sleeping in the uterus, rocked by the primordial sea, sails into life or returns to the sea of origin. The connection between wood and water is a recurrent link, a symbol for every living thing, of vegetative forces, circulation, movement, wind. It can signify movement perceived either as stimulation or as threat. Water is the origin of all life; Noah's Ark, a wooden ship, is a related image. With a ship one can sail upon the waters of life, one can escape the flood, one can reunite with that from which one became separated. The green-blue color of water is a symbol of truth, and its waves suggest perpetual activity. Psychologically water is the womb of the unconscious. It can also indicate the obstacle that a regression of the libido may create.

The Wheel is psychologically a symbol of the Self, the virtual point around which the manifest unfolds. With each revolution another level or stage of existence becomes actualized. With reference to the ego, the Wheel could be conceived as the supraordinate level at which the opposites are transcended and reconciled. The Wheel contributes to the awareness that the divine manifests in creation. In her commentary to *Aurora Consurgens*, von Franz notes that

> The earth in our text . . . [is called] the "Promised Land" . . . and can be regarded as a symbol of the self. . . . It is evident that this earth or "second body" is something that unites in itself the qualities of all the other elements:

> it is an airy earth, a fiery water, a fluid fire, etc., and as
> such it is a mystery known to God alone. In the cabala it
> is compared with *Malchuth* (von Franz, 1966, p. 344).

Card X is really the pivot and the balance point between the first series of trumps and the second, the point at which a transformation takes place in relation to the contents of the unconscious. The first half of the major arcana presents us with unconscious archetypal images carrying the collective energies that form the spiritual background of our lives. After the critical point has been passed, these same archetypal potencies are brought into the individual realm as landmarks to guide our ascent. The great eight-spoked wheel of the "accomplishment of the Great Work" becomes the Wheel of Fortune.

Up to card X, the great First Outpouring appears as the Magician (card I) or the active masculine principle, which creates by connection to superpersonal powers; the High Priestess (card II) or feminine wisdom, the inspirational feminine principle; the Empress (card III) or the great pregnant, nurturing, and preserving mother; the Emperor (card IV) or the kind, benevolent ruler; the High Priest (card V) or spiritual energy, organizing and directing; the Lover(s) (card VI) or the balanced masculine and feminine able to function as one; the Chariot (card VII) or the vehicle for outgoing enthusiasm; Justice (card VIII) or the formulation of forms; the Hermit (card IX) or the wise collector of all energies at the completion of the first lap of the journey.

Card X, like all pivotal symbols, expresses both the cycle that came before it and that which comes after. At the four corners of the card the four symbolic figures—angel, eagle, bull, and lion—represent the great fourfold division of the cosmos. They stand as the conventional symbols for the four fixed signs of the zodiac—Aquarius, Scorpio, Taurus, and Leo. The angel (Aquarius) stands for the air division of the zodiac, which includes also Gemini and Libra; the eagle (Scorpio) stands for the water division, which also includes Pisces and Cancer; the bull (Taurus) stands for the earth division, which also includes Virgo and Capricorn; and the lion (Leo) stands for the fire division, which also includes Sagittarius and Aries. These divisions correspond to the four functions—sensation (earth), feeling (water), thinking (air), and intuition (fire). In card X, because of their peripheral position in the corners, the four symbols indicate a cosmic, rather than a personal , representation of the realms to be approached or apprehended by the four functions.

In the center of the card is the great eight-spoked wheel of Perfect Manifestation, which tradition tells us, is made up of two four-spoked wheels rotating in opposite directions. These signify the balance of the four positive and the four negative aspects of the great tools pictured in the four suits of the minor arcana, acting in the dual rhythm of involution and evolution. In the Rider-Waite deck, one wheel is marked with the alchemical signs of mercury (mind), salt (body), sulphur (spirit), and water (feeling).

In native American tradition, the Medicine Wheel is a symbol for the Wheel of Life, which is forever evolving and bringing new lessons and truths to the walking of the path. The Earthwalk is based on the understanding that each one of us must stand on each spoke of the great wheel of life many times and that every direction is to be honored. It is said that until one has stood on another's spoke of the Wheel, one cannot know his/her heart. Every living creature will one day see and experience each spoke of the Wheel and know its truth. The circle is never-ending (life without end), and the Wheel teaches us that all lessons are equal, as are all talents and abilities. In experiencing the Good Red Road, running from south (birth) to north (death), one learns the lessons of being human and embodied. After graduation, the experience of death, one enters the Blue or Black Road of the Spirit, running from east to west. The golden door to illumination is the eastern door; this is the place through which the spirit enters and fills the space inside the circle. West indicates the internal solution to the present life challenges, how to reach a desired end, and north shows the way to integrate the lessons of the other directions.

Part II
THE PATH OF THE SERPENT

INDIVIDUATION, ALCHEMY, AND THE TAROT

Rumpite libros, ne corda vestra rumpantur.

Tear up your books that your hearts be not torn into shreds.

It is indeed doubtful whether in the last analysis the intellectual understanding is a fitting instrument or not.

—M. Esther Harding
Woman's Mysteries

Individuation designates the still-unexplored and very dark territory of the personality-mirroring reactions of the unconscious. It concerns the processes of life, which lie behind phenomena and are sensed but never known. They are secret, they present riddles, and for this reason they give the most significant impulse toward symbol formation. The symbol points to something unknown; when it is amplified by comparison with similar mythologems, we can perceive what the unconscious intends it to mean and we can become enriched by integrating the contents of the unconscious (Jung, CW 13, ¶ 480).

In each individual there is, according to Jung, a peculiar combination of qualities held together by a kind of formative principle or principle of individuation.

> The statistical proof of natural conformity to law is . . . only a very limited way of describing nature, since it grasps only uniform events. But nature is essentially discontinuous, i.e., subject to chance. To describe it we need a principle of discontinuity. In psychology this is the drive to individuation (Jung, CW 18, ¶ 1198).

It is this drive that is the starting point for the arcane preparation in alchemy.

The alchemists were pioneers, people open to the worlds within, who projected their inner perceptions onto outer symbols and thus found a universal language, transcending words, for communicating their experiences of the soul's architecture and dynamics. The alchemical manuscripts of the 13th through the

18th centuries can be regarded as ancient monuments, and like an archaeologist, one can begin to dig into their symbolic material, down through past layers of the psyche, in order to find new insights into and understanding of that which works in our souls today.

The outcome of a long development, lost to us like so many of the mysteries of the esoteric tradition, where it came from, how it originally looked, and the exact message it carried is no longer certain. We cannot build on what went before because we no longer have that precise knowledge. Intuitively, however, we can speculate that it coincides with all the other systems that took form as a result of the turmoil that overturned the values of antiquity in the Middle Ages and Renaissance times. Like them, in our troubled world in transition, we may find in the symbols they offer a vivifying and individual path that will enable us to reconnect with the spiritual world and the Divine.

Bernoulli describes "Al Chimiya," "the garden of inner speculation," with the following parable:

> If you have expected to find a neat, well kept garden full of flowers, you will be greatly disappointed. What confusion, what disorder, what a hopeless tangle! Weeds everywhere, the paths scarcely discernable beneath the rank verdure! It is almost impossible to distinguish a plan according to which the garden was laid out. And if we ask ourselves what our task in this garden should be, one of us may say that useful work might be done with the pruning shears; another may suggest that we remove the many rotting plants and roots. . . . To me it seems that, justified as these proposals may be, they do not strike at the core of the matter. Let us sit quietly for a while in our garden . . . and let us listen to what the common wild flowers, the scraggly bushes have to tell us. Perhaps they will tell us of the task that is to be found in this garden. We need only to harken; soon they will begin to speak, softly disclosing their secrets (1970, pp. 305-306).

Probing differently, Jung asks the fundamental question:

> [W]hat, in the end, do we know about the causes and motives that prompted man, for more than a thousand

years, to believe in that "absurdity," the transmutation of metals and the simultaneous psychic transformation of the artifex? We have never seriously considered the fact that for the Medieval investigator the redemption of the world by God's son and the transubstantiation . . . were not the last word, or rather, not the last answer to the manifold enigmas of man and his soul. If the *opus alchymicum* claimed equality with the *opus divinum*, . . . the reason for this was not grotesque presumption but the fact that a vast, unknown Nature, disregarded by the eternal verities of the Church, was imperiously demanding recognition and acceptance (Jung, CW 13, ¶ 196).

Even if the alchemists never produced any gold, they were on the track of

. . . a process of psychic transformation that is incomparably more important for the happiness of the individual than the possession of the red tincture (Jung, CW 13, ¶ 196).

Indeed, the alchemists were attempting in their own way to compete with the Creator insofar as they strove to do analogous work and therefore likened their own microcosmic opus to the macrocosmic labor of the world Creator.

The process of change involves enduring a difficult situation, confronting whatever unconscious attitude locks us in a frantic attempt to find a solution or to make us feel better. But finding an anesthetic is not the issue of the process of individuation. The aim of the confrontation with the unconscious is to abolish the dissociation between consciousness and the unconscious.

This means not only bringing the conflict to consciousness; it also involves an experience of a special kind, namely, the recognition of an alien "other" in oneself, or of the objective presence of another will (Jung, CW 13, ¶ 481).

No better words can be found to describe the alchemical opus and the process of individuation than this passage from Jung:

[T]he alchemical opus consisted of two parts: the work in the laboratory, with all its emotional and daemonic hazards, and the *scientia* or *theoria,* the guiding principle of the opus by which its results were interpreted and given their proper place. The whole process, which today we understand as psychological development, was designated the "philosophical tree," a "poetic" comparison that draws an apt analogy between the natural growth of the psyche and that of a plant. For this reason it seemed to me desirable to discuss in some detail the processes which underlie both alchemy and the modern psychology of the unconscious. . . . [M]erely intellectual understanding is not sufficient. It supplies us only with verbal concepts, but it does not give us their true content, which is to be found in the living experience of the process as applied to ourselves. . . . [N]o understanding by means of words and no imitation can replace actual experience. Alchemy lost its vital substance when some alchemists abandoned the laboratorium for the oratorium, there to befuddle themselves with an ever more nebulous mysticism, while others converted the oratorium into a laboratorium and discovered chemistry. We feel sorry for the former and admire the latter, but no one asks about the fate of the psyche, which thereafter vanished from sight for several hundred years (CW 13, ¶ 482).

The alchemists were decided solitaries; they rarely had disciples, and there is no evidence of secret societies. Each worked in the laboratory for himself, and there seems to have been very little direct tradition for them to follow. Their writings are relatively free of polemic, and the way in which they quote each other shows a remarkable agreement on first principles even if one cannot understand what it is that they agree about. True alchemy was never a business or a career but a genuine opus to be achieved by quiet, self-sacrificing work.

From the very earliest times, all alchemists agreed that their art is sacred and divine and that their work can be completed only with God's grace. This science of theirs is given to only a very few, and none understand it unless God or a master has opened one's eyes and heart. The knowledge thus acquired may not be passed on to others unless they are worthy of it (Jung, CW 12, ¶ 422-423).

The alchemist imagined the psychological structure of his opus and was aware that its secret was its association with the invisible forces of the psyche. In order to express this secret he readily resorted to allegory. The fantasy processes connected with the opus were semi-spiritual in nature, a "subtle body." Of this Jung says:

> In an age when there was as yet no empirical psychology such a concretization was bound to be made, because everything unconscious, once it was activated, was projected into matter—that is to say, it approached people from outside. It was a hybrid phenomenon, as it were, half spiritual, half physical; a concretization such as we frequently encounter in the psychology of primitives (CW 12, ¶ 394).

Imagination, like meditation, is of particular importance in the alchemical opus. The act of imagining was an activity that could actually bring about physical changes and was in turn brought about by them. But it is precisely because of this intermingling of the physical and the psychic that the determination of whether the ultimate transformations in the alchemical process are to be sought more in the material or more in the spiritual realm remains obscure. There seems to exist a realm intermediate between mind and matter, the psychic realm of subtle bodies that characteristically manifest in a mental as well as a material form. This is the only view that makes sense of alchemical thought, which must otherwise appear nonsensical.

> Obviously, the existence of this intermediate realm comes to a sudden stop the moment we try to investigate matter in and for itself, apart from all projection; and it remains non-existent so long as we believe we know anything conclusive about matter or the psyche. But the moment when physics touches on the "untrodden, untreadable regions," and when psychology has at the same time to admit that there are other forms of psychic life besides the acquisitions of personal consciousness—in other words, when psychology too touches on an impenetrable darkness—then the intermediate realm of subtle bodies comes to life again, and the physical and the psychic are once more blended in an indissoluble

unity. We have come very near to this turning-point today (Jung, CW 12, ¶ 394).

The alchemical opus was considered a process begun by nature but requiring the conscious art and effort of a human being for completion. In one sense, the opus is against nature, but in another sense, the alchemist is helping her to do what she cannot do for herself, and this surely refers to the evolution of consciousness. Although the urge to consciousness may exist, an ego is needed to realize that urge. The individual psyche is and must be a whole world within itself in order to stand against the outer world and fulfill its task as carrier of consciousness. Jung warns:

> The greatest danger about unconsciousness is proneness to suggestion. The effect of suggestion is due to the release of an unconscious dynamic, and the more unconscious this is, the more effective it will be. Hence the ever widening split between conscious and unconscious increases the danger of psychic infection. . . . With the loss of symbolic ideas the bridge to the unconscious has broken down. Instinct no longer affords protection against unsound ideas. . . . Rationality without tradition and without a basis in instinct is proof against no absurdity (CW 9/2, ¶ 390, n. 79).

Individuation is the process that enables a creative dialogue between the unconscious and consciousness. It can be experienced and becomes visible through the symbol, the means whereby something from within can be seen without, something invisible becomes visible, something concrete is given spiritual perspective, something specific and limited reveals universal dimensions. Individuation is a world-creating process. Jung sees the individual as one who in living consummation of the individuation process becomes the person he or she was meant to be. This is the human task; this is the human virtue. Our search for self-understanding is at the same time an obligation to go beyond the rational limitations of our intellect because reality can be experienced as meaningful only when it extends into a transcendent spiritual dimension. Becoming who one was meant to be is not a process of becoming perfect; rather, it means becoming aware of one's sharp angles and edges, of moving closer to the unknown and the potential in us.

The other aim of individuation, just as important as self-becoming, and intrinsically interwoven with it, is the achievement of autonomy. The process of individuation is, on one hand, a subjective internal integration, on the other, it is an interpersonal, intersubjective, rational event. We have to become independent individuals, freed from parental complexes, from collective standards, norms, and values, and from the social role expectations that were imposed upon us. Self-becoming also means "coming of age." By the same token, it means independence emerging from within and increasing awareness of the inner archetypal energies that may manipulate us as long as we remain unconscious of the power they have over us. Individuation is therefore liberation from forces of both the collective unconscious and collective consciousness.

Symbols are often the expression of resolution of conscious/unconscious conflicts. The unconscious and its symbols must be activated in order to find a creative way to deal with one's existential problems. The symbol is at first an ordinary everyday thing that points beyond its concrete reality to a background whose meaning we can barely apprehend initially. Often symbols are encountered in existential situations that they may help clarify; the meaning and importance of the situation is thus revealed. The symbolic approach creates the perspective needed to see the foreground of everyday reality embedded in the background of a much greater reality, whereby this universal background and the everyday reality can and do reciprocally influence each other. The symbol is thus the visible aspect of an invisible ideal layer of our psyche; it refers to an idea, a general concept, an abstraction. The symbol operates on two levels: one specific and personal, the other general and impersonal. The symbol is never completely comprehensible; it always contains a meaning that remains elusive. It also has emotional overtones and belongs therefore in the wider realms of religion, philosophy, art, and literature.

> *Symbols* are not allegories and not signs: they are images of contents which for the most part transcend consciousness. We have still to discover that such contents are real, that they are agents with which it is not only possible but absolutely necessary for us to come to terms (Jung, CW 5, ¶ 114).

Symbols enable us to gain access to the archetypal background of the psyche. The supportive elements from the collective unconscious with which one can connect through dreams, myths, and fairytales help transcend our conflicts and, according to Kast (1992, p. 192), affect the ego structure, its transformation, and healing. I believe that this restructuring effect of the symbolic process is nowhere more evident than in alchemy.

> Not much effort is needed at the beginning of the work; it is sufficient to approach it with "a free and empty mind." . . . But one important rule must be observed: "the mind (*mens*) must be in harmony with the work" and the work must be above all else. . . . [O]ne must keep the eyes of the mind and the soul well open, observing and contemplating by means of that inner light which God has lit in nature and in our hearts from the beginning (Jung, CW 12, ¶ 381).

Jung quotes from Seneca:

> "We do not need to uplift our hands toward heaven, or to beg the keeper of a temple to let us approach his idol's ear, as if in this way our prayers were more likely to be heard. God is near you, he is with you, he is within you. [A] holy spirit indwells within us, one who works our good and bad deeds, and is our guardian. As we treat this spirit, so we are treated by it. Indeed, no man can be good without the help of God. Can one rise superior to fortune unless God helps him to rise? He it is that gives noble and upright counsel. In each good man 'a God doth dwell, but that God we know not'" (CW 5, ¶ 114, n. 73).

In the alchemists' conception, the drama of the human psyche shows man taking upon himself the duty of carrying out the redeeming opus; they attribute the suffering and the subsequent need for redemption to the *anima mundi* imprisoned in matter.

> [A]lchemy is interested in the fate and the manifest redemption of the substances, for in them the divine soul lies captive and awaits redemption that is granted to it at the moment of release. . . . For the alchemist, the one primarily in need of redemption is not man, but the deity

who is lost and sleeping in matter. . . . His attention is not directed to his own salvation through God's grace, but to the liberation of God from the darkness of matter. By applying himself to this miraculous work he benefits from its salutary effect, but only incidentally. He may approach the work as one in need of salvation, but he knows that his salvation depends on the success of the work, on whether he can free the divine soul. To this end he needs meditation, fasting, and prayer; more, he needs the help of the Holy Ghost . . . (Jung, CW 12, ¶ 420).

The alchemists' work is the same work of redemption that God himself accomplished, and what comes out of the transformation is an ineffable material being named "the stone" that displays the most paradoxical qualities apart from possessing *corpus, anima, spiritus*, and supernatural powers (Jung, CW 12, ¶ 420).

The fact that visions allied themselves to the alchemical work and that dreams and dream-visions are often mentioned as important sources of revelation is another element in support of the parallelism between individuation and alchemy.

It is repeatedly stressed in the alchemical literature that the much-sought-after "philosopher's gold" would be revealed in a dream. The *prima materia*, the stone itself, or the secret of its production may be revealed to the alchemist by God. The production of the stone

> . . . transcends reason and . . . only a supernatural and divine knowledge knows the exact time for the birth of the stone. This means that God alone knows the *prima materia* (Jung, CW 12, ¶ 356).

The basic theme of the opus is that its purpose is to create a transcendent, miraculous substance—the philosopher's stone, the elixir of life, the universal medicine. The process involves finding the *prima materia* and subjecting it to a series of operations that will turn it into the philosopher's stone.

The work of the alchemist was based on the premises that spirit pervades all matter and that metals, which grow in the earth, ripen into gold if left there long enough. This ripening is a phenomenon extending also to the vegetal and animal kingdoms. In order to expedite this process and thus help God's purpose, the alchemists attempted to imitate nature in their laboratories. The initial task was to discover the *prima materia* from which the world had been created so that they could then release the spirit imprisoned in it and use it to accelerate the transmutations. They also knew that a "philosophic gold" had to be created. The main task of the alchemists was, therefore, to release the hidden spirit of God in matter, a spiritual work involving the transmutation of man himself, to cleanse himself of his impurities so that the *prima materia* of his own soul could be reunited with God. It seems to me that, although the images are different, the process of individuation has the same ultimate goal.

The sequence followed by the alchemists in their pursuit has been described thus:

> To the alchemists . . . there was no reason to believe that a transmutation of substances could not be achieved given the proper working conditions. The problem was simply one of ridding an element of one quality and substituting another. In alchemy this altering of a metal's form was symbolized by such images as "torturing," "separating," and all other images symbolic of death. If one could reduce a metal far enough, one would gain *prima materia*.
>
> This achieved, the alchemist would have the seed of things that would then have to be treated in much the same manner mother earth cradled the elements, in a warm vessel. This vessel would be the womb where the resurrection of the thing that had been killed would eventually take place. The important thing was to separate the four elements from each other and from the material worked on, . . . then to reduce each element down to each predominating quality, and finally to reunite the four primary qualities so that they would form a chaotic state of the first matter (Poncé, 1975, pp. 171-172).

The difference between the *prima materia* and the *lapis*, representing the beginning and the end of the opus, is that whereas the *prima materia* is chaotic, the stone is perfect. The stone resists the action of fire; it is more pure than the purest gold; it is the father of all miracles

> . . . containing as it does all elements in such a way that
> none predominates, but all form a certain fifth essence
> (Poncé, 1975, p. 175).

The "treasure hard to attain" whose presence was suspected in
the *prima materia* is potentially contained in it as a *massa confusa*.
Our intellect, our understanding, must transform this work of
mother nature into the celestial quintessence, into the life-giving
essence of heaven. Jung points out that understanding and intelligence are insisted upon throughout the alchemical literature not
only because intelligence above the ordinary is needed to perform so difficult a work, but because it is assumed that

> . . . a species of magical power capable of transforming
> even brute matter dwells in the human mind. . . . "[T]he
> intellect of man is the beginning, middle, and end of
> the procedure; . . . man is the greater and the principle
> form in the spagyric *opus*" (CW 12, ¶ 366).

The life-giving essence hidden in the dark *prima materia* can be
found only by descending into a region of danger, variously
described as cavern, forest, island, watery abyss—all images pointing to the unconscious. This obscure realm of the unknown creates

> . . . dread and resistance which every natural human
> being experiences when it comes to delving too deeply
> into himself [and] is, at bottom, the fear of the journey to
> Hades. If it were only resistance that he felt, it would
> not be so bad. In actual fact, however, the psychic sub-
> stratum . . . exercises a fascinating attraction that threat-
> ens to become the more overpowering the further he
> penetrates into it. The psychological danger that arises
> here is the disintegration of personality into its func-
> tional components (Jung, CW 12, ¶ 439).

However, the alchemist related himself not only to the unconscious
but also directly to the very substance that he hoped to transform
through the power of imagination. Imagination becomes, therefore, a concentrated extract of life forces, hence the quintessence
(Jung, CW 12, ¶ 394). Jung quotes an ancient alchemical text
describing the relation between consciousness and the *lapis*:

"This stone is below thee, as to obedience; above thee, as
to dominion; therefore from thee, as to knowledge; about
thee, as to equals" (CW 13, ¶ 287).

According to the text, when applied to the Self this means that
although the Self is subordinate to the individual, it is his ruler.
The Self is dependent on one's own efforts and knowledge, but
transcends one and embraces all of like mind. As the Self epito-
mizes the wholeness of the personality, it is not difficult to see the
parallel between the alchemical opus and the process of individuation, the aim of which is wholeness. The goal of all the
alchemists' strivings was the creation of an incorruptible substance that not only brought things to perfection but was also
capable of healing.

Tempting as it may be to find one-to-one parallels between
alchemical images and tarot trumps, I believe it is more important to decipher the symbolic language that points to the essence
of the process, the inner spiritual nature of the work. McLean
points out in his commentaries to the series of twenty-two plates
of the *Splendor Solis* that

> . . . on first encountering these 22 symbols, one might be
> excused for trying to connect them directly to the 22
> Major Arcana of the Tarot. Under deeper consideration,
> it becomes obvious that these cannot be related in such a
> simplistic one-to-one correspondence. However, these
> 22 figures work very much like a Tarot, as archetypal
> figures that can open the questing soul to facets of its
> own being.
>
> This cycle of illustrations . . . is not to be seen as 22 sep-
> arate independent symbols, but rather as an integrated
> pattern of archetypal ideals (1991, p. 94).

McLean sees behind these twenty-two illustrations an underlying structure forming the pattern depicted in Table 8. The arrangement proposed by McLean is one that could also fit the major
arcana perfectly. The first four cards offer a double *coniunctio*—
the Magician and the High Priestess, the higher masculine and
feminine; the Empress and the Emperor, the feminine and masculine in nature. Cards 5 through 10 follow the Lightning Flash,
and card 11, Strength, mirrors the archetypal background pro-

TABLE 8. PATTERNS UNDERLYING THE 22 PLATES IN *SPLENDOR SOLIS*.*

							The Primal Material of the Work (The First and Second Treatises)
1	2	3	4				
							The Seven Phases of the Process in Allegory (The Seven Parables of the Third Treatise)
5	6	7	8	9	10	11	
							The Seven Retorts of Transformation (The Seven Degrees of Heat of the Fourth Treatise)
12	13	14	15	16	17	18	
							The End of the Work (The Four Chapters of the Fifth Treatise)
19	20	21	22				

* From Trismosin, p. 94.

vided by the preceding ten. Cards 12 through 18 depict the painful ascending road of the Path of the Serpent, and cards 19 through 22 describe the higher realms where soul can unite with spirit.

The beauty of alchemy lies both in its materialized and symbolic language. According to Hillman (1980, p. 124), alchemy gives us a language of substance that cannot be taken substantively and concrete expressions that are not literal. It forces metaphor upon us, we are carried by its language into an "as if," into both the materialization of the psyche and the psychization of matter.

It is not the literal return of alchemy that is necessary, but a restoration of the alchemical mode of imagining, for in that mode we restore matter to our speech and we restore soul to matter and mind. The "as if" metaphor is healing because it joins in the heart what has been kept apart in the mind.

Alchemical analysis is qualitative not quantitative, a characteristic it shares with astrology. What alchemy has to say about who we are and what we are in danger of losing if we reject it was formulated thus:

> The alchemist accepts . . . himself for what he is in order
> to change himself into what he might be. The lonely
> struggle with substances in still or alembic becomes the

struggle of all men to free themselves from existing fetters and to advance into a qualitatively new sphere of
experience . . . (Grossinger, 1983, pp. 258-259).

Ultimately, it is this unity of craft and process with theoretical
thought that is the great revolutionary mark of alchemy. When
the scientific method was established in the 17th century, the qualitative values and the direction of change was left out and set
aside for the sake of "objectivity." To this position the alchemist
would have replied that

> . . . if you exclude humanity (the concrete object of qual-
> ity) you exclude reality in any consequential sense and
> your results have a limited and ultimately antihuman
> bias. . . . The complete science . . . would know how to
> grasp and define at the same time all crucial points of
> change, in which new qualities emerge; and it would
> vitally link its inquiries into natural process with the
> needs of a humanity that knew where it was going
> (Grossinger, 1983, p. 259).

Today it is the "invisible reality" in nature with which science is
concerned, and it is the same invisible reality in ourselves with
which we need to be concerned.

> [W]e are the product of this exact nature, folded in on
> itself; the subtleties, paradoxes and invisible realities that
> we contain, as we look outward, or inward, are of the
> same order as the invisible realities in objective nature at
> large (Grossinger, 1983, p. 261).

The profound darkness that shrouds the alchemical procedure
comes from the fact that every alchemist endeavors to devise a
nomenclature for the psychic transformations to which he was
witness. Every original alchemist built himself an individual structure made out of miscellaneous analogies to the fundamental concepts of alchemy. The method of alchemy is one of boundless
amplification, which forms the theoretical part of alchemy; the
other part is practical and is constituted by the opus. However,
the alchemical meaning of the most commonly used substances,
such as quicksilver, salt, and sulphur, is one of the secrets of the art.
The obscurity of the texts makes them impenetrable for us, and

the alchemists, themselves, were not always able to understand their own symbols and symbolic figures (Jung, CW 12, ¶ 401).

The single most important "theory" was the conviction of the inner property of substances. It was the so-called "quality" of sulphur or mercury that was used in alchemy, not the measurable substance. It was their characteristics and behaviors that made them recognizable and useful.

> Alchemists asked what the nature of the substance was and what were the links between the nature and the forms of the substance. The uniqueness of each substance could be in form: roundness, squareness, yellowness, blackness, whiteness, or in molecular aspects: airyness, wateryness, earthyness, fieryness . . . (Grossinger, 1983, p. 255).

The basic components of alchemy are considered to be the convictions that nature is composed of primary elements, that there is a gradual evolution and transformation of substance existing in nature, that there are systems that can be used to hasten and to induce this transformation, that there exists an interaction between one's inner being and the alchemical events that occur during an experiment, that the knowledge of the system of correspondences between planets, herbs, minerals, animals, and body parts, which is known as the Doctrine of Correspondences, is vital for the work, and that the ultimate aim is to arrive at that extraction of a spiritual essence believed to exist in matter and sometimes called the Philosopher's Stone. Additionally, the method used complementary pairs of opposites: sun/moon, gold/silver, sulphur/mercury, king/queen, male/female, husband/bride, Christ/man, to reach the integration of these opposites in the ultimate symbol of reconciliation of inner/outer conflict. Spiritual and chthonic elements were

> . . . united with the azure quintessence, the *anima mundi* extracted from inert matter, . . . that is to say, the whole of the conscious man is surrendered to the self, to the new centre of personality which replaces the former ego . . . . [T]he *filius macrocosmi*, the son of the great luminaries and of the dark womb of the earth, enters the realm of the psyche and seizes the human personality, not only in the shining heights of consciousness but in the dark

depths which have not yet comprehended the light
(Jung, CW 14, ¶ 704).

To enter the alchemical realm, one has to leave at the door one's
allegiance to orderly, logical systems of thought, one's need to
make sense of and to understand, as the only way to connect with
whatever lies before us. Alchemical texts, like the mysterious
workings of the psyche, confront the investigator with a challenge
to linear thinking, which in the labyrinthine paths ahead is totally
useless. I cannot help but recall the image of the Hanged Man
(card XII) losing all his carefully collected coins as he dangles
upside down, a position that can open a new perspective on the
world. As Klossowski de Rola put it:

> Only through reliance on inspired intuition, the golden
> thread of Ariadne, will the puzzle fall into place and
> light replace darkness. . . . Zen masters, for instance, use
> koans. . . which while unbalancing the intellect, may
> suddenly trigger satori or enlightenment (*Alchemy*, p. 9).

In sum, while working on his experiments, the alchemist experienced certain psychic phenomena, which appeared to him to be
the behavior of the chemical process. He was naturally unconscious of the fact that he was projecting and that the experience
had nothing to do with the chemical reaction he observed.

> He experienced his projection as a property of matter;
> but what he was in reality experiencing was his own
> unconscious. . . . Such projections repeat themselves
> whenever man tries to explore an empty darkness and
> involuntarily fills it with living form (Jung, CW 12,
> ¶ 346).

THE WORK

By all accounts, the first great labor of alchemy was the quest for
the *prima materia*. To secure this single, essential, raw substance,
one must begin at the right time, as determined by astrological
aspects, which are most favorable in Aries, Taurus, or Gemini.
The alchemist must be purified and must prepare a secret fire, or
first agent, described as "dry water that doesn't burn the hands,"

or as "fire burning without flames, which is tartar (the under-world, the unconscious) and spring dew." Although elaborate information has been given regarding the procedures after the *prima materia* was found, there is practically no information about the road leading to the mine from which it was to be extracted.

The description of the processes, and even the number of their phases, varies considerably. Indeed, Edinger (*Anatomy of the Psyche*) lists seven: *calcinatio, solutio, coagulatio, sublimatio, mortificatio, separatio,* and *coniunctio,* whereas Jung and Grossinger each list twelve operations: *calcinatio, solutio, separatio, coniunctio, putrefactio, coagulatio, cibatio, sublimatio, fermentatio, exaltatio, augmentatio,* and *projectio.* (It is interesting to note that in the Hebrew alphabet there are seven double and twelve single letters, and that astrologically seven corresponds to the number of planets, whereas twelve is the number of the signs of the zodiac.) Be this as it may, the alchemical operations provide basic categories by which to understand the life of the psyche, and they illustrate almost the full range of experiences that constitute individuation. Grossinger (1983, p. 298) divides the operations into three sequences of four stages, wherein the first sequence describes the creation of a black essence and the extraction of spiritualized substance; the second is "conceivably a series of signs and operations occuring during the first," but with different emphases; and the third sequence involves for him only what happens after the philosopher's stone has been obtained and involves the transformation of substance. Jung comments on this variability:

> The arrangement of the stages in individual authors depends primarily on their conception of the goal: sometimes this is the white or red tincture (*aqua permanens*); sometimes the philosopher's stone, which, as hermaphrodite, contains both; or again it is the panacea (*aurum potabile, elixir vitae*), philosophical gold. . . . The conceptions of the goal are as vague and various as the individual processes. The *lapis philosophorum*, for instance, is often the *prima materia,* or the means of producing the gold; or again it is an altogether mystical being that is sometimes called . . . *filius macrocosmi.*

> . . . Besides the idea of the *prima materia,* that of water (*aqua permanens*) and that of fire (*ignis noster*) play an important part. Although these two elements. . . constitute a typical pair of opposites, they are yet one and the same.

> . . . Like the *prima materia* the water has a thousand
> names; it is even said to be the original material of the
> stone. In spite of this we are on the other hand assured
> that water is extracted from the stone or the *prima mate-*
> *ria* as its life-giving soul (CW 12, ¶ 335-336).

Any given author may also intentionally (or unintentionally)
scramble the steps in order to keep his secret from falling into the
hands of the uninitiated. But Edinger's observation points out a
natural protection:

> The secret of the psyche is safe because it is not com-
> municable to those who have not yet experienced it for
> themselves (1985, p. 8).

Calcinatio or reduction is the first stage. Through calcination the
compound is converted into black powder. Some materials are
prepared for etheric isolation by reduction, while others must be
dissolved. At any rate, calcination is followed by dissolution, *solu-*
tio, or digestion.

By *solutio* and *sublimatio* the spirit is converted into a body,
and the body (the black ashes) sinks to the bottom of the vessel
where it is cleansed until it rises above the liquid solvent as a white
substance called, at times, the "gander" or the "bird of Hermes."

The original state of unconsciousness was known to the
alchemist as the *nigredo*, the chaos, the *massa confusa*, an interweaving of the soul with the body, forming together a dark unity
(the *unio naturalis*). From this enchainment to matter the soul is
freed by means of the *separatio*, achieving a conscious and rational counterposition immune to the influences of the body. This
means withdrawing projections that falsify one's view of the
world and prevent self-knowledge. But projections can be withdrawn only when they come within the scope of consciousness.
Thus it is that alchemists did not differentiate between psychic
contents and chemical substances. The psychic sphere representing the body miraculously appeared to the adept to be identical with the chemical preparation in the retort (CW 14, ¶
696-697). *Separatio* corresponds to liberation from the initial state
of chaos and darkness:

> From the successive unions arise an active principle
> (sulphur) and a passive (salt) as well as a mediating,
> ambivalent principle, Mercurius. This classical alchemi-

cal trinity then produces the relationship of male to female as the supreme and essential opposition. . . . [T]he four elements do not constitute a circle, i.e., a totality. This is produced only by the synthesis of male and female. Thus the square at the beginning corresponds to the quaternio of elements united in the *quinta essentia* at the end (Jung, CW 14, ¶ 656).

After *separatio* a union of opposites is performed, a crucial step meaning nothing less than the solution of the alchemical riddle and at the same time the redemption of a previously unconscious part of the personality.

Coniunctio has been rightly called the "central idea" of the alchemical procedure. The adepts were ultimately concerned with a union of substances, and by means of this union they hoped to attain the goal of their work: the production of the philosopher's gold, or a symbolic equivalent of it. The *coniunctio* precedes the production of the *lapis*, which is understood to be the product of the union of Sol and Luna. To that extent the *lapis* corresponds to the psychological idea of the Self, the product of the union of conscious and unconscious. The chemical process of conjunction was at the same time a psychic synthesis. Sometimes it seems as if self-knowledge brought about the union, but more often it is the chemical conjunction that facilitates the psychic. The *coniunctio* takes place in the retort, the vessel or matrix. The vessel is also called the "grave," and the union, a shared death (Jung, CW 14, ¶ 657). The *coniunctio* often needs a mediator, and this is Mercurius. He is the soul (anima), the mediator between body and spirit. The same is true for the synonyms of Mercurius: the green lion, the *aqua permanens*, which are likewise media of conjunction. Indeed, Mercurius *is* the conjunction because of his androgynous form (Jung, CW 14, ¶ 12).

> "[A]t the hour of conjunction the blackness and the raven's head and all the colours in the world will appear, 'even Iris, the messenger of God, and the peacock's tail'" (Khunrath, quoted in Jung, CW 14, ¶ 392).

Jung continues:

> Iris as the "messenger of God" is of special importance for an understanding of the opus, since the integration of

all colours points, as it were, to a coming of God, or even
to his presence (CW 14, ¶ 392),

which is a reminder that the alchemical transformation can occur
only *Deo concedente*, with the grace of God.

At times *coniunctio* has to be followed by the death of the
product of the union through *putrefactio*, a natural decay from
internal heat, or through *mortificatio*. This is the *nigredo* of the second phase, which is then followed, or not, by *congelatio* or *coagulatio* and then by a renewed washing (*ablutio*) or wetting with dew
(*cibatio*) (Jung, CW 12, ¶ 334). Exposing oneself to the storm and
stress of action solidifies personality; the churn of reality and the
battle with it promote ego development. It is no wonder, then,
that most creation myths present us with turning wheels and
churning oceans.

> The substance to be coagulated is elusive quick-
> silver. . . . Essentially it is the autonomous spirit of the
> archetypal psyche, the paradoxical manifestation of the
> transpersonal Self. To subject the spirit Mercurius to *coag-
> ulatio* means nothing less than the connecting of the ego
> with the Self, the fulfillment of individuation (Edinger,
> 1985, p. 85).

Not surprisingly, an alchemical recipe for coagulation recommends: "Take quicksilver, coagulate in the body of magnesia, in
lead, or in sulphur which does not burn." To Edinger the use of the
sulphur that does not burn makes it clear that a psychic meaning
has been superimposed upon the chemical reality wherein mercury
combines with sulphur to form the solid, red, mercuric sulphide.

Finally, the last operation in this phase is *sublimatio* or
distillation.

> The purpose of distillation in alchemy was to extract the
> volatile substance, or spirit, from the impure body. This
> process was a psychic as well as a physical experience
> (Jung, CW 13, ¶ 185).

When the distillate was made to run back into the belly of the
retort, or in a vessel sometimes called the "Pelican," the "circu-
latory distillation" resulted, an operation much favored by

alchemists, as they hoped to achieve particularly refined results by means of this "thousandfold distillation."

The alchemist accompanies his work with a simultaneous mental operation, the purpose of which is to cleanse away the impurities of his "interior anatomy."

> While the artifex heats the chemical substance in the furnace he himself is undergoing the same fiery torment and purification. By projecting himself into the substance he has become unconsciously identical with it and suffers the same process (Jung, CW 13, ¶ 173).

Jung even went so far as to present us with a tentative parallel between the logical sequence of psychological changes and the alchemical symbolism. See Table 9.

The powder made during the first eight operations is now put to use in the final phase of the work. *Fermentatio* involves mixing the substance with a metal (antimony, iron, gold, or silver) in order to increase the capacity of transmutation; *exaltatio* is a purer form of sublimation; and *multiplicatio* increases the quantity and perhaps the quality of the substance by adding mercury or by repeated sequences of *solutio* and *coagulatio*. The last stage is one in which the material prepared in the previous eleven is used to increase the virtue of some other metal to silver or to gold (Grossinger, pp. 316-317). This gold, or stone, or elixir of life is the final product of the alchemist's search. This is the hidden treasure in the *prima materia* in which it is potentially contained. It may be

TABLE 9. PSYCHOLOGICAL CHANGES AND ALCHEMICAL SYMBOLISM.*

Ego-bound state with feeble dominant	Sick king, enfeebled by age, about to die
Ascent of the unconscious and/or descent of the ego into the unconscious	Disappearance of the king in his mother's body, or his dissolution in water
Conflict and synthesis of conscious and unconscious	Pregnancy, sick-bed, symptoms, display of colors
Formation of a new dominant; circular symbols (e.g., mandala) of the Self	King's son, hermaphrodite, rotundum

* From Jung, CW 14, ¶ 523.

the quintessence extracted from chaos or the white dove contained in lead, an allusion to the inner opposite. It may be the invisible spirit received from on high and

> nourished by the stars, and it gives nourishment to all the living things it shelters in its womb. . . . This invisible spirit is . . . at the same time the root of all the substances necessary to the alchemical process or arising therefrom (Jung, CW 12, ¶ 444).

THE *PRIMA MATERIA* AND THE *LAPIS*

The *prima materia* represents the unknown substance that carries the projection of the autonomous psychic content. Emanating from the individual, it is different in each case, and for this reason, was given a multitude of definitions.

> For one alchemist the *prima materia* was quicksilver, for others it was ore, iron, gold, lead, salt, sulphur, vinegar, water, air, fire, earth, blood, water of life, *lapis*, poison, spirit, cloud, sky, dew, shadow, sea, mother, moon, dragon, Venus, chaos, microcosm (Jung, CW 12, ¶ 425).

The *prima materia* the alchemists sought was actually a metaphysical substance believed to exist not only hidden and trapped in matter but also in human beings. According to Poncé (1975, p. 173), the true secret of alchemy is the fact that the alchemist, by freeing and purifying the spirit in himself, caused a reciprocal event to occur in nature: "as inside, so outside"; "as above, so below." This, however, could not be done without the creation of that which was born from the *prima materia*—the philosopher's stone. Therefore the *lapis* can be understood not only as the end product of the opus but also as the initial material.

> The *lapis* was thought of as a unity and therefore often stands for the *prima materia* in general. But just as the latter is a bit of the original chaos which was believed to be hidden somewhere in metals, particularly in mercury, or in other substances, and is not in itself a simple

thing (as the name *massa confusa* shows), so too the *lapis* consists of the four elements or has to be put together from them (Jung, CW 9/2, ¶ 375).

In nature the elements are merely coexisting; they can be combined only by the alchemical procedure. The *lapis* is said to be produced by the splitting and putting together of the four elements, from the *rotundum*, "a highly abstract, transcendent idea, which by reason of its roundness and wholeness refers to the Original Man, the Anthropos" (Jung, CW 9/2, ¶ 388). Jung reiterates:

> This primary substance is round . . . like the world and the world-soul; it is in fact the world-soul and the world-substance in one. It is the "stone that has a spirit." . . . The alchemists describe the "round element" now as primal water, now as primal fire, or as pneuma, primal earth, or . . . the little body of our wisdom. As water or fire it is the universal solvent; as stone and metal it is something that has to be dissolved and changed into air (pneuma, spirit) (CW 9/2, ¶ 376).

For the alchemists the *prima materia* was the radical moisture, the *spiritus aquae* and the *vapor terrae*. It was called the soul of the metals, the *sperma mundi*, Adam's tree of paradise, which grows on the sea. It was also Adam and the accursed man, the hermaphroditic monster, the One and the root of itself, the All, and so on.

> The symbolical names of the *prima materia* all point to the *anima mundi*, Plato's Primordial Man, the Anthropos and mystic Adam, who is described as a sphere (= wholeness), consisting of four parts (uniting different aspects in itself), hermaphroditic (beyond division by six), and damp (i.e., psychic). This paints a picture of the self, the indescribable totality of man (Jung, CW 13, ¶ 173).

Some of the qualities ascribed to the *prima materia* include ubiquity, the fact that it can be found anywhere and everywhere, that projections can occur at any time and at any place; autonomy and everlastingness, meaning that it is without beginning and without end; miraculousness, that is, things arise from the invisible and immovable God; hiddenness, referring to the initial state that by the art of the alchemist and the grace of God can be transmuted into a manifest state of wholeness. Hyle alludes to that which the divine creation brought forth from chaos as a dark sphere; blackness is the initial stage of the process, the black earth in which the gold or the *lapis* is sown like wheat; and fluidity is the material principle of all bodies, including mercury (Jung, CW 12, ¶ 432-433). These qualities also describe the *filius philosophorum*, the *elixir vitae*, or the *lapis*. Further, the attributes of the stone, insistently emphasized, are incorruptibility, permanence, divinity.

> What unconscious nature was ultimately aiming at when she produced the image of the lapis can be seen most clearly in the notion that it originated in matter and in man, that it was to be found everywhere, and that its fabrication lay at least potentially within man's reach (Jung, CW 13, ¶ 127).

The absolute aim of the whole process is the stone, the *lapis,* the product of the *coniunctio* of the red king and the white queen. It is also a mystic being having spirit, soul, and body, with the power to give life to all mortals, to purify all corruption, to soften all hard and harden all soft bodies. It is said that this miraculous stone is found "when the search lies heavy on the searcher" (Jung, CW 12, ¶ 360-361). This means that a certain psychological condition is necessary for attaining the place where it dwells. Whereas the secret of the art lies hidden in the unconscious, the gateway to reach it is "exceeding narrow" and "none may enter save through affliction of the soul" (Jung, CW 12, ¶ 386).

The alchemists were well aware that there is danger connected with the work, not only if one makes a mistake, but adepts repeatedly warned to take care, to recognize, and to guard against the "deceptions of the devil," who often

> " . . . instills negligence, impeding our intentions; everywhere he creeps about, within and without, causing oversights, fear, and unpreparedness, and at other times he seeks by harassments and injuries to make us abandon the work" (Olympiodorus, quoted in Jung, CW 13, ¶ 430).

When we look at the synonyms for the *lapis*, we may be surprised to see that as the *prima materia* it is called *vilis*; as a substance in the process of transmutation it is called *servus rubeus* or *fugitivus*; and in its true apotheosis it is the *filius sapientiae* or even *deus terrenus*; it is the "light above all lights" and a power that contains in itself all the power of the upper and nether regions (Jung, CW 9/1, ¶ 289). The identity of the chaotic *prima materia* and the perfect *lapis* may seem less incomprehensible if we remember what Jung has called a "curious sport of nature": the fact that diamond, the "purest water," is carbon in crystalline form, whereas coal, carbon in its amorphous form, is black; moreover, the chief chemical constituent of the human body and all organic matter throughout nature is carbon.

One cannot imagine a greater contrast between two different forms of the same substance (namely, carbon), a relationship that suggests the one existing between the highest and the ordinary state of consciousness. Identification of the *prima materia* with the *lapis* (or at least the image of the *prima materia* as a pre-stage of the stone) suggests that the end result of the process of individuation utilizes very ordinary preexistent elements of the psyche, and through a process of transformation, achieves the mysterious transmutation symbolized by the alchemists in the *aurum non vulgi*, the philosopher's gold. This teaches that symbolically there is a fundamental identity of all substances, that they have an inherent faculty of transformation, and that in order to make the *lapis*, divine providence is needed, the stone being ultimately a gift of God. I am reminded of the situation in therapy in which all the elements of transformation are, at least to me, obviously there, yet there is no movement, because in the dark night of the soul, the Self seems to be inactive and the saving grace of faith is lacking. This is the time when the optimistic view of the alchemist can transform the soul's affliction by reminding one that

> . . . the dark background of the soul contains not only evil but a King in need of, and capable of, redemption . . . [and who] "at the end of the work . . . will go forth for thee, crowned with his diadem, radiant as the sun . . . constant in the fire" (Jung, CW 13, ¶ 183).

We have seen so far that, for the alchemists, the symbolic rite performed in the laboratory aimed at creating the celestial balm, or life principle, sometimes called *coelum*, a celestial substance hidden in the human body, a secret truth, a "good that passeth not away," which is taken hence after death (obviously, the immortal part of the soul). Psychologically, it is a representation of the individuation process by means of certain procedures of transformation of chemical substances from dark lead (a synonym for the *prima materia*, a matrix of the *filius philosophorum*) to the sought-for celestial substance, the *coelum*, the *quinta essentia* (Jung, CW 14, ¶ 703-705).

THE SEQUENCE OF THE WORK

> [T]he adept produces a system of fantasies that have a special meaning for him. Although he keeps within the general framework of alchemical ideas, he does not repeat a prescribed pattern, but, following his own fancy, devises an individual series of ideas and corresponding actions . . . (Jung, CW 14, ¶ 694).

Based on this description, it is not surprising that the sequence of operations from the "cheapest thing" to the "treasure which is not eaten into by moths nor dug out by thieves" (Jung, CW 14, ¶ 693) varies greatly from one text to another, from one commentator to another. Klossowski de Rola recounts it in this order:

The first matter and the first agent are placed in a mortar and pulverized with a pestle, mixed with the secret fire, and moistened with dew before being placed in the egg, the alchemical container in which the two principles contained in the *prima materia* interact; these are the hot, dry, masculine, solar principle (i.e., sulphur) and the cold, moist, feminine, lunar principle (i.e., mercury). The first work ends when, from the mutual destruction of these two opposites, the metallic, volatile humidity of the mercury of the wise appears. This is the end of the first phase of *nigredo*, likened to a starry night sky or the star that guided the magi to the birth place of the divine child.

The volatile principle of mercury flies through the alchemical air within the philosopher's egg, the hermetically sealed vessel, where it receives celestial and purifying influences. It then falls again, sublimated, onto the new earth, from which it eventually reemerges. The outer fire is now slowly increased until the coagulation and dessication of the emerging content is complete. In the process, beautiful colors, called the peacock's tail, appear. This is the end of the second work, the stage of *albedo*. The subject is said to now have enough strength to resist the fire. What is expected to occur is the emergence of the red king, or sulphur of the wise, out of the womb of the mother/sister Isis, or mercury, the white rose.

The third work recapitulates the first, with a new significance. It begins with a royal wedding, the King being united to the Queen with the help of the secret fire or salt; the red sulphur fixes the white mercury. From their union, the ultimate perfection, the quintessence, the philosopher's stone, is born.

In sum, there are three substances, three works, and three degrees of perfection. The first work ends when the subject is purified by repeated distillation and solidification and reduced to pure mercurial substance. The second degree of perfection is attained when the subject has been cooked, digested, and fixed into incombustible sulphur. The work is done when the third stone appears after the stone has been fermented, multiplied, and brought to ultimate perfection as a fixed, permanent, tincture, the philosopher's stone (Klossowski de Rola, 1973, pp. 10-12).

No matter the sequence described, several processes seem to recur: there are three substances, mercury, sulphur, and salt, which interact to produce the stone; there are four elements, earth, water, fire, and air, which are in some relationship to the three substances; and there are basically three colors, black (*nigredo*), white (*albedo*), and red (*rubedo*), which appear during the work, although green (*viriditas*), yellow (*citrinitas*), and the multicolored peacock's tail (*cauda payonis*) have also been described. There are three alchemical themes: conjunction of opposites, death of the product, and the resurrection, birth, and exaltation of the ultimate result, the *coelum*. All this can be expressed in a multitude of images from the mineral, vegetal, and animal kingdoms.

THE NUMBERS

One of the central axioms of alchemy is the saying attributed to Maria Profetissa: "One becomes two, two becomes three, and out of the third comes the one as the fourth." For Jung this shows that

> ... the even numbers which signify the feminine principle, earth, ... and evil itself are interpolated between the uneven numbers of the Christian dogma. . . . Thus the higher, the spiritual, the masculine inclines to the lower, the earthly, the feminine; and accordingly, the mother, who was anterior to the world of the father, accommodates herself to the masculine principle and, with the aid of the human spirit (alchemy or "the philosophy"), produces a son . . ., not a divine man but a fabulous being

conforming to the nature of the primordial mother. And just as the redemption of man the microcosm is the task of the "upper" son, so the "lower" son has the function of a *salvator macrocosmi* (CW 12, ¶ 26).

This process displays all the characteristics of psychological compensation; it shows that the gulf between the mother-world and the father-world is not unbridgeable, seeing that the unconscious holds the seed of the unity of both. After all:

> "the mask of the unconscious is not rigid—it reflects the face we turn toward it. Hostility lends it a threatening aspect, friendliness softens its features" (CW 12, ¶ 29).

Elsewhere Jung connects Maria Profetissa's axiom to the one transforming substance, the red gum, the resin of the wise, the "glue of the world," which is the medium between mind and body and the union of both. Of the four natures of the stone, three are earthy, or in the earth, but

> ". . . the fourth nature is the water of the stone, namely the viscous gold which is called the gum and with which the three earthy natures are tinted." We learn here that gum is the critical fourth nature: it is duplex, i.e., masculine and feminine, and at the same time the one and only *aqua mercurialis* (CW 12, ¶ 209).

So the union of the two is a kind of self-fertilization, a characteristic associated with the uroboros, the mercurial dragon, and hints (according to Jung) of the original man or Anthropos of Gnosticism.

In the center of the natural wisdom, whose circumference, closed in itself, forms a circle, the alchemist sees the fulfillment of the mysteries.

> "Here is the number four, within whose bounds the number three, together with the number two combined into One, fulfills all things, which it does in miraculous wise." In these relations between four, three, two, and one is found . . . the "culmination of all knowledge and of the mystic art, and the infallible midpoint of the center" (Dorn, quoted by Jung, CW 13, ¶ 187).

One

Therefore, the symbolic meaning of "one" is to be found in the idea of wholeness, totality, center, and origin. The Anthropos idea stands for human wholeness. It is the conception of a unitary being who existed before the human and at the same time represents humanity's goal. Another symbol for the one is the *rotundum*, the vessel of transformation, which is synonymous with the skull, the golden head, and the *filius sapientiae*. In the alchemical view, the soul is round and the vessel must be round too, like the heavens or the world. There seems to be no difference between the vessel and its content: the round Hermetic vessel in which the mysteries of transformation occur is the world-soul and humankind's wholeness (CW 9/2, ¶ 379-380).

Two

"Two" is the symbol of polarity, of the opposites: King/Queen, above/below, dry/moist, hot/cold, right/left. In the Middle Ages, two was considered the first number because with it division and multiplication begin. Also associated with the number two is the idea of good/bad, favorable/unfavorable. With the appearance of two, another emerges alongside the one, and this other can have a sinister significance, wherein one feels something alien, opposite, unknown.

> Therefore, argues a medieval alchemist, God did not praise the second day of creation, because on this day (Monday, or the day of the moon) the *binarius*, alias the devil, came into existence. . . . [A]s soon as the number two appears, a unit is produced out of the original unity, and this unit is none other than that same unity split into two. . . . The "One" and the "Other" form an opposition, but . . . the "One" seeks to hold to its one-and-alone existence, while the "Other" ever strives to be another opposed to the "One." The "One" will not let go of the "Other" because, if it did, it would lose its character; and the "Other" pushes itself away from the "One" in order to exist at all. Thus there arises a tension of opposites between the "One" and the "Other" (Jung, CW 11, ¶ 180).

Since the number two is feminine, it also signifies Eve, whereas the number three was equated with Adam. For this reason it is not difficult to see why Eve is associated with the devil, whereas Adam is related to the divine trinity. Dorn goes so far as to attribute not only duality but even the quaternity to the devil, thus breaking with the alchemical tradition in adopting the rigid Christian standpoint that Three is One but four is not, because four attains to unity in the *quinta essentia* (Jung, CW 11, ¶ 104).

Three

As the opposites never unite at their own level (*tertium non datur*), a supraordinate third is always required, in which the two poles can come together.

> [S]ince the symbol derives as much from the conscious as from the unconscious, it is able to unite them both, reconciling their conceptual polarity through its form and their emotional polarity through its numinosity (Jung, CW 9/2, ¶ 280).

Therefore the tension of opposites culminates in a release, out of which comes the "third." In the third the tension is resolved and the lost unity is restored. However, unity, the absolute One, cannot be known; it is undefinable. Therefore, three can be seen as an unfolding of the One to a condition wherein the unity becomes perceptible, recognizable.

> Three therefore appears as a synonym for a process of development in time, and thus forms a parallel to the self-revelation of the Deity as the absolute One unfolded into three (Jung, CW 11, ¶ 180).

The trinity is of exclusively masculine character. In antiquity it was represented by the three "spirits," namely, water, air, and fire. Jung believes that the unconscious transforms the trinity into a quaternity, which is at the same time a unity, just as the three persons of the Trinity are one and the same God. Whereas

> . . . three can be regarded as a relative totality, since it usually represents . . . a spiritual totality that is a product of thought. . . . Psychologically, however, three . . . should

be understood as a defective quaternity or as a stepping stone towards it. Empirically, a triad has a trinity opposed to it as its complement. The complement of the quaternity is unity (Jung, CW 9/2, ¶ 351).

With the distinct leaning of alchemy and of the unconscious toward quaternity, there is always a vascillation between the three and the four. There are three as well as four procedures, three as well as four colors. There are always four elements, but often the fourth is omitted. For Jung, the number three is not a natural expression of wholeness, since four represents the minimum number of determinants in a whole judgment (CW 12, ¶ 31).

The central ideas in alchemy seem, therefore, to be ternary as well as quaternary.

The psychologist cannot but mention the fact that a similar puzzle exists in the psychology of the unconscious. ... Four signifies the feminine, motherly, physical; three the masculine, fatherly, spiritual. Thus the uncertainty as to three or four amounts to a wavering between the spiritual and the physical—a striking example of how every human truth is a last truth but one (Jung, CW 12, ¶ 31).

Four

The quaternity is an organizing system of coordinates that are used for sorting out, as when we divide the year into seasons, the surface of the earth into cardinal points, the cycle of the moon into its phases, the human personality into temperaments or psychological functions. For the alchemists as well as for the Gnostics, it was "an attempt, more or less conscious, to organize the chaotic medley of numinous images that poured upon them" (Jung, CW 9/2, ¶ 381).

[T]he quaternity as produced by the modern psyche points directly not only to God within, but to the identity of God and man. Contrary to the dogma, there are not three but four aspects. ... The voice of nature is clearly audible in all experiences of quaternity ... (Jung, CW 11, ¶ 105).

For the Pythagoreans, the *tetraktys* emphasized four as the origin and root of eternal nature (Jung, CW 11, ¶ 61, n. 6). The *quaternio* is the union of inner opposites, the *hieros gamos*, the inclusion of passive/active and shadow/light within male/female, that is, within ourselves. In her commentary to *Aurora Consurgens*, von Franz quotes from a sermon of Pythagoras:

> The perfection of all counting is. . . Four, for Ten is perfected by Four. . . . Thus did God create all creatures from the four different natures; after they had come to ten in number, they were joined to one another . . . and God brought forth everything from them (p. 254).

For Jung, four signifies a *conscious* totality: it describes the ideal, spiritual man and formulates him as a totality, in contrast to the pentad.

Five

Five is the number assigned to the "natural" man, inasmuch as he consists of a trunk and five appendages.

> It is significant that the swastika symbolizes the "ideal" man, whereas the five-pointed star symbolizes the material and bodily man. The dilemma of four and five corresponds to the conflict between "culture" and "nature" (Jung, CW 9/1, ¶ 680).

However, five is also the quintessence and the number of the Anthropos, of Adam Kadmon, identified with the *filius philosophorum*. Indeed, the spirit of the fifth essence is

> ". . . the spirit of truth, whom the world cannot comprehend without the inspiration of the Holy Ghost. . . .He is the soul of the world," and moving all preserving all. In his initial earthly form . . . he is unclean, but he purifies himself progressively during the ascent through his watery, aerial, and fiery forms. Finally, in the fifth essence, he appears as the "clarified body." "This spirit is the secret that has been hidden since the beginning of things" (Paracelsus, quoted in Jung, CW 13, ¶ 166).

Six

According to an old tradition , six means creation and evolution, since it is the union of two threes, the even and the odd, female and male. The hexad, often represented by the seal of Solomon, consists of two intermingled triads, which alchemists used as a symbol of their art depicting the union of opposites. Although the triads sometimes represented water and fire, or earth and air, they ultimately indicate the male/female energies. The fact that one triangle points upward and the other downward may demonstrate "the not uncommon fact that the personality needs to be extended both upwards and downwards" (Jung, CW 9/1, ¶ 679).

Seven

Seven corresponds to the sequence of alchemical operations quoted in some texts and portrayed in the seven-petaled rose (see Jung, CW 12, fig. 29) or in the mandalas of the *Philosophia Reformata* (1622) or of the *Musaeum Hermeticum* (1625). The seven stages of transformation are depicted on the Tree of the Soul (CW 12, fig. 221) and in the Mountain of the Adepts (CW 12, fig 93. Reproduced in figure 23, p. 144). Seven is the number of metals and the number of planets; parallels between them are shown in Table 10 on page 145.

Also, the seven stars were originally

> . . . the seven great Babylonian gods, but . . . they had become the seven Archons, rulers of "this world," fallen angels condemned to punishment. . . . According to other sources the number seven is by no means sinister, since it is on the seventh mountain of the western land that the tree with the life-giving fruit is to be found, i.e., the *arbor sapientae* (Jung, CW 12, ¶ 298).

Psychologically, this image may refer to the building blocks of the ego and the seven fruits as earthly representatives of transpersonal principles. It is therefore not surprising that the *Sapientia* is also depicted by some alchemists wearing a royal crown of seven glittering stars (Jung, CW 12, ¶ 467). Finally, seven is the mysterious, numinous mixture of the masculine trinity and the feminine quaternity.

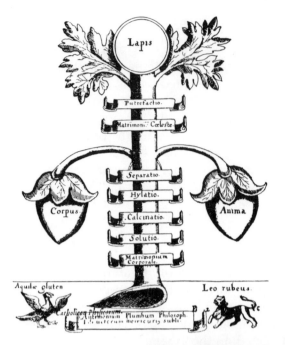

Figure 23. Stages in alchemical transformation. Top: *Arbor philosophica*, the tree as symbol of the stages of transformation (from Norton, *Catholicon physicorum*, 1630). Bottom: The mountain of the adepts (from Michelspacher, *Cabala*, 1654).

TABLE 10. PLANETS AND METALS.

Planet	Metal
Sun	Gold
Moon	Silver
Mercury	Quicksilver
Venus	Copper
Mars	Iron
Jupiter	Tin
Saturn	Lead

Eight

Just as three was deemed sacred and four was not, in the collective opinion seven is also sacred and eight is somewhat inferior, different. Whereas seven forms an uninterrupted series, the step to the eighth signifies entry into a new order, as illustrated by the musical octave in which the eighth note is the beginning of a new cycle. The motif of the double quaternity, or *ogdoad*, represents something that is at once heavenly and earthly, spiritual and corporeal, an image of totality (Jung, CW 14, ¶ 8). According to Scholem (1974, p. 19) "*ogdoad* is a Gnostic concept that signifies the eighth firmament above the seven heavens," where divine wisdom dwells.

Nine

Nine is the number of the muses and of the eagles of passion, the archers of Hermes Trismegistus (Jung, CW 14, ¶ 416). It is a number of completion, the end of pregnancy for woman, the end of the sequence of single-digit numbers, the end of a developmental sequence that has to become conscious because

> [U]nless the conscious mind intervened, the unconscious would go on sending out wave after wave without result, like the treasure that is said to take nine years, nine months and nine nights to come to the surface and, if not found on the last night, sinks back (Jung, CW 12, ¶ 111).

Ten

There are ten sephirot on the Tree of Life. They have also been concentrically imaged in a diagram that is practically identical to the one described by Origen as

> . . . a drawing of ten [presumably concentric] circles,
> which were separated from one another and held
> together by a single circle, which was said to be the soul
> of the universe (Jung, CW 14, ¶ 574, n. 119).

The Monad, the original unity and goal of the opus, reappears as
"denarius" (the number ten); "it is the unity of the personality
projected into the unity of the stone" (Jung, CW 14, ¶ 294).
Athanasius Kircher, in his *Arithnologia* (1665), produced a quaternity system in which ten was designated the "second monad"
and represented the spiritual world formed from duality and
opposites (Jung, CW 9/2, ¶ 416). There exists also an illustration
in the *Philosophia Naturalis* of Albertus Magnus (Jung, CW 14,
fig. 117), depicting the Anthropos as the *anima mundi*, containing
the four elements and characterized by the number ten, which
represents perfection $(1 + 2 + 3 + 4)$. See figure 24 . Ten is therefore
the perfect unfolding of unity, and the numbers one through ten
signify a completed cycle.

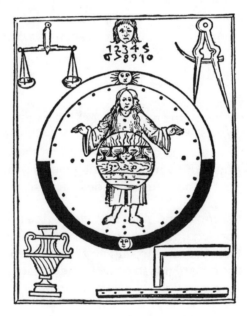

Figure 24. *Anthropos* as *Anima Mundi* and the number 10. (From Albertus
Magnus, *Philosophia Naturalis*, 1650.)

Eleven

Eleven, as ten plus one, denotes the beginning of a new cycle. In some areas of the world, the great Carnival begins on the eleventh day of the eleventh month at the eleventh hour (PM); this may be connected to the moment in the sun's journey just before it completes its cycle through the zodiac.

Twelve

Twelve is the number of alchemical operations, of the signs of the zodiac, of the months of the year. It is said that there exists a tree of faith, which grows from above downward, for its roots are in the Godhead. This tree has twelve branches, which are the twelve articles of faith. I cannot help but wonder if this alchemical image has not found its way into Card XII of the major arcana. Indeed, the two trees between which the Hanged Man is suspended grow downward; additionally, they have six stumps each where the twelve branches had been.

THE ELEMENTS

In alchemy there are always four elements, but often three of them are grouped together with the fourth in a special position; sometimes this fourth is earth, sometimes it is fire (Jung, CW 12, ¶ 31).

The squaring of the circle, a symbol of totality (figure 25, p. 148). is usually represented by a circle containing a square that in turn has a triangle within:

> [T]he philosophers maintain that the quadrangle is to be reduced to a triangle, that is, to body, spirit, and soul ... the body, or earth, in Saturnine blackness; the spirit in lunar whiteness, like water; and the soul, or air, in solar yellow. The triangle ... must change into a circle, that is, into unchangeable redness. Here the fourth is fire ... (Jung, CW 12, ¶ 165, n. 41).

The center and its periphery represent the totality of the psyche, the Self, defined by Jung as both the center and the circumference of the conscious and unconscious systems. These two heterogeneous systems intersect in the Self in functional relationship to one another. They are regulated by three rhythms, regimens, or procedures, expressed alchemically as the conversion in three steps of the four elements (or synthesized in the quintessence):

1st regimen: earth to water
2nd regimen: water to air
3rd regimen: air to fire (Jung, CW 12, ¶ 310).

These correspondences are also expressed in an old saying from Pseudo-Aristotle:

"When thou hast water from earth, air from water, fire from air, earth from fire, then shalt thou fully and perfectly possess our art" (Jung, CW 12, ¶ 475).

According to Klossowski de Rola (p. 17) Aristotle believed that the link between the four elements was mediated by their properties:

Heat + Dryness   = Fire
Heat + Humidity = Air
Cold + Dryness   = Earth
Cold + Humidity = Water

Figure 25. The elements and the squaring of the circle. Left: Maier, *Scrutinium chymicum*, 1687; right: Jamsthaler, *Viatorium spagiricum*, 1625.

TABLE 11. PRIMA MATERIA, THE BASIC PRINCIPLES AND THE ELEMENTS.*

Alchemical Principle	Element
SULPHUR	Earth (visible, solid state)
Fixed Principle	Fire (occult, subtle state)
SALT	Quintessence, comparable to ether
MERCURY	Water (visible, liquid state)
Volatile Principle	Air (occult, gaseous state)

*Modified from Klossowski de Rola, p. 19.

Klossowski de Rola further mentions (p. 19) correspondences between the *prima materia*, the three principles of the art, and the four elements as shown in Table 11.

Another version, quoted by Jung (CW 14, ¶ 655), states that fire working upon air creates sulphur, air working upon water creates mercury, and water working upon earth creates salt. As the earth has nothing to work upon, it brought forth nothing and thus it became the nurse and the matrix of the others.

Earth

Said to be wisdom and world soul but also accursed, the element earth is as ambiguous as the other alchemical substances (Jung, CW 14, ¶ 279). The earthly effect is "first a perfection of minerals, then a resuscitation of souls and a transfiguration of the animal body" (Jung, CW 14, ¶ 292). As *prima materia*, the earth is not a dead body. Although it sometimes coincides with the initial stage of the process (the *nigredo*, in which case it is called black earth), it is also inhabited by a spirit that is its life and soul, from which all created things can draw their strength. Through the spirit received from on high, the earth can incubate minerals, particularly gold, known as the imprint of the sun upon the earth, in her womb (Jung, CW 12, ¶ 444-445). Indeed, the earth is the "mother of metals," and of all creatures (figure 26). She is the fruitful "white earth" (Luna), the virgin earth that "undergoes the last degree of cultivation, that the fruit of the sun may be sown and ripened." The earth is here identified with the moon for "the lowest part of all the world is the earth, but the lowest part of the aether is the moon" (Jung, CW 14, ¶ 629, n. 271). This lowly status is illustrated by the animal assigned by the alchemists to the earth, the toad, which cannot fly but is firm and solid. It seems to confirm the saying: "Were it not for the earth in our work the air would fly

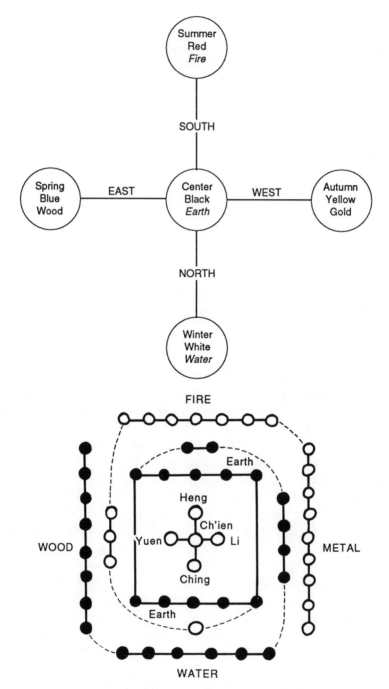

Figure 26. The earth. Top: The Central Element. Bottom: Mother of Metals, receiving into itself the creative power of heaven.

away, neither would the fire have its nourishment, nor the water its vessel" (Jung, CW 14, ¶ 2).

The elements have been used to symbolize the basic idea of ascent and descent as well as the stages of transformation depicted again and again by the alchemists in an attempt to apprehend the unconscious process of individuation. Jung quotes Dorn's proposal (CW 9/2, ¶ 420) that circular movement comes from the earth where fire originates; fire transforms water into air, which then rises, condenses, and comes down again. But during the ascent the volatized elements take from the higher stars "male seeds," which they bring down into "four matrices," the elements, in order to fertilize them. So earth is the crown of victory, the incorruptible "glorified body," and is called *terra alba foliata*. But it is also called black, based and accursed, painful to bear, a "moral turpitude that cannot be washed off." The alchemical earth is the arcane substance equaled with *adamah*, the red earth of paradise; it is the *prima materia*, black ash, of which it is said: "Despise not the ashes . . . for in them is the diadem, the ash of the things that endure (Jung, CW 14, ¶ 691, n. 102).

Water

The "one font of the four qualities" is the *aqua permanens* or *aqua pontica*, the primal water that contains the four elements. Also called "blessed water," the "water of harsh and bitter taste, . . . it is hard and difficult for any man to find that spring" (Jung, CW 14, ¶ 341). The good tidings announced by alchemy are that

> . . . as once a fountain sprang up in Judea, so now there is a secret Judea the way to which is not easily found, and a hidden spring whose waters seem so worthless and so bitter that they are deemed of no use at all. We know from numerous hints that man's inner life is the "secret place" where the *aqua solvens et coagulans* . . . the spark of the light of nature are to be found (Jung, CW 14, ¶ 344).

Thus alchemy announced a source of knowledge in the unconscious that yields a bitter taste, for it is a bitter thing to accept the darkness and the blackness of the passage in the valley of the shadow (Jung, CW 14, ¶ 346).

> Spirit in alchemy almost invariably has a relation to water. . . . The steam arising from boiling water conveys the first vivid impression of . . . the transformation of the corporeal into the incorporeal, into spirit or pneuma. The relation of spirit to water resides in the fact that the spirit is hidden in the water, like a fish. . . . From the alchemical transformation . . . is produced a collyrium (eyewash) which will enable the philosopher to see the secrets better (Jung, CW 13, ¶ 101).

Again, water can be a favorite symbol of the *albedo*, the regained state of innocence, the water of paradise that makes man whole and immortal. However, it is also the dark background of the soul, the "mire of the deep," the sea of the unconscious full of impurity that needs to be "purged" or "purified" (Jung, CW 14, ¶ 246). For the alchemists, the *prima materia* was at times the *humidum radicale* (radical moisture), or water (the *spiritus aquae*). Water was used as uniting symbol, the wonder-working "divine" water of alchemy:

> The healing and renewing properties of this symbolical water . . . point to the therapeutic character of the mythological background from which this idea comes (CW 9/2, ¶ 281).

Alchemical texts make known to us

> ". . . how the highest descends to the lowest, and the lowest ascends to the highest, and the midmost draws near to the lowest and highest, so that they are made one with it, how the blessed waters come down from above to awaken the dead, . . . how the elixir of life comes to them and awakens them, rousing them out of their sleep. . . . (CW 13, ¶ 191).

Finally, we find that water is the "hiding place and the dwelling place of the whole treasure" (CW 9/2, ¶ 201). The threefold process that holds the body, soul, and spirit of the transforming substance together in order to produce the end-result of the opus, the *lapis*, the treasure hard to behold, was formulated in the *Aurora Consurgens* thus

"For three months water preserveth the foetus in the womb; air nourisheth it for the second three; fire guardeth it for the third three" (Jung, CW 12, ¶ 477-478).

Air

Air is depicted in an ancient alchemical text thus:

"There are two offshoots from all the Aeons. . . . Standing opposite one another, they pair together and cause to arise in the space between them an incomprehensible Air, without beginning or end . . . " (CW 14, ¶ 160).

This passage describes a *coniunctio* between Sol and Luna, and as a result of the pairing:

. . . there was begotten a masculo-feminine pneuma, curiously designated as "Air," . . . [A]ir is used here in the spiritual sense of pneuma [whereas] Sol and Luna . . . are . . . endowed with an originally pneumatic character (Jung, CW 14, ¶ 161-163).

Air is the life of everything; the son of wisdom is born in the air. It is said that air is the mediator between fire (Sol) and water (Luna) by reason of its heat and moisture (Jung, CW 14, ¶ 162, n. 219).

"The air is a pure uncorrupted element, in its kind the most worthy, being uncommonly light and invisible, but inside heavy, visible, and solid. Enclosed within it is the spirit of the Highest that moved over the waters before the Creation, according to the testimony of the Holy Scripture: 'And . . . he did fly upon the wings of the wind.' All things are integrated in this element by the imagination of the fire" (Sendivogius, in Jung, CW 12, ¶ 397).

Jung points out that the pairs of opposites, namely, light/heavy, visible/invisible, are shown in their paradoxical identity, characteristic of unconscious psychic events. Thus

. . . the air's heavy, solid kernel is at the same time the *spiritus creator* which moves over the waters, and just as

"the images of all creatures" are constrained in the creative spirit, so all things are imagined or "pictured" in air
"through the power of fire" . . . because fire destroys all
composite things and infuses their images back into the
air in the form of smoke (Jung, CW 12, ¶ 398).

It would seem that inspiration and spiritual exaltation are appropriately represented by this image of the soul taking wing and
being uplifted, soaring in the lofty heights through the air. But
Jung warns:

We should not rise above the earth with the air of
"spiritual" intuitions and run away from hard reality, as
so often happens with people who have brilliant intuitions. We can never reach the level of our intuitions and
should therefore not identify ourselves with them. Only
the gods can pass over the rainbow bridge; mortal men
must stick to the earth and are subject to its laws. . . .
Man may have lost his ancient saurian's tail, but in its
stead he has a chain hanging onto his psyche which
binds him to the earth . . . [a] chain of given conditions
which weigh so heavy that it is better to remain bound to
them, even at the risk of becoming neither a hero nor a
saint. . . . That we are bound to the earth does not mean
that we cannot grow; on the contrary it is the *sine qua
non* of growth. No noble, well-grown tree ever disowned
its dark roots, for it grows not only upward but downward as well. The question of where we are going is of
course extremely important; but equally important, it
seems to me, is the question of *who* is going where. . . . It
takes a certain greatness to gain lasting possession of the
heights, but anybody can overreach himself. The difficulty lies in striking the dead centre. . . . For this an
awareness of the two sides of man's personality is essential: . . . these two aspects must never be separated
through arrogance or cowardice (CW 12, ¶ 148).

So earth is as necessary as air to the work, and soul as necessary
as body. The alchemical opus is based on the effect the soul has on
the body, but in all humility, one must remember that "thou canst
conceive the greater, therefore your body can bring it to reality

only with the help of the art and with God's permission (*Deo concedente*)."

Fire

Finally, the mystery of the art is enclosed in the invisible fire.

> The fire is "inextinguishable." "The philosophers call this fire the fire of the Holy Ghost." . . . "Just as . . . God the Father, God the Son, and God the Holy Ghost are united [i.e., as] the Holy Trinity in three Persons, and there yet remains the one single true God, so also the fire unites these three things: body, spirit, and soul, that is, Sun, Mercurius, and Soul." . . . This fire is "fire and water at once." The philosophers name it the "living fire" in honour of God, "who mingles himself with himself in the living water" (Jung, CW 9/2, ¶ 200).

Aqua permanens was the *spiritus mercurialis* in water form, hence, water is equated with fire. Although these terms were used indiscriminately, they are not the same because fire is active; so the spiritual fire as a form of *spiritus mercurialis* is spiritual, emotional, and close to consciousness, whereas water is passive, material, cool, and closer to the unconscious. Both are necessary to the alchemical process, since this is concerned with the union of opposites (CW 13, ¶ 187, n. 77-78). Fire seems to be contained at times in hylical water (CW 12, ¶ 433), and at times it is attributed to the element earth as hellfire. At times the hierarchy of elements begins with earth; at other times the primordial element is not earth, but water. In accordance with an ancient alchemical view, the earth is shown to emerge from the chaotic waters of the *massa confusa*. Air, the volatile element, rises from the earth and floats above it. Fire is highest of all; it is the "finest" substance, the "fiery pneuma which reaches up to the seat of the gods" (Jung, CW 12, ¶ 370).

THE SUBSTANCES

The dissolution of gold and silver in mercury, as well as the chemical reaction between mercury and sulphur forming red mercuric sulphide, may have been the original laboratory images that underlay the idea of the *coniunctio* of the King and Queen that gave birth to the red stone of the philosophers (Edinger, 1985, p. 211). Although the aim of the philosophers was the *aurum non vulgi*, it is worthy of note that gold can be produced in small amounts by nuclear bombardment of mercury, because mercury (80) immediately follows gold (79) on the periodic table of elements.

Mercury

In their concept of Mercurius, the alchemists included all the statements that mythology or natural philosophy ever made about him: he is God, daemon, person, thing, and the innermost secret man; he is psychic and somatic, he is the source of all opposites, he is duplex, ambiguous, and capable of taking conflicting positions at the same time (*utriusque capax*). The correct assessment of all the symbols connected with him leads to direct contact with that alien elusive inner reality: the unconscious (Jung, CW 13, ¶ 481). Mercurius stands for the beginning and the end of the opus; he is the *prima materia*, the *caput corvi*, the *nigredo*, and the stone. As the dragon he swallows himself, dies, and rises again as *lapis*. He is the colorful fan of the peacock's tail and the separation into four elements. He is the hermaphrodite of the *massa confusa* and of the end of the work; he walks separately in the brother/sister pair and reunites in their *coniunctio*, a symbol of reconciling opposites. Mercury is metal, yet liquid; matter, yet spirit; cold, yet fiery; poison, yet medicine. The changeability and multiformity of Mercurius is a key idea in alchemy. Child of Sol and Luna, born with the help of sulphur and salt, he seems to be a kind of universal formative principle—the principle of individuation (Jung, CW 13, ¶ 171, n. 10).

Mercurius is the divine winged Hermes manifest in matter, messenger of the gods, lord of thought, and sovereign psychopomp (Jung, CW 12, ¶ 404). The god of revelation, Hermes, is represented by the *serpens Mercuriri,*

> . . . a chthonic spirit who dwells in matter, more especially in the bit of the original chaos hidden in creation, the *massa confusa*. . . . Like the dragon, Mercurius is the slippery, evasive, poisonous, forerunner of the hermaphrodite, and for that reason he has to be overcome (Jung, CW 9/2, ¶ 371).

Since the opus was understood by the alchemists as a recapitulation or imitation of the creation of the world, the serpent Mercurius reminded them of the devil, the tempter, who on their own admission played all sorts of tricks on them during their work. Dwelling in the bowels of the earth, the snake, partly material and partly immaterial spirit, penetrates and sustains all things: this distant copy and counterpart of the Anthropos is equipped with the gift of wisdom and of supreme spirituality.

> Just as the serpent stands for the power that heals as well as corrupts. . . . so likewise the shadow is healthy instinctivity and the prerequisite for higher consciousness (Jung, CW 9/2, ¶ 402).

Therefore Mercurius is this "spirit-substance" that lurks unseen in the core of our psyche and must first be expelled if it is to be recovered: far from being merely curative and enobling in its effects, it may also act as a deadly poison that penetrates as pervasively as the pneuma penetrates the stone (Jung, CW 12, ¶ 406).

In the *Splendor Solis* we find a recipe for the production of the philosopher's quicksilver. It is said that when smoke and mist

> . . . seize upon the watery vapor with a pure, subtle, soily substance, the the Philosopher's Quicksilver is formed. But when it is brought to a fiery, earthy, subtle hardness, the Philosopher's Sulphur is formed (Trismosin, p. 30).

Sulphur

At the conscious level, sulphur represents will and motivation, whereas at the unconscious level it is the compulsive element, ranging from mere intent to possession. Sulphur is the symbol for that inflammable element in our psyche that thwarts our reason and our will, appearing now as consuming fire, now as life-giving warmth.

> Compulsion, therefore, has two sources: the shadow and the Anthropos. This is sufficient to explain the paradoxical nature of sulphur . . . (Jung, CW 14, ¶ 153).

Jung quotes from the *Turba philosophorum*:

> [T]here is in fact one substance in which everything is
> contained and that is the *sulphur philosophorum*, [which]
> is water and soul, oil, Mercurius and Sol, the fire of
> nature, the eagle, the *lachryma*, the first *hyle* of the wise,
> the *materia prima* of the perfect body. . . . and [is called] by
> whatever names the philosophers have called their stone
> . . . (CW 12, ¶ 336).

Sulphur is the light of nature, the supreme source of knowledge
for the natural philosopher; it is also the spirit of generative power.
Looking at its effects (as described by the alchemists), Jung has
concluded that sulphur is one of the many synonyms for the mysterious, active, transformative substance, which together with
Mercurius, forms the *lapis*. When it appears as a rainbow, it is a
divine and wonderful experience.

> Although a personification of evil, sulphur shines above
> earth and water with the splendour of the rainbow, a
> "natural vessel" of divine transformation (CW 14, ¶ 142).

The psychic factor that appears in projection in the qualities
ascribed to sulphur is the unconscious Self (Jung, CW 14, ¶ 144).
Indeed, sulphur is not only the medicine, it is also the *medicina*, the
wounded physician. As we know, symbols of the Self appear at
moments of violent collision between two opposite points of view,
as compensatory attempts to mitigate the conflict. Such is the role
of sulphur.

The qualities of sulphur have been described as follows: it
burns and consumes, causing (or signifying) putrefaction, corruption, imperfection, tincturing, and maturing, and blackness.
Luminous and corruptive, it is similar to Lucifer; masculine and
spermatic, it is connected to (perhaps imprisoned by) Venus, a
description fitting Eros, her son, and the passionate erotic energy
he generates.

The malicious, dangerous, and uncanny nature of sulphur
has been represented by the alchemists as snake, lion, eagle, fire,
cloud, shadow, fish, stone, unicorn, rhinoceros, dragon, raven.

Sulphur has a double nature, white and red. The former indicates the active substance of the moon; the latter, that of the sun.
Sulphur is one of the innumerable synonyms for the *prima materia* in its dual aspect as initial substance and end product. At the

beginning it is "crude and common"; at the end it is a sublimation product of the process (Jung, CW 14, ¶ 134).

Sulphur is the fire hidden in Mercury; it is a living fire, reviving dead bodies. Sulphur is *magna flamma*, a danger to the little life-flame of the alchemists. Its fieryness, unanimously stressed, refers not only to its natural combustibility but also to its occult fiery nature. As chthonic being, sulphur has close affinities with the dragon and the uroboros. These analogies make it difficult at times to distinguish between sulphur and Mercurius, since the same thing is said of both (Jung, CW 14, ¶ 135). The intimate connection with Mercurius emphasizes the importance of sulphur as a spiritual or psychic substance. It is not only the soul of metals but of living things; it produces the ferment that gives life or soul to the imperfect body (Jung, CW 14, ¶ 136).

Salt

Alchemical salt is usually in tandem with sulphur. Paracelsus frequently imaged salt as soul, sulphur as body, and mercury as the spirit combining them. For Jung, alchemical salt refers to feeling and to eros (CW 14, ¶ 330):

> Salt makes events sensed and felt, giving us each a sense of the personal—my tears, . . . my blood, my taste and value. The entire alchemical opus hangs on the ability to experience subjectively. Hence it is said in the "Golden Tract": "He who works without salt will never raise dead bodies" (Hillman, 1982, p. 117).

Since Paracelsus, the word *sal* often indicates the stable basis of life, ground, body. The term more particularly refers to alum, alkalis, bases, ashes, *sal ammoniac*, potash, as well as their equivalent sense qualities of bitterness, astringency, pungency, dessication, sharpness, dryness, capacity to sting and smart.

Salt is also a corrective, particularly a corrective of "lunatic *nigredo*" conditions, which it can isolate and fixate. A bitter despair,

> . . . a corrosive worry, a stubborn self-ignorance are leprous. . . . These conditions make the reflective power, which belongs to Luna, . . . come out only in spots, here

and there, perpetuating the condition rather than clearing it. Although "leprous" in alchemy generally meant "impure," Paracelsus seems to be speaking of a sickness of reflection itself. . . . Salt corrects this illness of reflection by means of fixing precisely what is wrong. . . .

Exactly what, when, where, and how must be felt, so that the "general imprecision of feeling" (T. S. Eliot, *East Coker*) can be spotted, and each spot cleared one by one. The larger disaster is corrected by the smaller sense of it. . . . The running-on of reflection in its wasting-away spottiness and self-eating leprosy can be purged by salt (Hillman, 1982, p. 128).

Crystallized reflection allows a way out by standing upon what one has already been through; "like cures like." Little depressions and solidified and salted experiences can yield small basic understandings that one is less likely to fight against. However, there is also the danger of too much salt, of becoming too fixated, "pickled," stuck in our past and our history, preserved from experiencing the present by experience of the past. Alchemical psychology protects itself from salt by its composite thinking

. . . where its salt is always yielding its body to sulphur and mercury. . . . For the function of salt is not its own conservation, but the preservation of whatever it touches (Hillman, 1982, pp. 132-133).

When events do not feel real enough; when the world tastes stale, flat, and unprofitable; when we feel uncomfortable in community and have lost our personal "me-ness"; when we feel weak, lost, alienated, and drifting—then the soul needs salt. The world can become earth, can become tangible, but progression from idea to grounded wisdom needs the salt of the earth. However, the very salt that is wisdom, truth, common sense, wit, and subjective feeling is also salt the destroyer by fanaticism and purism, indicating a hyperactivity of salt and loss of the mediating principle of dosage. Dosage is the art of the salt, and this dosage only our individual taste and common sense can prescribe (Hillman, 1982, p. 126).

When sulphur flares up it can be slain by a pinch of salt. . . . Salt wounds and slays the impulsive reactions, because it recalls the pain incurred in similar events. Salt gives us the awareness of repetition; sulphur only the compulsion. Perhaps the exalted wisdom of salt is nothing more grandiose than salt's ability to inhibit sulphur (Hillman, 1982, p. 124).

Hillman is of the opinion that alchemical substances offer distinctions between types of suffering. Whereas salt tastes the details of its pain by remembering precisely and with piercing agony, lead for instance, cannot see, does not know, remains paralyzed and sunk in a general obliteration of empirical memory. But problems cannot be resolved until they have first been acknowledged. At issue here is the capacity to internalize, to receive a problem into one's inner space. This would be to salt it. A problem reaches its solution only when it is adequately salted, for then it touches us personally. The taste of this experience may be bitter, humiliating, and lasting, but its solution is also lasting.

Our deep hurts are not merely wounds needing healing but salt mines from which we gain a precious essence, without which the soul cannot live. The soul needs to remember, to lick its wounds, deriving sustenance and a sense of reality thereby. We make salt in our suffering, says Hillman, and by working through our suffering, we gain salt, healing the soul (1982, p. 117). A trauma thus becomes a salt mine, a place of reflection offering a taste of the nature of one's personal being, a place where memory originates in the beginnings of personal history. These traumatic events initiate the soul.

> Who therefore knows the salt and its solution knows the hidden secret of the wise men of old. Therefore turn your mind upon the salt and think not of other things; for in it alone [i.e. , in the mind] is the science concealed and the most excellent and the most hidden secret of all the ancient philosophers (*The Rosarium*, in Jung, CW 12, ¶ 359).

Antimony

For Jung, antimony is the "black, magically fecund earth that Adam took with him from Paradise" described as "black, blacker than black (CW 12, ¶ 433). However, Jung also mentions that whereas antimony trisulphide, widely used as a dye (kohl), is black, the pentasulphide, also called "gold sulphur, " is orange-red

(CW 14, ¶ 466). Therefore, the antimony compounds known to the alchemists contained a substance that "clearly exemplified the nature of Rex and Leo, hence they spoke of the 'triumph of antimony'" (CW 14, ¶ 467).

Perhaps the value of antimony resides in its capacity to unite with all the known metals except gold, having been called the "wolf of metals" because it devoured them, or the *balneum regis* (the bath of the King) because it was used to purify molten gold, the impurities being removed in the form of scum (Edinger, 1985, p. 19).

Antimony is also the secret transformative substance that fell from the highest place into the darkest depths of matter where it awaits deliverance "though in its usage it has only the name in common with the chemical element" (Maier, quoted in Jung, CW 13, ¶ 183).

Grossinger suspects that prime matter could not have been mercury, but might have been a spirit of antimony. He lists some quotes from the alchemical literature: "The prime matter is antimony purified by iron, and finely pounded"; "The invisible mercury is the spiritual air of antimony which combines with vegetable or animal fluids"; "Antimony dissolves metals with as much ease as fire thaws ice"; "Nothing is better suited to alter the nature of metals than antimony"; and last, the most confusing of all the quotes:

> The mercury of the philosophers is not found in the earth, but must be prepared by art, by joining sulphur (of Mars) to the mercury (of antimony) (Grossinger, 1983, p. 301).

Elsewhere he confronts this confusion:

> [L]ately I have read . . . that mercury is simply a code word for something we know as antimony. . . . But I'm still not clear. Is it pure antimony? Is it antimony in solution with something else, say, iron? Because even if you identified it as antimony, you'd have to know what is meant to be calling it mercury. Mercury is a big word, like Sulphur, or Salt. . . . But there still are Sulphur, Salt, Mercury, and they have some relationship to the elemental principle. Since you need something to work

with, maybe antimony is a better source for elemental Mercury than the metal mercury. I don't know. Maybe antimony is the name for a stage within a process of occult chemistry. . . . Is the green lion which it becomes during the initial stage of the process really copper, or is copper a code name for the color green (Grossinger, 1983, p. 285)?

It seems to me that what we are confronting here in this confusion is similar to the confusion of people who, having survived pain by splitting off their feelings, have a very difficult time knowing that they feel and identifying what they feel once it is registered.

The ingredients of the work might . . . be anything. At any rate they are imaginary ones, even though they were expressed outwardly by chemical substances. . . . Even when, as is often undoubtedly the case, that procedure given by an author has no other aim than the production of the common gold, the psychic meaning of the opus nevertheless comes through in the symbolic nomenclature he employs in spite of his conscious attitude (Jung, CW 13, ¶ 355).

THE SEVEN METALS

In a passage from *Theatrum Chimicum*, Mercurius says, "I am the carbuncle of the sun, the most noble purified earth, through which you may change copper, iron, tin, and lead into gold" (Jung, CW 13, ¶ 267). This connection between Mercurius and the metals is encountered again:

Sun and moon supply the seeds that are planted in the earth (= Mercurius), and presumably the four other planets form the trunk of the tree. The four that are to be united into one refer to the tetrasomia of Greek alchemy, where, corresponding to the planets, they stand for lead, tin, iron, and copper (Jung, CW ¶ 13, 357).

Lead is the metal assigned to Saturn, tin to Jupiter, iron to Mars, copper to Venus, mercury (quicksilver) to Mercury; the moon and the sun were associated with silver and gold.

Lead

For a long time lead was the principal name for the arcane substance. Seth (Typhon) covered the coffin of Osiris with lead, which was also called the "sealed tomb of Osiris," and at times was the name for both Osiris and for sulphur. Lead as *prima materia* is said to be so "shameless and bedevilled that it drove the adepts mad" (Jung, CW 13, ¶ 139, n. 2)

> The inner driving-force behind the aspirations of alchemy was a presumption whose daemonic grandeur on the one hand and psychic danger on the other should not be underestimated (Jung, CW 13, ¶ 164).

When the ordering principles of consciousness are not in harmony with the unconscious and if the adept at this point orders his life according to rules traditionally regarded as rational, he brings himself into danger. The *prima materia*, "which is black outside and white inside, like lead," is hidden inside the whole man, who is threatened by the rational and socially accepted conduct of life, so that individuation is hindered.

> This danger . . . returns when the traditional, moral, and rational principles of conduct are put into force at a moment when something other than social life is in question, namely, the integration of the unconscious and the process of individuation (Jung, CW 13, ¶ 433).

There are times, however, when free autonomous spirit must be grounded in the restrictions of reality and personal limitations, all associated with Saturn and lead.

> Lead is heavy, dull, and burdensome. It is associated with the planet Saturn, which carries the qualities of depression, melancholy, and galling limitation (Edinger, 1985, p. 86).

Tin

Tin is the metal that corresponds to the planet Jupiter, of which it is said that it

. . . is often likened to the natural heat which generates all things; he dwells in the sky, and the earth is the place of his pleasure (Klossowski de Rola, plate 32).

The attributes that the soul acquires from Jupiter are the power to act and its fire (Edinger, 1985, pp. 134-135). Whereas Saturn represents death, Jupiter signifies life (Jung, CW 9/2, ¶ 130).

Iron

It is said of iron that it was begotten in the earth by the virtue of all the stars and planets but especially by the contribution of the pole star, called the Great Bear. It is the metal of Mars, the god of war, hot, choleric, and bilious. Mars was also called Daemogorgon, a god of the earth, or a "terrible god and iron" (Jung, CW 13, ¶ 176, n. 39). In one metaphor of *coniunctio*, it was recommended that iron be married to antimony, and when both turned red and single, they were to be married again to mercury; when mercury digested them, they were to be married, as one, to red gold.

Copper

Copper is correlated with Cyprian, another name for Venus, Aphrodite (Jung, CW 13, ¶ 228). Gold is said to owe its red color to the admixture of copper, mentioned in Greek alchemy as the transformative substance. Given that Venus stands for the spirit in nature, I wonder if copper in alchemy is not a reminder that, "nature *must not* win the game, but she *cannot* lose" (Jung, CW 13, ¶ 229). Nature is not only matter, she is also spirit.

Silver

The stages of transformation of the inner man are symbolized in alchemy by the stages that transform copper into silver and silver into gold, a gradual enhancement of value (Jung, CW 13, ¶ 118). Indeed, the moon condition, highly praised by many alchemists as if it were the ultimate goal, is nevertheless a transitional stage that has to be further pursued to the sun condition (Jung, CW 12, ¶ 334).

The soul of the whole man is drawn to the higher world where, according to Dorn, stacked (as it were) in a vertical row, there are four strongholds:

> The lowest is of crystal and shelters "philosophical love"; the second is of silver and contains Sophia; the third is of diamond . . . and only a few get there . . .; the fourth is golden but "not perceptible to the senses," "a place of eternal . . . joy" (Jung, CW 14, ¶ 731, n. 198).

Gold, silver, and mercury are the initial ingredients that are prepared and purified in order to become "symbolic" substances (Jung, CW 13, ¶ 357, n. 11); on the other hand, some texts indicate that Mercurius is the "soul" of gold and silver (Jung, CW 14, ¶ 713).

But it was also said that Luna is the sum and the essence of the nature of the metals; Luna is the "universal receptacle" of all things as well as the first gateway to heaven, and it was stressed that silver is yet another synonym or symbol for the *arcanum Luna* (Jung, CW 13, ¶ 218-219). Mercurius is also often identified with the moon, the quicksilver-silver connection being fairly obvious. Mercurius, like the moon, is a Lucifer, a light-bringer; he heralds the coming of the light of the sun (Jung, CW 13, ¶ 273).).

Gold

Gold and silver are the fruits of the sun-and-moon tree (Jung, CW 14, ¶ 181). It was also said that gold gets its qualities from Mercurius, just as because of the half-feminine nature of Mercurius he was also identified with the moon. Often the King is defined as gold refined from silver (Jung, CW 14, ¶ 354, n. 20). However, gold (the King) comes into being only through liberation of the divine soul (pneuma) from the chains of *Physis* (matter, in general). The gold that the alchemists sought, which originated in dung or in decomposed matter, was the shapeless and generally spurned content of the unconscious; yet gold is a favorite synonym for the *lapis*, being the *aurum philosophorum* or *aurum potabile* (Jung, CW 9/1, ¶ 543). Alchemy was not concerned with ordinary gold-making but with a philosophical secret. That gold has a symbolic nature is demonstrated by the attributes the alchemists gave it, such as *aurum non vulgi* or *aurum vitreum*. Owing to its analogy with the sun,

> . . . gold was denied the highest philosophical honour, which fell instead to the *lapis philosophorum*. The transformer is above the transformed, and transformation is

one of the magical properties of the marvelous stone (Jung, CW 12, ¶ 99).

THE STAGES

The number of operations and their sequence are very uncertain.

> We see the same uncertainty in the individuation process, so that a typical sequence of stages can only be constructed in very general terms. The deeper reason for this . . . is probably the "timeless" quality of the unconscious . . . (Jung, CW 16, ¶ 468, n. 8).

Not only are the number of operations variable, but also the number of stages. All texts describe the stages of *nigredo*, *albedo*, and *rubedo*. The stages of *citrinitas* (yellowing), *viriditas* (greening), and the *cauda pavonis* (peacock's tail) either are not mentioned or occur in different sequence, the yellowing preceding the greening or vice versa (Jung, CW 12, ¶ 333).

> The *nigredo* or blackness . . . is the initial state, either present from the beginning as a quality of the *prima materia*, the chaos or *massa confusa*, or else produced by the separation (*solutio*, *separatio*, *divisio*, *putrefactio*) of the elements. If the separated condition is assumed from the start, as sometimes happens, then a union of opposites is performed under a likeness of male and female (called the *coniugium*, *matrimonium*, *coniunctio*, *coitus*), followed by the death of the product of the union (*mortificatio*, *calcinatio*, *putrefactio*) and a corresponding *nigredo*. From this the washing (*ablutio*, *baptisma*) either leads directly to the whitening (*albedo*), or else the soul (*anima*) released at the "death" is reunited with the dead body and brings about its resurrection, or again the "many colours" (*omnes colores*) or peacock's tail (*cauda pavonis*), lead to the one white colour that contains all colours. At this point the first main goal of the process is reached, namely the *albedo*, *tinctura alba*, *terra alba foliata*, *lapis albus*, etc., highly prized by many alchemists as if it were the ultimate goal. It is the silver or moon condition, which still

> has to be raised to the sun condition. The *albedo* is . . .
> the daybreak, but not till the *rubedo* is it sunrise. The
> transition to the *rubedo* is formed by the *citrinitas*, though
> this . . . was omitted later. . . . The red and the white are
> King and Queen, who may also celebrate their "chymi-
> cal wedding" at this stage (Jung, CW 12, ¶ 334).

Thus the colors the alchemists used are primarily black, white,
and red to describe the basic stages and yellow, green, and "mul-
ticolor" to describe a particular substage.

The *prima materia* must be transformed by *putrefactio*, which
is synonymous with the *nigredo*, the grave, death (Jung, CW 14,
¶ 714).

There are two main divisions of the opus: The *opus ad album*
and the *opus ad rubeum* or *opus Lunae* and *opus Solis*. Both have to
be performed at certain fixed times. The first work to obtain whiteness must be brought to an end in the house of the moon, whereas
the second must be terminated in the house of Mercury (Jung,
CW 14, ¶ 181, n. 319).

> Psychologically they correspond to the constellation of
> unconscious contents in the first part of the analytic
> process and to the integration of these contents in actual
> life (Jung, CW 14, ¶ 181).

Nigredo

In the color sequence, black corresponds to the original destruction
of matter. The situation of distress corresponding to the alchemical *nigredo* was described as

> . . . the blackness of guilt that covered the bridal earth
> as with black paint. . . . There was a sundering of earth
> from heaven, the original paradise was shut down. . . .
> Malkuth became a widow, the fiery *yang* went back aloft,
> and the damp *yin* enveloped humanity with darkness
> (Jung, CW 14, ¶ 607).

Nigredo is often represented by the black raven although the
raven's head may represent the emergence from blackness, the
transition from *nigredo* to *albedo* (Klossowski de Rola, p. 118).

Because he dwells in caverns and dark places, the dragon also represents, at times, the initial state of unconsciousness. At the victorious conclusion of the battle of the hero with the dragon, the sun rises; consciousness dawns (Jung, CW 13, ¶ 118).

Albedo

This stage consists of shining whiteness, *leukosis*, white gold, *terra alba foliata*; it is lunar and feminine in imagery. Some consider the peacock's tail as part of the *leukosis* stage.

> Luna is really the mother of the sun, which means psychologically, that the unconscious is pregnant with consciousness and gives birth to it. . . . From the darkness of the unconscious comes the light of illumination, the *albedo* (Jung, CW 14, ¶ 219-220).

But sometimes one does not reach this state simply through *ablutio*, through washing. During the more painful procedure, the *dealbatio*, lye was added to the solution. This may be the reason that ash and salt are synonymous with the *albedo*, the connecting link between ash and salt being potash (lye is potash in solution) (Jung, CW 14, ¶ 320-321).

Rubedo

For Grossinger (p. 317) yellow and red are the main colors of the culmination of the opus. Red is *rubedo* or *iosis*. In Greek alchemy it was represented by the cinnabar of the philosophers, which was also called the "copper man turned to gold." Because of its redness it was often identified with sulphur.

Citrinitas

Citrinitas or *xanthosis*, the yellowing, may correspond to the ripening of the ears of barley springing up in the alchemical flask, or the fixed salt of urine, but (Grossinger insists) it is not gold, despite its color. For Jung this represents the phase in the work when one has reached some understanding and insight.

> When the *citrinitas* . . . (xanthosis, yellowing) appears, there is formed the *collyrium* . . . of the philosophers. If they wash their eyes with it, they will easily understand the secrets of the philosophy (Jung, CW 9/2, ¶ 195).

Viriditas

Green has a spermatic, procreative quality (Jung, CW 14, ¶ 137); it is also the color of the Holy Ghost, of life, procreation, resurrection (Jung, CW 14, ¶ 395). Not surprisingly the sarcophagi of card XX, the Judgement (representing resurrection), are green. In one alchemical text, the feminine personification of the black and rejected *prima materia* says:

> "I am alone among the hidden; nevertheless I rejoice in my heart, because I can live privily, and refresh myself in myself. . . [U]nder my blackness I have hidden the fairest green" (Eleazer, in Jung, CW 14, ¶ 622).

Jung interprets this passage as depicting a state of imperfect transformation, a state not only of torment but of hidden happiness.

> It is a state of someone who, in his wanderings among the mazes of his psychic transformation, comes upon a secret happiness which reconciles him to his apparent loneliness. In communing with himself he finds not deadly boredom and melancholy but an inner partner; more than that, a relationship that seems like the happiness of a secret love. . . (Jung, CW 14, ¶ 623).

THE OPUS IN FIGURATIVE LANGUAGE

In a 17th-century woodcut an alchemist stands on a hill within a grove of seven trees, which represent the seven planetary metals; the twelve fundamental substances of the opus (three of which have been previously discussed) are also depicted (see figure 27). McLean (1989, pp. 40-42) provides their astrological correspondences presented in Table 12.

Tartar, in alchemical language, means the underworld; it is the sediment in the bottom of the alchemical vessel. Tartar is also the *sal Saturni*, a sinister substance evoking death and hell (Jung, CW 14, ¶ 703). Auripigment (or orpiment) is one of the substances (along with arsenic, mercury, and antimony) that can be poisonous and healing at the same time, depending on the preparation (Grossinger, 1983, p. 40). Verdigris, the "leprosy of the metals," is the *benedicta viriditas*, the blessed greenness signifying the secret immanence of the divine spirit of life (Jung, CW 14, ¶ 623). Alum

TABLE 12. ASTROLOGICAL CORRESPONDENCES OF ALCHEMICAL SUBSTANCES

Fire	Earth
Salt/Sagittarius Sulphur/Aries Crocus Mars/Leo	Tartar/Capricorn Alum/Taurus Sal Ammoniac/Virgo
Water	Air
Auripigment/Cancer Vitriol/Scorpio Saltpeter/Pisces	Verdigris/Libra Cinnabar/Gemini Mercury/Aquarius

* From McLean, *Alchemical Mandala*, p. 40.

Figure 27. The alchemist, the seven planetary metals, and the twelve fundamental substances. (From *Hermetic Museum*, 1678).

is the metal that, along with vitriol, is brought forth by the stone (according to Dorn [Jung, CW 13, ¶ 375]). The water of alum is also said to be the source of mercury (Jung, CW 14, ¶ 683, n. 84). Cinnabar is connected to the dragon's blood, to philosophical sulphur, to copper (the associations between gold ☉, garnet ♁, and copper ♀, the metal of Venus, explain the similarities between their alchemical signs. Crocus Mars has the same alchemical sign as garnet and antimony, which is sometimes represented by ♁, and sometimes by ♯. *Sal ammoniac*, represented by the "Star of Bethlehem" ✳ (Klossowski de Rola, p. 126), was used to dry the pulverized corpse. It was primarily the preservative quality of both *sal ammoniac* and saltpeter (*sal nitri*) that was sought, but:

> secondarily, in the mind of the adepts, "marination" meant the "in-forming" penetration of *sapientia*. . . into the ignoble mass, whereby the corruptible form was changed into an incorruptible and immutable one (Jung, CW 14, ¶ 336).

Saltpeter is at times identical to salt in general; it is the *prima materia* in which Mercurius is stuck (Jung, CW 9/1, ¶ 534, n. 13). Of its sign, ✠, it is said:

> One can hardly imagine a better sign for the arcane substance, which salt was considered to be. . . . Salt, in ecclesiastical as well as alchemical usage, is the symbol of Sapientia and also for the elect personality (Jung, CW 9/1, ¶ 575).

The horizontal plane of the mandala depicts the alchemist integrating his unconscious, feminine side (represented by Luna on his left) with his light, conscious side (represented by Sol on his right). The vertical plane presents the three realms of the alchemical process. The hill of alchemy (below), with its grove of physical substances, provides the materials for the work. The realm of soul (middle) includes the seven spiritual stars and the five alchemical birds, symbolizing the inner psychic stages of transformation that the alchemist experiences during the opus. The black crow (or raven) represents the *nigredo*; the white swan, the *albedo*. The winged dragon, composed of the air principle (bird wings) and the chthonic principle (snake body), may at times represent Mercury, the winged, divine spirit manifest in matter, at times sulphur, its violent and pernicious effects exhaled in the dragon's fiery breath. But the dragon's head also contains the precious stone.

> [C]onsciousness contains the symbolic image of the self, and just as the lapis unites the opposites, so the self assimilates contents of consciousness and the unconscious (Jung, CW 14, ¶ 141).

The dragon is the oldest picture/symbol in alchemy, and it represents the oldest layer of the psyche; it is the image of untamed and unintegrated emotions; it cannot be destroyed without irreparable loss, as it stands for the raw energy, the fire that is needed for the process of transformation (McLean, 1989, p. 34). Whereas the pelican symbolizes the cyclic distillation (on which the alchemical opus is based) needed to obtain the "exaltation of the quintessence" (Klossowski de Rola, text accompanying plate 21), the phoenix symbolizes the transforming substance itself; it represents the miracle of transformation and rebirth, of the *nigredo* becoming *albedo*, of the passage from unconsciousness to illumination; the phoenix "after consuming itself . . . each time rose renewed, like the reborn sun . . . (Jung, CW 14, ¶ 281). The light-filled realm of the spirit presents three symbols of the divine: the Father (YHVH), the Son (lamb), and the Holy Ghost (dove). In the center is the statement. "Four kinds of fire are required for the work," which may be a reminder of the "squaring of the circle," a symbol of the *opus alchymicum* because it breaks down the original chaotic unity into the four elements and then combines them again in a higher unity. This unity is represented by the circle. The four elements are represented by a square that is usually contained in or containing a triangle. See figure 28 on page 174.

> [T]he production of the one from the four is the result of a process of distillation and of sublimation . . . so that the "soul" or the "spirit" shall be extracted in its purest state. The product is generally called the "quintessence" (Jung, CW 12, ¶ 165).

In figure 28, we are presented with a tree: its roots reach into the earth, here represented by a toad. Its center is formed by a square inside a triangle, surrounded by a circle, a symbol of totality and of Mercurius (Jung, CW 13, ¶ 272). On the outermost circle, representing the elements, are blood and primordial matter (hyle). The inner circles represent the three colors: black, white, and red, correlated with Mars, Jupiter, and Venus and with earth, water, and fire, respectively. On the sides of the triangle are the body (Saturn) in the area of earth, *anima* in the area of fire, and *spiritus* in the area of spirit. Within the triangle are earth, moon, and the feminine (bottom) and sky, sun, and the masculine (top). For McLean (1989, p. 98) the upward-pointing triangle integrates spirit, soul, and body and seems to form a six-pointed star (the seal of Solomon) with the triplicities (in the circles) black/earth, white/water, and red/fire. Above the circle the tree is crowned, a reminder that the topmost sephira on the cabalistic Tree of Life is *Kether*, the crown. With the next two sephirot (*Hochmah* and

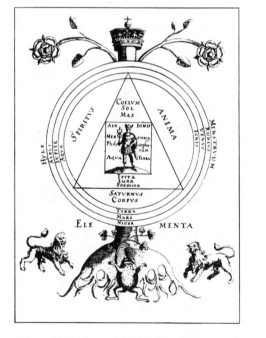
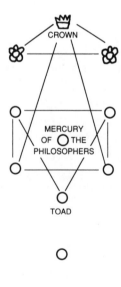

Figure 28. Alchemical transformation and the Tree of Life. Left: Symbol of hermetic transformation, the *Homo philosophicus Mercurius* (from *Mercurius redivivus*. 1630). Right: *Mercurius philosophorum* at the center of the Tree of Life in the place of Tipheret (from McLean, *The Alchemical Mandala*, p. 100).

Binah), represented here, perhaps, by the two roses, it forms the supernals. In the center of the square stands Mercury with his caduceus. On his left are fire and earth; on his right, air and water.

The caduceus represents a snakelike path that unites the opposites; its labyrinthine way, its twists and turns, are sometimes terror inspiring. It is on this *longissima via* that we meet with those experiences that are not readily accessible.

> [T]hey cost us an enormous amount of effort: they demand the very thing we most fear, namely the "wholeness" which we talk about so glibly. . . though in actual life we give it the widest possible berth (Jung, CW 12, ¶ 6).

The caduceus (figure 29) may represent the antinomial character of the **S**elf, which is in essence both conflict and unity. Indeed, the Self is a union of opposites par excellence; however, it is absolutely paradoxical in that it represents, in every aspect, thesis and antithesis and at the same time synthesis (Jung, CW 12, ¶ 22-24).

In the lower section of figure 29, three hearts, each with a snake protruding from its base, represent the three principles (salt,

Figure 29. Left: The Caduceus, conflict and reconciliation (from a Swiss woodcut, 1615). Right: The three principles and the four stages (from Valentinus, "Duodecim claves," *Hermetic Museum*, Vol. 1).

mercury, and sulphur) and the three realms (body, soul, and spirit). Contained in a circle, they seem to generate a churning that moves out from the essence (heart) of the three principles to their polarized outer expression (snakes) and is intensified by their endeavor to unite by grasping each other's tail. Above the circle, two figures, a male and female form a cross- or swastika-like shape, their heads polarized on the horizontal plane with their feet forming the vertical, while their arms reach back to touch each other's feet (replicating the snakes' movement). At each point of the cross stands one of the alchemical birds. First, the crow (*nigredo*) is north at the man's feet; the swan (*albedo*) is west at the woman's head; the peacock (the stage of all the colors) is south at her feet; and the phoenix (resurrection and final transformation) is east at the man's head. They also represent the four elements—earth, water, air, and fire, respectively (McLean, 1989, p. 78). Four above and three below suggest the symbol of antimony, ☿ or ♁ , a substance that symbolizes the complete opus.

Figure 30 depicts the end of the process. The alchemist as hermaphrodite has achieved integration of the opposite

Figure 30. The end of the alchemical process. (From *Rosarium philosophorum*, 1550, in McLean, *The Alchemical Mandala*, p. 39.)

(male/female) polarities. His/her golden crown symbolizes ruler-ship of the conscious solar element while the moon crescent underfoot indicates mastery of the unconscious lunar element. At the left foot stands the raven, a reminder of the inner dark spaces of which one must remain aware indefinitely. On the right, a tree with thirteen "moonleaves" may depict the *arbor philosophica*, which symbolizes spiritual growth and the highest illumination at the end of the transformation of the inner man (Jung, CW 13, ¶ 119); the thirteen leaves suggest the image of "the One who stands within the Twelve," a representation of the process of initiation into higher awareness (McLean, 1989, p. 37).

In his right hand the alchemist holds a crater, chalice, the divine cup of *Nous* (spirit or consciousness) sent by God to free humankind from its natural, imperfect sleeping state and enable participation in a higher state of consciousness and enlightenment (Jung, CW 12, ¶ 409). The three snakes within it represent, perhaps, the three primary alchemical substances (sulphur, mercury, and salt) or spirit, soul, and body. The left hand holds a coiled snake: this is the *spiritus Mercurialis*, "the soul of the world or of matter freed from its fetters" (Jung, CW 14, ¶ 700). The snake is the vegetation *numen* that dwells in the interior of the earth, the pneuma that lies hidden in the *prima materia* and, therefore, in the stone (Jung, CW 9/2, ¶ 386).

The vertical axis within the flask of figure 31 on page 178 connects the water of the unconscious (below) with the air of spirit (above). At their interface is the torso of the alchemist who, having achieved some awareness (as depicted by the sun and moon from which he arises and which he holds in his right and left hands respectively), emerges from the water. This entire process takes place in the sealed flask or alembic, the inner world, which receives heat from the outer world (the fire under the flask). In the water, above the precipitate, are the sign for sulphur (on the alchemist's left) and the sign for mercury (on his right) (McLean 1989, p. 31).

As we know, the sulphur of the philosophers is one element contributing to the production of the "body that is at the same time spirit"; it is "that which makes the spirit itself firm and fixed; [it] is fixed and eternal and cannot be burned." (Jung, CW 12, ¶ 511, n. 202) Mercurius corresponds outwardly to quicksilver, but as previously described, he is a *deus terrenus*, that part of God that

Figure 31. Connecting the water of the unconscious with the air of the spirit in the alchemical *vas*. (From Barchusen, *Elementa Chemiae*, 1718.)

was left behind in his creation and holds the soul captive in Physis, for which reason it must be liberated and emerge as *anima mundi*. Between the emergence from the waters of the unconscious and this liberation is the black bird, the raven, the necessary darkness through which one must struggle before the final transformation. Finally, in the neck of the flask is the mandorla (salt) containing the transformed alchemist. This plate evokes the analytic process in which that part of the analysand's soul that is too anchored in the concrete needs the fire of sulphur. Thus it will lead from gross to subtle while the part of the soul that at times takes to the clouds to avoid painful reality will have to be brought back to earth by salt. Mercurius mediates and interweaves between the two polarities; his is the energy behind the turning wheel of soul making.

TAROT AND
ALCHEMICAL IMAGERY

> If one wants to form a picture of the symbolic process,
> the series of pictures found in alchemy are good exam-
> ples, though the symbols they contain are for the most
> part traditional despite their often obscure origin and
> significance. . . . It also seems as though the set of pic-
> tures in the Tarot cards were distantly descended from
> the archetypes of transformation. . . . The symbolic
> process is an experience *in images and of images* (Jung,
> CW 9/1, ¶ 81-82).

Certain images encountered in the plates accompanying alchemical texts seem to have found their way into the major arcana.
Because juxtaposing the alchemical and the tarot images may be of
interest, a number of such collocations have been included so that
the reader can compare them and discover whether there is a common background (see figures 32 through 47 on pages 181 to 197).
At times it is the very idea that is expressed, as in Death (card
XIII) and the alchemical image of *putrefactio*, Judgement (card XX)
and the alchemical image of *resurrectio*, and in the variant of the
Lover(s) (card VI) that shows a man and a woman and the alchemical images of *coniunctio*. There is also correspondence between
the Empress and the Emperor (cards III and IV) and the alchemical images of Queen and King; the same can be said of the Sun
and the Moon (cards XIX and XVIII) and images of the sun and
moon repeatedly encountered in alchemical imagery. The Hermit
(card IX) is very like the alchemist, whereas the Devil (card XV)
presents us with an image almost identical to Mercurius as *prima
materia*, encountered in his son Pan, while the World (card XXI)
shows an impressive similarity to the image of Mercurius as *spiritus mundi*. The Chariot (card VII) is frequently used in alchemical
imagery (see figure depicting the sulphur of the philosophers as
Apollo). In other instances, a detail in one of the tarot cards is also
seen in one of the alchemical plates, such as the decanting of the
two jars seen both in Temperance (card XIV) and in a plate of
Maria Prophetissa pointing to a similar image. The Wheel of
Fortune (card X) resembles a detail of a 16th-century plate depicting allegorically the blinded Fortuna subjected to the laws of

chance that bring people randomly to ascendency, only to hurl them down at the next turn. In a 15th-century engraving, the Wheel of Fortune is connected to planetary influences, a major contributor to the outcome of the alchemical work. The papal cross, with its three crossbars, held by the High Priest (Card V) is shaped like the flowering branch held by the central female figure in plate six of Mylius' *Philosophia reformata* (1622). Finally, there are some alchemical images, such as the one from *Elementa chemiae* (1718), depicting sulphur as sun and Mercurius as moon bridging the river of eternal water, that bring to mind the ominous atmosphere of the Moon (card XVIII) in which the two towers guard a path similar to that of the eternal water. Some similarities can also be found between images depicting the alchemical opus and the tarot cards depicting the Fool, the Magician, and Strength.

Figure 32. The Magician. Top left: Holding a staff in his raised left hand, the Magician stands with the tools of his trade before him. Top right: Two alchemists similarly address their instruments (from Geber, *De Alchimia*, 1529). Bottom: The adept on the left also raises his staff in his left hand (from *Speculum Veritatis*, a 17th-century manuscript).

Figure 33. The Empress. Left: The left foot of the Empress rests on a crescent moon; her head is surrounded by stars. Right: Here the virgin stands on a crescent moon with her head encircled with stars (from *Speculum humanae saluaciones*, a 15th-century manuscript).

Figure 34. The Emperor. The orb held in the left hand and the black eagle are symbols that the Emperor (left) shares with the king (right). (From an anonymous 15th-century manuscript).

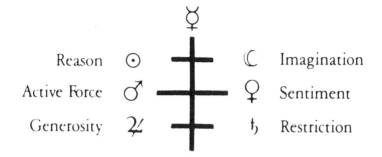

Reason	☉		☾	Imagination
Active Force	♂		♀	Sentiment
Generosity	♃		♄	Restriction

Figure 35. The Pope. Top left: In card V, the Pope wears a three-tiered crown and holds, in his left hand, a staff with three crosspieces. Bottom left: The Pope in this image also wears a tiara (from Scaliger, *Explanatio imaginum*, 1570). Top right: Oswald Wirth argues that this configuration represents a septenary formed by the rounded ends of the transverse lines and the rounded top of the cross thus formed. According to him, seven is the number of harmony and of planetary influences, known to have played a major role in alchemical procedures (Wirth, 1985, p. 82). Bottom right: Here a woman holds in her left hand a plant identical in shape to the papal cross (from Mylius, *Philosophia reformata*, 1622).

Figure 36. The Lovers. Top: An angel blesses the Lovers. Bottom: In this *coniunctio* engraving, the King and Queen are blessed by a priestly figure (from Mylius, *Philosophia reformata*, 1622).

Figure 37. The Chariot. The charioteer in Card VII (top) displays the same determination as the crowned Apollo (bottom). (From an anonymous 15th-century manuscript.)

Figure 38. The Hermit. The posture of the Hermit (top) is very similar to that of the alchemist (bottom) pointing to his *vas* (from *Splendor Solis*, a 16th-century manuscript).

Figure 39. The Moon. Top: Card XVIII. Bottom: The river of eternal water and the ominous mood in this 18th-century alchemical image (Barchusen, *Elementa chemiae*) are reminiscent of the winding path of card XVIII that leads beyond the howling dogs and the threatening towers into the unknown.

Figure 40. Top: Wheel of Fortune. Bottom left: Fortuna, blindfolded, brings individuals randomly into ascendancy on her wheel (from a 16th-century engraving
in Kenton, *Astrology*, figure 55). This is markedly similar to the wheels shown in
Card X (bottom right) and in another figure from Kenton (figure 45) that comes
from a 15th-century German manuscript.

Figure 41. Strength. Top left: Card XI. Bottom left: In an alchemical *vas*, the lion's jaws are forced open by a youngster (from *Splendor Solis*, a 16th-century manuscript). Top right: Here a lion eats (or disgorges) the sun (from *Rosarium philosophorum*, a 16th-century manuscript), an image as ambiguous as that of the woman opening (or closing) the lion's jaws in Card XI. Bottom right: A woman, having tamed the lion, is riding it (from Mylius, *Philosophia reformata*, 1622).

Figure 42. Death. Top: A skeleton moves through a field of severed limbs in Card XIII. Bottom left: In this putrefaction image, the skeleton stands on the black sun (Mylius, *Philosophia reformata*, 1622). Bottom right: Severed limbs also litter the ground in this alchemical engraving representing death and rebirth (*Splendor Solis*, a 16th-century manuscript).

Figure 43. Temperance. Top: The continuous flow between the two jars in card XIV is seen also in the symbol of the union of upper and lower, to which (bottom) Maria Prophetissa points (from Maier, *Symbola aureae mensae*, 1617).

Figure 44. The Devil. Goat's legs and horns are shared by the devil in card XV (top) and the god Pan (bottom). (Pan as depicted in an anonymous 14th-century manuscript.)

Figure 45. Judgement. Top: Card XX in which the angel blows its horn, holding a banner. Bottom left: An angel (lower right) blows its horn, announcing to the figure arising from the grave that the last hour is at hand (from Stolcius de Stolcenberg, *Viridarium chymicum*, 1624). Bottom right: Here it is the Christ who has arisen and who exhibits the same banner (from *Rosarium philosophorum*, 1550).

Figure 46. The World. Mercurius as *Anima Mundi* (from *Turba philosophorum*, a 16th-century manuscript) is surrounded by a mandorla and seems about to take wing, as does the dancing figure within the mandorla of Card XXI.

Figure 47. The Fool. Like the Fool of the tarot (top left), this youngster (top right) carries his bundle on a staff over his shoulder, and he seems likewise to have left the cities in the distance—or perhaps he avoids them—as he heads toward the wide horizon (bottom) and the rising—or setting—sun. (From *Splendor Solis*, a 16th-century manuscript.)

ALCHEMY AND CABALA

Directly or indirectly the Cabala was assimilated into
alchemy. Relationships must have existed between them
at a very early date, though it is difficult to trace them in
the sources. Late in the sixteenth century we come upon
direct quotations from the Zohar. . .(Jung, CW 14, ¶ 19).

A. E. Waite (*The Secret Tradition in Alchemy*, p. 379) refers to an
alchemical text of the third century A.D. in which the author claims
to have drawn out of "Jewry" his mystical ideas about man in his
original perfection, his fall, his redemption and restoration to paradise, as well as his knowledge about the vocation, aims, and
habits, of the "philosophers." Waite also quotes from a Hebrew
alchemical text, the *Aesh Mezareph* (Purifying Fire) an 18th-
century English translation of the 17th-century Latin manuscript,
in which there seems to exist a place of "whitening splendor," a
haven for medicine and for healing.

> Herein lies the restoration of metals. . . which is to be
> understood as the free operation within them of the three
> principles of the Supernals of the World of Metals. This
> analogy constitutes. . . that other gate of Alchemy (Waite,
> 1926, p. 393).

Waite's description of the sephirotic bridge that spans the gulf
between the Divine and the world of earthly elements points out
that the first three sephirot form the *habitaculum* of the deity, the
world of *Aziluth*, the *fons dietatis*, the true region of emanation of
"Divine Persons proceeding from one another." The next three
sephirot constitute the world of *Beria*, or of creation, an archetypal world, the pattern of ideas in the Divine Mind that manifests
in *Yetzirah*, or the world of formation, the formed but not the exter-
nalized universe.

Finally, the world of *Assiah*, represented by *Malkuth*, the last
sephira, presents us with the earthly substance, the spirit of which
must be helped to reunite with the creator. These four worlds are
encountered again and again in alchemical imagery. The Tree of
the Soul (Cook, *The Tree of Life*, 1988, p. 33) is the cabalistic Tree of
Life, with its four worlds (see figure 48 on p. 199). In the *Mutus
Liber*, the alchemical coat of arms represents attainment of the
spiritual goal of the opus and of the process whereby the alchemist

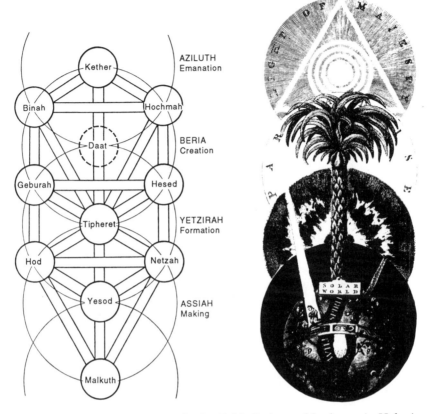

Figure 48. The four worlds. Left: the Kabbalistic worlds shown in Halevi, *Kabbalah*, p. 40. Right: the 18th century Tree of the Soul from Jacob Boehme.

was able to ascend from the earthly substance, here shown (see figure 49, page 200) as three waves that symbolize the sea of the unconscious with its three links to consciousness (salt, sulphur, and mercury). On the next level, three spheres depict the inner potential, now separated and purified. Above, a chevron forms a boundary between the higher realms of the psyche and the level below; the upper level is represented by three shells, the spirit descending into matter. It is not difficult to see in these three an image of the supernals, nor in the level below a depiction of the worlds of *Beria*, *Yetzirah*, and *Assiah*.

Another illustration from *Mutus Liber* (figure 50, page 202) shows the cosmic spiritual world represented by Jupiter, the Sun and the Moon far above the created world. The earth below this spiritual realm is divided into three concentric regions, the outer circle mediating between the spiritual sphere above, the middle transitional region and a dark innermost center. This alchemical image parallels the ancient cabalistic representation (figure 51, page 203) of the condensation of the divine energy from Ain, Ain-Sof, and Ain-Sof-Aur above the Tree of Life depicted in ten concentric circles of increasing density of matter from Kether, the outermost circle, to Malkuth at the center. Conceived at different historical times and in different cultures, these images present us with an archetypal commonality of similar concepts in almost identical visual form.

Scholem insists (1974, p. 187) that alchemy and astrology had little influence on the cabala, that for the cabalist gold (represented by the fifth sephira) is not the highest value, and that silver (represented by the fourth sephira) had a higher rank.

Waite, on the other hand, does describe cabalistic alchemy and the hypothesis it proposes about the evolution and generation of the sephirot from a metallic root (see figure 52, p. 204). In fact, those metallic attributions are discussed extensively in his text (Waite, 1926, p. 338), which does not keep him from affirming that in orthodox cabalism there is no trace of any symbolism concerning the metals, thus agreeing with Scholem. He further states (pp. 390-391) that the allocation of certain sephirot to certain metals stretches the "Doctrine of Correspondences" to the breaking point unless the metals themselves are spiritualized. It is obvious from the alchemical texts that the alchemists did just that. Moreover, neither for the alchemist was gold the highest value; as we know, their search was for the *elixir vitae*, the transformative substance that can redeem whatever it touches.

Figure 49. The alchemical coat of arms.

The alchemical images emphasize once again that

> ... in psychic matters we are dealing with processes of
> experience, that is with transformations which should
> never be given hard and fast names if their living move-
> ment is not petrify into something static ... for the sym-
> bol not only conveys a visualization of the process; ... it
> also brings a re-experiencing of it, of that twilight which
> we can learn to understand ... but which too much clar-
> ity only dispels (Jung, CW 13, ¶ 199).

Alchemical imagery is an attempt to penetrate extremely complex phenomena. It has an inevitable unconscious component
resulting from the underlying archetypal energy. It may also
become through active, intentional visualization, a refined system for attaining higher consciousness.

> Fundamental to alchemy is a true and genuine mystery
> which ... has been understood unequivocably as psy-
> chic. ... Certainly I believe that psychology can unravel
> the secrets of alchemy, but it will not lay bare the secret
> of these secrets (Jung, CW 14, ¶ 213).

The alchemists whose writings we have inherited describe a
method of liberating and containing the vital spirit within matter.

> In the last analysis every life is a realization of a whole,
> that is, of a self, for which reason this realization can also
> be called "individuation." All life is bound to individ-
> ual carriers who realize it, and it is simply inconceivable
> without them. But every carrier is charged with an indi-
> vidual destiny and destination, and the realization of
> these alone makes sense of life (Jung, CW 12, ¶ 330).

The tangle of ideas that form the body of alchemy have their
source in a variety of traditions. That alchemy has served as receptacle for every type of speculation about the nature of the soul,
spirit, and body, indicates that in it we have a collection of ideas
about what is basic in existence, whether or not we accept the
terms employed to define it. For Poncé, alchemy represents a
legitimate expression of Western mystical tradition. In his view

Figure 50. The Cosmic Spiritual Worlds (from *Mutus Liber*, 1677).

Figure 51. The ten attributes of the Divine Will.

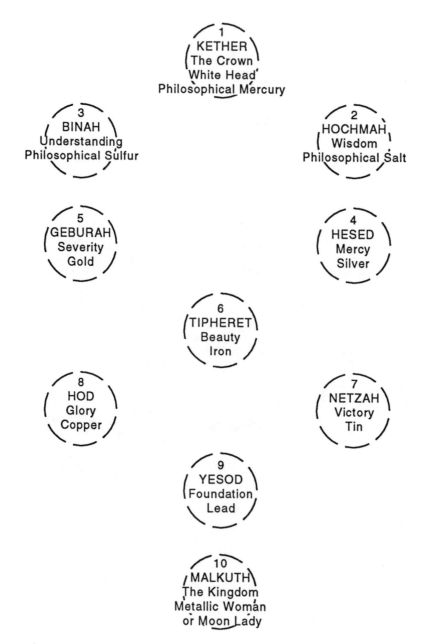

Figure 52. The *Sephirot*, their significance, and their metal allocations (from A. E. Waite, "Kabbalistic Alchemy," *The Secret Tradition in Alchemy*, pp. 381, 384).

the alchemists were involved in a perpetual Genesis, in an endless imaginal world (Poncé, 1988, p 136).

Finally, the fundamental correspondences between mind and matter provide assurance that the alchemical symbols will not die (Grossinger, 1985, p. 279).

It is not difficult to identify the goal of alchemy with the goal of individuation. On our difficult journey toward reunion with the Divine Spirit, alchemy, the cabala, and tarot seem to offer us similar images that may make our road, if not less arduous at least more endurable, and they may offer us hope in those dark moments when no light will appear.

The chapters that follow explore the last twelve tarot cards in terms of their correspondences with astrology, alchemy, and the cabala. The emphasis is, however, on their connections to alchemical imagery, as we follow the ascending Path of the Serpent, itself symbolic of the individuation process.

The letter that corresponds to card XI is *caph*, which means power principle, the grasping hand, fixation of light in matter, assimilation, selection, classification, compression, progress. It also means conflict, resistance. In its negative sense, it suggests hatred, violence, or numbness.

With card XI and the lion tamer, the influence of secret subliminal energies begins in the darkness of inner space. Should the instinctual forces symbolized by the lion be rejected and not consciously lived and should one fail to integrate their polarity in the total personality, they will exert their complete, wild destructiveness. In the apocalypse they are represented by Woman riding upon Beast.

Whereas the Wheel (card X) presented us with incessant revolutions, this card depicts the pole of repose, the transitional point between past and future, the present moment, and the work individuals must carry out within themselves. Indeed, the two symbols of good and evil that chased each other in the previous card are set here in sharp confrontation. Animal past and enlightened future are watched over by the eternal present, represented here, as in card I (the Magician), by the lemniscate that forms the brim of the lion tamer's hat and suggests the macrocosmos, the world soul activating the magical powers of the human spirit. It seems to be the actual place for the human being: below the ten sephirotic powers but not yet immersed in the ten images that follow, we find the point of stillness where the needed strength for the journey ahead can be gathered.

The number 11 (see ideogram) is composed of 5 (the pentagram, the human creature) and 6 (the hexagram, the capacity to relate). The reappearance of the lemniscate begins a new sequence of eleven cards and emphasizes that infinity is both the origin and the goal of conscious and unconscious energies in the search to reconnect with the Divine.

> "The soul is above nature and through it nature is comprehended, but the intelligence is above the soul and through it the soul is comprehended, and the intelligence is comprehended by that which is above itself, and is surrounded by the One God whose nature is not to be comprehended" (*Liber Platonis quatorum*, in Jung, CW 12, ¶ 372).

THEMES, ASSOCIATIONS, CORRESPONDENCES

Card XI depicts encounter with unknown powers, both freeing and confining. It also portrays the stimulation and concentration of intuitive insights that allow achievement of mastery. Activation of contrasexual spiritual and psychic powers are intimated as well. This card suggests becoming conscious through self-examination of the constructive and destructive potentials that reside in all these powers and of the effect they may have in everyday life.

The ideogram for this card is

Astrological amplification: Strength has been occasionally associated with the planet Mars and with the sign Aries; most attributions, however, connect it with the sign Leo, a fire sign ruled by the Sun. Leo is also related to the mystery of individuality (Greene, 1983, pp. 203-211). The fated path of individual maturation seems to imply the development of a unique individual essence and its quest for its source within. We are dealing here with the confrontation between the individual ego and its instinctual roots that must be tamed before a person becomes individuated. Indeed, for Jung the lion

> . . . represents the king in his theriomorphic form, that is, as he appears in his unconscious state. The animal form emphasizes that the king is overpowered . . . by his animal side and consequently expresses . . . nothing but emotions. Emotionality in the sense of uncontrollable affects is essentially bestial, for which reason people in this state can be approached only with the circumspection

proper to the jungle, or else with the methods of the animal trainer (Jung, CW 14, ¶ 405).

The lion also signifies healthy impulses that need to be expressed assertively, not only destructive, aggressive impulses that have to be tamed. It seems that fate does not allow the lion to remain in his bestial form. Leo's deepest urge is the search for the Self; in the process of becoming aware of the problem of the opposites, the central value of life is uncovered. Compassion and understanding, the means by which to reach the deeper source, are also the way to the redemption for which Leo is in search. One can engage on this arduous path only with the steadiness and caring of a feminine stance; impatient irritability or impulsive/compulsive action can only be destructive.

Cabalistic amplification: The first step in the training of a cabalist focuses on the elementary experience of being embodied. The body must be known in order to recognize its analogies with and its resonance to the higher world. The process of self-discovery must begin with a thorough knowledge of the ways in which the body can interact with the psyche. Only thus will the cabalist, or anyone engaged in the process of enlightenment, be able to move from Malkuthian body-consciousness to the psyche/spirit world of *Yesod* and *Tipheret* (Halevi, *Work of the Kabbalist*, p. 44).

Alchemical amplification: Jung observed that the chief star in the constellation Leo, called *Regulus* or *Little King*, was regarded by the Chaldeans as the lion's heart and that "cor" (heart) is one of the names of the arcane substance that signifies fire or any great heat (CW 14, ¶ 493, n. 353). *Fermentatio*, provided by seething emotional excitement, is needed to sustain the alchemist during the *opus magnus*; only when the heat of the furnace is raised to a sufficient intensity can the goal be attained. In alchemy the lion, the "royal" beast, is a synonym for Mercurius or for a stage in his transformation.

> He is the warm-blooded form of the devouring. . . dragon. . . . Like him, the lion appears in dual form as lion and lioness. . . . [T]he fiery lion is intended to express. . . the passionate emotionality that precedes the recognition of unconscious contents. . . . It is, how-

ever, psychologically correct to say that emotion unites as much as it divides (Jung, CW 14, ¶ 404).

Indeed,

> According to the statement of the alchemists the king changes into his animal attribute, that is to say he returns to his animal nature, the psychic source of his renewal (Jung, CW 14, ¶ 406).

Psychological interpretation: The lion tamer signifies integration of affects, beautiful forms, self-control, being cultured. Seen positively, the subduing of the lion means self-assurance, heroic endeavor. In a negative sense, it means rapacity, devouring intrusiveness. The lion brings to mind the feared, denied, dark, primitive instincts. In *Mysterium Coniunctionis* Jung points out that elevation of the human figure to a king or divinity or, on the other hand, its representation in subhuman, theriomorphic form are both

> . . . indications of the *transconscious character* of the pairs of opposites. They do not belong to the ego-personality but are supraordinate to it. . . . The pairs of opposites constitute the phenomenology of the paradoxical *self*, man's totality (Jung, CW 14, ¶ 4).

Jungian interpretation: Card XI depicts a female figure taming a lion. This fiery lion evokes

> archetypal energy storms . . .[that] have traditionally been represented by myth and religion as the negative side of God. It is not far afield to interpret these harrowing experiences as being influenced by the gods, for their scale is monumental, always far larger than the ego. In Egyptian myth the devil Set, who is the enemy of order, represents overwhelming affects. . . . Much Egyptian ritual revolves around the creation of a stable counterposition in imagery of principles of order, such as those represented by Horus, Osiris, or Isis (Schwartz-Salant, *The Borderline Personality*, p. 21).

Jung describes the lion as

> . . . a "fiery" animal, an emblem of the devil, and stands
> for the danger of being swallowed by the unconscious
> (Jung, CW 12, ¶ 277).

He points out:

> The lion, the zodiacal sign for the torrid heat of summer,
> is the symbol of . . . "frenzied desire" ("My soul roars
> with the voice of a hungry lion, " says Mechthild of
> Magdeburg) (Jung, CW 5, ¶ 425)

and

> . . . the devaluation of the psyche and other resistances to
> psychological enlightenment are based in large measure
> on fear—on panic fear of the discoveries that might be
> made in the realm of the unconscious. . . . These "archaic
> vestiges" or archetypal forms grounded on instincts and
> giving expression to them, have a numinous quality that
> sometimes arouses fear. They are ineradicable, for they
> represent the ultimate foundation of the psyche. . . . It is
> this fear of the unconscious psyche which not only
> impedes self-knowledge but is the gravest obstacle to
> a wider understanding and knowledge (Jung, CW 10,
> ¶ 530).

This conflict between consciousness and the unconscious is
brought nearer to a solution through our becoming aware of it
(Jung, CW 11, ¶ 392), and the image with which card XI confronts
us may represent just this quiet fortitude that is needed to face
the unconscious and, by doing so, to achieve the ultimate goal of
individuation.

> So long as the self is unconscious, it corresponds to
> Freud's superego and is a source of perpetual moral con-
> flict. If, however, it is withdrawn from projection and is
> no longer identical with public opinion, then one is truly
> one's own yea and nay. The self then functions as a union
> of opposites and thus constitutes the most immediate
> experience of the Divine which it is psychologically pos-
> sible to imagine (Jung, CW 11, ¶ 396).

SYMBOLIC LANGUAGE OF THE IMAGE

A young woman wearing the colors of the High Priestess (card II): a blue dress with a red cape and yellow sleeves (indicating intelligent handling) subdues a lion without using violence but through the magic power of her femininity. Once its wildness is tamed, its strength can be put to unanticipated use.

She invites us to leave the plane of quantity (for she is obviously weaker than the lion in terms of physical force) and to raise ourselves to the plane of quality, for it is evident that her superiority can only be found on that plane. Illuminated by the supreme clarity and compassion of her faith and filled with tolerance, patience, and calm steadfastness, she can face whatever power the lion represents. Not only is she not swept away, but she is also able to ground him, and his *élan vital* is thus redirected.

Earth goddesses tamed lions, rode lions, or became lionesses in their devouring, destructive aspect. Greeks and Phoenicians knew this goddess as Anatha, Athena, or Neith, the Strength of Life. Indeed, the tarot card of Strength sometimes bore the name of Neith (Gettings, 1973, p. 66), who, according to Jung, is both masculine and feminine in nature. He quotes an ancient invocation to Neith:

> Nit [or Neith], the Ancient, the Mother of God, Mistress of Esne, Father of Fathers, Mother of Mothers, who is the Scarab and the Vulture, who was in the beginning (Jung, CW 5, ¶ 358).

We cannot help but remember that *Hochmah*, the second sephira and one of the three supernals (mediators of the divine energy of *Ain Sof*), was addressed with the same homage in identical words: "Father of Fathers, Mother of Mothers." Here we find another link to the High Priestess.

The image shows feminine energy taming elements of masculine force; she is active, inspiring, encouraging through her certainty. The image also indicates spiritual growth through contact with primordial powers, that is, the creative energy that the lion represents. Confrontation with destructive forces that endanger development and the transformation of chaotic energies increases personal strength. The lion tamer reminds us of the Empress (card III) and of Justice (card VIII), who also see to it that limited interests do not damage the organizational whole. The lion tamer masters life power in conformity with universal law.

The lion, symbol of undisciplined, brutal force, evokes the "dog days" of summer in which the sun radiates with destructive force. In the psychic realm the lion stands for the power of the instincts. The lion with the golden mane denotes the creative fire of spirit that works on the outside. It shows both the spiritual and the demonic aspects of instinctual and of latent affective powers.

In Egypt the lion-headed goddess Sekhmet of Memphis, who was the goddess of fright and of murder, personified the deadly heat of the desert sun. Her twin, the cat- or lion-headed Bastet, was connected to the life-giving aspects of the sun, sexuality, and fertility. The apocalyptic image of the woman riding the beast may be interpreted as denoting the overwhelming power of sexual passion; it may also mean revolution, anarchy, and destruction of the established order. Circe, who transforms men into animals, is related to it as well. These formidable images all reflect the unbridled power of the unconscious.

Spiritual forces must be acquired through an experienced mastery of power. When human will surrenders to God's will and becomes one with it, the individual becomes a participant in immeasurable forces. He or she is then able to tame with goodness and softness the brutal violence, malice, hate, jealousy, and envy that might otherwise take one over. Spiritual authority comes from a religious spirit strong in its belief. It influences others who may not even be aware of it.

Here, at the beginning of the upward road, straining to reconnect with the divine energy that the Magician first mediated, we pause to gather all available strength for the arduous task that lies ahead.

"In the Cabala it is the Union of man, reduced to the simplicity of the monad, with God; in Physio-Chemistry it is the Fermentation (of) man reduced to (the simplicity of) our stone, with the Macrocosm" (Khunrath, *Amphitheatrum Sapientiae* . . .(1609), in Jung, CW 12, ¶ 427, n. 4).

Alchemically the operation facilitating this union is *fermentatio*. We need to remember that when grapes are fermenting, an incredible amount of energy is generated and the ultimate product of this fermentation is spirit.

XII
THE
HANGED MAN ל

The letter that corresponds to card XII is *lamed*. It means trial, voluntary sacrifice or pain-induced progress, being forced ahead by a goading prodder. It denotes all that stretches out, unfolds, arises, the open hand, the extended arm, expansion, realization. In its negative sense it indicates the arrogance of objective sciences or of power. In card XII the image is most clearly related to its corresponding number; we are presented here with two tree trunks each bearing six branch stumps. Between the two polarities hangs our hero, an image that connects this card to card VI (the Lover[s]), in which he appeared to hesitate between two attractive opposites represented by two women and two roads ahead. In card XII that indecision has now become fatal, having escalated to inescapable, paralyzing passivity. One sees no exit, no means to reach freedom, no way to success. Suspended in the great solitary void in which everything appears overwhelmingly unlimited, one is utterly alone in the vastness of the universe. The only outcome of this situation is transformation by some form of ego death.

Twelve is the number of the signs of the zodiac, the astrological wheel of life. Here the wheel is stuck: everything seems equally unattainable and unachievable—the old solutions have all failed.

THEMES, ASSOCIATIONS, CORRESPONDENCES

This card indicates a reversal in the direction of applied will, an interruption in the former flow of action. It recommends quieting down mental busyness, being suspended in timeless space, patient waiting. It can also suggest giving up egotism or tapping the deepest layers of the unconscious. It may indicate spiritual death. The Hanged Man connotes sacrifice of the ego and the breakdown of obsolete structures.

The ideogram for this card is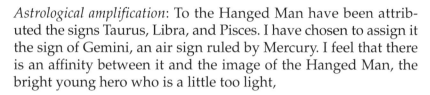

Astrological amplification: To the Hanged Man have been attributed the signs Taurus, Libra, and Pisces. I have chosen to assign it the sign of Gemini, an air sign ruled by Mercury. I feel that there is an affinity between it and the image of the Hanged Man, the bright young hero who is a little too light,

> . . . a little too invulnerable and a little too far away from ordinary human suffering and ordinary human longing to perform his appointed task of redemption (Greene, 1984, p. 193).

Too much light constellates darkness, and he stands as a reminder of the sacrifice demanded of those who cannot let go of patterns of behavior that may have at one time helped them to survive but that are now creating their very destruction. It is this needed sacrifice that they are determined, with fierceness and single-mindedness, to avoid. Yet even as the spiritual darkness spreads, caused by growing estrangement from the divine Source, the spark of heavenly wisdom is preserved.

For the Egyptians, Sirius (a star just below the constellation Gemini) was the guarantor that, even in the spirit-estranged chaos of the earth, order and harmony would be restored (Sucher, 1982, pp. 82-84). The Gemini symbol Ⅱ may be seen as joining a higher and a lower world and is reminiscent of the two trees and the horizontal bar from which our youthful hero hangs upside down. Gemini is the sign that represents a fundamental dichotomy and an inherent antipode: masculine/feminine, intellect/emotion, spiritual/material, light/dark, day/night, heaven/earth, negative/positive, and the clash and collision between them. The conflict is usually projected, and most of the time it is only in the second half of life that one recognizes the inner enemy who is also the brother, who cannot ever be conquered yet who must be constantly fought. Thus, Gemini reflects a cyclical experience as it portrays the conflict between bondage to a mortal body (and thus limitation and death) and the yearning for exaltation of the spirit and the realm of eternal life. The polarity and contradiction suspend our young man in midair for as long a he refuses to see that while opposites are inseparable they may not be irreconcilable.

Cabalistic amplification: The "Tree of Emanation," or the cosmic tree, the tree of the sephirot, grows downward from its root, the first sephira, and spreads out through those sephirot that constitute its trunk to those that make up its main branches or crown (Scholem, *Kabbalah*, p. 106). Similarly, man is seen as an inverted tree growing down from heaven; "the soul takes root in man from heaven, " quotes von Franz in her commentary to *Aurora Consurgens* (p. 163, n. 36). The Hanged Man may be a reminder that, in order to reconnect with the divine roots, one must take the Tree of Life as a model. Again in *Aurora Consurgens* (p. 253), von Franz quotes a Gnostic text that connects the number 12, the dodecad, to evil and earthly fate:

> The number two advancing from itself up to six—two, four, six—produces the Dodecad. . . . They therefore called the Dodecad . . . the Passion . . . for they assert that a fall took place from the Dodecad. In the same way they oracularly declare that, a power having departed from the Dodecad and perished, this was represented by the woman who lost a drachma and . . . found it again.

Alchemical amplification: In alchemy the number 12 plays a role as the number of months, hours of the day and of the night, and the signs of the zodiac, with which the phases of the *opus* were often correlated. It also shows the number of operations of the *opus*. It signifies the number of cornerstones of the Heavenly Jerusalem and the number of the tribes of Israel, representing the virtues of simplicity of heart, unquestioning faith, humility, etc. (von Franz, *Aurora consurgens*, p. 215).

In the alchemical tradition, the ruling principle of the conscious ego and its power demands must undergo *mortificatio*, which has to do with darkness, defeat, and torture. It means the transformation of the collective, dominant, and ruling principles that the Emperor (card IV) represented. Indeed, owing to *mortificatio* and *sublimatio*, the body takes on "quintessential" or spiritual form and consequently is not very different from spirit. "It may shelter spirit and may even draw it down to itself" (Jung, CW 16, ¶ 499). The extraction of the soul from the *prima materia* is equivalent to the *mortificatio* (Jung, CW 14, ¶ 401, n. 139), which is an essential part of the mystery of transformation.

> It signifies the overcoming of the old and obsolete as well as the dangerous preliminary stages . . . (Jung, CW 14, ¶ 169).

> The alchemists understood the return to chaos as an essential part of the opus. It was the stage of the . . . *mortificatio* which was then followed by the "purgatorial fire". . . .The unconscious is both good and evil and yet neither, the matrix of all potentialities (Jung, CW 14, ¶ 253).

Psychological interpretation: Giving up past certainties, one feels exposed in fear and anxiety, to the insecurity of the unknown ahead. Only a reversal of values and standpoints makes transition to the second half of life possible. In order to transcend the anguish of our present condition, we must reverse our stance. This means seeing behind appearances the true essence of things. We must recognize that, based on our abilities alone, we are powerless; our actions must come, not out of the ego, but the Self must be allowed to act through us.

Jungian interpretation: The Hanged Man may indicate the shift from ego-centeredness to centroversion and from the ego to the Self.

> The idea that man is an inverted tree seems to have been current in the Middle Ages . . . . "It pleased the Physicists to see man as a tree standing upside down, for what in the one is the root, trunk, and leaves, in the other is the head and the rest of the body with the arms and feet" (Andrea Alciati, in CW 13, ¶ 412).

The mystical world-tree, the tree of the sephirot also signifies man implanted in paradise by the roots of his hair (CW 13, ¶ 411).

Regarding contemplatives who are minded to understand the purpose of existence, Jung says:

> A great reversal of standpoint, calling for much sacrifice, is needed before we can see the world as "given" by the very nature of the psyche. It is so much more . . .

impressive, and therefore more convincing, to see all things that happen to me than to observe how I make them happen. Indeed, the animal nature of man makes him resist seeing himself as the maker of his circumstances. That is why attempts of this kind were always the object of secret initiations, culminating as a rule in a figurative death which symbolized the total character of this reversal . . . .[This is] an initiation process whose purpose it is to restore to the soul the divinity it lost at birth (CW 11, ¶ 841-842).

The Hanged Man shows a situation created by being stuck in an extreme one-sided attitude. The only way out of the conflict between persona and shadow, between ego and Self, is to turn upside down, a most painful task for an ego reluctant to let go of the only way of being that it knows. The following passages from Jung seem to evoke the Hanged Man and the energies he may represent.

Natural life is the nourishing soil of the soul. Anyone who fails to go along with life remains suspended, stiff and rigid in midair (CW 8, ¶ 800).

. . . the law of life demands that what [one] take[s] from outside and inside will be the very things that were always excluded before. This reversal of one's nature brings an enlargement, a heightening and enrichment of the personality, if the previous values are retained alongside the change—provided that these values are not mere illusions. . . .[T]he development of personality is one of the most costly of all things. It is a matter of saying yea to oneself, of taking oneself as the most serious of tasks, of being conscious of everything one does, and keeping it constantly before one's eyes in all its dubious aspects—truly a task that taxes us to the utmost (CW 13, ¶ 24).

All these moments in the individual's life, when the universal laws of human fate break in upon the purposes, expectations, and opinions of the personal consciousness, are stations along the road of the individuation process. This process is, in effect, the spontaneous realization of the whole man. The ego-conscious personality is only a part of this whole man, and its life does not yet represent his total life. . . . [S]ince everything living strives for wholeness, the inevitable one-sidedness of our conscious life is continually being corrected and compensated by the universal human being in us, whose goal is the ultimate integration of consciousness and unconscious, or better, the assimilation of the ego to a wider personality (CW 8, ¶ 557).

It has become abundantly clear to me that life can flow forward only along the path of the gradient. But there is no energy unless there is a tension of opposites; hence it is necessary to discover the opposite to the attitude of the conscious mind. . . . [T]he repressed content must be made conscious so as to produce a tension of opposites, without which no forward movement is possible. The conscious mind is on top, the shadow underneath, and just as high always longs for low and hot for cold, so all consciousness, perhaps without being aware of it, seeks its unconscious opposite, lacking which it is doomed to stagnation, congestion, and ossification. Life is born only of the spark of opposites (CW 7, ¶ 78).

He . . . has possibly come to realize that what originally meant advancement and satisfaction has now become a boring mistake. . . . The energy streaming back. . .falls into the unconscious and activates all the things he had neglected to develop (CW 7 ¶ 90).

The counterpart of his conscious attitude . . . will leave him no peace and will continue to plague him until it has been accepted (CW 7, ¶ 88).

[L]ibido fights against libido, instinct against instinct, [and] the unconscious is in conflict with itself. . . . [M]ythological man perceived the unconscious in all the adversities and contrarieties of external nature without ever suspecting that he was gazing at the paradoxical background of his own consciousness (CW 5, ¶ 395).

[The] burden the hero carries is *himself*, or rather *the* self, his wholeness. . . the totality of his being, which is rooted in his animal nature and reaches out beyond the merely human towards the divine. His wholeness implies a tremendous tension of opposites paradoxically at one with themselves. . . . Sunk in his own depths, he is like one buried in the earth; . . . a Kaineus "piled with a hundred burdens" and pressed down to death, groaning beneath the intolerable weight of his own self and his own destiny (CW 5, ¶ 460).

Quoting from Nietzsche's "Birds of Prey,"

Encaved within thyself,
Burrowing into thyself,
Heavy-handed,
Stiff,
A corpse —
Piled with a hundred burdens,
Loaded to death with thyself. . . (CW 5, ¶ 459).

[S]acrifice means. . . relinquishing all the ties and limitations which the psyche has taken over from childhood into adult life. . . . Life calls us forth to independence, and anyone who does not heed this call because of childish laziness or timidity is threatened with neurosis (CW 5, ¶ 461).

[W]ithout the co-operation of the unconscious and its instinctive forces the conscious personality would be too weak to wrench itself free from its infantile past and venture into a strange world with all its unforeseen possibilities. The whole of the libido is needed for the battle of life. But [he] cannot bring [himself] to this decision, which would tear aside all sentimental attachment to childhood . . . CCW 5, ¶ 463).

The Hanged Man may be suspended in midair by his unwillingness to step into his own future and thus sacrifice childhood attachments, at times to a destructive parent. Suspension is the symbol of unfulfilled longing or tense expectation (suspense) (CW 5, ¶ 594). He could also represent a one-sided dedication to unrealistically high ideals. In a Swiss deck, the expression on his face is similar to the one usually associated with Don Quixote, the knight with the dolorous countenance, whose delusional system kept him away from the stream of life.

On the other hand, situations in cases in which an image of a rite of passage could help the flow of psychic energy might be furthered by this card. Indeed, initiation was often attended by all sorts of tortures necessary to free the individual from the inertia of the unconscious, which offers the "utmost resistance to any kind of spiritual development" (CW 7, ¶ 172). Shakespeare comments:

> And so, from hour to hour we ripe and ripe,
> And then from hour to hour we rot and rot,
> And thereby hangs a tale.

> —*As You Like It*
> Act II, Scene 7

SYMBOLIC LANGUAGE OF THE IMAGE

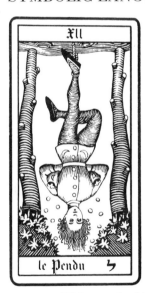

In Cards I through XI, the emphasis was on active development. Their model and hero was the Magician (card I), master of himself and of creation. The model with which the human being is now presented calls for realigning the center of consciousness, for the readiness to live up to intuitive impulses emerging in inner stillness, for subordination of his own will to God's will. It is in stillness that life condenses in a focal point, which activates psychic contents.

With his arms and head forming a triangle and his feet crossed, the Hanged Man evokes the alchemical symbol ☿ that indicates the completion of the *opus magnus*. This symbol is the inverse of that for sulphur ☍, which appears in card IV (the Emperor). If the Emperor denotes the old established order, to one for whom this order has never worked or is no longer working, card XII presents a solution, a way out. In contrast to card IV, the 4 here is placed above the 3, signifying subordination of action to cosmic law. When one feels one is being tested or is on trial, one has to choose carefully the images upon which to focus; we must place our striving for wholeness upon the universal totality in order to find the renewal we seek. The crossed legs also connect to the image of the sun, as their shape suggests the swastika encountered in the Wheel of Fortune (card X).

The red and white motley clothes are only in apparent contradiction to the passivity of the figure. Its activity is expressed by its having to choose from among several possibilities. The color red stands here for active endurance, while white means tolerant receptivity. Whereas the lion-taming feminine figure of card XI (Strength) must integrate her masculine, fiery component, here the task is to passively allow things to happen and to accept the ensuing events in order to attain a higher order of awareness. The white also refers to the purity of the creative imagination. The two half-moons encountered on the shoulders of the Charioteer (card VII) have drifted here below the waist and emphasize the need for humility and correct intuition. The gold and silver coins falling out of the two bags held under the Hanged Man's arms shows the necessity of letting go of obsolete values. The accumulated experiences of the past are now being lost, and rightly so; old currency is of no use in a new territory. This situation is reminiscent of the one depicted by T. S. Eliot in "East Coker" (*Four Quartets*).*

The fact that the coins are shown scattered around his head represents spiritual richness and strength freed by introversion. It also depicts potentially fertilizing seeds falling on the earth below. The two trees bring to mind the two pillars of the temple, which appear in some decks flanking the throne of the High Priestess and which suggest a link to the spiritual powers that she represents. This link is also behind the image of the twelve red branch stumps, a reminder of the twelve signs of the zodiac through which the sun travels. An astrological chart is a circle divided in twelve. It represents the ground plan of the world order upon which each individual destiny is entered. It is not a diagram, but the signature of cosmic order in the schema of self-becoming. All mandalas and schematas originate in it. The space between the two trees shows the gap between time and timelessness, the lack of continuity between here and there, the missing link.

---

* We regret that we could not reproduce T. S. Eliot's verses from Part III, lines 25 through 30 and 39 through 48, expressing the pain of a soul having lost its old bearings and spending agonizing time in an unknown space. The T. S. Eliot estate and the publisher Harcourt Brace have denied us permission to quote those verses.

Card XII depicts a helpless man deprived of his physical means. Hanging from a yellow crossbeam, he embodies the painful process by which a state of consciousness that interrupts the flow of interfering thoughts is achieved. This fixation of attention opens the door leading to contact with the unconscious. The *I Ching* says (Wilhelm/Baynes, p. 321):

> He who walks in truth and is devoted in his thinking . . .
> is blessed by heaven, . . . and there is nothing that would
> not further.

This card stands for contemplation and self-examination as tools for "working on what has been spoiled" (*I Ching*, hexagram 18). It means acceptance of fate, awareness, discipline, and submission to the knowing spirit. It shows that mindfulness opens necessary doors and leads to the strength to contemplate the void and to transform inner emotional landscapes. Preparation for the new life entails perception and assimilation of the formless and nameless, through concentration of the mind in silence and stillness. New insights can be consolidated by perseverance, leading to increasing self-realization and capacity for adaptation, as well as by giving up striving for conventionally accepted modes of success and distraction. The dangers are impatience, loss of self-control, intolerance for outward stillness and the incapacity to reach inner quietude, fear of uncertainty, and the feeling of being lost in the reversed world beyond logic.

The mythic hero corresponding to the Hanged Man is Theseus, who defeated the minotaur with the help of Ariadne's thread. At first glance, they do not seem to have much in common. But, although motionless, the Hanged Man has at his disposal spiritual and occult powers; through the subtle energy that he radiates, he exerts an irresistible influence. He brings to mind the Nordic myth of Odin, who became a magician and a reader of runes only after his sacrificial hanging:

> I ween that I hung / on the windy tree
>   Hung there for nights full nine;
> With the spear I was wounded, / and offered I was
>   To Odin, myself to myself.

> [From the Rune poem of Odin
> quoted in Neumann, *The
> Great Mother*, p. 252]

In the way of Zen, insight into the nature of Self does not belong to any dualistic category; it is beyond relativity. We must free the spirit that takes care of things and that cannot be captured in any form. This may be the aim of the clown who can personify death only by hanging upside down.

> [A]s such, he is a figure of great, even ultimate, power —
> a Superman, or better, an upended "Batman," who can
> swirl all the roiling energies of the psyche into a single
> bolt of existential lightning (Belmonte, p. 55).

The Fall that brought about the change of man's state from "paradise" to the terrestrial state of "toil, suffering, and death" implies the force of gravitation. It suggests that the Fall is a shift from a spiritual gravitational system, the center of which is the divine, to a terrestrial gravitational system, the center of which is materiality, earthiness, needs, desires, passions, etc. The Fall can then be understood as a change from one gravitational field to the other. The Hanged Man is proposing the possibility of reversal, what Jung called *opus contra naturam*, that is, individuation, which realigns us with the spirit. We are reminded here of the cabalistic Tree of Life, conceived as having its roots in heaven and growing toward the earth. Indeed, in some tarot decks, the two trees supporting the beam from which the Hanged Man is suspended grow upside down, their roots in the spirit, their crowns toward earth. Thus there is a field of gravitation other than that of the elemental forces of the lower order. Insofar as the soul is capable of transcending the engulfing gravitational pull of the lower order, it can form a bridge to the gravitation center of the spirit. We can conceive thus that spiritual man is under the sway of the gravitation of "heaven" and that carnal man is under the sway of the gravitation of "earth," whereas psychic man lives in equilibrium between these two gravitational fields. Terrestrial gravitation enfolds of and coagulates mental, psychic, and physical elements around foci such as earth, possessions, power, and enjoyment; whereas celestial gravitation is radiation and extension of mental, psychic, and physical elements toward transcendence. Finding the balance between them is the goal of individuation.

The Hanged Man, with solid ground under his feet above, seems to "know" that his head still does not know. His vision is focused beyond intellect, and he will act out of this knowledge. This is the leap of faith, the inner act that changes *my* will into *"Thy* will be done." It is this change in perspective, in the locus of control, that can allow us to get out of a situation that seems hopeless, in which we feel stuck, locked in with no exit.

> Nobody who finds himself on the road to wholeness can escape that characteristic suspension which is the meaning of crucifixion (Jung, CW 16, ¶ 470).

XIII
DEATH

The letter *mem* means female, mastery, movement, transformation, procreative power, multiplicity, eternal life through death and resurrection. Its symbol is the water that incessantly flows through all empty spaces and channels. In its negative sense it means occultism and black magic. Death represents a terrifying passage, a prerequisite stage to rebirth, a separation of consciousness from its present limited modality of expression. The number 13, assigned to this card, is associated with the sun in the manner of a permanent point following it through its passage through all the signs of the zodiac (1 + 12). Thirteen can also be seen as the central point of three interlocked squares [1 + (3 × 4)], which form a circle of the highest tension and solidity. See figure 53.

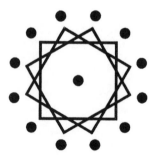

Figure 53. Three interlocked squares and the center point. (From Bernoulli, *Zur Symbolik Geometrischer Figuren und Zahlen*, p. 409.)

THEMES, ASSOCIATIONS, CORRESPONDENCES

Movement, change, transformation, and dissolution are all in the domain of this card, as well as transition and renewed beginning at a higher level. Death is seen as a life process with ceaseless cycles of retraction and expansion. This card helps us conceive of death as the great equalizer, and it reminds us that death can establish a balance of polarities, the inner center. Death is seen as a catalyst, a regulating principle.

The ideogram for this card is

Astrological amplification: To Death was assigned traditionally the planet Saturn or Mercury and the signs Aries, Gemini, and Scorpio. Capricorn, an earth sign ruled by Saturn, seems to fit card XIII; in winter the earth lies fallow, the sun is weakest, and the world is darkest. Barrenness and death lie everywhere, not least within the souls of men. Old forms of consciousness must die to allow the birth of new. The theme of the wasteland and the long wait for the redeemer in depression, despair, and deadness is the Capricorn pattern. Characteristic of the Capricorn rite of passage is crucifixion by fixation in matter: not only imprisonment, limitation, and bondage but also decay, decomposition, and rotting. The very principle that causes Capricorn the greatest suffering—the rigid, guilt-ridden, narrow, timorous Saturnian energy—is that which endows Capricorn with the endurance, determination, and foresight to struggle through the dark night of the soul. While on one level something seems to create symptoms, problems, and destruction, on some very hidden level something seems to be working toward the greater wholeness of the individual (Greene, 1984, pp. 242-250). Capricorn is also symbolic of the soul's imprisonment in physical reality; the world seems to be a place of bondage to the body, to responsibility, to the law, to consciousness, to God. The valuing of tradition and the forms of the past also belong to this sign. Mastering the world by the ego is Capricorn's intent; therefore, the relativization of the ego is experienced as death.

Cabalistic amplification: It is said by the cabalists that upon death the Malkuthian body returns to the elements. While the vital-energy triads slowly disintegrate and the body decays, the *Neshuma* (soul) finds its home in an upper region, and the spirit, when the processes of purification are complete, returns through *Kether* to the Absolute (Halevi, *Tree of Life*, p. 94). Through the curtain of *Hochmah*, a bright world beyond is perceived. The silent, deep thought of the inner intellect illuminates the path back to *Kether*. Thus death separates the soul of man from his coat of flesh and draws him up into the next world (Halevi, *Tree of Life*, p. 160).

Alchemical amplification: In alchemy, as in many Gnostic systems, water has the dual meaning of life and death. In her commentary to *Aurora Consurgens* (p. 259), von Franz quotes:

> "This water makes the dead to rise and slays the living, it lightens the darkness and darkens the light. . . ." "And it is the sharpest vinegar, which decomposes everything."

The success of the first operation is indicated when the *nigredo* and the darkness appear: matter is dead and disintegrates; the fine is separated from the coarse. (See figure 54 .) With their *mortificatio, putrefactio, combustio, incineratio, calcinatio*, etc., the alchemists imitated the work of nature. Their labors can be likened to human demise without which new and eternal life cannot be attained. Jung quotes the alchemical literature:

> "The old philosophers named this work or labour their descension, their cineration, their pulverization, their death, their putrefaction of the *materia* of the stone, their corruption, their *caput mortuum*. You must not despise this blackness . . . but persevere in it in patience, in suffering, and in silence . . . until the days of its tribulations are completed, when the seed of life shall waken to life, shall rise up, sublimate or glorify itself, transform itself into whiteness, purify and sanctify itself, give itself the redness, in other words, transfigure and fix its shape. . . . Therefore, if the human will is given over and left, and becomes patient and still and as a dead nothing, the Tincture will do and effect everything in us and for us, if we can keep our thoughts, movements, and imaginations still, or can leave off and rest (CW 16, ¶ 512).

Psychological interpretation: We are under the unavoidable obligation to transcend the ego and its limitations. Without relativizing

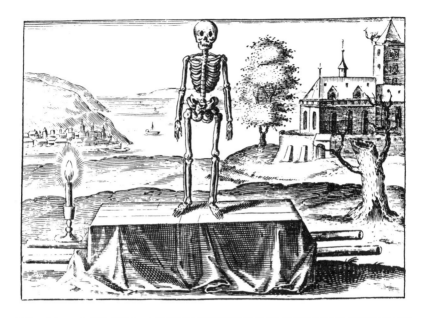

Figure 54. Top: *Mortificatio* (from *Hermetic Museum*, 1678). Bottom: *Mortificatio* (from Mylius, *Philosophia reformata*, 1622).

the ego no rebirth is possible, no transformation of consciousness. The death of the old must occur for the energy locked within it to be released and directed toward maturation and connection to higher levels of consciousness.

Psychologically death represents the most definitive and painful of all sacrifices that must be comprehended, accepted, and worked through in its entire significance. We are liberated from the deceased and the past through renunciation.

Jungian interpretation: The descent into the dark world of the unconscious, the perilous adventure of the night sea journey, aims at the restoration of life and resurrection and triumph of life over death. Death therefore represents the completion of the spirit's descent into matter (CW 12, ¶ 436). Jung also warns:

> By descending into the unconscious, the conscious mind puts itself in a perilous position, for it is apparently extinguishing itself. . . . [T]he deliberate and indeed wanton provocation of this stage is a sacrilege (CW 12, ¶ 437).

Rites of passage are death-and-rebirth rituals through which the individual "dies" to his previous circumstances and is born to the new. In the past these rites were sacred ceremonies in which a radical psychic transformation was ensured by the powerful symbolism of the ritual, which activated archetypal components. In these solemn rites conducted within a sacred context, individuals were ritually mutilated with the absolute approval of the gods who sent the dreams that were required for the ritual's completion. For Jung death means

> . . . the total extinction of consciousness and the complete stagnation of psychic life, so far as this is capable of consciousness. So catastrophic a consummation, which has been the object of annual lamentations in so many places (e.g., the laments for Linus, Tammuz, and Adonis), must surely correspond to an important archetype. . . (CW 16, ¶ 469).

Perera, in *Descent to the Goddess* (1981), describes such a "catastrophic consummation" in Inanna's impaling:

> Suffering can lead to a terrible passivity, a negative iner-
> tia. . . . And in Ereshkigal's realm there is a standstill
> where all is miasmic and inhuman and inchoate. Inanna
> is. . . passive, empty of life, reduced to meat. There is no
> motion, no obvious quickening. There is only the place-
> ment of the body on the peg (p. 37). . . . The enstakement
> continues the process that permits the birth of the capac-
> ity to be separate and whole unto oneself. . . the capacity
> to negate and to assert, to endure firmly grounded, to
> destroy and to create (p. 40).

Dismemberment is thus a central image, a kind of sacramental
act undertaken for the purpose of transformation. It is a familiar
motif common to the Dionysian mysteries, the Orphic mysteries,
the cult of Osiris, etc. The main points of resemblance among the
manifestations of these redemption mysteries are as follows: in
Osiris, his god-man nature (which guarantees human immortality) is associated with dismemberment and resurrection; in
Orpheus, the taming of passions and teaching of wisdom is connected to the descent into the underworld and its torments; in
Dionysus, the ecstatic revelations are paralleled with dismemberment and resurrection (CW 12, ¶ 416, n. 36).

> Dismembering the victim corresponds to the idea of
> dividing the chaos into four. . . parts. The purpose of the
> operation is to create the beginnings of order in the *massa
> confusa*. . . . The pyschological parallel to this is the reduc-
> tion to order, through reflection, of apparently chaotic
> fragments of the unconscious which have broken
> through into consciousness (CW 13, ¶ 111).

Jung refers to S. Spielrein's case of schizophrenia in which she
reported dismemberment and recomposition, and cites Eliade:

> Dismemberment is a practically universal motif of prim-
> itive shamanistic psychology. It forms the main experi-
> ence in the initiation of a shaman (CW 13, ¶ 91, n. 4).

He points out (CW 13, ¶ 116, n. 111) that the alchemical *mortificatio*, dismemberment, flaying, etc., pertain to the birth and revelation

of the inner man and that *separatio* is also often represented as the dismemberment of the human body (CW 13, ¶ 89). Furthermore:

> The corpse in our picture is the residue of the past and represents the man who is no more, who is destined to decay. The "torments" which form part of the alchemists procedure. . . the reiterated death. . . consist in . . . cutting up the limbs, dividing them into smaller and smaller pieces, mortifying the parts, and changing them into the nature which is in [the stone] (CW 16, ¶ 478).

Elsewhere he states:

> [T]he picture represents the *putrefactio*, the corruption, the decay of a once living creature. Yet . . . this death is an interim stage to be followed by a new life. No new life can arise, say the alchemists, without the death of the old. They liken the art to the work of the sower, who buries the grain in the earth: it dies only to waken to new life (CW 16, ¶ 467).

SYMBOLIC LANGUAGE OF THE IMAGE

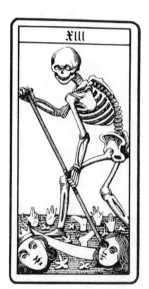

Every end bears within itself a new beginning. This transformation is foreshadowed by cards VII (the Chariot), X (the Wheel of Fortune), and XII (the Hanged Man), which all point the way toward development, destiny, and being put to the test. Death can liberate the energy contained in and devitalized by the increasingly burdensome inertia of matter.

Card XIII presents us with symbols of regression, that is, reduction to the elemental forms of the vegetal and mineral realm. Forgetting, sleep, and death are different levels of manifestation of the same process: remembering is to forgetting as awakening is to falling asleep and as birth is to death. The tufts of grass on which Death walks are symbols of sleep because deep sleep is a state in which we live a vegetative life: we are like plants when we are in deep sleep. The flower, withered but not destroyed, reawakens to new life, just as the burgeoning greenery emerges from the ground. This image is reminiscent of the passage "On Death" from Una Thomas' *Scrapbook* of quotes from Jung:

> If we listen to the quiet voices of our deeper nature, we become aware that already, soon after the middle of our life, the soul begins its secret work of getting ready for the departure. Out of the turmoil and terror of our life, the one precious flower of the spirit begins to unfold— the four-petaled flower of the immortal light—and even if our human consciousness is unaware of its inevitable operation, it nevertheless does its secret work of purification.*

The skeleton is the symbol of death because it reduces the phenomenon of a conscious, mobile, living human being to that which is mineral: the bare bones.

The crescent form of the scythe connects this card with card II, the High Priestess in her Terrible Mother aspect. The crown on the ground indicates a crossing over into a new and unknown realm; it suggests the influence of a new principle, being guided toward a spiritual renewal, and the sacrifice of the past. This ground is strewn with cut-off feet, heads, and hands.

> Beheading is significant symbolically as the separation of the "understanding" from the "great suffering and grief" which nature inflicts on the soul. It is an emancipation . . . a freeing of the soul from the "trammels of nature." Its purpose is to bring about . . . a *unio mentalis* "in the overcoming of the body" (Jung, CW 14, ¶ 730).

The heads seem to be alive, the male head standing for wisdom and the female for perceptive knowledge, qualities that are not lost with death. They may evoke the experience of higher states of consciousness that are not connected with the coarse substance of matter. The experience of the Self is always a defeat for the ego, according to Jung, and alchemy expresses this through the sym-

---

* The "Scrapbook" has been privately mimeographed at the C. G. Jung Institute in Zurich.

bols of death and mutilation (CW 14, ¶ 788; CW 16, ¶ 472). Hands, feet, and heads taken together mean loss of consciousness, of standpoint, giving up ideals, arrest of activity, either deliberately or passively. Scattered on the ground, they evoke old fertility rituals in which dismemberment preceded resurrection and the new life it promoted. Dismemberment was an act invoking divine magic and grace without which infusion of life into that which was dead could not be accomplished.

Those who bear death within know that it is only divine grace that can resurrect what is dead in them. This also evokes the concept of psychic dissociation encountered in psychotic and neurotic manifestations, as well as in states of fragmentation anxiety.

In Egyptian mythology Seth is the murderer of Osiris, and this introduces the notion of murder as prerequisite for resurrection and transformation.

Death has been represented in many forms—dancer, embryo, reaper, etc. As dancer, it suggests liberation from matter, from obsolete patterns of behavior; Shiva the destroyer is one of its images. Death as reaper evokes mortal anxiety of extinction or incisive discrimination. When represented as water, it reminds us that when heated it rises as a cloud; when cooled it falls as rain, snow, or ice/hail until it returns to the ocean from which it originated. It is the ocean itself, awesome and overwhelming; it is bottomless abyss and endless space. As fire, the eternal burning in Hades is one of its images; it is the immaterial flame that burns all forms, leaving the essence untouched. As mother's lap, death depicts overpowering yearning to return to the only place of safety left, the only possible alternative. The same feeling may be expressed in the image of death as eternal sleep. When represented as embryo, it is regeneration, a holistic process of transformation, or by contrast, sorrow for an unlived life. Death as bridegroom means fear and hope: fearing the alliance with something alien or relishing new life. Death as the unknown can denote an experience that cannot be shared or a conflict with negative, destructive inner forces lying in wait in any attempt to explore new ways of being. It may also indicate self-encounter in the struggle with belief in God. Lastly, Death as air evokes annihilation or being removed from places that had been ours, so poignantly expressed by Rilke (1981, p. 28):

Erkennst du mich, Luft, du, voll noch einst meiniger
　　Orte?
Du, einmal glatte Rinde,
Rundung und Blatt meiner Worte.

Do you know me, Air, you who fill my old places?
You, once smooth bark,
Surround, and support of my phrases.

The letter *nun* means reincarnation, regression, the fruit. It indicates that spiritual and material levels are interchangeable: fertility can be realized in artistic or intellectual creativity or by having a child. It also means multiplication, solidarity. In its negative sense, it indicates sexual magic, suggestibility.

Transformation and renewal are represented here by a winged figure, the power of the divine, pouring the contents of a silver jar into a golden one without spilling a drop either on the earth or in the water that it straddles. After the sacrifice of card XIII, the ego is in the process of reuniting with the Self; this death and resurrection bring no loss to the spiritual substance. The elements of the restructured personality are redistributed, gauged, refined, and a new balance is established. This figure seems to decant material into spiritual existence, transforming coarser matter into a more differentiated mode of being.

In some decks the figure is represented with one foot on the globe and the other on a cube (die), an image indicating the earthly form of the square transformed into the heavenly circle. Moreover, by adding the numbers in 3.1415 (which is π, the ratio of the circumference of a circle to its diameter), we obtain 14, the number of our card. The treasure of house of Wisdom has fourteen cornerstones containing the principal virtues of the whole foundation: it is built on fourteen pillars. In ancient Egypt the pharaoh had fourteen Ka's, described as moral and physical attributes of strength, light, intelligence, sight, hearing, etc. According to Boehme, the number 14 symbolizes the Holy Ghost as manifested unconsciously in nature (von Franz, 1966, p. 331). Furthermore, the double three (spirit) added to the double four (matter) also equals fourteen. See figure 55.

Figure 55. Double three and double four. (From Bernoulli: *Zur Symbolik geometrischer Figuren und Zahlen*, p. 409).

THEMES, ASSOCIATIONS, CORRESPONDENCES

Temperance denotes timelessness, balance, renewal of ideas, life in its changeable shapes, refinement, purification, verification, confirmation. It indicates heightened potentiality acting upon external circumstances, creating harmony between conscious, directed willpower and dreams and fantasy, greater effectiveness, and a new awareness of helpful forces of the unconscious becoming conscious. Temperance connotes the constant transformations of living matter, its slow liberation from imprisonment in a sensory and concrete mode of perception, and the reciprocal interaction of all forces. It represents moral judgment pondering all circumstances as well as the virtue of temperance.

The ideogram for this card is

Astrological amplification: To Temperance have been attributed the planet Jupiter and the signs Cancer, Sagittarius, and Aquarius. Cancer, the Crab, was called by the Chaldeans the "Gate of Man" through which souls descend from the heavenly spheres into incarnation. Cancer represents the first emergence of life, the entry of the spirit into a corporeal body. It is associated with the end, as well as with the beginning, for it is the point of the sun at midnight when the old day dies and the new day is born. In Cancer, both a regressive longing for the womb and a mystical yearning for God find expression. Like the actual crab, which must stay close to both the water and land, Cancer is driven to anchor its energy in the concrete earthly world, with one foot eternally in the water of feeling so that Cancer itself can ultimately become the womb through which nascent souls may be born (Greene, 1984, p. 203).

Cabalistic amplification: Although water is the symbol of the passive, feminine left pillar (Halevi, *The Way of Kabbalah*, p. 145) and is represented by the Hebrew letter *mem* (one of the three mother letters), it is on the central pillar of the Tree of Life that water finds its deepest meaning. The sephira *Yesod* was said to receive the waters from on high, bringing to *Malkuth* (the earth, the body) the spirit of *Kether* (aleph, air). The waters of the soul may thus provide a bridge not only for the descent of the spirit but also for the ascent of those yearning to reconnect with the Divine.

Alchemical amplification: Immersion in water signifies *solutio*, a dissolution in the concrete sense of the word, but also the solution of a problem. Thus, after *putrefactio*, *solutio* follows. As the dissolved matter is being boiled, droplets of vapor can flow upward or back toward the source of the Water of Life.

> Water is the *deus ex machina* of alchemy, the wonderful solvent, the word *solutio* being used equally for a chemical solution and for the solution of a problem (Jung, CW 10, ¶ 628).

Solutio is, at times, a return to the dark initial state, to the amniotic fluid of the womb. The alchemists frequently point out that their stone grows like a child in its mother's womb; they call the *vas hermeticum* "the uterus," and its contents, "the fetus" (Jung, CW 14, ¶ 454). The fixed, static aspects of the personality that allow for no change must be decomposed and washed in order that "they may be regenerated or born again, and made more healthy, more noble, and more strong" (Edinger, *Anatomy of the Psyche*, p. 48). The alchemists used the image of the Red Sea as a form of the *aqua permanens*, the universal solvent, the liquid form of the philosophers' stone.

> Thus, that which has passed through the *solutio* of the Red Sea is the goal of the *opus,* the Self. Or. . . the Red Sea is the totality of the psyche, the agency of *solutio* that the ego must encounter and pass through on the way to individuation (Edinger, *Anatomy of the Psyche*, p. 72).

The Red Sea is thus equated with the redemption of the lost value hidden in the darkness of matter and with the whole alchemical process of transformation.

Psychological interpretation: Temperance indicates renewal of life through the continuous exchange between conscious and unconscious, and through the reconciliation of opposites resulting from the sacrifice of the ego and from having had the courage to face the void. Through the progressive process of becoming conscious, the ego connects dynamically with psychic contents. The firmness of the will to pursue higher aims is thereby strengthened, and spiritual realization can occur. Once the fetters of a rigid, fixated ego are broken (card XIII Death), connection to the suprapersonal can be established, confusion is replaced by order, and the capacity to distinguish and face reality is sharpened. Clinically this transformation is expressed by a fear of water and swimming, changing to the capacity to entrust oneself to an alien element, symbol of the unknown, within and without. Indeed:

> "The first step in the ascent to higher things is the study of faith, for by this is the heart of man disposed to solution in water. . . " (Dorn, in Jung, CW 14, ¶ 363).

Jungian interpretation: After describing the blackness, which is the *immunditia*, the uncleanliness (CW 16, ¶ 468), as well as the *separatio, divisio, putrefactio*, and *mortificatio*, all of which represent the original chaotic state of conflict between the four hostile elements, Jung continues:

> . . . there can be no more doubt that the black darkness is washed away by the *aqua sapientiae* of "our science," namely the God-given gift of the royal art and the knowledge it bestows. The *mundificatio* (purification) means. . . the removal of the superfluities that always cling to merely natural products, and especially to the symbolic unconscious contents which the alchemist found projected into matter (CW 16, ¶ 486).

This *aqua sapientiae* is also

> . . . the *aqua benedicta*, the lustral water, wherein the birth of the new being is prepared. . . . The *aqua permanens* . . . and the terms *oleum, oleaginitas, unctuosum, unctuositas*, all refer to the arcane substance which is likewise *Mercurius*. The idea is a graphic reminder of the ecclesiastical use of the various unguents and the consecrated water . . . a

possible reference to the *commixtio* of the two substances in the chalice of the Mass (CW 16, ¶ 454).

Further, we find that

> . . . the water I have spoken of is a king descending from heaven, and the earth's humidity absorbs it, and the water of heaven is retained with the water of the earth, and the water of the earth honours that water with its lowliness and its sand, and water consorts with water and water will hold fast to water. . . (CW 16, ¶ 483).

SYMBOLIC LANGUAGE OF THE IMAGE

The sun symbol on the angel's forehead signifies differentiated awareness; it also implies things kept in balance, behavior adapted to circumstances, increase and decrease, growth and decay. The sun symbol appears also in cards VII (the Chariot), VIII (Justice), and XX (Judgement). In these cards it points to the coordination and steering of constructive energies. Here in card XIV, it represents insightful definition of vital forces, whereas in card XX it will indicate enlightened action of spirit. The blue mantle worn over the red gown also recalls these cards. Angels warm and nourish spiritual embryos so that introverted willpower becomes actively supported. This angel is winged, as is the Empress (card III), but it does not dwell in unreachable realms; it renews and revives all life, even the fading tulip at its feet, with heavenly water. (The ebb and flow of this live-giving water indicates further that psychic energy modulates bodily functions and that such changes can be experienced daily.) Winged figures represent "guardians of the threshold" and guardian angels, fearlessness and individual spirituality. This angel, winged genie, also signifies guidance from above, divine grace, and timelessness. It is winged yet firmly implanted on both the earthly and heavenly planes. It depicts the interaction of Self and ego. It suggests an awareness of and pre-occupation with archetypal images and figures, which can appear in human form or in any shape in order to make the essence of the divine more understandable and graspable and the effect of its power more evident.

The stream of water between the jars signifies integration of duality and mediation; the liquified matter corresponds to spiritual change. The silver and gold jars are symbols of the dual psychic uplifting qualities, feeling and reason, which are burdened by corporeality. The silver jar represents the well of the water of life, the moon. The golden jar represents spiritual recognition, the sun.

Temperance (card XIV) is connected to the Hermit (card IX); she attempts to achieve passively that for which he actively searches. *Yesod*, the sephira corresponding to card IX, is called "The Recipient of the Waters From Above," a reminder that the element water is active in both cards.

This card is also called "Path of the Bow," the path of spiritual progress. The arrow on the taut bowstring of card VI (the Lover[s]) expresses the intense wish to reach its aim, the integration of polarities, the reconciliation of the opposites, of which the sexes are the evident symbol. This arrow points to the genitals, out of which the seed of new life comes, and to the womb, in which new life is contained and nourished.

When the Tree of Life is looked at from below, the direct ascending connection on the central pillar between *Yesod* and *Tipheret* depicts the ecstasy into which a soul is swept upward toward a higher spiritual level. This connection was named "The Path of the Arrow" and was associated with Sagittarius. In astrology Sagittarius is related to fire, to burning zeal, and is connected by many to the Chariot (card VII). It is represented by a centaur (half-horse, half-human) with a bow and arrow pointed toward the sky. It is the symbol of the passionate yearning to overcome animal nature. The image of Temperance makes the same statement: with one foot on earth and the other in water, it bridges duality. Given the water symbolism connected with this card, the astrological association with Cancer (a water sign) seems to be more appropriate. Indeed, the zodiacal symbol of this sign ♋ is made up of two small circles connected by two crescents, each like a cup or bowl. The upper cup is inverted, pouring water into the lower one, just as the angel in our card is pouring the Water of Life into the lower jar of material experience, thereby transforming it.

The winged figure mediates the flow and endless alternating current of psychic energy between outer and inner, conscious and unconscious. This play of the Water of Life renewing the soul can only happen by the grace of God.

Life's creative energy cannot be directed by sheer willpower.

> It does not lie in our power to transfer "disposable" energy at will to a rationally chosen object. . . . Psychic energy is a very fastidious thing which insists on fulfillment of its own conditions (Jung, CW 7, ¶ 76).

Through this, our guardian angel, we can learn to trust the powers operating in the universe and in ourselves. We can let these deeper currents dissolve the obstruction keeping our psychic energy blocked. This "spirit which is water, or water which is spirit, is essentially a paradox, a pair of opposites. . ." (Jung, CW 13, ¶ 98). The water being poured from one jar into the other may be a symbol of the union of opposites, mixture of oil and water, and/or of decanting a coarser liquid into a more purified form of the same fluid. Indeed, the liquid poured from one jar into the other is

> ". . . the water from which everything [originates] and in which everything [is contained] and that is . . . water and soul . . ." (quoted in Jung, CW 12, ¶ 336, from Turbam philosophorum exercitationes in *Artis Auriferae*).

Just as life is born of the spark of opposites, so divine water possesses the power of transformation; it renews through its "miraculous" washing, and it animates inert matter. In this new balance, in the flow of opposites, the libido finds its proper gradient; thus an inner knowing, a center of hidden silence and strength becomes manifest. This image shows that there is a particular way to integrate the opposites that will generate a third element—a Golden Mean—between them, a proportion of great value that may be symbolic of the ego's relation to the Self. All consciousness, perhaps without being aware of it, seeks its unconscious opposite, lacking which, it is doomed to stagnation, congestion, ossification. But moisture heralds the return of the soul, the recovery of feeling after the barren state of intellectual abstraction.

The falling dew signals resuscitation and a new light: the ever deeper descent into the unconscious suddenly becomes illumination from above. . . . This dewiness partakes of the nature of the psyche, . . . while on the other hand dew is synonymous with the *aqua permanens*, the *aqua sapientiae*, which in turn signifies illumination through the realization of meaning (Jung, CW 16, ¶ 493).

Sameck means wrath, prop or support, a Tent peg. A tent peg is to a tent as a foundation is to a house; the Self is the foundation of our house of life. It is the Self that offers trials and tribulations, ordeals that provide the opportunity to respond to their challenge. *Sameck* suggests not only the creative potential in humankind but also the conflict and contradiction that must be endured in order to become better fitted for a higher mission, for we cannot know our strengths or our weaknesses until we have met temptation. The letter *sameck* is a modification of the circle. It is said to represent the *uroboros*, the serpent biting its own tail, a symbol of eternity, timelessness. In *sameck* time has become timeless; the first and the last are one.

This card, symbol of difficult transitions, describes the vortex of fateful powers, the crucible of earthfire, the priceless hidden treasures guarded by the gnomes. It shows that egotistical weaknesses and fears can only intensify and become barriers to further development if not recognized. Each human being must learn to cope with the fire of instincts; only thereafter can it transform itself and become the source of spiritual enlightenment. It is our own spirit that is the tempter, the destroyer, and the liberator. Inner forces become satanic when they act autonomously, when their potential strength is out of consonance with the harmony that lawfulness and wholeness provide. Indeed, evil can be defined as misplaced force: misplaced in time, it is out of date; misplaced in space, it turns up in the wrong place; misplaced in proportion, it is either too little or too much. The road ahead is free only when we become aware of ourselves striving for power, distorting the truth, manipulating unfairly to our own advantage. Then the cloud of unknowing can dissipate, the multiplicity in the unity can be recognized, and we can cease to be tempted and distracted by plurality and polytheism. The figure of the Devil must not be interpreted exclusively in negative terms: temptation as challenge also serves knowledge and enlightenment; it also connotes the unexpected and unavoidable and is linked to fateful destiny.

When 15 is seen as 3×5, it is the trinity and its relation to the human being that becomes emphasized. Five is the number of the human; its symbol is the pentagram, which here (see ideogram) points downward and signifies sinking into matter. The three is represented by a caricature of the Trinity: a devilish trio, the threatening demon, guardian of the threshold, barrier to any further movement standing on a square pedestal to which the two small devils are fettered. We are similarly enslaved when taken over by their negative energy. Fifteen, the sum of the numbers 1 through 5 ($1 + 2 + 3 + 4 + 5 = 15$), is also the small number of the moon.

THEMES, ASSOCIATIONS, CORRESPONDENCES

This card indicates testing, confirmation, affirmation, servitude, and the consequences of unconscious negative contents that contradict our ideal self-image. It depicts limitation and inertia; resistance that opposes massive form to force; the passive, evil concretization that nevertheless provides a basis for further development.

The supreme spiritual structure is represented by the Trinity with the addition of a fourth, reprehensible aspect of the quaternity, the Devil. (See figure 56.) This quaternity confirms the Holy Ghost as the resynthesis of the original One, which had been split. It issues from a source that is both light and dark (Jung, CW 11, ¶ 263).

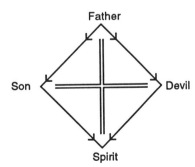

Figure 56. Father-Son-Devil-Spirit quaternity.

The ideogram for this card is

Astrological amplification: To the Devil are attributed the planets Saturn and Neptune and the signs Leo and Sagittarius, the latter due to the letter *sameck*, assigned to this card. Saturn is the planet of boundaries, limitation, inertia, bondage to circumstances that devour emerging creativity. Indeed, Chronos/Saturn was known to devour his children as soon as his wife Gaia gave them birth. In medieval astrology, Saturn was believed to be the abode of the Devil and his spawns were "dragons, snakes, scorpions, vipers, foxes, nocturnal birds of prey, and other devious breeds" (Jung, CW 9/2, ¶ 129). Just as "the Devil is any God who begins to exact total obedience" (Greene, 1984, p. 53), so Saturn is the form builder who rigidly insists on maintaining what he has built. Yet the tempter is also the redeemer: the higher levels of enlightenment are reached by going through hell, and it is through our shadow that we are connected to our depths. The Devil is the ruler of our personal hell—the thoughts, conflicts, aspects of ourselves that repel, disgust, elicit fear, and generally disrupt or disturb our life and our self-image. In Saturn (lead) there is a "shameless demon that drives men mad" (Jung, CW 13, ¶ 164, n. 86), yet the Devil is the saturnine form of the *anima mundi* (Jung, CW 13, ¶ 163, n. 85). Saturn, full of contradiction, cold, sterile, mournful, and pernicious, is also wise, judicious, reliable, the "old man of the mountain" in whom the "natures are bound with their complement" (Jung, CW 13, ¶ 173, n. 39).

Saturn clearly shows us the cost of our desires and attachments; it reveals the true nature of the material plane. Saturn is the principle of self-preservation and contraction. It can manifest itself as defensive, rigid attitudes rejecting any new venture or self-righteously fulfilling one's duties and responsibilities. Saturn is also connected with old patterns of adjustment to life and of personality that get increasingly rigid over time and become self-oppressive and life limiting. However, Saturn can also represent an inner pressure to become and achieve; it is the principle of commitment, structure, stability, self-reliance, seriousness, and caution. With Saturn we are confronted with time, death, and fateful destiny.

Cabalistic amplification: The ultimate source of evil resides in the second light in *Ain Sof*: "the light which did not contain thought." This light has no other purpose but to rest in itself and passively resist the structure of emanation, which the first light in *Ain Sof*, "the light which contained thought," had built. Thus, the duality between amorphous and structured forms of matter (being the root of good and evil), originates in *Ain Sof*, and the root of evil, a principle within *Ain Sof* itself, holds itself aloof from creation, seeks to prevent the forms of light that contain thought from being actualized, and strives to frustrate and destroy whatever is constructed by that light. Evil is therefore the outcome of a dialectic between two aspects of the light in *Ain Sof*, and its activity arises from its opposition to change (Scholem, *Kabbalah*, p. 126). The cabala also discusses the *qliphot* (*kelippot*), the realm of demons or the world of shells, a mirror arrangement of the Tree of Life. Caused by distortion, imbalance, and atrophy, these forces manifest when excess is reached in overactivity or overresistance. The symbolism of shells indicates their fixity, their stop of flow, their separation from the living body. All qliphotic phenomena reveal a disturbance in the natural interplay of the sephirot. Any permanent distortion in the Tree generates a disastrous circumstance (Halevi, *The Tree of Life*, p. 79).

Alchemical amplification: The alchemists knew the danger of demonic energy, which manifests by opposing the work. According to them, the devil

> . . . instils [sic.] negligence, impeding our intentions; everywhere he creeps about, within and without, causing oversights, fear, and unpreparedness, and at other times he seeks by harassments and injuries to make us abandon the work (Jung, CW 13, ¶ 430).

> The Devil causes impatience, doubt, and despair during the work (Jung, CW 11, ¶ 139, n. 22).

In their *Mercurius duplex* the alchemists saw, on one hand, Hermes the mystagogue and psychopomp, and on the other hand, the poisonous dragon, the evil spirit, and the trickster (Jung, CW 9/1, ¶ 689). The *filius philosophorum* of the alchemists is one of the numerous manifestations of Mercurius duplex, ambiguous and capable of anything. His dark side has an obvious affinity with the devil, the true *principium individuationis* (Jung, CW 11, ¶ 470). Indeed, from the psychic depths that cast up the powers of destruction, the rescuing forces will also come (Jung, CW 11, ¶ 532).

In the alchemical tradition, *prima materia* is saturnine and the malefic Saturn is the abode of the devil, or again, it is the most despised and rejected thing, found in filth. These epithets suggested to Jung that the alchemists discovered in projection the qualities of the unconscious (CW 13, ¶ 209). *Caogulatio* is explicitly associated in alchemy with evil, lead, and Saturn, the malefic principle. Lead, according to Jung (CW 14, ¶ 472n), signifies the vexations and troubles wherewith God visits us and brings us back to repentance. Ego development is associated with the experience of evil: consciousness of our own evil, that is, awareness of our shadow, coagulates. It is necessary to leave room for evil if one is to contribute to the real world, and being an ego is inextricably connected with guilt, which is punished by *coagulatio*, confinement within the limits of one's own personal reality. Embodied existence is experienced as bondage, as *coagulatio*, and as evil because it confines the soul. The entire early process of individual psychic development, that is, the ego emerging from the original state of oneness with the "objective psyche," can be considered a process of *coagulatio* and may be connected to eating of the fruit of the tree of knowledge of good and evil and to the temptation by the devil, who brought it about.

Psychological interpretation: The Devil is a primordial image belonging to the dawn of existence, the great tempter representing the essence and energy of the creative counterforce; the less acknowledged, the more dangerous. He is the fascination with the downward pull that one must discriminatingly accept and integrate or resist and reject. Facing the dark forces inside us is just as inevitable as facing death. It is only by courageously confronting our built-in flaws and faults that we prevent their turning into the dragons of our destruction. Nature must not be despised because in its revenge it will either enslave or annihilate us.

Jungian interpretation: Mephisto describes himself as "Part of that power which would/Ever work evil, but engenders good (Goethe, *Faust*, Part I). Goethe here describes the libido as a force of nature, good and bad at once or morally neutral. Similarly, Lucifer is not simply evil as such, but good and evil, or a system of higher powers in the lower. As the uroboros dragon, he impregnates, begets, bears, and devours himself, a description pointing to his basic identity with the collective unconscious.

> Coming to terms with the unconscious is on one hand an endeavor to understand the archetypal world of the psyche and on the other hand a struggle against the sanity-threatening danger of fascination by the measureless heights and depths and paradoxes of psychic truth. . . . Here the human mind is confronted with its origins; the finite consciousness with its immortal Self. . . . Kinsman and stranger at once. . . the more it is bound by time and space, the more it will feel the *other*, as that difficult higher striving who crosses its purpose at every misguided step, who gives fate an unexpected twist and sets it as a task the very thing it feared (CW 13, ¶ 210).

The stirrings in the darkness necessarily seem like a devilish betrayal of the ideal of spiritual development. But the devil, too, is endowed with the same spiritual substance, albeit an evil and corrupt one. For Jung, this original identity of substance

> . . . is still expressed . . . in the close connection between Jehovah and Satan in the Old Testament. There may be an echo of this primitive connection in the Lord's Prayer, where we say "Lead us not into temptation"—for is not this really the business of the *tempter*, the devil himself? (CW 9/1, ¶ 394).

Jung also suggests that in Christian dogma the morally ambiguous Yahweh became an exclusively good God, while everything evil was assigned to the devil.

> It seems as if the development of the feeling function in western man forced a choice on him which led to the moral splitting of the divinity into two halves . . . . Thanks to the development of feeling values, the splendor of the "light" god has been enhanced beyond measure, but the darkness supposedly represented by the devil has localized itself in man. . . . [T]he devil was largely, if not entirely, abolished, with the result that this metaphysical figure, who at one time was an integral part of the Deity, was introjected into man. . . . We think that the world of darkness has thus been abolished for good and all, and nobody realizes what a poisoning this is of man's soul (CW 9/1, ¶ 189).

The devil represents the shadow, one that goes far beyond anything personal and could therefore best be compared with the
principle of evil.

> Evil is the necessary opposite of good, without which
> there would be no good either. It is impossible even to
> think evil out of existence. . . . The view that we can sim-
> ply turn our back on evil and in this way eshew it
> belongs to the long list of antiquated naïveties (CW 9/1,
> ¶ 567).

The danger in our culture of having divested the godhead of darkness and evil has had tragic consequences:

> . . . since the reality of evil and darkness could not be
> denied, there was no alternative but to make man
> responsible for it (CW 9/1, ¶ 189).

> It is a psychological rule that when an archetype has lost
> its metaphysical hypostasis, it becomes identified with
> the conscious mind of the individual. . . . [S]ince an
> archetype always possesses a certain numinosity, the
> integration of the numen generally produces an infla-
> tion of the subject. . . . In recent times this type has
> extended . . . into the field of political psychology, and its
> incarnation in man has had all the consequences that
> might have been expected to follow from such a misap-
> propriation of power (CW 11, ¶ 472).

Indeed:

> [E]very spiritual truth gradually turns into something
> material. . . . An alchemist could still pray: "Purge the
> horrible darkness of our mind," but modern man is
> already so darkened that nothing beyond the light of his
> own intellect illuminates his world. . . . That surely is
> why such strange things are happening to our much
> lauded civilization, more like a *Götterdämmerung* than
> any normal twilight (CW 13, ¶ 302).

In therapy we may become aware of the presence of destructive forces associated with this card whenever the therapeutic process comes to a halt. Jung says:

> Behind the mandala lurks the devil. . . . This shadow aspect of the mandala represent[s] the disorderly, disruptive tendencies, the "chaos" that hides behind the self and bursts out in a dangerous way as soon as the individuation process comes to a standstill, or when the self is not realized and so remains unconscious (CW 9/1, ¶ 689).

Jung also points out that

> . . . evil has no substance of its own but arises from a "mutilation of the soul.". . . If the devil fell away from God of his own free will, this proves . . . that the devil already had a "mutilated" soul for which we must hold a real cause responsible (CW 9/2, ¶ 85).

The implications of this statement for both analyst and analysand seem to be far reaching for understanding those cases of "soul murder" and their clinical manifestation. Jung has also observed that

> Since [the trickster] has on occasion described himself as a soul in hell, the motif of subjective suffering would seem not to be lacking either. . . . There is something of the trickster in the character of the shaman and medicine-man. . . . [T]he "making of a medicine man" involves, in many parts of the world, so much agony of body and soul that permanent psychic injuries may result . . . in confirmation of the mythological truth that the wounded wounder is the agent of healing, and that the sufferer takes away suffering (CW 9/1, ¶ 547).

SYMBOLIC LANGUAGE OF THE IMAGE

The figure of the devil is depicted as a hermaphrodite. It brings together the four elements: the dark legs correspond to the obscure depths of the earth, the scales covering them are related to the element water, the wings are associated with the element air, and the red head evokes the element fire. The mixture of such diverse elements as male/female, human/animal, bird/fish creates an impression of chaotic disorder, of a reversal of all the basic qualities into their opposites. However, the material of which our world is made takes shape through the relationships among the four elements. Thus, life and creativity are experienced through harnessing the polarities of the opposites.

By suffering the tension between these opposites, we are confronted with our shadow, our blind spots, our actions, and our "acting out," and although exclusive reliance on a personal ego is the basis of all vanity, all inordinate sensuality, and all lack of knowledge about one's spiritual powers, it is also the basis of all differentiation.

The devil, the dark side, is the other face of the heavenly nature; it is the grotesque and uncanny aspect of the unconscious. We are reminded here that *Geburah*, the fifth sephira (see the chapter on card V, the High Priest), is called "the left hand of the Holy One blessed be He" and "a quality whose name is evil." This spirit has many off-shoots in the constricting and limiting powers of the universe (Scholem, 1974, p. 123). The devil is often identified with the snake in the Garden of Eden, the tempter, but it is also known as the liberator from musty instinctuality. The black magic associated with the devil seems to have been captured in figure 57.

8	1	6
3	5	7
4	9	2

Figure 57. The magic square.

The odd numbers in the grid form a central cross; the even numbers are relegated to the corners, another link to the four elements (and an anticipated connection with the four evangelists of card XXI [the World]). In this unique arrangement of the numbers 1 through 9, each row, each column, and each diagonal adds up to 15, the number of the Devil. Fifteen is also the number of Pan, the wild nature god and earthy ruler of generativity who represents the untamed power of instinctuality (suggested by the goat legs with which he is usually depicted). Because materialistic solidity is a condition of all manifestation, it is not surprising that for those who are unmindful of Lucifer the *lumen naturae*, who could have brought light, he becomes instead the father of lies, a psychopomp changed into diabolical seducer. Nevertheless, the light of nature is the *quinta essentia* that is extracted by God himself from the four elements and dwells in our hearts (CW 13, ¶ 148). Yet,

> . . . what will [the doctor] do when he sees only too clearly why his patient is ill; when he sees that he has no love, but only sexuality; no faith, because he is afraid to grope in the dark; no hope, because he is disillusioned by the world and by life; and no understanding, because he has failed to read the meaning of his own existence. . . . [W]hat he needs in order to live, namely faith, hope, love, and understanding, . . . these four highest achievements of human endeavor are so many gifts of grace (CW 11, ¶ 499-501).

It is precisely these gifts of grace that are lost when the devil takes over and the light vanishes. The incapacity to connect love and light, on one hand, with darkness and bondage to circumstances, on the other, devours any emerging creativity so characteristic of Saturn. The brighter the light, the darker the darkness.

> The growing darkness reaches its greatest intensity on the day of Venus (Friday), and changes into Lucifer on Saturn's day. Saturday heralds the light which appears in full strength on Sun-day (CW 13, ¶ 301).

The Devil holds a downward-turned torch illuminating the world of illusion, the counterinspiration unleashing the forces of destruction. Excessive knowledge of evil may lead to possession by it and its chaos; at the same time it may lead to loss of faith in the hidden order within chaos. We certainly have the power to generate destructive images, but the use of destructive force renders the generator a slave to the generated.

The pentagram on the Devil's forehead points downward, indicating that insight into the totality of interactions remains incomplete as long as we are disconnected from our biological natures out of egotistical motives or we distort truth through lies and injustice. Such efforts enslave us to the powers we would bring into service. It is essential that we not deny our instinctuality as long as we are bound to our body, while at the same time it is imperative that we avoid its misuse.

The Devil's golden hooves and horns point out the high value of instinctuality; the red head depicts the burning intensity of unfettered passion, the overwhelming and terrible power of the animalistic demand for brutal lust. Nevertheless, this can also be the pulsating power that renews all forms and arts of life and allows them to persist. The horns are also a symbol of spiritual renewal for those who are aware of all within them that remains undomesticated until the conflict between the opposites is overcome. Because the bat (like the horse) can find its way in the dark, the batlike wings signify intuitive ascending evolution.

The scaly legs are reminiscent of the gnomes that guard the treasures of the earth, the scales themselves symbolizing the life-supporting element water. Their eyelike appearance brings to mind the secret eye of the phallus and the snake of the Garden of Eden [card VI, the Lover(s)], as the yoni and lingam signs in his raised left hand seem to point out. The two chained figures represent the bondage of humankind to materialism and the resultant lack of knowledge about our potential for spiritual powers and capacities. They can also stand for the conscious and the unconscious or for the alchemical *solve et coagula*. The pedestal recalls the Emperor's throne (card IV); the shape is not square, however, but suggests, rather, the tartar of the alchemist 🜿, a substance that the alchemists connected with "tartarus," or hell. The red of the pedestal reveals the activity of the central fire, which is connected to the fire from above. The pedestal also represents the resistance that the element earth (form) opposes to power, the negative evil that nevertheless provides the opportunity to grab a foothold.

The Devil impinges upon Justice (card VIII), a warning that evil is the result of justice untempered by mercy. However, from the victory of justice over unbridled instinct, a new creative course can develop. The Devil represents the individual and the collective shadow, the limitation of the total personality through being taken over by a complex (becoming unconscious), identification with the persona (becoming inflated), or possession by the anima (becoming moody, fickle, or mendacious) or by the animus (becoming rigid, power hungry, or generally conflict-prone). Shadow seen positively serves the expansion of consciousness through assimilation of contents that were previously incompatible and through recuperation of the energy used to repress them.

XVI ע
THE TOWER
OF DESTRUCTION

The letter *ayin* means destruction, transformation, regeneration by discarding what has hardened. It means ruin, transmutation, disgrace, inhibition of premature development. When all dangers seem to be overcome, overblown self-satisfaction builds a Tower of Babel. One imagines one has become godlike; one believes one's goal is reached; the tower is then designated *The House of God*, built to celebrate one's self-perceived godliness. But pride is the primordial sin and is, therefore, punished with the greatest severity: the thunderbolt smashes the tower to pieces and throws its builders to the ground. All has now come to an end. In its negative sense the Tower means conspiracy or exorcism.

The number 4 is squared: $4 \times 4 = 16$. Sixteen can also be seen as $10 + 6$, connoting (X, the Wheel of Fortune) circular perpetual motion, the temporary structures of the cycle of human lifetime, involution and evolution, increase and decrease, plus [VI, the Lover(s)] masculine and feminine, yin and yang.

THEMES, ASSOCIATIONS, CORRESPONDENCES

The Tower of Destruction suggests that the individual can reach insight only by setting aside her or his presumption. This card denotes sin, awakening, and redemption; it indicates egocentricity and may point to loss of means.

The ideogram for this card is

Astrological amplification: To the Tower of Destruction have been attributed the planets Mercury, Mars, or Jupiter, and the signs

Virgo or Capricorn. I have chosen to assign to it the planet Uranus, which at its best is the great liberator, the awakener, the illuminator that stirs up a person's inner and outer life with such intensity that things are never the same afterward. Uranus symbolizes a force that manifests as sudden changes of life pattern, sudden alterations of consciousness, flashes of insight, bursts of new ideas, and original conceptions. It is a channel through which powerful forces flow into awareness. Uranus also is expressed as rebelliousness, independence, the unconventional, and the erratic. It does not always act destructively, but the destructiveness is always there when there is resistance to its influence. The sweeping changes Uranus brings disorganize the old and organize the new. Uranus speeds up the rhythm of nature; as a result, an individual may often feel excitable, restless, driven by an overwhelming desire for change and freedom. Uranus provides heightened psychic sensitivity and intuitive insight beyond the barriers of space and time and beyond conventional wisdom. However, under Uranian influence one can become so absorbed in the excitement of discovery and experimentation that one can go to extremes of utter disregard for tradition and for human limitation; willful obstinacy may then obliterate any sense of proportion (Arroyo, 1978, pp. 40-42).

Cabalistic amplification: To gain access to the higher worlds requires great responsibility, for there are the dangers of excess, weakness, irresoluteness, temptation, inflation, and many other hazards unknown to those who do not seek the door of immortality.

Direct involvement in the Work of Unification, as the cabala is sometimes called, so as to bring the inner and outer worlds, the upper and lower levels of existence, together in consciousness, means that after reaching a certain point of ascent the phase of imparting begins, an obligation of service that necessitates a redescent. The product of having really reached the top is the perspective that the peak conveys, and it is this perspective that generates the urge to return to the ground. Apprehending the divine and mysterious laws of life is a gift of grace that has to be translated in all humility into giving to others what has been given to us.

Alchemical amplification: When the process brings the operation of unification only to the level of a magical exercise concerned with personal inflation and private interest, which are the very opposite of the aim of the Work, diametrically opposed energy is constellated and an explosive, destructive event will bring the entire work down. Whenever *coagulatio* fixates the ego in an inflated position, *sublimatio* will follow. *Sublimatio* can be experienced as grinding and hammering to bring about the necessary movement to sublimate the body or coagulate the spirit. *Sublimatio* is not only the purification of something transcendent from defilement by gross and opaque materiality; it is also the grinding and hammering of something artificially lofty, the rigid identification with spiritual heights as a refuge from and avoidance of the recognition that the appropriate stage of the *opus* is *mortificatio, combustio, incineratio* , or *calcinatio.*

I am reminded of one analysand who, three months into analysis, came with a dream in which she was given a beautiful silver rectangular plaque, exquisitely hammered. She immediately identified it as an indication of the stage of *albedo*, knowing that silver is a symbol for the alchemical *luna* and that

> . . . illustrious Luna imparts a beautiful white to the Tincture, the most perfect white hue and a brilliant splendor. And thus is the darkness transformed into light, and death into life. And this brilliant whiteness awakens joy and hope in the heart of the artist, that the work has gone so well and has fallen out so happily. For now the white color reveals to the enlightened eye of the soul cleanliness, innocence, holiness, simplicity, heavenly-mindedness, and righteousness, and with these the Tincture is henceforth clothed over and over as with a garment. She is radiant as the moon, beautiful as the dawn (Jung, CW 16, ¶ 514).

This was at best a prospective dream, but in her interpretation it became the support to a premature restructuring of the ego in a "lesser" *sublimatio.* The task of "hammering" the feminine, as symbolized by the silver, still lay ahead. Very much a daughter of the patriarchy, she had survived through her thinking function and a fairly aggressive animus. In order to reach the "higher" *sublimatio,* she had to descend into her inner depths, a painful, slow work of decomposition, before the ascent to a new and authentic feminine spirit could be approached. The image of the Tower is a typical *sublimatio* symbol (Edinger, 1985, p. 127). When matter and spirit are entangled, *sublimatio* raises us above the concrete and the personal. The danger is that one can get tragically caught in the archetypal dynamism of *sublimatio*, which then impels us to go farther and farther away from earthly reality until the inevitable enantiodromia sends us crashing to the ground. This unwilling leap into the unknown may then get us involved in the very fate from which we were assiduously fleeing and for which we were suited (Jung, CW 7, ¶ 236).

Sublimatio and *coagulatio* are repeated again and again until all aspects of one's being are revealed by this *circulatio* and one has made the circuit of complexes often enough to bring about their transformation (Edinger, 1985, p. 143). The relative freedom and perspective of the sublimated state is an important achievement in psychic development, but it can be disastrous if one remains stuck in the sky (figure 58); ascent and descent are both needed. A unified personality is able to connect the below (personal) with the above (archetypal).

In both alchemy and the cabala, the movement is not a one-way ascent to heaven. In contrast to the route followed by the Christian redeemer, who comes from above to below and returns

Figure 58. The Tower of Babel. The tower at the left is from *The Bedford Book of Hours*; on the right is the ruined tower in the Gringonneur Tarot, a deck dating from the 14th century.

to the above, in alchemy the *filius macrocosmi* starts below, ascends on high, and with the powers of above and below united in himself, returns to earth again (Edinger, 1985, pp. 144).

Psychological interpretation: Whenever the ego identifies with the transpersonal energies of the psyche and uses them for personal pleasure or power, the result is destruction and defeat.

> Passion raises a man not only above himself, but also above the bounds of his mortality and earthliness, and by the very act of raising him, it destroys him. This "rising above himself" is expressed mythologically in the building of the heaven-high tower of Babel that brought confusion to mankind. . . (Jung, CW 5, ¶ 171).

The common similarity among the diverse types of people who share puer/puella traits is a consistent refusal to take the more difficult path of ordinary adaptation and perseverant labor. What is preferred is the habitual escape into the extraordinary, the exciting, the unique, the path of grandiose flight into an "over-the-rainbow" fairyland or into an idealized, fictitious, spiritual Garden of Eden; magnificent isolation in an ivory tower is preferred to common, pedestrian, human interaction. Yet, paradoxically, this nostalgia of the absolute may express a striving to redeem the Self from an unconscious state, and the yearning for the spirit and the spiritual remains at the core of all human effort for development.

Jungian interpretation: In "The Type Problem in Poetry" Jung says:

> The tower undoubtedly has the meaning of something solid and secure, as in psalm 61:4: "For thou hast been a shelter for me, and a strong tower from the enemy." Any resemblance to the Tower of Babel would involve an intense inner contradiction (CW 6, ¶ 390).

And yet, the image our card presents us is one of destruction—the lightning strikes, the battlement topples. The similarities between card XVII and the Tower of Babel are strickingly evident when we compare the Tower of Destruction card of the 14th century Gringonneur deck and the Tower of Babel from the *Bedford Book of Hours* (see figure 58, p. 259). What inner attitude could have brought this about? Isolation in the ivory tower can be the result of either

> . . . stifling of self-confidence or else an unconscious heightening of the ego's importance to the point of pathological will to power. . . . If, through assimilation of the unconscious, we make the mistake of including the collective psyche in the inventory of personal psychic functions, a dissolution of the personality into its paired opposites inevitably follows. . . . One man arrogates collective virtue to himself as his personal merit, another takes collective vice as his personal guilt. Both are as illusory as megalomania and a sense of inferiority (CW 7, ¶ 235, 237).

Jung further states:

> Through his identification with the collective psyche, he will infallibly try to force the demands of his unconscious upon others, for identity with the collective psyche always brings with it a feeling of universal validity—"godlikeness.". . . The person then becomes a collective truth, and that is always the beginning of the end. . . (CW 7, ¶ 240).

The Tower of Destruction (or *La Maison Dieu* [House of God], as this card is called in the Tarot de Marseilles and the Oswald Wirth decks; see figure 58, page 259), can thus be seen as a symbol of hubris, inflation, and megalomania, an expression of self-aggrandizement, illustrated in the building of the Tower of Babel:

> Then they said, "Come, let us build ourselves a city, and a tower whose top may reach to heaven; and let us make a name for ourselves, lest we be scattered abroad upon the face of the whole earth" (*Genesis* 11:4).

Challenging the *numinosum* constellates the *tremendum* and has the dreaded fragmenting effect.

> [I]f the individual identifies himself with contents awaiting integration, . . . inflation results. . . [which] comes very near to a more or less conscious monomania. . . .

In alchemy, inflation evidently develops into a psychic oedema (CW 16, ¶ 472).

The rational man, in order to live in this world, has to make a distinction between "himself" and what we might call the "eternal man.". . . . [E]ternal truths become dangerously disturbing factors when they supress the unique ego of the individual and live at his expense. . . . The separation of the empirical ego from the "eternal" and the universal man is therefore of vital importance, particularly today when mass-degeneration of the personality is making such strides. Mass-degeneration does not come only from without; it also comes from within, from the collective unconscious (CW 16, ¶ 502).

SYMBOLIC LANGUAGE OF THE IMAGE

Originally the tower—as phallic symbol—represented individual creative endowment; however, this endowment was erroneously assigned to the ego as part of the original sin. Adam's sin and the descent into matter can be seen as his inability to transform matter through self-less acts. The same spirit was active in the builders of the Tower of Babel. This tower was composed of seven superimposed squares symbolizing the law of septenary, also active in card IV (the Emperor) and represented there by the scepter that the Emperor holds. The tower was constructed to exalt the macrocosmos; condemned to destruction, it expresses the relativity of all creation. The tower can also stand for a place of refuge. It may be seen as the spinal cord supporting the body. It is the site of divine powers represented by church, temple, lighthouse, observation tower, signaling tower, hospital, home. It means defense, protection, isolation, egotism.

Arrogant humankind constructs the tower as a sign of its own divinity; this brings about divine wrath and destruction by the thunderbolt. In reality it is belief in the omnipotence of the personal ego, the source of all limitation and suffering oppressing humankind, that is destroyed. The toppling of the battlement represents human willpower gone astray, which may create openness and perspective by its removal and provides the possibility of a new beginning on a higher plane. It suggests that disasters can liberate us from ego fixation or from rigid intellectual constructions through the destruction of a false value system. The rows of bricks evoke the image of humanity composed of individuals, just as the individual body is composed of individual cells. The three windows represent a limited perspective; the third window may suggest an attempt at synthesis through abstract speculation or belief. The two failing figures symbolize action and reaction. The winding stairs within are the connection between heaven and earth, the possibility of escaping isolation.

Seen as a whole, the tower reveals that the forms that have served the spirit as tools tend to become coarse and to solidify until they no longer allow the living truth to shine through. The ruins in the background are such solidified forms, which survive as witness to the past. They are the germs that decompose our thoughts if we cling to them. This is the danger for arrogant occultists who believe they are mastering astral powers when the astral powers are, in reality, possessing them. They expose themselves to the danger of losing sanity or of being driven into death.

In the Visconti-Sforza deck the two falling figures are an adolescent (puer) ad an old man (senex), suggesting perhaps, that the puer/senex archetype is not the appropriate one for this encounter with the sights and sounds of the upper worlds. Indeed, these worlds are extremely disturbing and unsettling if one is ungrounded, unstable, and ill prepared; that is, when one's physical and psychological bodies are not in a healthy condition or are ill matched (Halevi, *The Work of the Kabbalist*, p. 24). Glimpses of a higher form of existence come by God's grace and can change a whole attitude of life. To hold the gift from heaven, one has to have a degree of maturity, stability, and strength; one has to acknowledge that one is a recipient and, at most, a collaborator, but certainly not the originator or the owner of the high-quality energy one is allowed to utilize.

Round shapes float in the air around the tower. They represent disembodied thoughts that take shape in the visible world; their power originates in the vital force. They can also be interpreted as surviving fragments of the past or as seeds of the future:

they are instinct, combative energy. They may also signify forces that are acquired individually. The green spheres, connoting passive vitality, show that we are dealing with spiritual forces apportioned to help humankind in an entire range of possible worldly endeavors; they come from a variety of realms. The red and the yellow spheres bring to mind the reality of the *yang* principle, numinous forces, fire or sulphur energy. The group of ten to the right of the tower bring to mind the Tree of Life; they also represent the ten intelligible aspects of life power. The group of twelve to the left of the tower represent the signs of the zodiac. The thunderbolt signifies insight, illumination, or destruction. It is the sheaf of flames that burns everything. The green plants point out that new life can sprout through human effort; they connect fertility with destruction.

The free-falling figure with outstretched arms symbolizes the active pole in restrained fall, whereas the other figure, in unrestrained vertical fall, shows the lack of mastery over thought or body. Taken together, the two falling figures may represent thinking and feeling liberated from the prison of duality.

Psychologically, worldly goal-oriented thinking must be sacrificed. Through identification one thinks one is something one is not and will never be; that is why it can and must be destroyed. Looking at the sequence of Death (card XIII), Temperance (card XIV), and the Devil (card XV), we may become aware that, after darkness and decomposition (represented by card XIII), the suggestion of a new beginning (card XIV) seems to reactivate the forces of darkness that the Devil embodies. Indeed, premature restructuring of the ego creates a grandiose, arrogant stance represented by the Tower, which must be destroyed in order to allow further development.

In the alchemical tradition, the coarse must be separated from the fine so that the latter can become volatile; thus the crow will be able to soar and will become the swan. This is the work of *sublimatio* that "is part of the royal art where the true gold is made" (Jung, *Letters* 1:171). Comparing the figure representing a pair of alchemists kneeling by the furnace and praying for God's blessing with our card, one is struck by the similarity of shape between furnace and tower (figure 59). Could this mean that spiritual gold can be obtained only with God's help and that presumption and pride will bring God's wrath upon any work tainted by inflation?

Figure 59. Alchemists kneeling by the furnace (from *Mutus Liber*, 1702).

Just as for card XIII (Death) and in contrast to the other cards, the Tower of Destruction is to be given a less negative interpretation when it appears in reverse. The card then shows the possibilities of foreseeing the consequences, of not being deluded by appearances, and of avoiding unproductive controversy. It also shows a certain reticence to take on great works, a healthy, practical intelligence, and the good common sense of a Sancho Panza.

XVII
THE STAR

The letter *pe* means liberation, immortality. It represents the mouth and the tongue. It stands for inspiration, the influence of the macrocosmos upon humankind, the light of nature, initiation through the inner voice, eloquence. In its negative sense, it means misuse of words and hopelessness.

How should we read the number 17, a primary number that has almost no relation to its neighbors? Card XVII follows the catastrophe of card XVI (the Tower of Destruction). Above, we see eight stars; in the middle, there is a woman on the beach; and below, the sea's surface reflects the eight stars of heaven. The kneeling woman pours upon the earth and into the water the contents of the two jars that her predecessor in card XIV (Temperance) decanted from one into the other. We are thus not dealing here with transference to a new form; the contents are poured from above to below, thereby suggesting an outpouring of needful help. The number 17 can also be interpreted as 10 + 7: as cycle of renewed life, wholeness, and transformation, or by reduction as 1 + 7 = 8: the feminine, the Great Female Goddess, procreation and birth, as well as the pleasures and the experience of love. Indeed, this card has been associated with the Sumerian Goddess Inanna and with Venus, the evening and the morning star:

> [J]ust as evening gives birth to morning, so from the darkness arises a new light, the *stella matutina,* which is at once the evening and the morning star (Jung, CW 13, ¶ 299).

According to the Arabic alchemist Dshabir ibn Hayyen, the number 17 is composed of the sequence 1, 3, 5, 8: numbers that form the basis of all other numbers.

THEMES, ASSOCIATIONS, CORRESPONDENCES

Meditation, revelation, union, and creativity are all contained in the Star(s). This card represents inner light, sensation as spiritual perception, and hope; it therefore mediates increased awareness of immortality and of the Self. It suggests giving up control and the need for security.

The ideogram for this card is

Astrological amplification: The planets Mercury and Saturn and the signs Gemini and Libra have been attributed to the Star(s). Aquarius, the Water Bearer, is an air sign with Saturn and Uranus as rulers, yet with enough energy to also fit card XVII. The Water Bearer, in Egyptian mythology, resides near the first cataract of the Nile, where he pours water to heaven and to earth from his urns. Most definitely a champion of light and of spirit, of the values of the mind and not of the instinctual plane of life, Aquarius is the immortal messenger of the gods, a perfect being liberated from the limitations of time and space. He can fly between heaven and earth, inspire, guide, instruct, guard, protect, and sometimes even struggle with us, as an angel once wrestled with Jacob.

> Seeker after the Holy Grail, his main motivation is to find the cup and pour it out upon the parched land for the rest of us, to help us revitalize, to guide us on our way to the inner kingdom (Burt, 1988, p. 427).

Cabalistic amplification: On the ascending journey, when the place of the soul is reached, the awesome possibility of establishing a permanent link with the Self arises. This point of entry into the first of the Seven Halls of Heaven is the coming of age in the Work and the beginning of spiritual adulthood. Although one has access to the higher realms, one is also tested on the various stages of devotion, purity, and sincerity that one may have reached, because even then the

> . . . middle path up through the Halls of Holiness and Sanctification to the place before the abyss that lies in front of the Divine Face will not be without its testing (Halevi, *Work of the Kabbalist*, p. 34).

Alchemical amplification: We are here in the presence of the "unfailing light" and the "rightful food," the stream of a spiritual substance coming from the *lumen naturae*, which the adept felt as divine illumination (von Franz, 1966, p. 163). As such, this light personifies that arcane substance, be it dew or *aqua permanens*, which unites the hostile elements into one.

In the alchemical tradition, the wasting that follows death ends with the appearance of a luminary that announces the birth of a child. The first stage of completion is reached with the emergence of the metallic inconstant humidity of the mercury of the wise, raising the heat of the fire to a high intensity. The washing leads to the many colors of dawn, the peacock's tail preceding *albedo*, the daybreak. Continuing to raise the heat of the fire even more brings about *citrinitas*, the yellowing, and finally, with the fire at its most intense, *rubedo*, the sunrise (Jung, CW 12, ¶ 334). The east or dawn is correlated not only with *rubedo* (blood and life), but also with the feminine, white, "dewey" substance fertilized by the spirit. "She is . . . 'thousand-named,' . . . the vessel and the matter of good and evil" (Jung, CW 14, ¶ 14). The appearance of the colors of the peacock's tail (*cauda pavonis*) in the *opus* represents an intermediate stage preceding the definitive end results. "The phenomenon of the colours owes its existence to the 'Imagination of the great Mystery, where a wonderful essential Life is born'" (Jung, CW 9/1, ¶ 580).

According to von Franz (1966, p. 206), dawn denotes a state in which there is a growing awareness of luminosity, of a diffused glow on the horizon, on the threshold of consciousness. It is the feminine light of the unconscious, bringing illumination, gnosis, or the realization of the Self, whose emissary she is. The dawn is midway between night and noon, shining with twofold hues, red and yellow. This is an evident reminder of the four alchemical stages whereby dawn shines yellow and red (*citrinitas* and *rubedo*) midway between night and day (*nigredo* and *albedo*).

Psychological interpretation: From ancient times the stars have symbolized eternity. "The soul comes from the stars and returns to the stellar regions" (Jung, CW 9/1, ¶ 343). In the relentless work of individuation, moments of reprieve are necessary if we are not to get lost in the dark night of the soul. It is in such moments that powerful archetypal images can appear, symbols of hope that can mobilize psychic energies and activate inner fortitude. Some of these symbols of an inner gathering take the form of an eight-spoked wheel or an eight-rayed star (Jung, CW 11, ¶ 90).

This card presents us with the renewed flow of the sap of life after the disastrous hammering, pulverization, and *sublimatio* of the preceding card (XVI, the Tower of Destruction). Here may be the difficult transition between ideal and real, between the agent that activates the passage and actualization.

Jungian interpretation: The goddess Inanna provides a many-faceted symbolic image, a wholeness pattern combining earth and sky, matter and spirit, earthly bounty and heavenly guidance. Many of her symbols are associated with this card, from her eight-spoked shield (see figure 60) to the morning star. Indeed, from very early times, this goddess of the radiant, erratic morning and evening star, the Lady of Myriad Offices (Perera, 1981, pp. 16-18), has symbolized consciousness of transitions and borders, places of intersection and crossing over that imply creativity and change.

Some authorities, having reached this multitudinous stage, are reluctant to go further or, at times, have declared there is nothing beyond polymorphism or polytheism. This stance disregards the clear indications that come from alchemy: after the *cauda pavonis*, *citrinitas*, and *viriditas* come the final stages of *albedo* and *rubedo*. The intermediary stages, significant when present, are not essential to the final goal of wholeness. Can it therefore be surprising that after the peacock's tail (card XVII) the tarot also presents us with *albedo* (card XVIII, the Moon), *citrinitas* (card XIX, the Sun), and *viriditas* (card XX, Judgement) before reaching *rubedo* (card XXI, the World)?

People assert, says Jung, that globes, stars, crosses, and the like are symbols for the center in themselves. When asked what they mean by this center, they confess that it is a vision that leaves them with a wonderful feeling of perfect harmony, at times reached in a moment of extreme pain or profound despair.

Figure 60. Inanna's shield.

> If you sum up their experiences, you can formulate it
> this way: They came to themselves, . . . they were able
> to become reconciled to themselves, and thus were
> reconciled to adverse circumstances and events (Jung,
> CW 11, ¶ 138).

The Star(s) is thus a symbol for renewal. We are reminded that
the goddess Inanna, the morning and evening star, concerned
herself more with life than with good and evil, that her sacrifice
was made more for life than for redemption of sins.

SYMBOLIC LANGUAGE OF THE IMAGE

The naked figure evokes the image of
Venus, symbol of expansive, streaming life
power. This impression is reinforced by
the name of the card and by the image
of the eightpointed morning star present
in the center. The eight stars remind us of
card VIII: Justice that aligns actions with
their consequences. In the masculine
realm, we may see a parallel to the energy
that this card represents in card VII, the
Chariot. The sun above the charioteer's
head (evoked in card XVII by the eight-
pointed star) directs his course as well as
the course of the stars. Moreover, the
seven small stars signify the seven small
planets, the seven days of the week, the
seven chakras, etc. They thus depict seven centers of psychic
energy, seven elements of embodied force. The Star(s) can be seen
as eyes of heaven, as discerning thought, as possibility of transcending the world of appearances. They may also show the
capacity to overcome personal disposition and anxieties.

The weight of the figure's body is supported by her left knee,
which is on the ground; her right foot stands on the mirror of
water. In this way a balance between consciousness and the
unconscious, between doing and being, is achieved in meditative
introversion.

The bird taking flight (in some decks) is an ibis; it represents
the interaction between above and below, outside and inside,

heaven and earth. It suggests both detachment from all entanglement and recognition without craving it. It is a symbol of Toth,
the moon god, and as such it is connected to the cyclic lapse of
time and its measurement. Here it signifies the vital force that
wants to soar in order to become active in other, higher realms.

The evergreen acacia branch is an image of hope; it indicates
that things can survive and remain alive even in times of drought.
After the storm of card XVI (the Tower of Destruction) comes mild
spring rain, the promise of renewed growth, the possibility of triumph over human limitation, and an invitation to explore the
healing powers of nature.

The Star(s) represents the beginning of true initiation. The
light of the Star(s) gives direction in the night as do position lights,
beacons, milestones, and timers. This card expresses a yearning for
that world that goes beyond recognition, conflict, and separation.
It describes maturity as a piety of the heart and faith in providence. It depicts the impact of new life forces resulting from integration of the opposites and insists that the life-relevant reality
of spiritual impulses can become understandable only when sensuality is not repressed. The Star(s) stands for the power of love
that radiates through the breath of life that is active in the body, a
power that is at the same time a prototype and a model in which
future and past, origin and end, come together.

The card brings into focus the eternal reciprocal love between
the Lord and his creature and makes us see that the totality of
God's name comprises the named and the naming, the Lord as
Being, a reality that is revealed in an act of shared suffering, of
empathy. The mystic's soul is guided by the stars; inspired by the
heart, he or she surrenders to their heavenly influences, which
leads to mystical enlightenment.

The central star of Venus represents the Great Feminine
Goddess, the self-renewing life. Venus is associated with Sirius, the
star of Ishtar, connected to the fertilizing cyclic flooding of
the Nile. In Christian symbolism, it is Maria as *Stella Maris* who
has this meaning. Some authors have associated the planet Venus
with the Star of Bethlehem, which announced to the world the
existence of Jesus. Venus as morning star represents Lucifer as
light bringer, the promise of a new morning. Venus as evening
star evokes the garden of the Hesperides in which the dragon
guards the golden apples of immortality.

The middle star has eight green-blue rays, showing that the
red rays have been transcended and that we are now dealing with

spiritual powers, the waters of eternal life, the colors of immortality and of hope. The eight yellow rays represent material forces, the fertility of matter and its longevity. (See figure 61.) As the stars shine above us and teach us a sense of beauty and humility, so we learn to accept a fate that the gracious figure seems to offer with such simplicity that she makes us love a task that destiny has imposed upon us without our choosing. Thanks to her, what may have seemed our earthly prison comes closer to paradise.

The two jars shown on the card depict the active and the passive poles. The ability to procreate and multiply is illustrated by the pouring of water into water; the flow creates concentric rings that signify circumambulation, the integration of the periphery into the center, possibilities of expression. It can also mean lusty, playful sexuality in its broadest sense, exchange of masculine and feminine forces, cross-fertilization.

The nakedness of the figure represents the unmasked truth. The mystery of card XVII is the mystery of the revealing vision, the apperception of suprasensory worlds that mirror themselves in constellations and images that shine in the heaven of the soul. It is found also in the mystery of sleep and dreams, which temporarily loosens bodily ties. We are part of two ways of being whereby nightly existence becomes understandable only by interpreting its symbols. Dreams must be interpreted also in relation to functional disturbances of the body. In the temple of Asklepios, the god showed the sleeper the healing medication. When the body of the sleeper no longer gets in the way with its reactions, the spirit can impart its knowledge.

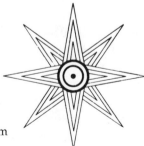

Figure 61. The eight-pointed star (from Wirth, *Tarot of the Magicians*, p. 132).

Psychologically, by giving up one's will, all fictitious formal attire is peeled off, and the simple, unavoidable truth of human nature becomes visible. The multiplicity-in-unity of spiritual contents appears.

Inanna, goddess of seasonal vegetation, depicts feminine nature embodied: playful, passionately erotic, independent, self-willed, ambitious, and multifaceted. Vital and complex, she represents a model in which joy, lust, and multiplicity can no longer be denigrated and dismissed as frivolity and fickleness. Her descent and return can provide a model for our own psychological and spiritual journeys. She emerges from the realm of the dark goddess Ereshkigal stripped naked like the figure on our card. With a deeper and more resonant awareness of her inner truth, she unites above and below in a new fluid pattern. Inanna is the image of a new feminine sensibility rooted in the depth of instinct, a wisdom capable of restoring creative wholeness by providing an inner rhythmic interplay between body, soul, and spirit to women and men alike.

In ancient times navigators were obliged to hug the coast from port to port. It is only after they discovered the fixed North Star in the sky above that they were able to find their way below, leaving the security of the coastline behind and daring to entrust themselves to the high seas. Finding the right star and using it as a guide to set goals that were previously unreachable does not mean, however, that one can aim to set anchor in the sky; those who do are the very ones who get lost.

Divine inspiration is needed when we have almost lost hope, but it becomes effective when it connects with and activates the spark of divine light that we all carry within.

> Therefore the heavens will open for him and like thunder will the voice sound of him who has the seven stars in his hands, whose spirits are sent out to testify to all the world. . . . He who has ears to hear shall hear what the spirit of wisdom tells the son about the doctrine of the seven stars through which the holy work is fulfilled (von Franz, 1980, p. 204).

Card XVII seems to represent the hope that the light is at hand.

XVIII THE MOON   צ

The letter *tsade* means shadow, reflex, roof. It indicates the activity of the spirit in physiological and material life, foresight, organization, individual regeneration through awareness of the body, ritual. In its negative sense, it means misleading imagination, erroneous moon rituals.

After card XVII (the Star[s]), which conveys an image of dawn promising a new day filled with "the perfect brightness of the internal vision" (von Franz, 1966, p. 204), the Moon indicates a return to earlier events. In the background two towers seem to stand guard at some invisible threshold, warding off the prowling evil that makes the hounds bay; in the foreground a ten legged crab (or crayfish) lurks in a pond. This image seems to represent a Charybdis-and-Scylla double-bind: the dangerous, regressive aspect of the ten-spoked Wheel of Fortune in the foreground, and the peril lurking between or beyond the two ominous towers in the background. The 10 below plus 2 × 4 above equals the number of our card, 18. The number 18 can also be seen as 9 × 2, in which 9 is a number associated with the moon and its connection with fertility, creativity, completion, and the unconscious.

In numerology the number 18 is an astral-cycle number; the solar and lunar eclipses repeat in the same sequence every eighteen years. In Christian symbolism 10 + 8 means the fulfilling of the law with mercy; 6 × 3 means belief in the Trinity, which is associated with just behavior.

THEMES, ASSOCIATIONS, CORRESPONDENCES

The moon evokes sleep, dream, introversion, passion, chaos, vegetative organization, expansion of consciousness. The bottomless abyss is its territory. It shows disconnection between feeling and understanding, lack of resistance to instinctual forces, and insecurity. The Moon also suggests disappointment and abandonment.

The ideogram for this card is (69)

Astrological amplification: The Moon represents our deepest emotional patterns and needs, our sensitivity and responsiveness, our rootedness in our being and in our past. It symbolizes our relationship to the inner feminine, influencing the way in which we seek to secure and protect ourselves and the types of relationships we form. It is the gateway to the outer planets; how we deal with our basic feelings affects whether these planets attack as enemies or serve as guides to illumine our paths. The Moon is connected with Neptunian energy: its vision, its imagination, its compassion, and its spirit of sacrifice. In a negative sense, the addictive quality of Neptune may overtake and overwhelm an imbalanced Moon energy. I have therefore chosen to assign Neptune to the Moon, although traditionally the Moon has been correlated with Aquarius, Cancer, Venus, and even Uranus.

According to Greene, Neptune is essentially a feminine planet that opens the gates of experience to the suffering of the world and to the agony of the spirit incarnated in the flesh (Greene, 1984, p. 117). Neptune symbolizes mystical consciousness longing for release from the body's prison and union with the divine source of the soul.

Cabalistic amplification: The gift of wisdom is synonymous with the full moon, and its loss is synonymous with the waning or dark moon. This special wisdom linked with the moon as the feminine principle of consciousness opens the door to the suprapersonal realm. Without the moon spirit, consciousness is incomplete because it needs not only the knowledge of the mind and intellect but also the wisdom of the heart (Poncé, *Kabballah*, pp. 272-274).

Alchemical amplification:

> [T]he Moon, standing on the borders of the sublunary world ruled by evil, has a share not only in the world of light but also in the daemonic world of darkness. . . . That is why her changefulness is so significant symbol-

ically: she is duplex and mutable like Mercury and, like
him, is a mediator; hence their identification in alchemy
(Jung, CW 14, ¶ 19).

The moon crescent is the symbol of the spark of light that slumbers
in the human soul, the hidden fire of the alchemists that is to be
awakened by the alchemical process (Silberer, 1971, p. 189). Earth
and moon coincide in the *albedo*, for on the one hand, the sublimated or calcinated earth appears as *terra alba foliata*, the sought-
for good, like the whitest snow, and on the other hand, Luna as
mistress of the *albedo* is the *femina alba* of the *coniunctio* and the
"mediatrix of the whitening." When the moon shines in her fullness, the "rabid dog," the danger that threatens the divine child,
is chased away (Jung, CW 14, ¶ 154).

In the alchemical tradition the whitening appears after the
nigredo phase has been overcome. In the silver light, feelings are
transformed and the divided returns to unity. The alchemists said
that *solutio* takes place in the moon, a statement that corresponds
to the dissolving, dark irrational side of the moon with its dangerous potential for dismemberment. One aspect of the Dionysian
solutio is the orgiastic instinctual immersion that expresses the
yearning of the lonely, alienated ego for containment in a larger
whole, in a desire to reestablish the lost connection with fellow
humans. The moon is not only an agent of negative or dangerous
solutio; it is also the source of dew, of fertilizing moisture, of healing and growth, and it is identical to the *aqua permanens*.

Psychological interpretation: Before the creation of the sun and
moon, it is as if the world were outside of time, in a kind of dawn
state. There was light in this world, but the luminosity was that of
the world of the archetypes in which as yet no discriminating ego
consciousness existed. Then the moon rises; consciousness is dif-
fuse, uncertain, changeable, ephemeral. This state is later followed
by a clear, steady state of consciousness—the sun. The eye that
saw hitherto only the darkness and danger of evil turns toward
the circle of the full moon where the ethereal realm of the immortals begins. The plenilunium is the gracious and serene complement of the sinister new moon and its perils. Once the malignity
is tempered, sinfulness and its evil consequences are also miti-
gated and that which has wings can embrace the earth (Jung,
CW 14, ¶ 207-211).

Card XVIII describes a difficult passage on the winding road toward the mystery of transformation and wholeness. We are faced with a triple reinforcement of the image of instability: the fickle Wheel of Fortune; the crab that can go backward, forward, and sideways; and the connection to the moon, whose cyclic modulations of shape have become the very symbol of variability. Thus, card XVIII marks entanglement in an unpredictable fate or, at any rate, the possibility of such. On the other hand, the Moon is also the ruler of the astrological sign of Cancer (the Crab), a sign in which feelings predominate and are the expression, the inspiration, and the creativity of the moon spirit presiding over the assembly of the nine muses. The moon, with her antithetical nature is, in a sense, a prototype of individuation, a prefiguration of the Self (Jung, CW 14, ¶ 217-220).

Jungian interpretation: As Neumann has pointed out, moon consciousness in both men and women represents a certain way of perceiving the world. The contribution of the ego consists in a readiness to accept emerging unconscious contents and to come into harmony with them. Moon consciousness depends upon the activity of the unconscious for inspiration, as well as for the functioning of instincts and for connection with the available libido.

> What emanates from moon-spirit is an emotional movement closely related to the activities of the unconscious. In active eruption it is fiery spirit, it is courage, anger, possession and rage; its self-revelation leads to prophesy, cogitation, and poetry, but also to lying. Along with this fiery productivity, however, goes another, more "measured" attitude which meditates, dreams, waits and wishes, hesitates and lingers; which is related to memory and learning, and whose outcome is moderation, wisdom, and meaning (Neumann, 1954, p. 85).

The act of understanding through moon consciousness involves the whole psyche; it is a conceiving through full-grown perception that makes experiences real and integrates the realization, thus bringing about a personality change. It is not under the burning rays of the sun that the creative process fulfills itself, but in the cool reflected light of the moon, in the dark and quiet, the secrecy, the silence, the hiddenness. The moist nighttime is also the time of

healing and recovery. It is the regenerating power of the unconscious that, in nocturnal darkness or by the light of the moon,
performs its task, in its own time, at its own pace. Neumann also
points out that moon time has periods and rhythms; it waxes and
wanes, is favorable and unfavorable:

> The waxing moon is more than a measurer of time. It is
> a symbol, like the waning moon, the full moon, and the
> dark moon, for an inner and outer quality of life and
> humanity. We can most clearly represent to ourselves
> the archetypal character of the moon's periods by the
> changing forces of the radiations. For they are centers of
> the waves of vibration, the streams of power, which from
> within and without, pulse through the world (Neumann,
> 1954, p. 86).

The seat of moon consciousness is not the head but the heart, and
understanding means an act of inclusive feeling accompanied by
affect participation. As Jung says:

> [Moonlight] does not show up objects in all their piti-
> less discreteness and separateness. . . but blends in a
> deceptive shimmer the near and the far, magically trans-
> forming little things into big things, high into low, soft-
> ening all colour into a bluish haze, and blending the
> nocturnal landscape into an unsuspecting unity (Jung,
> CW 14, ¶ 223). . . . It needs a very moon-like conscious-
> ness indeed. . . to talk and act in such a way that the har-
> monious relation of the parts to the whole is not only
> not disturbed but is actually enhanced. And when the
> ditch is too deep, a ray of moonlight smooths it over
> (Jung, CW 14, ¶ 227).

Neumann insists that it is essential to bear in mind that the
processes of moon consciousness have their relation to the ego
and cannot be described, therefore, as unconscious. Plain and simple masculine consciousness finds moon consciousness and the
knowledge it imparts unverifiable, willful, and mystical. What
the moon spirit perceives is, in large part, beyond scientific understanding. It relates to those general experiences of life that have

always been the subject matter of mysteries and belong to the domain of intuitive wisdom, not that of exact science. It is the wisdom relating to the indissoluble and paradoxical unity of life and death, of nature and spirit, to the laws of time and fate and growth. The wisdom of the moon/Sophia lacks abstract, impersonal, universal, and absolute character; it is nonspeculative, close to nature and life, bound to fate and to living reality. Its illusionless view of reality is related to its actuality as helper, nourisher, comforter. The moon wisdom of waiting, accepting, ripening admits everything into its totality and transforms it and, along with it, its own being. It is always concerned with wholeness, with shaping, that is, with creativity.

However, any development, at any stage that strives toward sun consciousness, looks on the moon spirit as regression, as the terrible mother, as witch; it is a symbol of the devouring unconscious. The dark moon (Hecate) especially becomes the bloodsucker, the danger of inundation by the unconscious, of moodiness, lunacy, and madness. (See figure 62.) The English phrase "to moon," to be melancholy, shows that to be withdrawn can mean to be "drawn to the moon" with its dangerous pull toward the unconscious.

Germination and decay, light changing to darkness, death was well as resurrection, all belong to the symbolism of the moon, which dies and is reborn each month (Edinger, 1985, p. 163).

Figure 62. Hecate. An engraved Roman gem from Neumann: *The Great Mother*, p. 169.

SYMBOLIC LANGUAGE OF THE IMAGE

The moon stands at the borderline between eternal, ethereal things and the ephemeral phenomena of the earthy, sublunar realm (Jung, CW 14, ¶ 173). Many old Hermetic texts contend that the light of God cannot be found before one has come up from the dark cloud of the unconscious. Similarly in *The Cloud of Unknowing* (1912), a mystical medieval text, it is observed that the closer the soul of the mystic gets to the godhead, the darker it becomes.

As we approach the end of our ascending journey, it is no wonder that the card we encounter presents us with the darkness of the moon. However, we must remember:

> Usually it is said that from the moon comes the dew, but the moon is also the *aqua mirifica* that extracts the souls from the bodies or gives the bodies life and soul. . . . As the water of ablution, the dew falls from heaven, purifies the body, and makes it ready to receive the soul; in other words, it brings about the *albedo*, the white state of innocence . . . (Jung, CW 14, ¶ 155).

The little droplets falling from the face of the moon may represent this heavenly dew. The winding, upward-leading path to the mystery beyond permits advance toward completion. The spiritual world is illuminated in the same measure as the material world is darkened; the transitional space is bathed by the light of the moon. Its pale yellow light testifies to an unfocused mental activity, inadequate to grasp the essence of things but essential to visionary perspective. The moon evokes night, its visions and its stillness, loneliness, feeling abandoned, removed, the intensity and inexorability of the numinous. Connected with ebb and flow, it suggests fullness and emptiness—the tides. It stands for enchantment, abduction, absurdity, variability, loss of orientation, disruption of the habitual, feeling trapped, bottomless pain.

The imprecise moonlight evokes an image of vague theories based on illusory concepts; nevertheless we must attempt to advance, at our own risk, on this swampy and uncertain ground. Human imagination will repeatedly objectify the subjective and thereby help the mind construct an image of the world from it.

Although the two towers of card XVIII stand in better relationship to wholeness than does the Tower of card XVI, they nevertheless offer a very narrow passage, suggesting a confrontation with the guardians of the threshold. Indeed, these foursquare towers are the eightfold guarded entrance to the underworld, through which only the unburdened and the righteous (card VIII, Justice) find passage. This narrow gate is the crossing from the world of the ego to the world of the Self; its prerequisite is the necessity of becoming conscious of, confronting, and accepting the shadow.

> For the gate is narrow and
> the way is hard that leads to life
> and those who find it are few (Matthew 7:14).

Here is potential access to spiritual power, but first it leads to and through the dark night of the soul.

The passage to the other world is full of contrasts: what is light here is dark there: what here is virtue, there is flaw (a connection to card XII, the Hanged Man). Only the one whom the dogs recognize as master—and at whose feet they lie still—is able to go through. He can never return. The passage to the nonworld, by contrast, stands for escape, distortion, disguise. It means lack of understanding and separation between cause and effect (a reminder of card XV, the Devil).

The two howling dogs warn against the forbidden regions in which the imagination can lose itself when prodded by fears and yearnings; they see to it that social order is maintained. But dogs are changeable, mythical beings, companions to Isis, Artemis, and Hecate. They are guides to the dead in the underworld after having accompanied them through life. The dog was also a psychopomp, a regular companion of Asklepios, the god of healing, and of Hermes. It is a symbol with ambivalent aspects: on one hand it represents the gift of healing, of second sight, a connection to the forces of the underworld, of the unconscious; on the other hand it represents knowledge of healing power and of fire in its sexual connotation. The dog is also a symbol of voracity and of cunning.

Anubis, the Egyptian guide of the dead in the underworld, the messenger of the gods, connected to thieves, werewolves, vampires, and changelings, had the head of a dog. Hecate herself, goddess of the underworld, the dark side of the moon, is at times also dog headed (Jung, CW 5, ¶ 354-355). To Hecate were dedicated the junctions of three roads, forked roads, and crossroads. Where roads meet, dog sacrifices were offered to her. This sacrifice occurred at the very point of union where roads cross, symbol of the reconciliation of opposites and of the mother as object and epitome of all union. This point is also, however, where roads divide, where there is a parting and a separation, reiterating that the mother means to us both embrace and farewell. The dog sacrifice at this spot propitiates the mother in both senses. The astral form of the dog, the Dog Star, which appears at the highest point of the summer solstice, suggests that the dog could have a compensatory significance, death being made equal to the sun at its highest point.

Another symbol in card XVIII that is connected with the summer solstice is the crab. In astrology Cancer is the sign of the zodiac in which the sun begins to retreat, when the days begin to grow shorter. It is the house of the moon, a feminine, watery sign, and is correlated with the breast. It signifies resurrection because the crab sheds its shell (Jung, CW 9/1, ¶ 604-605). However, because the crab also hides in its shell to protect its vulnerability, it signifies defensiveness, caution and foresight, intuition of coming events. The crab stands now for the sun and now for the moon, according to whether it moves forward or backward. In Egyptian mythology the scarab, the equivalent of the crab, is a symbol of the sun because it rolls untiringly its ball of dung, which warms, protects, and nourishes its eggs, the new life. The scarab is thus a life spender and a life protector.

The crab swims in the ocean of life, but it can be caught or captured. It stands for secret changes in the body. It connotes the danger of confrontation with the unconscious—its devouring, but also its cleansing, aspects. It can signify paralysis of will, loss of hope, the unexpected in its frightening aspects, but also fearlessness through helpful, instinctive knowledge. Emotional and feeling problems cannot be solved through thinking or through action but only through the awareness that comes from listening in stillness. The crab shell stands for introversion, immobilization by looking back, remaining caught in the past. Nevertheless the crab shell is the burden of the past that can be discarded as soon as one can recognize the possibilities available in the present.

The crab is thus a symbol of self-consciousness and self-examination because it walks backward; it is a symbol of moral and psychic renewal; its realm is the past and the hidden. Because it keeps the water pure by devouring rotted matter, the crab symbolizes the search of purifying consciousness that penetrates the organic core to remove the obsolete, discriminating between the reliable foundation and the relativity of the transitory.

The serpentine path between the foreground and the background represents the duality of light and dark that we encounter on all cosmic planes. It shapes and dissolves; it is both healing and dangerous. It is the helpful/dangerous aspect of the psyche, the delicate ray of hope, undauntedness. It emphasizes the moon as the symbol of love that leads from the impersonal to the personal, the shared.

> [P]sychologically. . . love and kindness are the antithesis of evil. The wings of the dove temper the malignity of the air, the wickedness of the aerial spirit (Jung, CW 14, ¶ 206).

The moon emphasizes the irreplaceable value of a relationship with a partner in facilitating our confrontation of personal problems projected upon the other, where they appear "outside" and can be better grasped, addressed, and clarified. This process forces us to take a concrete position because theoretical understanding alone never solves the problems of the practical, individual level of reality.

The moon directs ideation and fantasy, the power of our desires that would like to bring to fruition all our potentialities, with or without ego approval. The ego adapts or it is sacrificed. Instinctive patterns become conscious through awareness, and by becoming conscious, the compulsion to repeat is interrupted. Becoming conscious is introverted feeling from the action vantage point, whereas progressive, extroverted awareness becomes action. The numinous is experienced and expressed in ritual and thus becomes part of consciousness; ritual action has spiritual character. Our compulsions are transformed when we can challenge our decisions; when we can ask, "Do I have to do this?" We can achieve recognition when we have freed ourselves from the fetters of addiction to self-gratification. Then we become aware of the cosmic rhythm that does not imprison but becomes creative, freeing power.

However, there are some people who stand too close to the murky pond; the regressive pull of the crab draws them back into their fateful past. These cannot muster the courage to dare take the winding mysterious path that leads past the howling dogs and the ominous towers and toward the mythical land beyond in which they may find what they are yearning for: wholeness, connectedness, and creativity. For them the depressive moon spirit will be as far as they will go. Whenever moon consciousness is not tempered by the discriminating function of sun consciousness, an imbalance of gushing feeling and devouring dedication takes over. Discomfort, uneasiness, a sense of danger that one cannot identify seems to be present whenever one encounters someone taken over by this moon spirit. One cannot help being mistrustful, wary, and withholding, fearful of the unconscious elements at work in such a personality unaware of their power for destruction.

XIX
THE SUN

ק

The letter *coph* means light, enhanced life, hatchet, concretization, union of the individual with God in real life, the connection and reunion of humankind and nature with God, the sun of Osiris. Its symbols are gold, light, and salt. In its negative sense, it means lack of stability.

The sun with its four shining rays, four searing rays, and its sharply accentuated center brings to mind the number 9, the symbol of consciousness that here radiates and extends to the All, the Encompassing Consciousness. The flickering, uncertain light from the lantern of the Hermit (card IX) has now become the victorious brightness of the daily luminary. In front of it the twins, a boy and a girl, embody the polarity of the opposites and reborn humankind reuniting at this level with the consciousness of the All. The twins can be represented by pentagrams that express their diversity by their upward and downward orientation. (See figure 63.)

Thus $9 + 5 + 5 = 19$, the number of our card, a number of joining, of union, in which 9 can be either 3×3, a harmonious

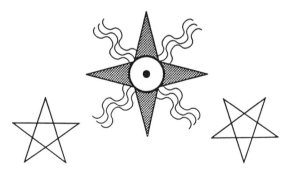

Figure 63. The sun symbol and two pentagrams. (From Bernoulli, *Zur Symbolik geometrischer Figuren und Zahlen*, p. 413.)

multiplication of two trinities, or 5 + 4, a new beginning at a higher level, self-affirmation through awareness of a higher power.

THEMES, ASSOCIATIONS, CORRESPONDENCES

The Sun means becoming conscious of the unity of life, of alternating times of fulfillment and void, fertility and infertility, transformation, revitalization. The Sun connotes the highest heaven, completion. It represents existential essence and signifies joy and enthusiasm.

The ideogram for this card is

Astrological amplification: According to Kenton, the Sun is the planet of individuation (Kenton, *Astrology*, p. 22). People living by their inner Sun sign live according to their individual nature. If a person follows his or her Sun, relating outer life to inner self, he is freed from the inner powers obscuring the horoscope, especially those governing the instinctual world. When a person lives by her or his Sun, the whole horoscope is altered in emphasis; one acquires vision and determination beyond the ordinary and can withstand or avoid disasters that others cannot bear or do not foresee. When guided by the inner Sun, fate is a prison from which the soul can escape and rise to reach the world of pure spirit.

Cabalistic amplification: The cabalists saw in the sun-moon *coniunctio* a replica of the *Tipheret-Yesod* coupling. *Tipheret*, the counterpart of the sun within the individual, lies on the axis of consciousness; through it passes the majority of forces flowing down the Tree of Life, as through the solar system. Above *Tipheret* is *Kether*, the Crown, through which streams the Divine Emanation. The sun not only illuminates the planet, it shines light on the smallest particles that the human eye can detect. Psychologically, the same phenomenon occurs within a person in touch with his or her inner truth, as focused in *Tipheret*. Although only miniscule compared to *Kether* (as is our sun compared to the galaxy), it nevertheless represents one's own individuality. *Tipheret* is the sun of the human being, the midpoint between Heaven and Earth, between *Kether* and *Malkuth* in each human being. It partakes of the upper and lower levels of the Tree except where it is prevented from scorching the Earth by *Yesod* or from losing itself in the inconceivable, eternal absolute (*Ain Sof*) through the invisible door of *Daat*.

> Tipheret is the Sun, almost impossible to look directly upon. Such was the face of Apollo that a glance at it by the unprepared might blind them for life. Seen from the view of a man this might well correspond to seeing more than a man could bear to know about himself; this is why most men live in Yesod—the moon of themselves—preferring to see only by reflection the light of their real nature (Halevi, *Tree of Life*, p. 59)

Alchemical amplification: Just as the cabalists attributed the sun to *Tipheret*, the heart is the Tree of Life, so the alchemists considered that the "heart is the seat of the imagination, and is also the 'sun in the microcosm'" (Jung, CW 13, ¶ 201). However, in order to be able to connect with the higher, more spiritual realms, it must be liberated from the restlessness and emotionality originating in the bondage to the body (Jung, CW 13, ¶ 202). Elsewhere Jung states:

> [T]he silver or moon condition. . . has to be raised to the sun condition. The *albedo* is, so to speak, the day break, but not until the *rubedo* is it sunrise. The transition to the *rubedo* is formed by the *citrinitas* . . .(CW 12, ¶ 334).

Indeed, although

> The sun is the image of God, the heart is the sun's image in man, just as gold is the sun's image in the earth, . . . and God is known in the gold (Jung, CW 12, ¶ 445)

and

> Gold, the royal colour, is attributed to God the Father (Jung, CW 12, ¶ 319),

the alchemists did not consider gold the goal of their *opus magnus*:

> For these alchemists the gold undoubtedly had a symbolic nature and was therefore distinguished by such attributes as *vitreum* or *philosophicum*. It was probably

owing to its all too obvious analogy to the sun that gold was denied the highest philosophical honor, which fell instead to the *lapis philosophorum*. The transformer is above the transformed . . ."for our stone, namely the living western quicksilver which has placed itself above the gold and vanquished it, is that which kills and quickens." . . ."Understand, ye sons of the wise, what this exceeding precious stone proclaims . . .'And my light conquers every light, and my virtues are more excellent than all virtues. . . . I beget the light, but the darkness too is in my nature . . .'" (Jung, CW 12, ¶ 99).

Hence, there is also a *Sol niger* (black sun), which coincides with the *nigredo* and *putrefactio* (death). Like Mercurius, Sol in alchemy is ambivalent (Jung, CW 14, ¶ 113). The *Sol niger* is synonymous with the *caput corvi* (head of the crow) and denotes *anima media natura* in the state of *nigredo*.

Psychologically, this means a provisional extinction of the conscious standpoint owing to an invasion of the unconscious. . . ."You must go through the gate of the blackness if you would gain the light of Paradise in the whiteness" (Jung, CW 14, ¶ 117, n. 40).

Because the Sun is not the last card of the major arcana, indicating that the journey does not end here, I have chosen to attribute to this card the alchemical stage of *citrinitas*, or yellowing, a transition stage toward the final *rubedo*.

The alchemical sun, with its active substance sulphur, is hot, dry, and yellow/red, qualities associated with Typhon (the Egyptian Set), the evil principle. The active sun substance enkindles inner warmth from which come all the motions of the will and the principle of all appetites. It is a vital spirit; it has its seat in the brain and its governance in the heart. It is therefore a substance believed to have a generative and transformative effect:

[T]here is in the heart a sunlike arcanum from which life and warmth stream forth. . . . It is a hot, daemonic principle of life, having the closest affinities with the sun in the earth, the "central fire" or "ignis gehennalis" (fire of hell) (Jung, CW 14, ¶ 113).

Although these statements indicate that the sun is a transitional and not a final state in alchemy, there are also statements such as:

> Truly the form which is the intellect of man is the beginning, middle, and end of the preparations, and this form is indicated by the yellow colour . . . (Dorn, quoted by Jung in CW 14, ¶ 390).

These statements seem to imply that the beginning is also the end, a uroboric image usually associated with card 0, the Fool. However, the circle described by the sun is "the line that runs back on itself, like the snake that with its head bites its own tail," evoking the alchemical *opus circulatorium* that takes the image of the sun's course through all the signs of the zodiac (Jung, CW 12, ¶ 470).

Because all the elements are contained in it, the sun can be identified with the quintessence, the universal power of growth, healing, mana. The alchemical sun is thus the spark of the divine fire implanted in man, the supreme treasure that the "animal man" understandeth not (Jung, CW 14, ¶ 114-115).

Psychological interpretation: The Sun means return to unity from multiplicity. Its regenerative rays coming from a central light are a symbol of wholeness and of the potential communion of conscious and unconscious forces that are no longer divided and fragmented by material, everyday occurrences.

Jungian interpretation: For Jung, the sun is the symbol of psychic life force, the libido (CW 5, ¶ 297). Indeed,

> Just as the sun, by its own motion and in accordance with its own inner law, climbs from morn till noon, crosses the meridian and goes its downward way toward evening, leaving its radiance behind it, and finally plunges into all-enveloping night, so man sets his course by immutable laws and, his journey over, sinks into darkness, to rise again (CW 5, ¶ 251)

The image of the Dioscuri, the divine twins—one mortal, one immortal—is interpreted by Jung as psychology projected into the heavens, the underlying idea could probably be paraphrased thus: just as man consists of a mortal and an immortal part, so the sun is a pair of brothers, one of whom is mortal, the other immortal. ...The sun comparison tells us over and over again that the dynamic of the gods is psychic energy. This is our immortality, the link through which man feels inextinguishably one with the continuity of all life (CW 5, ¶ 296).

SYMBOLIC LANGUAGE OF THE IMAGE

The Sun, perennially identical to itself, shines impartially, exposing truth freed from illusion. The sun spirit rises out of primordial opposites: out of evening/morning a day emerges. The sun, image of the creative, sinks into the sea at night: it is in chaos that the foundation is laid. In the morning the sun— an active, generative, existential center within the life of the body/soul/spirit— rises above the earth. This is a faithful image of self-determination, authority, extroversion, the masculine principle, and reconnection with universal spirituality. The Sun is clarity of consciousness, tuneful emerging, fertility or a threat to fertility through drought. It means reaching the optimum, seeing the goal in meaningfulness, an organizing principle missing in our times. It is enlightenment of the deepest purpose of willpower, of the most profound unconscious communication; it is memory of past lives. The two children, connoting new life about to develop and grow, receive the light of the sun from its straight golden rays as well as from its flaming red rays; the former are linear, forming, penetrating, gathering together, symbolic of light as wave; whereas the latter are oscillating, shaping, encompassing, symbolic of light as particle (see figure 64). Taken together, gold and red rays symbolize the numinous forces, fertility, love, power, and time; but also burden, toil, and disruption.

Figure 64. The Sun-god Shamesh. (From *New Larousse Encyclopedia of Mythology*, p. 50.)

The paradisiacal garden in which the children play is protected by a wall of red and yellow stones, square-cut and fitted, connected to blue supports, which signify that only feeling (blue) can reconcile the basic opposition between the active energy of work (red) and acquired knowledge (yellow). The wall is boundary, protection, control, and channeling of growth through knowledge of the assumptions and rules of nature, the purity of one's own nature limited by collective space. The garden with its flowers represents the four realms of nature: mineral, vegetal, animal, and human. Reorganized nature reawakens to a higher level of consciousness. The thirteen orange spheres signify vital breath, the *prana* of the Hindus.

The child is an image of the harmonious cooperation of the individual with the community. It is the individual soul in the making, the warmth of empathy, cooperation in the redemptive strivings of humankind, spiritual effort. The two children hold hands, an image of innocence, inexperience, of undeveloped capacity for discrimination. The boy, the active pole, and the girl, the passive pole, depict life as awareness of "so-ness" in the here and now; a harmonious world evolves out of the play of imagination, and problems find solutions by themselves. The mystery is clarified through enlightenment.

Among the ancients half-divine, half-human twins protected navigators; as phallic gods they were associated with the concealed aspect of the divine, with the bottomless mystery of divine energy. The Egyptian god Ra and the Greek gods Apollo and Helios were all sun gods, patrons of philosophy and culture. We can also see a connection between the children and the Cabiri, who played an important part in the mysteries of Samothrace. They were assigned the task of keeping the unknown forces of the human spirit in reserve. During the festival held annually in their honor in Lemnos, all the fires were extinguished and new fire was brought from Apollo's temple in Delos. Symbol of rational, linear, Apollonian consciousness for the last 3000 years, the sun is nevertheless one of the cards that has been depicted in the widest range of variations. In the Visconti-Sforza deck, it is a wingless cherub dancing on a cloud holding aloft the severed, blood-colored head of the father, and in the Rider-Waite deck, it is the blond child riding a white horse. In the Gringonneur deck, on the other hand, it is the spinning woman, representing perhaps Clotho, one of the fates. Most of the other decks (Oswald Wirth, Marseilles) depict two children, two boys or a boy and a girl, an image that seems to foretell a coming *coniunctio*. Finally, one cannot help but wonder what compensatory image has been carried in the collective unconscious to counterbalance the deadly effects of the sun as represented by the scorpion of the Mantegna deck. At the present time we are faced with the results of Apollonian scientific consciousness: the devastation is experienced throughout the world in the destruction of our environment.

XX
JUDGEMENT
ר

The letter *resh* means gratitude, the human head, opposition of forces, disruption and regeneration through movement. It also means vegetative life, harmony as feminine principle, the spirit becoming visible in forms. *Resh* begins the Hebrew words *ra* (meaning wicked), and *rasha* (meaning evil), and also the name of God, *rahum* (meaning the merciful). It represents the possibility of renewal of the individual through comprehension of symbols; the ego can now establish a connection with the archetypal layer of the psyche. Card XX links punishment with transformation and purification, from devouring greed to cleansing repentance, warmth of heart, and balance.

The ultimate separation finds its expression in the Last Judgement. An angel, symbol of life-giving breath, announces the last hour by blowing its horn, whereby light separates from dark and lightness separates from heaviness. The angel is surrounded by an aura that seems in some decks to be formed by two intertwined pentagrams that emphasize the situation preceding the separation and sentencing. The moment the horn sounds, the pentagrams fall apart, good rises, and evil descends. The four modalities of five (i.e., the *quaternio*, symbol of totality, and the number of primordial man, the Anthropos) yield twenty, thereby preparing for further development. In many cultures the old limit of counting numbers was the number 20 (fingers and toes add up to this number). The Maya assigned their sun god the number 20. In Judeo-Christian religion, the number 20 represents the Ten Commandments realized into belief and action. Seen as $5 \times 4 = 20$, it refers to the five books of Moses and the four gospels or the four levels of consciousness (magical, mythical, logical, and integrative) in the evolution of humankind (5). Twenty, the number of this card, can also be seen as 10 + 10, symbols of individual and universal cycles. Individual consciousness unites with collective consciousness.

The unfathomable and undifferentiated (card 0) is active in the Judgement through natural wisdom (card II, the High Priestess), whereas the Magician (card I) executes purpose through the Wheel of Fortune (card X). In arcanum X the verdict is revealed as the inscrutable decision of fate, whereas in arcanum XX the individual recognizes its lawfulness. The High Priestess, Justice (card VIII), and Judgement are three different aspects of human knowledge about the eternal (card 0); together they bring to completion the *opus magnus*, the transformation of the mortal in the immortal.

THEMES, ASSOCIATIONS, CORRESPONDENCES

The present instant, realization, decision are the expression of the Judgement. This card connotes transition between one level of existence and another. It means versatility and indicates the relativity and equality of good and evil.

The ideogram for this card

Astrological amplification: King of the Underworld and of its unlimited treasures, possessing the cap of invisibility, Pluto is the monarch of those who have passed from our realm. He is ruler over death and resurrection, the most profound transformation that a person can go through. The gate through which one passes in order to reach Pluto's kingdom is said to induce the distillation of the essence of experience; the limited ego is evaporated, and the final reunion with the Creator is made possible. The great energy of Pluto comes from a transcendental source and manifests in the tension between opposites. He therefore symbolizes a kind of power that can be used creatively only when spiritual evolution and healing have occurred. Pluto is also said to be able to purge karmic residue, giving the individual a heightened perspective on life experience and a detachment potentially growing into wisdom. This energy can help one gain the courage to face one's deepest desires and transmute them through commitment to the work of transformation. Thus, Pluto represents spiritual rebirth.

Cabalistic amplification: The Judgement represents an image of the Work of Unification. Indeed, we find:

> Therefore was the Tree of Life sown in the earth, that what was accursed might obtain blessing and that the dead might be set free (von Franz, *Aurora Consurgens*, p. 368, n. 31).

Elsewhere von Franz brings a clear image of integration connected with resurrection:

> Wake up from Hades, stand up from the grave and come forth from the darkness. . . . The Medicine of life has entered into you. And the spirit rejoices again to dwell in the body, and the soul too, loves it (von Franz, *Aurora Consurgens*, p. 32).

Alchemical amplification: The alchemists sought transformation and discovered it in the transmutation of chemical substance. Some additionally were able to know:

> "It is my own transformation—not a personal transformation, but the transformation of what is mortal in me into what is immortal. It shakes off the mortal husk that I am and awakens to a life of its own; it mounts the sunbarge and may take me with it" (Jung, CW 9/1, ¶ 238).

In a note to this paragraph, Jung points out that the stone and its resurrection are represented as the resurrection of the *homo philosophicus*, the Second Adam.

The alchemists found themselves in the role of redeemers whose work was a continuation of the divine work of redemption, not "a precautionary measure calculated to guard against possible damnation at the Last Judgement" (Jung, CW 12, ¶ 436, n. 40). Also, Jung understood the work of the alchemist as being one in which:

> ". . . God will . . . take way [human] imperfection; then will that thing be strengthened and improved, as after the resurrection a man becomes stronger and younger than he was in this world. . . . Thus the philosophers have beheld the Last Judgement in this art, namely the germination and birth of this stone, . . . for on that day

the soul to be beatified unites with its former body through the mediation of the spirit, to eternal glory" (Rhazes, quoted in CW 13, ¶ 392).

Indeed, in his wanderings among the mazes of his psychic landscape, the alchemist came upon an inner partner, a relationship that seems like

> . . . a hidden springtime, when the green seed sprouts from the barren earth, holding out the promise of future harvests. It is the alchemical *benedicta viriditas*, the blessed greenness, signifying on the one hand the "leprosy of metals" (verdigris), but on the other the secret immanence of the divine spirit of life in all things (Jung, CW 14, ¶ 263).

Green is thus a color assigned to transformation and resurrection; it was also assigned by some to the Holy Ghost (Jung, CW 12, ¶ 319). According to Jung, "It is rust alone that gives the coin its worth" (CW 12, ¶ 209), a kind of alchemical quip that points out once more that there is no light without shadow and no psychic wholeness without imperfection.

> To round itself out, life calls not for perfection but for completeness; and for this the "thorn in the flesh" is needed, the suffering of defects without which there is no progress and no ascent. . . . The unconscious is always the fly in the ointment, the skeleton in the cupboard of perfection, the painful lie given to all idealistic pronouncements, the earthliness that clings to our human nature and sadly clouds the crystal clarity we long for. In the alchemical view rust, like verdigris, is the metal's sickness. But at the same time this leprosy is the *vera prima materia*, the basis for the preparation of the philosophical gold (Jung, CW 12, ¶ 207-208).

Thus, the birth of the alchemical stone could be interpreted as a resurrection, not merely the birth of the Self and, at the same time, the rebirth of a new ego-consciousness, for

> . . . the archetype of the Self, as such, is presumably "eternal"—only the archetypal image which represents it in

the psyche "dies" and changes in accordance with the changes in individual consciousness (von Franz, *Aurora Consurgens*, p 251).

Psychological interpretation: Resurrection means reestablishment of human existence after the death of an inner aspect. Change, transformation of one's being, transmutation to a higher level of aspects of ourselves that had for a long time remained stuck in the concrete and the material is occurring, mediated by an emerging awareness of and a connection to the "*corpus glorificationis, the subtle body in the state of incorruptibility*" (Jung, CW 9/1 ¶ 202). Jung points out:

> In Chinese alchemy [a] state . . . called the "Diamond Body" correspond[s] to the *corpus incorruptibile* of medieval alchemy, . . . the incorruptible body of resurrection. This [depicts] . . . the union of all opposites, and is embedded between *yang* and *yin*, heaven and earth; the state of everlasting balance and immutable duration. [Psychologically this expresses] . . . a shifting of the . . . centre of personality from the personal ego to the impersonal non-ego, which is now experienced as the real "Ground" of the personality (CW 9/1, ¶ 637-638).

Furthermore,

> . . .we can easily understand the central importance of the resurrection idea: we are not completely subjected to the powers of annihilation because our psychic totality reaches beyond the barrier of space and time. Through the progressive integration of the unconscious we have a reasonable chance to make experiences of an archetypal nature providing us with the feeling of continuity before and after our existence. The better we understand the archetype, the more we participate in its life and the more we realize its eternity or timelessness (Jung, CW 18, ¶ 1572).

Jungian interpretation: For Jung, the Last Judgement represents the possibility of resurrection through the spirit (CW 13, ¶ 392). He points out that

... on the day when the world comes to an end, or psychologically speaking, when individual consciousness is extinguished in the waters of darkness, that is to say when a *subjective* end of the world is experienced ... consciousness sinks back into the darkness from which it originally emerged. ... [O]n that day (the day of the Last Judgement) the light returns to eternal light and the darkness to eternal darkness. The opposites are separated and a timeless state of permanence sets in, which, because of the absolute separation of the opposites, is nevertheless one of supreme tension and therefore corresponds to the improbable initial state (CW 9/1, ¶ 256-257).

However, individuation is achieved through integration of the opposites and by activation of the ego-Self axis. This is established not only by relativizing the ego but also by developing a caring and merciful attitude toward oneself. Indeed, to accept oneself as one is may sound

... very simple, but simple things are always the most difficult. In actual life it requires the greatest art to be simple, and so acceptance of oneself is the essence of the moral problem and the acid test of one's whole outlook on life. That I feed the beggar, that I forgive an insult, that I love my enemy in the name of Christ—all these are undoubtedly great virtues. What I do unto the least of my brethren, that I do unto Christ. But what if I should discover that the least amongst them all, the poorest of all beggars, the most impudent of all offenders, yea the very fiend himself—that these are within me, and that I myself stand in need of the alms of my own kindness, that I myself am the enemy who must be loved—what then? Then, as a rule, the whole truth of Christianity is reversed: there is then no more talk of love and long suffering; we ... condemn and rage against ourselves ... we deny ever having met this least among the lowly in ourselves, and had it been God himself who drew near to us in this despicable form, we should have denied him a thousand times before a single cock had crowed (Jung, CW 11, ¶ 520).

To see where one has been hurt and to recognize how, because one has been wounded one has inflicted pain on others, and finally to see that this endless chain of being hurt and hurting can be stopped through awareness of and willingness to accept and integrate both sides, this is forgiveness and redemption. This is the Last Judgment.

> "O blessed nature, blessed are thy works, for that thou makest the imperfect to be perfect through the true putrefaction, which is dark and black. Afterwards thou makest new and multitudinous things to grow, causing with thy verdure the many colours to appear" (from the *Rosarium philosophorum*, quoted in Jung, CW 16, ¶ 479).

SYMBOLIC LANGUAGE OF THE IMAGE

The angel, representing the Self, is enshrouded by clouds because the true nature of things is veiled by their appearance. It may also represent the archangel Michael, leader of celestial hosts, winner of the battle against evil spirits, guide of souls, spiritual potential of humankind; or it may represent the archangel Gabriel proclaiming the divine message. The sun sign on its forehead signifies the spirit, which "bloweth where it listeth." The angel bears the mysterious elixir on his head and, by his relationship to the meridian, makes it clear that he is a kind of solar genius or messenger of the sun who brings "illumination," that is, an enhancement and expansion of consciousness (Jung, CW 13, ¶ 107). As bright as it may be, the light of the sun allows us to see only superficial aspects. The true essence of things can be perceived solely through interiorization and discrimination.

The cross on the square banner points to this discrimination grounded in measured judgment. It means reconciliation of opposites in a new unity. It also alludes to actualization and to the four-dimensional square stone of the wise.

> The idea of the cross points beyond the simple antithesis
> to a double antithesis, i.e., to a quaternio. To the mind
> of the alchemist this meant primarily the intercrossing
> elements, [the lapis, primordial man, the God within
> that] represents and suffers the discord of the elements,
> and at the same time brings about the union of the Four
> and . . . is identical with the product of that union (Jung,
> CW 14, ¶ 607).

The horn means vibration, movement, penetration into interstitial spaces. It evokes the experience of being immersed in music and in deeply felt emotion; it evokes consonance of existence and time, of development and regression. The spiritual strength of human beings helps them to escape the grave of the ego complex, to come to terms with evil, and to integrate the shadow.

The twelve rays represent the twelve signs of the zodiac, the elapsing year. The twelve fire tongues in the Wirth deck inspire the heroic spirit to generous gestures, the sensitive to self-sacrificing service, and give to the spiritual leader the capacity to transmit wisdom. The flames are white, blue, red, and gold, colors that bring to mind the four elements. The tongues also remind us of the Holy Ghost, the Comforter. In some old decks, instead of an angel, one sees a swooping swan, another symbol for the Holy Ghost, the divine spirit, the resurrection.

The man and woman represent newly resurrected humankind, wise human reason, religious uplift, the knowledge of the heart, the unconscious. The child is their heir, receiving the carryover from the past: in the child the previously fragmented truth reveals itself shining in its new wholeness.

> "God breathed into created things . . . a certain germi-
> nation of greenness, by which all things should multi-
> ply. . . . They called all things green, for to be green
> means to grow. . . . Therefore this virtue of generation
> and the preservation of things might be called the Soul of
> the World" (Mylius, quoted in Jung, CW 14, ¶ 623).

To awaken means to come face to face with God's light, to find a new center in the personality that has integrated ambivalence. It signifies seeing and hearing the primordial essence in its own dimension, transcending time and space, the polar opposites, and the three worlds. Here the resurrected must be God's witnesses, and this witnessing is at the same time the sentencing they must pass on themselves. The resurrected are the twice born, returned from the realm of the Mothers, released from rigid self-righteousness, opening the spirit to that which had been previously unconscious. Theirs is the resurrection of the forgotten past, the recovery of insights believed lost but preserved in collective consciousness, the revitalization of the inferior function. They undergo profound character change: what was obstacle is now help, sensitivity becomes the basis for action, and reality becomes the grounding of spiritual uplift.

The green sarcophagi signify boats on the primordial sea, the water of life; they bring to mind cards VIII (Justice), IX (the Hermit), and X (the Wheel of Fortune), the beginning and the end of a road. They also evoke the buried seed that becomes green again, transformation.

> It is the hope . . . that one day, at "vespertime," probably in the evening of life, she will become like Noah's dove, which, with the olive leaf in its beak, announced the end of the flood and appeared as the sign of God's reconciliation with the children of men (Jung, CW 14, ¶ 625).

While the Lover(s) (card VI) could only make a feeling choice between two alternatives, the Charioteer (card VII) has a wider range of conscious possibilities. He can utilize the abilities and the means acquired thus far; he can also run away. Justice (card VIII) requires an objective stand uninfluenced by the ego; it demands insight into the equal value of the opposites. Once acceptance, indicated by the Hermit (card IX), is reached, the Wheel of Fortune (card X) starts to turn upward. If the individual has not achieved relativization of the ego, he is again tested (the Hanged Man, card XII). Here he must sacrifice the ego to the Self and surrender to the protection that the Self promises. If this does not succeed, he may sink into a shadowlike existence or be reborn (card XIII). Should he now become inflated, the Tower of Destruction (card XVI) disrupts his work and forces him to reassess reality. By the light of the Moon (card XVIII), he is assigned new duties at a higher level; he may fall into the deep depression he had thus far avoided, afraid he would not be able to endure it. Catastrophes open the door to what had remained unreachable until now. With the help of spirit and enlightened consciousness (card XIX), he is able to face the truth (Judgement, card XX).

However, merely penetrating the darkness or plunging into the abyss and falling apart is not necessarily followed by transformation and redemption. Grace is not a given, not an assured thing. One needs the trumpet call of the Self, a transpersonal message, to awaken slumbering positive archetypal energies. One must also endure patiently and perseveringly the real suffering of the sacrifice demanded of us, to which we must now consent. Accepting what happened to us in the past and what we irretrievably, missed so far can open the door to something totally new, a great mystery beyond the realm of our past or present experience.

The letter *tau* means unity, quiver of arrows, receptacle of all thoughts, words, and works. The three flames that emanate from *Ain* give life to the world: the universal substance reveals itself in forms. In its negative sense *tau* means offense against the spirit. The number 21 can be given different interpretations. The central figure may represent the perfected human being, assigned the number 5, the mandorla surrounding it is the ultimate unity, and the four apocalyptic figures in the four corners represent the world elements that honor it. We may take the images in the corners not as elements but as representations of the four temperaments or qualities of human personality, and we may take the center as the image of wholeness toward which they strive: thus $(5 \times 4) + 1 = 21$.

The number 21 can also be conceived as the sum of the numbers 0 through 6 because they comprise all the concepts that this card illustrates. These different interpretations all point to reunion of the trinity in unity, the synthesis of the three roads to redemption (3×7), the end stage of the developmental process.

Card XXI means awakening from the bind of erroneous concepts and reaching enlightenment whereby one is capable of perceiving that the absolute and the relative are both the same and different.

THEMES, ASSOCIATIONS, CORRESPONDENCES

The World represents cosmic consciousness. This image connotes enlightenment, joy, the ability to see eternal meaning beyond concrete reality. It signifies knowledge animated by enthusiasm, and it indicates obedience graced by joyous acceptance.

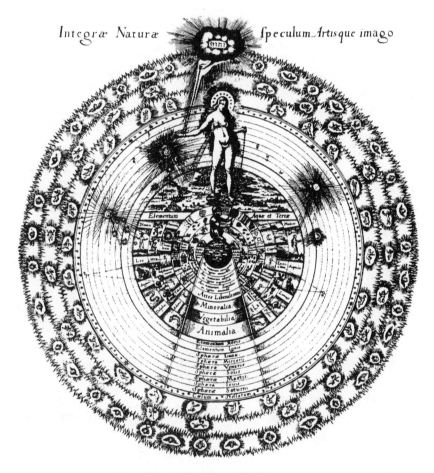

Figure 65. The Wisdom of God as *Anima Mundi,* guide of humankind, herself guided by God. (From Fludd: *Utriusque cosmi,* 1617.).

The ideogram for this card is

Astrological amplification: The sign of Pisces represents that phase of individual development in which one can achieve distancing from worldly attachments and where devotion to greater truth enables one to become a channel for a more comprehensive whole. Spiritually, Pisces is concerned with dissolving attachment without losing contact with kindness and compassion. In Greek mythology, Pisces is connected with that element in the cosmos that is represented as a female being. When the Olympians fled the wrath of Typhon, Venus and her son, Cupid, became fishes in order to escape him (Sucher, 1982, p. 101). In Pisces the individual has approached the spiritual goal after a long and painful road. Now Self and cosmos can be integrated and spiritual redemption can thus be achieved. As always the female element is an expression of soul forces that mediate between the individual and God (see figure 65) which shows *anima mundi*, guide of humankind, represented by a monkey, herself guided by God, hidden in the cloud overhead. The same long-haired, naked woman is represented in figures 66 and 67 (pages 306 and 307) this time surrounded by an oval-shaped aura, a mandora identical to the one that surrounds the feminine figure of card XXI. Although, according to Jung, the reddening (the alchemical *opus ad rubeum*) takes place in Libra, the second house of Venus (CW 14, ¶ 415), I have chosen to assign card XXI to Pisces because of mythological image of Venus and Cupid, mentioned earlier.

Cabalistic amplification: The non-sephira *Daat*, or spiritual knowledge, represents the capacity to perceive what is not perceptible to the senses by means of the imagination. *Daat* is a door between worlds through which consciousness can come down or go up (Halevi, *Work of the Kabbalist*, pp. 48-49). Here, on the threshold to the upper worlds, one can hear the Sacred Voice instructing the Self. That mysterious position, at which psyche, spirit, and the Divine can touch, has now been reached.

Alchemical amplification: The *opus magnus* is completed. The supracelestial spirit of the waters, united with the light, is aptly called the world soul, *anima mundi*. This is connected to the Holy Spirit, who was present at the creation and played the role of pro-creator, impregnating the waters with the seed of life. The end of the alchemical *opus* is assigned a multiplicity of images and terms: red tincture, quintessence, etc. An image that connects directly with that of astrology can be found in a manuscript quoted by Jung:

> "That noble whore Venus is clothed and enveloped in abounding colour." This colour "has a reddish appear-ance." . . . A variant says: "That precious substance is a

Figure 66. The Triumph of Venus (School of Verona, 15th century reproduced from Neumann, *The Great Mother*, p. 62.).

Venus of the ancients, the hermaphrodite, who has two sexes." . . . "In our chemistry there is Venus and Cupid. For Psyche is the female, Cupid the male, who is held to be the dragon" (CW 14, ¶ 415).

The red blood of this dragon was the tincture and:

> . . . the soul, which are extracted from the *prima materia* and bring "dead" bodies to life (CW 14, ¶ 420).

The growing redness (*rubedo*) that follows *albedo* denotes an increase in warmth and light coming from the sun, consciousness.

Figure 67. Anima Mundi, from *Quinta essentia*, 1574.

This corresponds to the accrued participation of consciousness, which now begins to interact with the contents of the unconscious. At first this process of integration is

> . . . a "fiery" conflict, but gradually it leads over to the "melting" or synthesis of the opposites. The alchemists termed this the *rubedo*, in which the marriage of the red man and the white woman, Sol and Luna, is consummated (Jung, CW 14, ¶ 307).

Elsewhere Jung quotes:

> "I found a certain stone, red, shining, transparent, and brilliant, and in it I saw all the forms of the elements and also their contraries." . . . For heaven, gold, and carbuncle are synonyms for the *rubedo*. . . . Ruby or carbuncle is the name for the *corpus glorificatum*. . . . [T]he bed-chamber of Venus is lit by carbuncles (CW 9/1, ¶ 580, n. 127).

So the goal is sometimes the red tincture, *aqua permanens*, sometimes the philosopher's stone, which as a hermaphrodite, contains both sexes, or again it is the panacea, *aurum potabile*, or *elixir vitae*, the philosophical gold, etc. The conceptions of the goal are as varied as are the stages of reaching it. However,

> . . . one cannot know the procedure unless it be a gift of God, or through instruction of a most experienced Master: and the source of it all is the Divine Will. . . . [T]he production of the stone transcends reason and . . . only a supernatural and divine knowledge knows the exact time for the birth of the stone. This means that God alone knows the *prima materia* (Jung, CW 12, ¶ 356).

The birth of the lapis was regarded by the alchemists as a gift of the Holy Ghost or of the *Sapientia Dei* (Jung, CW 14, ¶ 443). For von Franz, *Sapientia Dei* is a feminine hypostasis of the Divine, the sum of archetypal images in the mind of God. Considered the archetypal model world after whose likeness this sensible world was made, her image was interchangeably used with that of Wisdom, *anima mundi*, or Holy Jerusalem.

"Then the glory of the just shall appear like unto the sun in the kingdom of their father when the walls of Jerusalem are wholly complete and the whole number of the elect is filled up, and she shall appear glorious and happy. . ." (von Franz, *Aurora Consurgens*, p. 370).

Not surprisingly, therefore, one finds among the images used for this card, as in the Visconti-Sforza deck, two young boys holding a sphere in which the holy city is depicted.

Psychological interpretation: The World represents fulfillment, completion, reaching the goal, arrival at the central position where one can participate joyously in the dance of life within the equilibrium of the mature psyche and psychic wholeness. The image represents end and beginning, culmination of the search and seed of fresh endeavor. Contemplating this image, one may imagine the veil of space-time as parting to reveal a personification of the ground of being. An invocation proper to such an epiphany would be: "May I come, by this goddess, to the knowledge of my own radiant truth enclosed in the coils of my own temporal life" (Campbell, 1974, p. 34).

 Psychologically, card XXI represents the Self as highest spiritual unity that remains unchanged throughout all incarnations, the kernel of the individual. Its world can be intuited but not recognized.

Jungian interpretation: In the center of card XXI we see an ellipse, which like the shell of an almond, is meant to protect the kernel until it is ripe and can be released. We perceive an aura in almond shape, a mandorla meant to contain and, at the same time, to release something essential and more precious than itself. Rilke's poem seems to evoke it:

BUDDHA IN DER GLORIE

Mitte aller Mitten, Kern der Kerne,
Mandel, die sich einschliesst und versüsst.
dieses alles bis an alle Sterne
ist dein Fruchtfleisch: Sei gegrüsst.

Sieh, du fühlst, wie nichts mehr an dir hängt:
im Unendlichen ist deine Schale,

und dort steht der starke Saft und drängt.
Und von aussen hilft ihm ein Gestrahle,

denn ganz oben werden deine Sonnen
voll und glühend umgedreht.
Doch in der ist schon begonnen,
was die Sonnen übersteht.

◇ ◇ ◇

The core of every core, the kernel of every kernel,
an almond! held in itself, deepening in sweetness:
all of this, everything, right up to the stars,
is the meat around your stone. Accept my bow.

Oh, yes, you feel it, how the weights on you are gone!
Your husk has reached into what has no end,
there the strong sap works and fills you.
And from beyond a gloriole descends

to help, for high above your head your suns,
full and fulgurating, turn.
And yet, already in you is begun
something that will live longer than the suns.*

The mandorla is mother's mouth; it is a mystical diagram, an
abstract image, an ancient shape for meditation, serving self-discovery and Self-revelation, which in Buddhism are one and the
same. Wherever mandorlas are seen—above the entrance portal of
medieval churches, on the covers or title pages of ancient holy
books—it always seems that something is beginning, is opening,
is coming.

After the long journey through the second half of the major
arcana, in which the ego had to be defeated again and again and
was forced to give up its old ingrained behavioral patterns, the
true Self may now emerge. As above, so below; as inside, so out-

---

* The first six lines and the last line of *Buddha in der Glorie* are from the translation by
Robert Bly in *Selected Poems by Rainer Maria Rilke*, N. Y.: Harper-Colophon Books, 1981, p.
151. Lines seven through eleven are from the translation by C. F. MacIntyre in *Rilke, Selected
Poems*, Berkeley: Univ. of California Press, 1956, p. 127.

side. The new stance is one that Tillich has named "the courage to be rooted in God," the God that appears after God has disappeared in the fear and anxiety of doubt. It is belief, faith that is able to transcend meaninglessness by accepting it. The mandorla can bring us to self-discovery and discovery of faith, to an almond shell that contains its own kernel.

> [T]he goal of the opus was to deliver *anima mundi*, the world creating spirit of God, from the chains of Physis (Jung, CW 13, ¶ 404).

In our card, the *anima mundi* dances against a blue background, the blue of the sky, and the blue of faith. She is a constant reminder that the courage to accept the human condition frees and that this freedom is obtained by connecting with the inner kernel of the Divine planted in each of us.

SYMBOLIC LANGUAGE OF THE IMAGE

Light and weightless, a young woman dances, creating a vortex movement that begets the world. Her arms and head form a triangle, while her feet and lower legs suggest a square. This leg position, also encountered in card IV (the Emperor) and reversed in card XII (the Hanged Man), evokes the symbol for sulphur ⚵, the central fire of the alchemists, which burns immovable and by which all movement is sustained.

The two staffs in her hands symbolize integration and disintegration; both end in spheres: one blue, one red. The red sphere captures the fiery energies and returns them to matter under the direction of the blue, receptive sphere. The dancing figure can also be seen as a hermaphrodite, as a reconstitution of divine unity, man and woman in the material world. She signifies harmony, the stillness of the earth as yellow kernel, an image mirroring the pathways of the stars and planets.

In the dance of the dimensionless point, everything is present and concomitant and simultaneous at all times—knowing and not knowing, movement and stillness, beginning and end. The constant unfolding of the creative energy, the world soul, is symbolized by the swastika, which also depicts the movement on the vault of heaven, total recognition, movement as generator of life. The vital force is surrounded by a mandorla, an elliptically shaped wreath or garland that is at the same time its limitation and its concentration. (See figure 68.) A mandorla is that almond-shaped space created in the center of two partially overlapping circles.

> This symbol signifies nothing less than the overlap of opposites . . .[and] is described as the overlap of heaven and earth. There is not one of us who is not torn by the competing demands of heaven and earth; the mandorla instructs how to engage in reconciliation (Johnson, 1991, p. 99).

The mandorla has a wonderfully healing and encouraging function. When we are tired or discouraged or so battered by life that we can no longer live in the tension of the opposites, we are then in need of the mandorla to help us transcend the conflict by giving us a spiritual perspective.

> The mandorla binds together that which was torn apart and made unwhole—unholy. . . . It is the place of poetry.

Figure 68. The Great Goddess with swastika, one from Troy, one seventh-century Boetian (Neumann, *The Great Mother*, figure 20 and plate 134).

> . . . Great poetry. . . unites the beauty and the terror of
> existence. It has the ability . . . to remind us that there
> are links between the things that we have always
> thought of as opposites (Johnson, 1991, pp. 102-103).

The ellipse has two foci, suggesting a synthesis of two points of
view in a dynamic form. It depicts the mystery of the identity
of the One with itself in all its unfoldings and infoldings. It suggests the cyclic movement of light, the interaction between heaven
and earth, joy, peace, accomplishment, enlightenment. We are
shown here the Work and its completed task. The wreath also
represents the flow and the flame of life.

The aim of the process of individuation is timeless unity, the
return to the lost paradise, the heavenly Jerusalem (the central
image in the Visconti-Sforza deck), the temple precinct, the sanc-
tuary that protects against falling back into ambivalence.

The snake of paradise has changed into a veil floating around
the dancer. This is the veil of the High Priestess (card II). The void
becomes manifestation, but the essence is hidden by the flowing
form, the glowing, iridescent matter. This is the highest layer of
life, paradise.

The two staffs suggest handling the four magic weapons:
willing, knowing, daring, and silence. They are the image of the
polarity of the four elements balancing the double opposition,
involution and evolution, integration of the microcosm into the
macrocosm.

In the four corners, the ancient symbols of bull, lion, eagle,
and angel (the perfected human) correspond to the elements that
the Magician (card I) was about to use in shaping the world. These
four images are schemas of order, differentiating totality and serving as starting points for meditation. They show the cohesion of
four divergent elements:

> bull (earth): stability, endurance, patience, silence;
> lion (fire): incarnation, resurrection, intrepidity, reason;
> eagle (water): emotion, death and regeneration, temerity;
> angel (air): search for truth, coincidence of form and context.

For the alchemists, the *prima materia* was also called the "soul" of
substances. Jung (CW 13, ¶ 173) enumerates its symbolic names:
Adam and the accursed man, the hermaphroditic monster, the

One and the root of itself, the All, and so on. He considers that they all

> ... point to the *anima mundi*, ... the Anthropos and mystic Adam, who is described as a sphere (=wholeness), consisting of four parts (uniting different aspects itself), hermaphroditic (beyond division by sex), and damp (i.e., psychic). This paints a picture of the self, the indescribable totality of man (Jung, CW 13, ¶ 173).

The hermaphrodite is a reconstruction of the totality, the foundation and origin of all personality, the atemporal Self. It is the identity of the individual with the transpersonal, the unity of the fundamental preexisting structure of the universe and of humanity; it is thinking a thought to its end.

Further, Jung adds that the "alchemical retort is therefore equivalent to the *anima mundi*, which according to an old alchemical conception surrounds the cosmos" (CW 13, ¶ 245).

All these images point out that we are at the end of the journey so movingly depicted by Jung in one of his interviews:

> Only the total experience of being can transform this ideal state of the *albedo* into a fully human mode of existence. Blood alone can reanimate a glorious state of consciousness in which . . . the devil no longer has an autonomous existence but rejoins the profound unity of the psyche. Then the *opus magnum* is finished: the human soul is completely integrated (Jung, 1977, p. 228f.)

0
THE FOOL

ש

The letter *shin* means tooth, lap, combination, synthesis. It represents God's kingdom under the fourfold rule of the Tetragrammaton. It is the cross that connects the Tree of Life to the Tree of Knowledge, the completion of all things, the renewed individual.

The Fool is the only unnumbered arcanum. No record exists as to who was the first to number the major arcana, but the fact that the Fool has remained unnumbered complicates the question of its placement in relation to the other twenty-one arcana. As zero, the Fool has been placed before arcanum I, after arcanum XXI. In some authoritative tarots the Fool is placed between Judgement (card XX) and the World (card XXI), but in these same tarots that assign the Fool the number XXI, it is also assigned the number 0. Sadhu has no doubt that the Fool's place is between the twentieth and twenty-first arcanum, so logically the number should be XXI, which according to him, is accepted by those who comply exactly with tradition. It is interesting to note that in the Hebrew alphabet the number of the letter *shin* is 21 and that the letter *tau*, assigned to the arcanum of the World, bears the number 22; this agrees with the position of Papus and Haich—that arcanum XXI is misnumbered and should really be the final card, numbered XXII (Newman, 1983, p. 143).

The images of arcana I through XXI express constant movement and change. They form two concentric rings in which the inner ten represent our spiritual context, the archetypal backdrop placing our ephemeral materiality within the infinite and eternal, and the outer eleven depict a developmental sequence in which each image is constantly transformed into the next. The Fool does not participate. In contrast to the surrounding images, he remains set in eternal youth, passive and poor, without name or shape. He stands motionless in the center, in the hub of the wheel, where immobility within rotation is possible; he looks detachedly at the glittering carousel turning around him. Freed of the fetters of the ego, he has given up all worldly fame; he concerns himself with neither boasting about all the crowns of the emperor nor flaunting all the treasures of the wise. In his wanderings he has encountered all the wonders and horrors of the world; he has learned to know and to forget himself. He has freed himself from all torments and transformations. He does not feel that a foolish animal pulls his threadbare pants down. Although he is almost naked, he no longer desires anything.

Perhaps he has partaken to satiety of the dance of world events and now no longer has any taste for it. He has plunged courageously, or foolishly, into the surf, which has pulled him away from the friendly shelter of family and country, now obsolete. He has become homeless, a mockery to the wise and a nagging worry to those who love him. He has reached the other shore, the *un*knowing, the *un*formed. He has returned home to the void, the zero, the empty circle, ambiguous symbol of ultimate wisdom and/or fulfillment of poorest folly. The beggar's bundle that he carries has holes in it, showing that he knows how to let go; yet it remains filled with the breath of heaven and of life that pervades and animates all things. The name of the card, the Fool, originates in the word *follis*, meaning "bag full of wind." It refers to the limitless realm of the inconceivable as well as to that which does not exist at all, the unreal. The bag also contains seeds from the past that represent the individual's spiritual conquests.

The Fool endures his fate patiently and carries the wanderer's staff, which is also the Hermit's. The line returns on itself and at the same time contains all the letters of the Hebrew alphabet and the array of corresponding figures of the major arcana. The circle, the zero, symbolizes the cosmic egg, bearing in it all germination, a connection to the fulfillment of card XXI, the World. We have now come full circle.

THEMES, ASSOCIATIONS, CORRESPONDENCES

The Fool stands for the undifferentiated and the ten thousand things, the careless wanderings of the individual toward wholeness, spurred on by his dreams, his hopes and fears, and the burden of his past. This card indicates insight into the meaning of existence and the recognition of wholeness as well as misunderstanding of or disregard for universal laws. The Fool points beyond success or failure. Negatively it represents extinction, incomprehension, and spiritual death.

The ideogram for this card is

Astrological amplification: The Fool has been associated with the planets Neptune, Uranus, Pluto, and Venus, and with the zodiacal sign Pisces. Because it is assigned the Hebrew letter *shin*, traditionally related to the element fire, it seems that its affinity must be sought in this direction; however, as the Fool is also a card that indicates a new beginning, I have assigned it Aries, a fire sign and the first sign of the zodiac. Indeed, Aries is the constellation considered the leader of the host of the zodiac; its association with the phoenix in Egyptian mythology suggests the beginning of a new cycle. Aries thus points to inaugurating, initiating, or sponsoring a new spiritual element and is thus associated with creative initiative, beginning new projects, or reactivating stagnating ones by novel impulses (Sucher, 1982, pp. 78-81).

Cabalistic amplification: Having arrived at the lower face of the supernals, conversion in *Daat* takes place and the mystic's Self is transformed, allowing him to enter the Kingdom of Heaven. Here, in place of the Self, where the three lower worlds meet, the Way proper begins.

> This is where Vilon or Veil of day and night is rolled back and forth. In the Palace of the curtain between the natural and supernatural . . . called the Seat of Faith, this Hall opens out from the physical world of *Assiah*, through the psychological World of Formation and into the creative realm of the Spirit. This is the hidden door in the Heart of Hearts. . . . Into this, the first of the Heavens, a natural man can enter, sometimes apparently quite by accident, to gaze in awe at the Heavens above. . . . Only the man of deep devotion and conscious intention can sustain such a vision (Halevi, *The Way of the Kabbalah*, p. 210).

It is from this place of the Creator that all created things emerge, descend, ascend, and reemerge. The act of creation, we are told, occurs in the utterance of the Word, the first of all sounds, the supreme name of God: EHYEH, I AM. This first of the Divine Names originates from beyond *Kether* and is followed by the nine other names of God and their divine qualities. Known as the ten sephirot, they are eternally emanated. Should they cease to be, all the manifest World would vanish. Poised at the edge of the abyss, the Fool seems to say:

> But as for me, if thou wouldst know
> What I was;
> In a word
> I am the Word who did dance all things
> and was not shamed at all.
> 'Twas I who leapt and danced . . . Amen.
>
> —"The Hymn to Jesus,"
> *The Leucian Acts,*
> quoted by Godwin in *Angels*, p. 252

Having made contact with the crown of creation, an evolved human being must now turn back down and impart what has been received. This is vital for the universe, for without everyone's consciousness, parts of existence would remain dark and unknown and the Work of Unification would remain undone. In this labor of love there is no differentiation, even as there is no difference between the Self in one human being and another. "All is one," say the mystics, "and the One is in all" (Halevi, *Work of the Kabbalist*, pp. 189-190).

Alchemical amplification: The same intuition that supports Meister Eckhart's statements, "God is Nothingness," and "When all things were in the midst of silence, then leapt there down into me from on high, from the royal throne, a secret Word" has been central to the conviction of the alchemists that their art is a gift of the Holy Ghost. The Great Work can be done only if God himself, through the Holy Ghost, enters the work of man by divine inspiration and by direct intervention in the miraculous transformation (CW 14, ¶ 445). Even though a divine miracle was the decisive factor, Jung points out that the stone was still concocted artificially, by human hands, and in the retort (CW 14, ¶ 443) this was expressed in the saying: You can't do it alone, but you alone can do it. The questing religious spirit and the projection of unconscious content into matter provided the needed remedy for all "afflic-tions of the soul," and "as was only to be expected . . . though their purses shrank, their soul[s] gained in stature" (Jung, CW 14, ¶ 446). The Fool seems to evoke this complex attitude of the alchemist: awareness of the divine and of the awesome nothing-ness into which he may venture while stepping forward into the future and into fate.

Psychological interpretation: The Fool gives us the sense that the everyday roles we deem so important are transient vanities and inflated illusions. Image of a fringe experience on the edge of chaos, from which not intellect, collective conventions, or even the strongest will, but only faith, trust, and purity of heart can, in the end, pull us through, his easy flexibility emphasizes the rigidities that block our lives. The Fool points out that earthly concerns and ego boundedness are all precarious. Bravely he aban-dons all safety and enters those spaces in which nobody dares to tread, poised in midair between reckless naivete endangering his very existence and the leap of faith innocently achieved. The Fool takes us on a journey through all mythologies. One cannot escape the impression that, here at the end of one road, we can look back and perceive or imagine all journeys ever made. We can see the connection in Quispel's idea:

> All Gnostic systems start in heaven, run their course on earth, and return to heaven. . . . [T]oday, it is psycholog-ical analysis that continues the millenial process of com-ing-to-consciousness, producing the same symbols as did gnosticism, kabbalism, and hermetic philosophy. All these traditions [and the closest parallel to Christian gnosticism is to be found in alchemy] show the same tendency to integrate the figure of the Son of Man into the innermost core of the personality while expanding it to a dimension comparable to the *purusha atman* of Hinduism (Quispel, "Gnosis and Culture," in C. G. *Jung and the Humanities*, pp. 27, 34).

On one hand we are confronted by the

> . . . myth of the ignorant demiurge who imagined he was the highest divinity [which] illustrates the perplexity of the ego when it can no longer hide from itself the

> knowledge that it has been dethroned by a supraordinate authority. The "thousand names" of the *lapis philosophorum* correspond to the innumerable Gnostic designations for the *Anthropos*, which make it quite obvious what is meant: the greater, more comprehensive Man, that indescribable whole consisting of the sum of conscious and unconscious processes (Jung, CW 9/2, ¶ 296).

On the other hand we are faced with this fact:

> For most of us . . . a perspective that takes in the total field of relations is disorienting, if not unbearable. . . . Unless the image of the god-as-self is properly modeled, it can be neither recognized nor understood by that part of the mind that we identify as consciousness. . . . [E]ffective work with models implies a capacity for play and a readiness to forget. "To know God as He is," says Meister Eckhart, "we must be absolutely free from knowledge" (Belmonte, "The Trickster and the Sacred Clown," in *C. G. Jung and the Humanities*, p. 56).

Play and forgetting are the natural domain of the Fool, quintessentially "free of knowledge."

Jungian interpretation: Jung's perspective connects the fool/trickster with the savior and the divine.

> If we consider, for example, the daemonic features exhibited by Yahweh in the Old Testament, we shall find in them not a few reminders of the unpredictable behavior of the trickster, of his senseless orgies of destruction and his self-imposed sufferings, together with the same gradual development into a savior and his simultaneous humanization. It is just this transformation of the meaningless into the meaningful that reveals the trickster's compensatory relation to the "saint" (CW 9/1, ¶ 458).

The individuation process opens the way to a unique creativity in each moment and to a secret center of the personality, the mysterious source of life. This process leads to the realization of spontaneity that makes one unpredictable: others cannot see into the inner sanctum of one's heart from which the unexpected, creative reaction springs. These reactions can only originate in a state of oneness with the Self, because the quality of uniqueness in each moment belongs only to the Self. When one is centered around an unrestrained source of life, one also separates from collective entanglements, outwardly and inwardly distancing oneself from that which is not oneself. This is the state in which one may appear "foolish," but it brings to mind the last of the ten ox-herding pictures of Zen, showing an old man going to market (figure 69). He has a sweet smile on his face.

> [T]he man . . . goes to the market with his pupil and his beggar's bowl, and has even forgotten his *Satori* experience with the gods. That means he does not subjectively feel unique, but, the story adds, the cherry tree blossoms as he goes by and that is something you would not guess when an old fellow with a fat belly goes to the market with a rather insipid smile. Uniqueness springs from him as a creative act, but it is not intentionally on his mind. He does not feel unique; he *is* unique (von Franz, *Alchemy*, p. 160).

Figure 69. The Old Man going to market. (From Powell, *The Tao of Symbols*, p. 152).

In the writings of other Jungians (Hazard, Whitney, Hinton), the Fool appears as mediator between uniqueness and limitation and depicts the limitlessness of infinite possibility in the bewildering, overwhelming grandeur of the sacred cosmic energy of which we are a part. In "The Trickster and the Sacred Clown," Belmonte writes:

> If the original "psychologems" are neglected—if the process of self-constitution in the language of myth is blocked—the equilibrium of the person-in-society is disrupted and the contents of desire are experienced as threatening and alien. . . . [W]hen the mind's ordering eye is blinded and its mythic voice muffled, pathology will result. . . .[F]or Jung archetypal imagery allows the mind to view itself as a balanced totality. . . of contending but mutually interdependent processes. . . .
>
> Cultures of the voice and the book respectively bear a very different relationship to the realm of the invisible and the unseen. They take notice of different worlds and generate opposed notions of what is "obvious". . . .
>
> The clown himself might be a metaphysician . . . who lays the foundation of his culture's forward movement into an uncertain future. . . .
>
> The use of reversal and . . . analogic coding are fundamental to the mythic mentality. . . . Myth talk is doubletalk to the literal mind. . . .[T]he myth symbol always partakes of this duality. . . .Jung's [Trickster] archetype is embedded in a drama of ecstasy and awareness. . . .
>
> "No psychic value," Jung wrote, "can disappear without being replaced by another of equivalent intensity." If we banish Hermes the *psychopompos*, the escort of souls to Charon, he returns as a Hound of Hell . . . .
>
> Through catharsis [mythical language's] tragic poetry yields inner harmony to the soul. . . . All myth has a lamentative, grieving, as well as a laughing aspect [both represented in the image of the Fool, who] like grief and laughter, is restorative. . . .

[K]nowledge . . . is created when the biologically grounded mind achieves a means of coding the unspeakable (*C.G. Jung and the Humanities*, pp. 50, 53, 51, 55, 56, 49, 57).

If the archetype is a link or rebinding (*religio*) of the present with the past, we may paradoxically conceive that, by reconnecting past and present, we could achieve a new perspective allowing us to outgrow our past. This indispensable shift to healing may be mediated by the Fool, who could help us accept past shame and vulnerability. If we can achieve recognition of the Fool as a personification of the unacceptable side of our being, our frightful shuddering is transformed into carnival laughter and our stalled pilgrimage toward self-acceptance, self-knowledge, and Self-activation can proceed.

Finally, among the Winnebago Indians, the chief-who-would-be-trickster breaks the most sacred taboos and sheds the raiments of his worldly station before his metamorphosis into an infantile wanderer, that is, a Fool.

SYMBOLIC LANGUAGE OF THE IMAGE

Before considering the actual symbols of the card, we know that it must express a certain phase of the cosmic beginning. The name of the card and its number, 0, with its meaning of the Unmanifest, the *Ain Sof* of the cabala, the *enso* of Zen Buddhism, or the "One about which nothing can be said" of the Hindu philosophies, indicate that we are stepping out of the ordinary way of thinking. The alchemical element air, present in this card, expresses the first breath, *pneuma*, an outpouring of the spirit, a preparation. Indeed, the great white sun pictured in the upper right corner of the card in certain decks contains all the colors of the spectrum, encompassing all potential wavelengths before analysis and after synthesis.

The Fool, pictured as an eternal youth, is about to step off a high cliff down into the abyss. He is the *puer aeternus*, a force constantly equal to itself and in perpetual motion. His white undergarment means innocence, purity, freedom from covetousness, wisdom. The motley tunic indicates ignorance, deception, self-indulgence, and egocentricity. His belt represents the powerful and permanent circular movement of the sky, the completed circle that makes a day. The goal of his journey is nowhere and everywhere. Without knowing where the road leads, enmeshed in his fantasies, his hopes and fears, the Fool (like humankind) dances on the edge of the abyss, careless and aimless. He pays no attention to the path on which he travels, and thorns and thistles stab and scratch him until he bleeds. The road is his home; rarely is there an inn to welcome the pennyless. The Fool carries his assigned burden patiently. Like a newborn infant, he has no inkling of the battles and defeats that lie ahead, nor has he any knowledge about his possibilities. His bundle contains trifles and junk: illusions, fantasies, successes, ideas that can be potentially dangerous when they disregard concrete reality; however, it also contains the tools that he needs to live his life.

When tired, the Fool leans on the rugged branch that he uses as a wanderer's staff. At night this aids his groping progress; it helps him discover hidden obstacles, and when attacked, it can serve as a weapon.

The dog is the faithful companion that tries to hold his master back from the fathomless abyss. When the Fool abandons the beaten track, the dog spots the right path and urges him to keep to the road. However, if it finds a bone, its master is forced to stop, and if it uncovers the scent of some wild animal, it will drag our Fool along in hapless pursuit. At night the dog is its master's guardian, defending his sleep—but it may also disturb that sleep by baying at the moon. The wanderer can teach the biddable dog tricks that could bring joy to the children in the marketplace or could bring money when performed at a county fair.

The sun is the balanced center of all consciousness, the moving spirit in all animated things. It enlightens the meaning of life and shows the importance of all action, independent of its practical momentary function within or beyond time.

The red tulip at his feet, the same that was budding for the Magician (card I) and blooming for the Emperor (card IV), is here wilted, as it was in card XIV (Temperance), indicating that not in materiality but in pure contemplation of the divine is perpetual essence to be found.

The Fool submits to no rule. He passes by, leaves all roads behind, and trusts the light, the vital energy of individuality. He wanders along the abyss like a fish swims in water. In his ramblings he has or has not achieved enlightenment. Yet the legend of the "Wandering Jew," eternally accursed, is here changed into a positive image. The Fool, stopping nowhere, is constantly hopeful, perpetually transforming. It is in nothingness that the hope for things to come emerges.

In Japanese Zen the empty circle *enso*, floating free in space (figure 70) is the symbol of utmost transparency and fulfillment. For the mystics (whether Eastern, Christian, or Hebrew), this void is the inalterable precondition for the experience of transcendence. In the Hassidic mystical tradition, the void is one of God's names—God himself in his most hidden aspect.

The Fool seems to guide us toward a place alternatively described as enlightenment, which is somehow connected with the void. Jung quotes from the text of the *Bardo Thodol*:

> Thine own intellect, which is now voidness, yet not to be regarded as of the voidness of nothingness, but as being the intellect itself, unobstructed, shining, thrilling,

Figure 70. Enso from Addiss, *The Art of Zen*, p. 135.

and blissful, is the very consciousness, the All-good Buddha (CW 11, ¶ 837).

Thine own consciousness, shining, void, and inseparable from the Great Body of Radiance, hath no birth, nor death, and is the Immutable Light . . . (CW 11, ¶ 839).

For Jung the soul is the light of the godhead and the godhead is the soul, a paradox that the East can sustain, but one that is difficult for us in the West (CW 11, ¶ 840). However, he continues (¶ 884 ff.), one cannot escape the impression that enlightenment is a natural occurrence, which is a simple concept, yet attempts to explain it provoke the greatest confusion. Nevertheless, one can venture to assert that enlightenment implies both insight into the nature of self and emancipation from illusion concerning self. It may thus express a change of consciousness as a result of the supersession of the ego by the Self. Quoting from the *Theologia Germanica*, Jung notes:

In whatsoever creature the Perfect shall be known, therein creature-nature, created state, I-hood, selfhood, and the like must all be given up and done away.

Then the man says: "Behold! I, poor fool that I was, thought it was I, but behold! it is, and was, of a truth, God!" (CW 11, ¶ 886).

Jung associates this passage with one of Meister Eckhart's sayings:

. . . for I am the unmoved mover that moves all things. Here God can find no more place in man, for man by his emptiness has won back that which he was eternally and ever shall remain (CW 11, ¶ 887).

The universality of the Fool archetype is illustrated by a passage from *Charley Bland* by Mary Lee Settle, a contemporary author of African-American descent, describing

. . . the happiest summer dominated by the Fool in the Tarot pack . . . whirling, timeless, joyful fool, pure balance, clown, heaven and earth, scapegoat and ritual sacrifice. Because he is the center of things, and outside at the same time, he is pure balance, invisible. . . . [I]t is the seventh sense, the sense of balance. There is no word for it. . . . Athletes know it . . . it is sensed, hardly registered, simply lived. In music it is called true pitch. We had it for a few months that first summer. Love was the Fool at the center of things, poised there, not hidden, but invisible (1989).

The Fool is always true and a truth to face, a paradox, the ultimate integration of opposites. In dreams he can stand laughingly beside the dreamer, giving support and that comfort that the Fool gives: nonsupport and noncomfort that nonetheless is comforting because it is so absurdly and ridiculously human. Above all else, the true Fool is humanness and fallibility and erring. One needs him to balance the pedantic and unrelated side of exaggerated rationality. Jung asks:

> . . . how else can one perceive the light without the shadow, hear the silence without the noise, attain wisdom without foolishness? (CW 11, ¶ 953).

T. S. Eliot, in his "Little Gidding" (in *Four Quartets*) said that we human beings will never cease exploration, that after we have explored everything we can, we come back to where we started, but after this exploration, we will know the place—actually for the first time. After light has traveled through all the arcana and has transformed them, it returns, victorious, back on itself, guided by the Fool.

Appendix I
TAROT AND ASTROLOGY

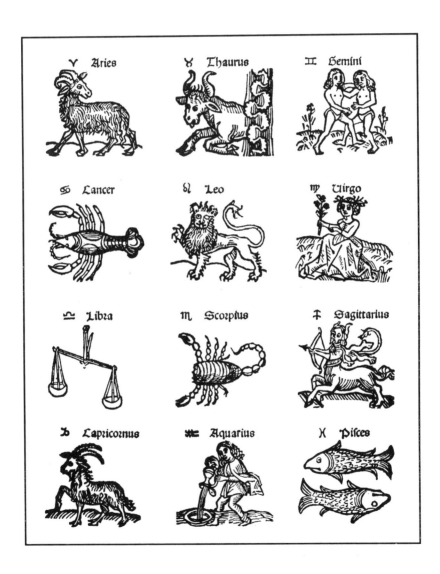

TAROT AND ASTROLOGY

> The collective unconscious. . .appears to consist of
> mythological motifs or primordial images, for which rea-
> son the myths of all nations are its real exponents. In
> fact, the whole of mythology could be taken as a sort of
> projection of the collective unconscious. We can see this
> most clearly if we look at the heavenly constellations,
> whose originally chaotic forms are organized through
> the projection of images. This explains the influence of
> the stars as asserted by astrologers. These influences are
> nothing but unconscious, introspective perceptions of
> the activity of the collective unconscious (Jung, CW 8,
> ¶ 325).

If we accept that the major arcana may be a set of such primordial
images, exploring their astrological dimension can only bring us
closer to the motifs of the collective unconscious that they express.

The arguments presented thus far attempt to demonstrate
that the tarot can be a major resource for understanding archetypal energies available to us in the alternate layer of the psyche,
the realm of the Self. Moreover, the tarot can activate the transformative power of the symbolic world and may thus become a
vehicle for the transcendent function integrating contradictions,
solving conflicts, and assisting wholeness and individuation.
On the other hand, it is generally accepted that astrology is probably the oldest language that expresses the processes of life in
nature as well as in everyday existence (Mann, p. 18). In the search
for a greater understanding in interpreting the tarot, it was
thought that finding relationships with astrological imagery might
be of help. And although I agree with Mann that "[t]he greatest
advantage of synthesis of tarot and astrology. . . is that using the
two symbol systems together allows a greater depth of interpretation" (Mann, p. 20), the result of this synthesis, as found in the
literature, has unfortunately resulted more in confusion than in
clarification or revelation of deeper connections.

Most of those who proposed these incongruous correlations
adopted the already available Hebrew letter-astrological attributions. Because the Hebrew alphabet was held to encapsulate the
entire order of creation within its twenty-two letters, it was
believed that any physical or spiritual quality could be represented graphically through these letters (Pennick, p. 214).

TABLE 13. HEBREW LETTERS, SIGNS, ELEMENTS AND ALCHEMICAL SUBSTANCES.

Correlations between Simple Letters and Signs of the Zodiac		Correlations between Mother Letters, Elements, and Alchemical Substances		
Simple Letter	Zodiac Sign	Mother Letter	Element	Alchemical Substance
He	Aries	Aleph	Air	Mercury
Vau	Taurus	Mem	Water	Salt
Zain	Gemini	Shin	Fire	Sulphur
Heth	Cancer			
Teth	Leo			
Yod	Virgo			
Lamed	Libra			
Nun	Scorpio			
Sameck	Sagittarius			
Ayin	Capricorn			
Tsade	Aquarius			
Coph	Pisces			

TABLE 14. THE DOUBLE LETTERS AND THE PLANETS.

LETTER	PLANET			
	Kaplan	Innes	Wirth	MacGregor-Mathers
Beth	Saturn	Moon	Sun	Mercury
Ghimmel	Jupiter	Mars	Venus	Moon
Daleth	Mars	Sun	Mercury	Venus
Caph	Sun	Venus	Moon	Jupiter
Pe	Venus	Mercury	Saturn	Mars
Resh	Mercury	Saturn	Jupiter	Sun
Tau	Moon	Jupiter	Mars	Saturn

TABLE 15. ASTROLOGICAL ATTRIBUTIONS TO THE SEPHIROT

SEPHIRA	ASTROLOGICAL ATTRIBUTIONS			
	Halevi	Kaplan	Zain	Doane & Keyes
Kether	Neptune	Pluto	Pluto	Pluto
Hochmah	Uranus	Uranus	Neptune	Neptune
Binah	Saturn	Neptune	Uranus	Uranus
Hesed	Jupiter	Jupiter	Jupiter	Jupiter
Geburah	Mars	Mars	Saturn	Saturn
Tipheret	Sun	Sun	Venus	Venus
Netzah	Venus	Venus	Mars	Mars
Hod	Mercury	Mercury	Mercury	Mercury
Yesod	Moon	Moon	Moon	Moon
Malkuth			Sun	Sun

According to the *Sepher Yetzirah*, a cabalistic text dating back to somewhere between the third and the sixth century C.E., God formed the seven planets and the seven days of the week from the seven double letters (Pennick, pp. 8-12). Setting aside for the moment the fact that the Hebrew letters were assigned to the major arcana only late in the 19th century and looking strictly at the Hebrew letter-astrology correspondence, one cannot help but observe that there seems to be an overall consensus on the correlations between the twelve simple letters and the twelve signs of the zodiac. It also appears that this consistency of attribution extends to the three mother letters, to which were assigned the three elements. Table 13 depicts these correlations as described by Innes (p. 86), MacGregor Mathers (in Innes, p. 88), Wirth (1990, p. 216), and Pennick (p. 12).

The astrological attributions to the seven double letters are unclear and contradictory. Pennick mentions that the seven planets have been assigned to the seven letters but fails to identify them specifically. Although all available sources trace the derivation of these correlations to the *Sepher Yetzirah*, as Table 14 shows, they differ considerably. A study of the astrological attributions to the sephirot, as Table 15 also shows, only increased the confusion. Investigation of the thirty-two paths and their celestial correspondences complicated the picture even further (see figure 71 on page 334).

The ways in which the major arcana have been associated with astrological energies have followed three distinct paths: one is offered by the European school, headed by Wirth, in which *aleph* is assigned to the Magician. The second alternative follows the esoteric school of the Golden Dawn (Crowley, Case, MacGregor Mathers), which connects *aleph* with the Fool, because according to them, the Fool heads the major arcana. The third approach looks at their astrological dimensions without using the intermediary of a Hebrew letter.

Hurwitz (p. 185), quoting the Zohar (I, 30a), says that *aleph*, the first letter of the Hebrew alphabet, represents the masculine principle, and *beth*, the second letter, represents the feminine. If we are to connect Hebrew letters with tarot card images, then the *aleph*/Magician and *beth*/High Priestess associations are justified, whereas the *beth*/Magician association proposed by the Golden Dawn school is not. Looking at the esoteric meanings of the Hebrew letters (Pennick, p. 229), it is the European school that seems to have the higher number of fitting equivalences (e.g.,

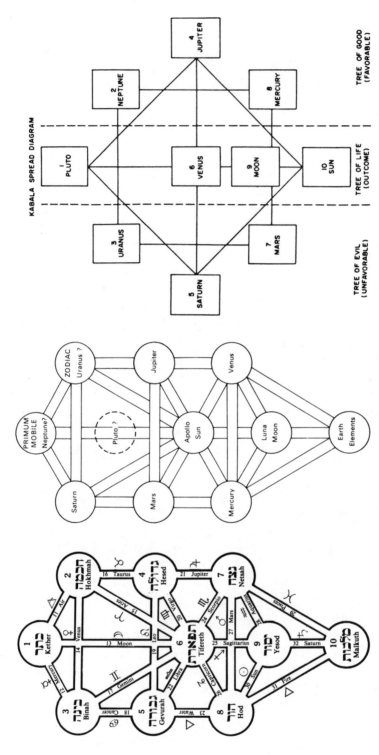

Figure 71. Astrological correspondences of the Tree of Life. (From Poncé, *Kabbalah*, p. 161; Halevi, *Tree of Life* [Introduction to the Cabala], p. 52; Doane and Keyes, p. 60)

TABLE 16. HEBREW LETTER ATTRIBUTIONS TO MAJOR ARCANA FROM WIRTH AND THE GOLDEN DAWN.

Hebrew Letter	Esoteric Meaning	Major Arcana	
		Wirth	Golden Dawn
Aleph	Wealth, father	Magician	Fool
Beth	Mother	High Priestess	Magician
Gimel	Nature	Empress	High Priestess
Daleth	Authority	Emperor	Empress
He	Religion	High Priest	Emperor
Vau	Liberty	Lover(s)	Hierophant
Zain	Ownership	Chariot	Lover(s)
Cheth	Distribution, discrimination	Justice	Chariot
Teth	Prudence	Hermit	Strength
Yod	Order, destiny	Wheel of Fortune	Hermit
Caph	Force	Strength	Wheel of Fortune
Lamed	Sacrifice	Hanged Man	Justice
Mem	Death	Death	Hanged Man
Nun	Reversibility	Temperance	Death
Sameck	Universality	Devil	Temperance
Ayin	Balance, foresight	Tower of Destruction	Devil
Pe	Immortality, cosmic mother	Star	Tower of Destruction
Tsade	Shadow, reflection	Moon	Star
Coph	Light	Sun	Moon
Resh	Recognition	Judgement	Sun
Shin	Sacred fire	World	Judgement
Tau	Synthesis	Fool	World

TABLE 17. MYTHOLOGICAL AND ASTROLOGICAL ATTRIBUTIONS TO MAJOR ARCANA.

Trump	Gods and Goddesses (Greene)*	Sign and Planet (Thierens)†
Magician	Hermes	Aries
High Priestess	Persephone	Taurus
Empress	Demeter	Gemini
Emperor	Zeus	Cancer
High Priest	Chiron	Leo
Lover	Paris	Virgo
Chariot	Ares	Libra
Justice	Athena	Scorpio
Hermit	Cronos	Sagittarius
Wheel of Fortune	Moirai	Capricorn
Strength	Heracles	Aquarius
Hanged Man	Prometheus	Pisces
Death	Hades	Saturn
Temperance	Iris	Mercury
Devil	Pan	Mars
Tower/Destruction	Poseidon	Uranus
Star	Pandora	Venus
Moon	Hecate	Moon
Sun	Apollo	Sun
Judgement	Hermes (Psychopomp)	Jupiter
World	Hermaphrodite	Neptune
Fool	Dionysus	Part of Fortune

* Adapted from Sharman-Burke and Greene's *The Mythic Tarot*.
† Found in *Astrology and Tarot*, pp. 38-39.

TABLE 18. PLANETS AND METALS ASSOCIATED WITH THE MAJOR ARCANA.

Planet	Symbol	Metal	Trumps
Mercury	☿	Quicksilver	1-3
Venus	♀	Copper	4-6
Mars	♂	Iron	7-9
Jupiter	♃	Tin	10-12
Saturn	♄	Lead	13-15
Moon	☽	Silver	16-18
Sun	☉	Gold	19-21

* From Roberts: *Tarot Revelations*, p. 57.

nature/Empress; religion/High Priest; authority/Emperor; prudence/Hermit; destiny/Wheel of Fortune; force/Strength; sacrifice/Hanged Man; death/Death; shadow, reflection/Moon; light/Sun; recognition/Judgement), whereas by contrast, the Golden Dawn and its adherents seem to present us with some pairings that are particularly difficult to accept (e.g., father, wealth/Fool; mother/Magician; balance, foresight/Devil; immortality, cosmic mother/Tower of Destruction). See Table 16, page 335. Knight, perplexed by the multiplicity of contradictory attributions, explains them thus:

> [Although] Thierens is an eminent astrologer, his knowledge of the Qabalah seems very limited, and ... though Zain's propagandizing efforts on behalf of esoteric philosophy are highly commendable, his Qabalism is somewhat unorthodox to say the least. ... Stenring, on the other hand, is a Qabalist of no mean erudition, but his knowledge of the Tarot, which is non-Hebraic, seems doubtful (Knight, p. 230).

An investigation of the way renowned astrologers have correlated the trumps with astrological symbols also proved disappointing. Surprisingly, Greene related them to mythological figures rather than to the planets or zodiacal signs; by extension, then, it is left to the reader to connect those Greek gods with the planets with which they have become associated: Hermes/Mercury, Zeus/Jupiter, Ares/Mars, Cronos/Saturn, Hades/Pluto, Poseidon/Neptune, Hecate/Moon, Apollo/Sun.

Why Greene pairs the Star with Pandora (p. 69) and not with Venus is a puzzlement, as is the merely mechanistic correlation between the sequence of the first twelve trumps with the twelve signs of the zodiac, which Thierens (p. 38) proposed. See Table 17. Even more difficult to accept is the clustering offered by Roberts (*Tarot Revelations*, pp. 52-56). For him there exists a "stairway of planets" in which the major arcana (or "keys," as he calls them) are clumped into triads, as illustrated in Table 18. Whereas Death (XIII) and the Devil (XV) can easily be associated with Saturn, pairing Temperance (XIV) with that restrictive and dark energy is incomprehensible. Granted that ". . . science began with the stars, and mankind discovered in them the dominants of the unconscious, the "gods," as well as the curious psychological qualities of the zodiac: a complete projected theory of human character, [and that] astrology is a primordial experience similar to alchemy" (Jung, CW 12, ¶ 346), to add yet another dimension to an already bewildering entanglement only muddles further the embroiled jumble. Admittedly, astrology was an all-encompassing global concept, which—due to the multiplicity of its aspects—came to touch every human activity. Undoubtedly the symbols used by astrologer and alchemist alike represent primordial elements and processes that were developed to a great extent in the middle ages, but they assuredly originate in a much earlier period. (See figure 72) The mythological quality of consciousness at that time produced images that have survived in the collective unconscious and that emerge whenever an appropriate stimulus occurs.

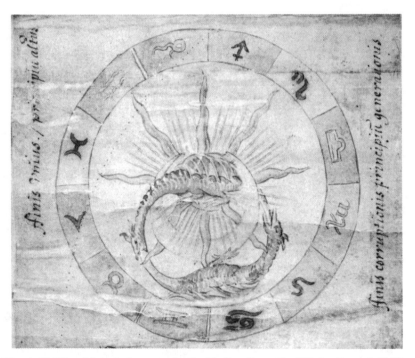

Figure 72. The alchemical process in the Zodiac. From the "Ripley Scrowle" MS., 1588.

Because the tarot are perennially alive and imaginative descriptions of our inner selves, they have the capacity to reconnect us with the ancient and eternal design lying dormant in the collective unconscious layer of the psyche. It does not seem impossible that myths are behind that mysterious and, at times, mystifying, energy of the major arcana. This would explain the survival of the trumps, which transcended the changes in culture and consciousness. Going far back thus seems justifiable, but to do so indiscriminately is hardly of any help. Finding correspondences to a tarot image in the cabala or in alchemy, although a complex and arduous task, is gratifying when limited to a one-to-one comparison; when the attempt is made to compare tarot to astrology, however, the task becomes one of sorting out from among clusters of ill-fitting, predetermined pairings. The historically "accepted" planetary and zodiacal correspondences that attributed the planet and sign not to the tarot trump but to its assigned Hebrew letter is, as we have seen, at the origin of this confusion.

Whether it is the shape of the Hebrew letter that is the criterion for astrological allocations (Wirth's choice in pairing *aleph* with Orion, *beth* with Cassiopeia, *ghimmel* with Virgo, *ayin* with Scorpio, *he* with Aries) or its place on the Tree of Life (specifically on one of the twenty-two paths—Crowley's attributions), one is faced with the fact that, by reaching for the astrological equivalent of the tarot card in the Hebrew letter associated with it, one allows oneself to be diverted from the main task of the astrological attribution to the trumps—an elaborate and sensitive endeavor in itself.

Some associations of the major arcana and their astrological correlations are better than others, and some have been mentioned in the literature again and again, no matter what the esoteric school or whether the Hebrew letter was considered or not. For example:

Often Mentioned	Less Often Mentioned
Magician/Mercury	Lover(s)/Taurus
High Priestess/Moon	Chariot/Sagittarius
Empress/Venus	Temperance/Cancer
Emperor/Jupiter	Sun/Sun
Justice/Libra	
Strength/Leo	

In proposing my own attributions, I have tried to stay as close as possible to what, intuitively, I perceive to be the common features that link the tarot card with an astrological sign or planet:

Magician/Mercury	Hanged Man/Gemini
High Priestess/Moon	Death/Capricorn
Empress/Venus	Temperance/Cancer
Emperor/Jupiter	Tower of Destruction/Uranus
HighPriest/Mars	Devil/Saturn
Lover(s)/Taurus	Stars/Aquarius
Chariot/Sagittarius	Moon/Neptune
Justice/Libra	Sun/Sun
Hermit/Scorpio	Judgement/Pluto
Wheel of Fortune/Virgo	World/Pisces
Strength/Leo	Fool/Aries

Although at first glance it might seem difficult to accept a World/Pisces association, I quote Hand, an astrologer of world renown, who wrote (1989, p. 239), "In the language of mysticism, Pisces symbolizes the surrender of the soul to God." If, therefore, the twenty-first arcana represents the point in the return journey of the soul, in which one is at the gates of the infinite, then this attribution seems appropriate. It may also be that for some the Moon/Neptune correlation is not satisfactory; in this case Hand argues that Neptune is:

> . . .probably misnamed from an astrological point of view, since it has little similarity to the boisterous Roman sea-god. It is more like the Hindu goddess Maya; . . . its nature eludes definition because it is associated with aspects of the universe that are unclear, illusory, and even imaginary (p. 75).

This description fits well the Moon energy. I am also less than satisfied with the Star/Aquarius pairing, which certainly has many flaws, not the least of which is that despite its "watery" aspects, Aquarius is an air sign, and as such it is not a good fit with the feeling quality of the Star. There is much to support a Venus/Star correlation, as Venus seems closer to the Inanna quality that this card emanates. That would have left the Empress associated with Ceres/Demeter, which has been proposed by Greene (in *The Mythic Tarot*, p. 24); although certainly well-rooted in mythology, this latter pairing remains astrologically in the still controversial area of the asteroids.

Finally, my greatest ambivalence about my own proposed equivalences concerns the Death/Capricorn and Judgement/Pluto pairings because I can also easily accept that Hades/Pluto, the Lord of the Underworld, may be a better attribution to the Death card, symbolizing as it does the necessary journey into darkness where one can tap into the hidden treasures of one's soul and return transformed by this death-of-the-old experience. I can also easily accept a Judgement/Capricorn correlation. Somehow I cannot help but see in Judgement elements of the patriarchal Judeo-Christian commandments enforced by the authority of the fathers, and according to Hand, it is Capricorn that is overly serious, tends toward self-importance, and is the manifestation of the father complex at the zodiacal sign level. Furthermore, Capricorn allows the world to define its criteria about what is important and acceptable; it is concerned with an objective idea of the truth and is "unusually subject to the influence of authority figures and of those who claim knowledge that is universally applicable" (Hand, pp. 233ff.).

Although the flow of time and events is continuous, we perceive it as being composed of discrete events. These can be units of time or individual objects, actions, people. This perception, which originates in our consciousness, is the basis for our understanding of the universe: it is the origin of (and is expressed in) language and numbers. Any system of notation can only be one fragmentary means of describing one way of seeing one "reality." Whereas most human perception is of a fragmentary nature, existence is a holistic continuum: and within any of the chosen notational systems, whether numerical, alphabetical, or symbolic, for those who can find it, a deeper reality is encoded (Pennick, p. 225). Each of these notations is but a particular expression of a magical structure that acts at all levels in the material as well as in the nonmaterial worlds. The esoteric approaches and techniques that exist within all cultures can provide a means of coming to a creative understanding of that transcendent reality.

> In our lives, we are all writers on the unfolding blank pages of existence (Pennick, p. 225).

Hopefully, the major arcana and their cabalistic, alchemical, and astrological correspondences can provide us with a key to the inner magical secrets that will enrich those blank pages with all the colors found in the most beautiful "book of hours."

In the imaginal world of the psyche, experiences are not connected by causality but by meaning. Connections between events and the images of the tarot exist because there is shared meaning (Sharman-Burke & Greene, *The Mythical Tarot*, p. 12). This is the basis of Jung's method of amplification, which has proven not only legitimate but profitable in the present approach to tarot imagery. As long as one stays close to the image, circumambulating it and finding correspondences and similarities can only deepen insight, provided our associations are not allowed to lead to intellectual constructs or esoteric systems far from the center of meaningful and restorative truth: enlivening the images never means burdening them with prejudice.

Traditional meanings may thus cloud rather than clarify, especially if one is unwilling to suspend belief in the confining concepts by which the world is often structured. More than ever, it is important to start from a viewpoint that allows for a greater understanding of life; one must look at the world and one's involvement in it with an increased awareness that can encompass more than one layer of reality.

> You are the creator of your own experience and the true source of all intentions in your universe. . . . You are, in the totality of what you are, the creator and focus for divine energy in your universe (Hand, p. 17).

Because "individual consciousness is based on and surrounded by an indefinitely extended unconscious psyche" (Jung, CW 11, ¶ 140), by reaching into its richness and drawing from it, a more comprehensive personality can emerge in the course of development. Since this growth comes from the unconscious, which is by definition unlimited, the extent to which the personality can realize itself is also unlimited; this is, in fact, individuality in the highest sense. Jung has called this realization the "individuation process."

> So far as the personality is still potential, it can be called transcendent, and so far as it is unconscious, it is indistinguishable from all those things that carry its projections. . . [that is,] symbols of the outside world and the cosmic symbols. These form the psychological basis for

the conception of man as a microcosm, whose fate, as we know, is bound up with the macrocosm through the astrological components of his character (Jung, CW 11, ¶ 390).

For the alchemists the process of individuation was analogous to world creation, and the alchemical *opus* itself was an analogy to God's work of creation. Jung believed that alchemy was inconceivable without the influence of her elder sister astrology (CW 14, ¶ 222), that it is no longer useful to investigate how far "off" these fields might be, but rather to recognize that there is an eminently psychological reason for their existence, and that one can benefit from investigation of the psychological foundations on which they rest. When the old alchemists and astrologers ascribed their secrets to matter or to the stars, they recognized a reality of the soul beyond the capacity of linear consciousness to comprehend. Citing Jung, Harding (*Redemption Ideas in Alchemy*, p. 24) affirms that those who accept their not knowing are no ignoramuses, but not so those whose consciousness has not yet reached the point in its development where they know their not knowing.

Individuation concerns the processes of life, which are sensed but never known; these processes present riddles to linear understanding, which we can grasp only fleetingly, in intuitive glimpses, while circumambulating images, reflecting other images, suggesting connections that may help apprehend the unfathomable. It could be the reason why the sephira Daat (knowledge) is surrounded by a dotted circle and not completely traced upon the Tree of Life at the crossroads of the supernals with the pillar of equilibrium. There, at the door that opens to direct revelation of the eternal spirit, dances, in its mandorla glory, the major arcanum the World. May it be your guide into the magic of the unknown.

Appendix II
TAROT AND DIVINATION

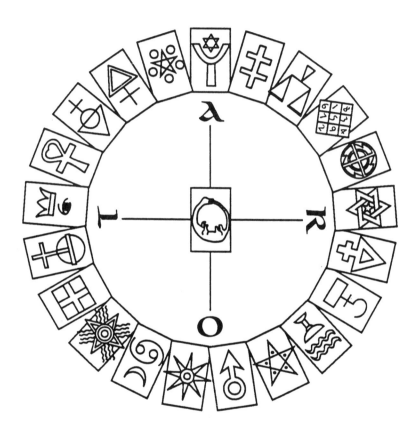

DIVINATION AND THE TAROT

It is a dubious task indeed to try to introduce a collection of archaic "magic spells" to a critical modern public with the idea of making them more or less acceptable (Jung, CW 11, ¶ 999).

The use of tarot cards for fortune-telling has discredited their archetypal wisdom in the eyes of many who would otherwise be inclined to investigate and explore the unfamiliar more open-mindedly. People using the *I Ching* for divination, on the other hand, had only to suspend their incredulity that anything valid might come their way from beyond the well-established, rigorous inquiry of the logical mind with which they were familiar. They never had to overcome a distaste for swindlers, gypsies, and mountebanks; or the charlatans sometimes associated with palmistry, ESP readings, tarot cards and fortune-telling used as a "game" to take advantage of the gullible. What *I Ching* users do have to overcome is reluctance to accept as valid any hidden, mystical knowledge—an object of derision in our linear, rational Western culture. Jung stated:

> I have no answer to the multitude of problems that arise when we seek to harmonize the oracle. . .with our accepted scientific canons. . . . The irrational fullness of life has taught me never to discard anything, even when it goes against all our theories (so short-lived at best) or otherwise admits of no immediate explanation. It is of course disquieting, and one is not certain whether the compass is pointing true or not; but security, certitude, and peace do not lead to discoveries. . . . Clearly the method aims at self-knowledge, though at all times it has also been put to a superstitious use (CW 11, ¶ 1000).

Jung continued:

> Could there be a more uncomfortable position intellectually than that of floating in the thin air of possibilities, not knowing whether what one sees is truth or illusion? . . . [T]he decisive thing here is. . . the subjective condition, that is, whether one believes oneself to be "sincere" or not (CW 11, ¶ 1003).

Given the exclusively Apollonian, linear, rational system of education of the Western scientific mind, any alternative mode of exploration under circumstances in which logic does not yield satisfactory answers is usually dismissed with contempt. The method of choice usually is to examine all aspects of the problem at hand, all arguments, for or against, which come to mind. As a result, one is faced with a number of equally valid considerations and no indication of the way out of the confusion. In times of transition in our life, times of uncertainty that arouse high anxiety, seeking logical answers can only increase our sense of helplessness. The search, if not for answers, then at least for some form of guiding clues, inevitably has to include a willingness to approach the unknown layers of our psyche, in which synchronicity and not causality rules.

> Just as causality describes the sequence of events, so synchronicity. . . deals with the coincidence of events. The causal point of view tells us a dramatic story. . . . The synchronistic view on the other hand tries to produce an equally meaningful picture of coincidence (Jung, CW 11, ¶ 973).

Indeed, synchronicity takes the coincidences of life occurrences as meaningful beyond any apparently random quality. There seems to be a strange interdependence between objective circumstances and subjective, psychic states that becomes palpable, provided we are open to it and prepared to contemplate it. If we could be willing to suspend our incredulity, then we could also accept the idea that responses that make sense come to us by means of

> . . . a technique which at the outset seemingly excludes all sense. . . . But oddly enough, the answer received apparently coincide[s] with the questioner's psychological blind spot remarkably well. . . . The method . . . does indeed take into account the hidden individual quality in things and men, and in one's own unconscious self as well (Jung, CW 11, ¶ 984, 983).

There are layers of our psyche that can only be approached with the imagination and the inspiration provided by an ancestral wisdom that is able to tap into them. In his "Foreword to the *I Ching*," Jung reminds us that at one time the *I Ching* was considered

. . . a cult utensil serving to provide spiritual nourishment for the unconscious elements or forces . . . that have
been projected as gods. . . .[a means] to give these forces
the attention they need in order to play their part in the
life of the individual. [It has now become a resource]
whose value is neither generally recognized nor even
widely known (CW 11, ¶ 982).

Everything Jung stated regarding the I Ching seems to be easily
applicable to the tarot; in particular:

Like a part of nature [the I Ching] waits until it is discovered. It offers neither facts nor power, but for lovers
of self-knowledge, of wisdom, it seems to be. . . right. . .
. He who is not pleased by it does not have to use it. . . .
Let it go forth into the world for the benefit of those who
can discern its meaning (CW 11, ¶ 1018).

I am convinced that the tarot is perhaps more compatible than
the *I Ching* for the Western psyche because of its greater flexibility.
Whereas consulting the I Ching entails throwing coins or yarrow
sticks six times, thus obtaining one of sixty-four hexagrams (with
or without changing lines), the approach to tarot seems to allow
for the level of complexity of the question asked as well as for the
level of sophistication of the questioner.

For those unfamiliar with the cards, the first encounter may
come through a dream image. If this is followed by identifying
the particular trump that most closely resembles the dream image,
meditation on this tarot figure will provide a subtle tuning and
realignment of energy that permits a fresh look at the situation
that triggered the dream. A greater familiarity with the cards
enables questioners to select from several layouts the one corresponding to the complexity of the answer they seek. An even sub-
tler approach matches the significance of the shape of the selected
spread to the question. For instance, a question about a love relationship is best answered by using the six-card star spread because
the Star of David expresses appropriately the interaction between
the masculine and feminine energies involved. But whatever the
level one has selected, one needs to remember that

. . . [i]t is not wise to tempt the Gods. Only when our
minds fail to apprehend the graver issues of our lives,
so that higher guidance alone can resolve our doubts

and anxieties, is it advisable to resort to the divinatory offices of the Tarot (Hoeller, p. 15).

The primary function of the tarot is to take something that is at first implicit and make it explicit and meaningful. Beyond the wish for an answer, the question is a way of focusing consciousness, the process of divination taking place between aspects of being within the individual and what is sought as a response from the soul. Whenever we ask our questions with merely the stubborn desire of finding out whether we will get what we want, the way we want it, and when we want it (which is usually this very minute!), we can only remain stuck in an inner-isolating, self-centered, vicious circle. As soon as we realize that all our personal actions are related to the play of universal forces, we can benefit from events that, although difficult and painful to bear, may enhance our awareness.

Learning from our experiences, neither bitter nor revolted nor resigned, can be the occasion for important changes, such as escaping from self-defeating old patterns, trying new ways, and adopting new directions, as much on the spiritual as on the mundane plane. We will feel freed from the chains of concreteness— and be able to go beyond the materiality that obscures our vision and our perspective—whenever we are able to reach into the symbolic realm. The tarot can provide us with a bridge between the subjective and the symbolic layers of our psyche only if we approach it with the desire to move out of the blind spot of egotistical illusions in which we have been imprisoned. Discovering the "will of the spirit" through divination is one way in which we can open the door to another level of reality and distinguish what is not available to our usual mode of perceiving and thinking. Tragically today

> [w]e are no longer supported by the wise counsel and deep insight of the oracle; therefore we no longer find our way through the mazes of fate and the obscurities of our own natures (Jung, CW 11, ¶ 981).

I am convinced that the tarot can help us attain a deeper understanding of ourselves and of the world when we abandon our disjunctive thinking; divination can then become a means to strengthen the ego-Self axis. The tarot can show us how to leave the prison of our limited natures and arrive at a higher level of awareness. Like the *I Ching*, it can be seen as

> . . . a spring of living water . . . ,[as] a deep and danger-
> ous water-hole in which one might easily be bogged
> down, [but also as] an old well that needed only to be
> renovated in order to be put to useful purposes once
> more (Jung, CW 11, ¶ 1014-1015).

The tarot will speak to you to the extent to which you are willing to listen; the images respond to the inner questions asked,
even if you have not fully formulated them or don't know how to
ask them.

THE LAYOUTS

Most interpreters of the tarot, in the books I have consulted, use
the entire deck for their readings. In the selection of layouts that
follows, the spreads presented are only those that can use the
major arcana exclusively, with the exception of the Ten Thrones-
spread, which also uses aces. Of the spreads selected, those most
often encountered were the Celtic Cross and some variant of either
the Yes/No or the Past, Present, Future spreads, which use anywhere from three to seven cards. Next in order of frequency were
the Horoscope spread, the Seventh Card, or 21-Card spreads, and
the Tree of Life spread. Three or four authors described the Name
spread, the Wish spreads, some form of the Horseshoe spreads, the
Pyramid spreads, and one of the frequent either five-, six-, or
eight-pointed Star spreads. Criswell, Doane and Keyes, Fairfield,
Greer, Paterson, Roberts, and Walker each presented one or more
original spreads that form the basis for the following collection.

GENERAL PROCEDURES

Shuffling: Meditation on the question asked must precede any
reading: only then can the answer reflect back the problem with a
deeper and wider perspective. Whether we shuffle the cards hand-
over-hand or riffle them (by separating the deck into two packs
and flipping them with the thumbs so that the cards intermix) or
spread them face down on a table, mixing them around with both
hands or only with the left, we end up creating a *massa confusa*
out of which, as in alchemy, the spirit will sort out and select the
important features in the correct order. Alternatively, one can cut
the deck into three packs to the left and reconstruct it by picking
up the righthand pile first, the middle next, and the left one last.

Should the chosen layout require a card to represent the questioner (the so-called "significator"), this card must be selected before shuffling. The significator is the card that represents the questioner or the circumstances for which one seeks guidance. In order to identify it, one sorts through the deck, looking at all the cards, until the one is found that best gives expression to the quest or the querent. Depending on the layout, the significator is either kept aside or replaced in the deck and shuffled and spread with the other cards. There are certain layouts for which having inverted cards in the spread is a requirement; this must be kept in mind when shuffling in order to ensure a mix of upright and reversed cards. Inverted cards can have a delayed, weakened, or even a reversed meaning. The number of reversed cards, as compared to upright ones, may determine the answer, as for instance, in a "yes/no" spread.

Selection: After concentrating on the question while shuffling the deck, visualizing the pattern of layout that best fits, one then selects the number of cards (face down) necessary for that spread from a well-shuffled deck. This can be done in several ways: by picking the cards one-by-one intuitively, or by counting out the number of cards necessary from the top or bottom of the shuffled-and-cut deck. One can also deal singly selected cards into three piles or form the piles by cutting. The questioner then chooses one pile intuitively and spreads the cards in the preselected pattern. If a significator is necessary, it is set aside (face up) before shuffling. The cards can also be spread out two or three at a time (face up or face down, depending on the spread). It is often advisable to draw the layout on paper; this sketch can be used as a reminder of the way the cards are going to be read or to reconstitute the layout at a later date, to look at the pattern in a new light.

Reading: Whatever the meaning attached to a card (its name, description, number, the Hebrew letter associated with it), its interpretation must always remain open to one's inspiration. When intuition takes in all the elements of a spread, the meaning will emerge from all the interrelations perceived. The relationships between the cards may, for instance, indicate a trend or pattern in a particular area of life, or it may reveal a change in the making. Some authors recommend rearranging the sequence and positions of the cards after the initial reading in order to obtain a different perspective. These permutations permit a deeper understanding of the energies and forces involved in the situation (Greer, 1984, p. 89).

At times a layout does not use all the cards for the spread; in this case the unused cards can serve as clarificators. When a card or group of cards in a spread continues to pose a dilemma, at the end of a reading one can select one, two, or three additional cards from the left-over pack, placing them over or near the ambiguous cards. If it is the general message of the reading that needs a more pointed focus, one to three cards may be placed above the layout (from left to right) and read as a final complementary clarification.

Certain spreads, especially the multilinear ones, require that the cards be interpreted in a predetermined sequence. If a significator has been chosen for the layout, one begins with that card. The value of the significator also determines the way the cards are counted for interpretation; if, for instance, the significator is one of the elemental cards (I, XIII, or 0), one counts *by threes*; that is, every third card is interpreted in relation to the next third card. One counts *by sevens* if the significator is one of the planetary trumps (II, III, IV, XI, XVII, XX, XXI) and *by twelves* if the significator is one of the zodiacal trumps (V, VI, VII, VIII, IX, X, XII, XIV, XV, XVI, XVIII, XIX). When no significator is chosen, the cards in the spread are counted *by fives*, beginning either from the upper left or the upper right corner (counting from left to right or from right to left, respectively) if the cards are laid in rows; if they are spread in a circle, the counting begins with the key card. There will be three cards between each two consulted; that is, cards one and five are read in relation to each other, card five then becomes card one, and the process is repeated until all the cards in the spread have been consulted.

If a final outcome is needed, the card expressing that outcome is selected by reduction of the cards in the spread until a number under 22 is obtained. The number of all cards are added together and reduced; the cards associated with that number represent the outcome. This is possible only in spreads involving a maximum of seven cards. (For example, if cards IV, XVIII, II, and XIV are drawn in a four-card layout, their sum is 38, which reduces to 11 [3 + 8]; thus the outcome card is arcanum XI).

THE SIMPLER SPREADS

THE SINGLE-CARD SPREAD

After the cards are shuffled and cut, the top card (or, alternatively, the bottom card) is turned over: the seeker meditates and dialogues with the card thus obtained. This method is appropriate for a short answer or for focusing or grounding at the beginning of a difficult day.

THE TWO-CARD SPREAD

Also known as *The Crossing Challenge*, the two cards form a cross. A card is selected (as above), and a second card is chosen—either intuitively, or by simply alternating the top with the bottom card, or even more simply, by taking the next (following) card. This second or crossing card represents a challenge to the question asked: it could show a resistance or inner block that must be faced and removed, or it may also bring precision and focus to the question asked. Focusing and removing resistance may help to look beneath the apparent situation and reveal the core issue, which may redirect the entire approach (Mann, p. 138).

THREE-, FOUR-, AND FIVE-CARD SPREADS

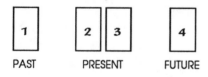

To determine the contribution of past events to the present and future, three, four, or five cards can be laid linearly, such that (in the case of four, for instance) the first card represents the past; the middle two, the present; and the last, the future.

The "Yes/No" Spreads

To answer a simple "yes/no" question, Golowin (p. 241) suggests the following single-card spread. After the cards are shuffled and cut, one card is drawn from the deck; an odd-numbered card means "yes," and an even-numbered card means "no."

Usually, however, three cards are selected for this spread (although five, seven, or even nine cards can be used). There are several methods of interpretation: the simplest counts the number of inverted versus upright cards, with a majority of the former indicating "no" and a preponderance of the latter meaning "yes." For more details, the middle card indicates the present situation and cards on either side represent the past and future, respectively.

Another method assigns the far-left card (card 1) the "pivot" card: if it is upright, the answer is "yes" and if inverted, "no." Cards 2 and 3 show influences that either help produce a positive response or describe the reason for a negative answer. Alternatively, the middle card provides the reason for the answer ("yes" or "no"). In some three-or-more-card linear spreads, the middle card is given a value of 2 and the others have a value of 1. In this case, cards to the left of middle indicate the reasons for the favorable or unfavorable answer and cards to the right may show the basis for the outcome and the favorable forces at work.

Additionally, the three-card linear spread can be used to answer the question: What is happening now? (Fairfield, p. 141). Here card 1 indicates the nature of the present situation, card 2 shows one's attitude toward it, and card 3 focuses on the primary thing that the questioner must bear in mind. This layout can also be used to clarify the contributions made by the body, mind, and spirit (Greer, 1984, pp. 28ff.).

A Four-Card Spread

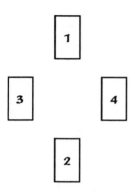

To answer everyday problems, four cards are shuffled, cut, and laid out as shown.

Card 1:   One aspect or force at work in the situation;

Card 2:   Another aspect or other force at work;

Card 3:   Critical assessment of the situation or attitude toward it;

Card 4:   Decision based on all factors; prognosis.

The vertical axis can also represent the conscious/unconscious (above/below) polarity, while the horizontal (left/right) axis may show the personal/partner or the inner-personal/outer-personal, or simply the past/future polarity.

CONFLICT-SOLVING SPREADS

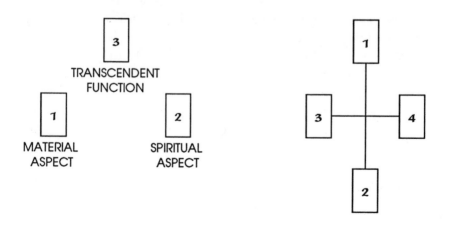

Whenever one finds oneself with a choice between two alternatives, or an inner conflict that one is at a loss to resolve, one may
select three cards, bearing in mind the supernals on the Tree of
Life. One must concentrate and choose, one-by-one, a card for the
first alternative (or material aspect), for the second possibility (or
spiritual aspect), and finally a last card that will help transcend the
situation.

When the conflict seems more complex, the *quaternio* model
may be kept in mind. In this case, the pairs Magician/High
Priestess and Emperor/Empress are visualized while selecting
the cards. The solution may be found after the interpretation. If a
final outcome is needed, the numbers of the four cards may be
added together and reduced to a number under 22. The card associated with this number represents the outcome. (See p. 353 for
reduction technique.)

THE TRIAD AND PENTAD METHODS

Variants of the three-card "yes/no" layout, these spreads indicate past, present, and future events. The left card represents the
past as remembered. The middle card shows the present as
the seeker sees it, and the right card reveals the future as it will
probably unfold.

The Five-Card Spread

When five cards are used to clarify past/present/future interrelations, the middle card is the key or pivot, the present, inner, and
outer blocks and challenges. The two cards to the left are usually
read as past components, causes, or events leading to the present
situation. The cards to the right of key show the outcome and the
seed of the future evolving from the present.

Wirth's Five-Card Spread

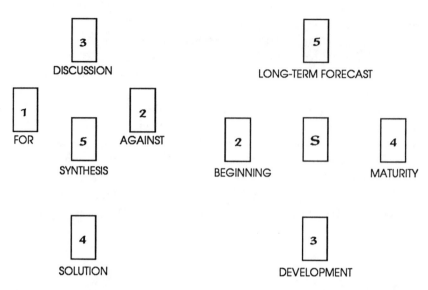

Sometimes five cards are spread in a cross-pattern. For instance, after drawing four cards from the deck, Wirth reduces their numbers to determine the fifth card. Cards 1 and 2 show favorable and unfavorable elements, respectively. Card 3 is a commentary card; card 4 is the solution; and card 5 is the synthesis.

Developmental Five-Card Spread

In a variation of the Wirth spread, a significator is chosen and placed in the middle. Card 2 represents the beginning; card 3, the development; card 4, the maturation; and card 5 is the long-term forecast. See illustration above.

The Seasons Spread

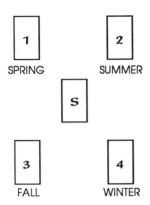

SPRING   SUMMER

FALL   WINTER

LeMieux's "New Year's Eve Reading" (p. 156) or Seasons Spread presents a different five-card spread with the significator in the middle. Cards 1 through 4, representing the seasons (spring, summer, fall, and winter, respectively), are placed in the corners. As a variant, he proposes using twelve cards, three for each season (one for each month of the year). He also suggests that this spread be used on or around one's birthday. (The four-card reading takes about fifteen minutes, whereas the twelve-card method can take up to an hour.)

SIX-, SEVEN-, AND EIGHT-CARD SPREADS

The Six-Card Hungarian Method

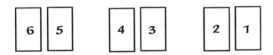

After shuffling, the cards are cut into three piles. Beginning right, a single row is formed, using the bottom card from each pile (cards 1-3), followed by the top card from each pile (cards 4-6). Cards 6 and 5 represent the future; cards 4 and 3, the present; and cards 2 and 1, the past.

The Six-Card Cross

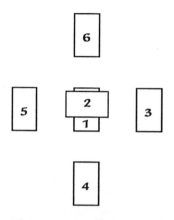

These six cards can also be laid out in a cross, which may help to focus on a particular situation, as it gives more details than the linear spreads; it can also provide a basic picture of the person and the situation in question.

Card 1: The role the questioner plays in the current situation;

Card 2: The true nature of this situation;

Card 3: What created it;

Card 4: How it affects the questioner;

Card 5: Where it can lead;

Card 6: The key to the situation.

The Seven-Card Spread

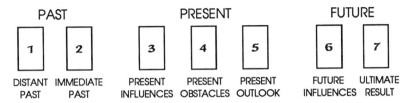

PAST   PRESENT   FUTURE

| 1 | 2 | 3 | 4 | 5 | 6 | 7 |

DISTANT IMMEDIATE   PRESENT   PRESENT   PRESENT   FUTURE   ULTIMATE
PAST   PAST   INFLUENCES OBSTACLES OUTLOOK   INFLUENCES RESULT

For a "yes/no" question, it is the number of inverted ("no") cards versus the number of upright ("yes") cards that determines the answer. However, if four cards are inverted, the answer is either "no" or a delayed "yes." Moreover, the middle card indicates why this particular answer is given. The three cards to the left suggest consequences of acting on it. The cards to the right indicate what might have contributed to the situation and lead to the answer received. At times the cards to the left may also reveal what might happen should one disregard the advice. This spread is appropriate for questions regarding past/present/future sequences of a problem.

Card 1: Distant past—the basic events and influences that may have created the present outlook and attitude;

Card 2: Immediate past—recent events that may have had a specific influence and may be on their way out;

Card 3: Present influences—read with the previous card, it indicates what may modify the present outlook;

Card 4: Present obstacles, hazards—even if a favorable card, in this position it may mean a diversion from the true goal;

Card 5: Present outlook—usually an extension of cards 3 and 4, it often indicates the way the current situation extends into the future;

Card 6: Future influences—a summary of all the preceding cards; shows the way they combine to create coming events;

Card 7: Ultimate result: the culmination brought about by all the preceding suggested interactions between past attitudes and the present.

The Grand Gallery

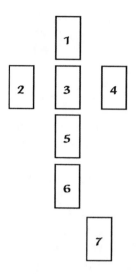

Seven cards are selected from the shuffled deck and placed face up in the form of a cross. The separate seventh card is the key to future progress. The cards are studied individually and together. Inverted cards indicate negative factors that could hinder progress.

The Eight-Card Spread

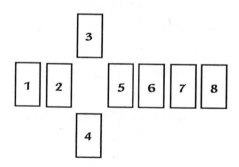

Used to clarify options before taking an important step or making a critical decision, the cards are laid out after shuffling as shown.

Card 1: Underlying state of mind—feelings about the step to be taken;

Card 2: Precipitating events forcing the step under consideration;

Card 3: Effect it will have on others;

Card 4:   Effect it will have on the questioner;

Card 5:   Main concern—anxieties and fears;

Card 6:   What the seeker hopes will be obtained by taking this step;

Card 7:   What will probably happen as a result;

Card 8:   Key factor.

NINE-CARD SPREADS

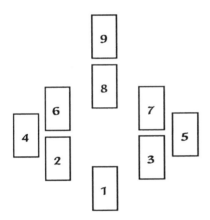

As an alternative that is used for options clarification, this spread can be laid out as depicted (Fairfield, p. 148; Greer, 1984, p. 131).

Card 1:   Reason for considering the option;

Card 2:   What it represents to the questioner;

Card 3:   Its true nature;

Card 4:   Resources that support it;

Card 5:   Obstacles that block it;

Card 6:   Advantages of pursuing it;

Card 7:   Disadvantages of pursuing it;

Card 8:   What will most likely happen if the option is chosen;

Card 9:   The key factor.

The Simple Cross Layout

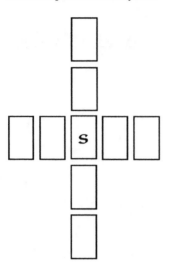

After selecting the significator, the cards are shuffled and dealt. If preferred, the deck can be cut into three piles, one of which is chosen for the spread. The remaining cards can be used for clarification by placing one or two cards on or near the card or group needing elucidation.

Cards right: Events leading up to the situation;

Cards left: Future trends;

Cards below: Negative influences;

Cards above: Action to be taken.

TEN-CARD SPREADS

Goal Setting Ten Card Spread

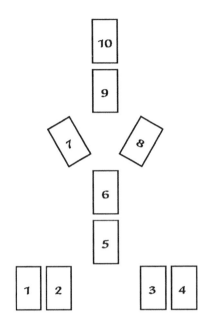

This layout focuses on steps to be taken, resources, and obstacles that affect those steps toward a set goal. After shuffling, the cards are spread as shown:

Cards 1 & 2:   What's wrong with the situation;

Cards 3 & 4:   What's right about it;

Card 5:   What kind of thing the seeker could do well;

Card 6:   Step(s) to be taken toward the goal;

Card 7:   Resources for taking the step(s);

Card 8:   Obstacles in the way;

Card 9:   Where the step(s) will probably lead;

Card 10:   The key factor.

The Three-Row Spread

```
┌─┐  ┌─┐  ┌─┐
│ │  │ │  │ │
└─┘  └─┘  └─┘
    PAST

┌─┐  ┌─┐  ┌─┐
│ │  │ │  │ │
└─┘  └─┘  └─┘
   PRESENT

┌─┐  ┌─┐  ┌─┐
│ │  │ │  │ │
└─┘  └─┘  └─┘
   FUTURE
     ┌─┐
     │S│
     └─┘
```

After choosing the significator, nine cards are selected from the shuffled deck and spread in three horizontal rows of three cards each. The top, middle, and bottom rows represent the past, present, and future, respectively. When interpreting the cards, one begins with the middle card of each row, which shows the basic conditions of the situation and also connects and reflects the influence of those in the preceding row. Cards to the left illustrate conflicting influences and opposing forces. On the right, the final outcome shows interaction between or antithesis to the preceding two.

THIRTEEN-CARD SPREADS

The Magic-Cross Spread

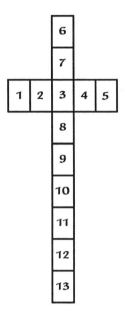

After shuffling and cutting, the cards are dealt as shown.

Cards 1 & 2:   The past;

Card 3:   The present;

Cards 4 & 5:   The opposition;

Cards 6 & 7:   Hopes, expectations;

Cards 8-13:   The future.

The Planning Mandala

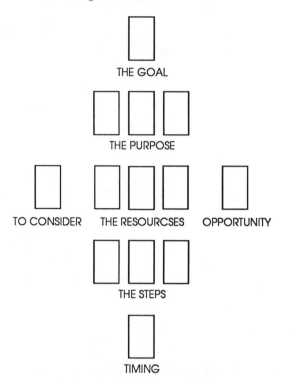

Used when analyzing a problem, this layout helps define the goal and the steps needed to get there. The cards are shuffled and selected intuitively, one-by-one, and spread as shown.

The goal: Practical or spiritual intentions;

The purpose: Reason it is wanted from the concrete, the logical, and the symbolic, spiritual points of view;

Resources: What must be learned in order to carry out the project, including skills and abilities, knowledge and information, and attitudes and feelings;

The steps: Concrete action that must be taken;

Timing: Specific sensibility concerning an opportune moment for action: if the card is clearly associated with an astrological sign (e.g., Justice/Libra), the timing is very precisely stated by the card selected for this position;

Fate: The unseen or unknown factors—what must be considered and to what opportunity one must be alerted.

THE FIFTEEN-CARD SPREAD

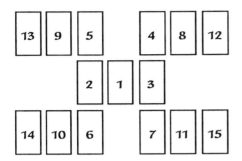

For this layout, the cards are shuffled, cut, and spread in the following pattern:

Card 1:   The questioner;

Cards 2 & 3:   Inner and outer situations;

Cards 4, 8, & 12: Direction in which life will flow without intervention;

Cards 5, 9, & 13: Potential alternative action, positive or negative;

Cards 6, 10, & 14: Information that will assist in decision making (for a young person, the future; for an old person, the past);

Cards 7, 11, & 15: Forces beyond control that cannot be changed and to which one must adapt.

THE SIXTEEN-CARD SPREAD

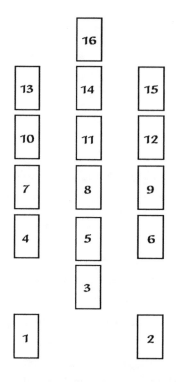

This spread is used to answer in-depth questions about one's job. The cards are shuffled, cut, and spread as shown.

Card 1:   What's wrong with current job;

Card 2:   What's right with current job;

Card 3:   Type of work one is good at;

Cards 4-6:   Steps to be taken to obtain the job;

Cards 7-9:   Resources that would help;

Cards 10-12: Blocks that would hinder;

Cards 13-15: Where steps will most likely lead;

Card 16:   The key factor.

THE HORSESHOE SPREADS

These layouts usually utilize five, six, or seven cards spread in a semicircle with the convexity toward either the top or the bottom.

The Five-Card Horseshoe

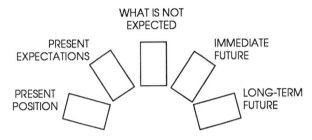

Card 1:   Present position;

Card 2:   Present expectations;

Card 3:   The unexpected;

Card 4:   Immediate future;

Card 5:   Long-term future.

The Six-Card Horseshoe

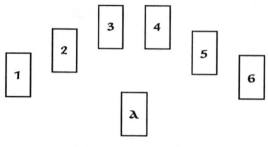

PRESENT STATE OF AWARENESS

When one has two or more options to choose from, this spread is suggested. It is important to be precise and to state the alternatives very clearly and specifically. After writing out the options, the cards are shuffled and cut in as many piles as there are identified alternatives (at times there may be more than, at times fewer than six). The top cards from each pile are placed face down in a semicircle. Before turning them over, the questioner must become aware of any feelings about the option being focused on, any hopes that the card to be uncovered will be favorable or unfavorable. One may be afraid to look—if so, why? What feelings accompany each card as it is turned over and interpreted? What do inner reactions reveal? What is really wanted, hoped for? Is there fear that it will never come to pass? Several other cards (e.g., cards A through D) may be added to help clarify the issue and bring greater insight to making the decision.

Card A: Awareness of any personal bias;

Card B: Key factor that may have been omitted;

Card C: A need that must be fulfilled no matter what the option chosen;

Card D: What might help in making the decision.

Seven-Card Horseshoe Spreads

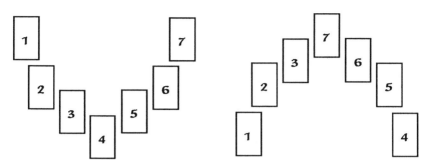

These layouts give a direct answer to a specific question. After the deck is shuffled and cut, the first seven cards are taken from the top and placed face up in the following order:

Card 1: Influences from the past;

Card 2: Present circumstances;

Card 3: The future (general);

Card 4: Recommended course of action;

Card 5: Attitudes in the environment;

Card 6: Obstacles;

Card 7: Probable outcome.

Alternatively, three cards can be spread beginning bottom left and going up toward the apex, followed by three cards beginning bottom right, also going up toward the apex. The seventh card is placed in the middle of the arch thus formed.

Card 1: Has the necessary action been taken?

Card 2: Present situation;

Card 3: Unconscious fantasies;

Card 4: Hidden obstacles;

Card 5: How are the people involved behaving?

Card 6: What should be done next;

Card 7: Final result.

The Churchyard Spread

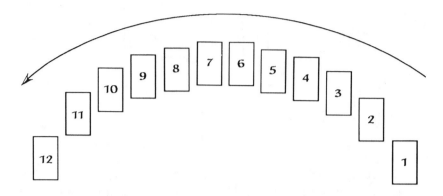

Suitable for answering a precise question, this spread also allows the answer to a second question, of which the questioner was not aware, to emerge. The significator is preselected, and the cards are shuffled and cut into three piles, right to left. After restoring the deck, twelve cards are counted from the top of the pack. The rest of the cards are set aside. The significator is then reinserted among the twelve cards, which are reshuffled and cut as before. The cards are dealt face up from right to left in a fan or horseshoe shape. The position of the significator is important because it indicates the end of one answer and the beginning of the response to the unasked, unconscious question. Should the significator fall at the beginning, it means that the question asked is not the relevant, substantive one. Should it appear at the end, it indicates that the question asked is the only relevant one and the primary problem to be addressed at this time. This spread can therefore give answers such as, "Not only———but also———,"""Only this:———," and, "Not this, but that."

The Quest

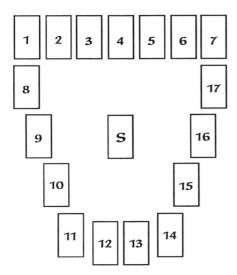

Seventeen cards are individually chosen and placed as shown. If so desired, a significator can be preselected and placed in the center.

Cards 1-7:   Desire and future prospects;

Cards 8-17:   Obstacles and opposition.

THE PYRAMID SPREADS

The Seven-Card Pyramid Spread

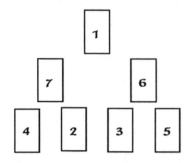

After preselecting the significator, the cards are shuffled, cut, and placed one-by-one in the following pattern.

Card 1: Significator

Card 2: Roots of the problem

Card 3: Depth; unconscious contribution

Card 4: Strength

Card 5: Opposition

Card 6: The future

Card 7: Unknown factor

The 21 Card Pyramid Spread

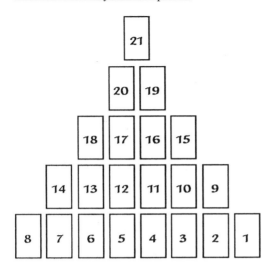

To answer a question, solve a problem, or simply depict general trends that may be at work in a person's life, shuffle, cut, and deal the cards face down according to the diagram. Some authors begin with the bottom line and end at the top with card 21: others recommend starting at the top and ending bottom right. In addition, there are readers (Doane and Keyes, pp. 39ff.) who consider that every fifth card has a key significance; it is known as a "key" card and is treated as the first card of each group of five, the four following cards representing past events leading to the time to which that key refers.

Key I: The present;

Key II: The immediate future;

Key III: The next turn of events;

Key IV: The distant future;

Key V: The final outcome.

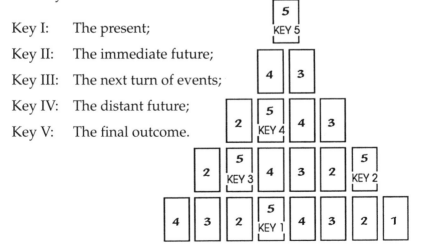

THE MORE COMPLEX SPREADS

The Celtic Cross

This is apparently the oldest spread, believed to be in use since the 17th century. Once the significator is selected, the cards are shuffled, cut, and dealt from the top of the deck, with two cards placed on top of the significator. The rest of the cards are arranged according to the following diagram.

Card 1:   The covering card is placed over the significator and shows the current situation, the prevailing atmosphere surrounding the questioner, the basis of the problem, what fate has contributed to the state of affairs.

Card 2:   The crossing card indicates the immediate influences that may affect or conflict with the interests of the questioner; it reinforces or clarifies card 1.

Card 3:   The crowning card describes the ideal solution or outcome, the ultimate goal, or possible development in the future or in the conscious awareness of the questioner.

Card 4:   The card beneath represents the heart of the matter, the foundation, the basic events and concerns upon which the question is based—unconscious awareness.

Card 5:   The card behind points to the recent past and its effects on the present situation; what is passing out of the questioner's life.

Card 6:   The card before suggests future influences that are likely to come into play; the probable direction in which the situation will develop.

These six cards are interpreted in detail: after their meaning has been fully grasped, one proceeds to interpret the next four. Some readers recommend that they be dealt only after the first six have been thoroughly interpreted.

Card 7:   The answer card describes strengths and weaknesses contributing to the future; it also describes what is within the questioner that may contribute to the answer.

Card 8:   The strengthening card illustrates the questioner's environment; those factors with positive effect, e.g., home, family, friends.

Card 9:   The defining card discloses inner feelings, secrets, intuitions, hopes, and fears that the questioner brings to the situation.

Card 10: The end card reveals the result of everything represented by the preceding cards; it can be read as the conclusion of a story told by all the others.

Alternatively, card 7 has been interpreted as fears; card 8, as the home; card 9, hopes and ideals; and card 10, final outcome (LeMieux, p. 147). Elsewhere, Douglas (pp. 196-197) has interpreted cards 7 through 10 as a sequence of events, from the most recent (card 7) to the most distant (card 10).

Similar to the Celtic Cross, the Nine-Card Spread omits one of the cards covering the significator. Either the card describing the current situation (card 1) or the card representing immediate influences (card 2) is left out; all the other card positions have the same meaning and are interpreted in the same way.

The Major Arcana Spread

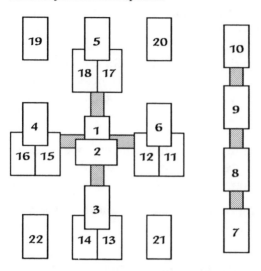

A development of the Celtic Cross, this layout uses all twenty-two trumps. After shuffling and cutting, preferably three times, the first ten cards are laid out, face down, in the pattern of the Celtic Cross. Two cards are then selected to cover card 6, plus two for card 3, card 4, and card 5 (eight in all); these cards modify and give additional information about the card they cover. Finally, the last four cards of the deck complete the spread, as shown in the accompanying illustration.

Card 1:	Inner focus of energies
Card 2:	Outer focus of energies
Cards 3, 13, 14:	Needs and desires forming the basis of one's attitude
Cards 4, 15, 16:	Talents or abilities that assist or hinder; opportunities to which the questioner is most sensitive
Cards 5, 17, 18:	Thoughts, ideals, ambitions
Cards 6, 11, 12:	Decision making; the use of abilities based on
Card 7:	The way the questioner sees him- or herself
Card 8:	How others see the questioner
Card 9:	Lessons that must be learned

Card 10:   The outcome

Card 19:   Feminine energy

Card 20:   Masculine energy

Card 21:   Limitations and obstacles

Card 22:   Possibilities and hidden strength

The Seventh-Card Spreads

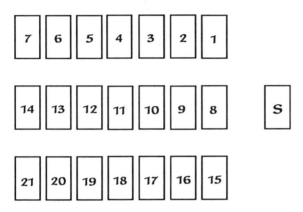

Seven is a synergetic number indicating a return to unity of the active (3) and passive (4) elements.

Before shuffling, the significator is selected and placed on the table, face up and to the right. After shuffling, every seventh card is removed from the deck and placed on the table to the left of it. The first septenary pertains to the life-giving spirit; the second, to the soul and life; and the third, to concentrating and sublimating principles.

As the cards are counted out, the six not chosen are transferred to the bottom of the pack; the layout proceeds until all twenty-one cards are placed, face up or face down, in three rows of seven. If face down, the cards are counted according to the value of the significator (see p. 353) and interpreted as they are turned up. The counting and reading is done from right to left. When all the cards have been turned up, one can interpret by clusters, by rows, or by the general meaning that the entire spread seems to suggest.

Four-Corners Spread

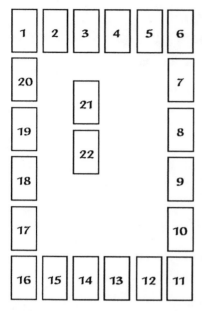

A variation of the Seventh-Card spread is the Four-Corners Spread. The cards are drawn by the same procedure, however, no significator is pre-selected. Starting at the top left corner, the cards are spread in a square as shown. The center cards, 21 and 22, are beacons to the way ahead.

The Italian Method

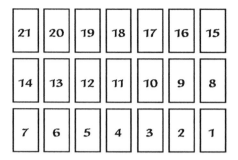

21	20	19	18	17	16	15
14	13	12	11	10	9	8
7	6	5	4	3	2	1

Although very similar to the Seventh-Card Spread, the Italian Method does not include a significator and the cards are laid face down after shuffling, having been picked one-by-one from the deck. The three rows of seven represent the past (top), the present (middle), and the future (bottom). The last card indicates the final solution. The reading then proceeds by counting every fifth card (there will be three cards between every two consulted), turning it over, and interpreting it in relation to the one just uncovered. The reading begins at the top and proceeds from left to right. An additional dimension to the reading can be obtained by pairing cards 1 and 21, 2 and 20, 3 and 19, etc. and interpreting the resulting combination. Alternatively, the cards can be spread from the bottom row up, in which case the bottom row represents the past and the top stands for the future.

Alternative Italian Method

In another variation of the Italian Method a significator is preselected and re-introduced in the deck before shuffling. The cards are then laid face up in three rows of seven as in the Italian Method. The significator will be the starting point of the reading which proceeds by counting over the cards in the direction in which the significator faces. Should the significator card face neither right nor left, the nature of the enquiry will determine the direction: for business questions one counts to the right; for the relationship questions one counts to the left. The meaning of the divinatory reading is given by the sequence of cards; it is as if each card selected by the counting procedure becomes a "word" in the divinatory sentence. The number of cards in the counting is determined by the Hebrew letter associated with the significator one has pre-selected: three for a mother letter, seven for a double letter and twelve for a simple letter. Should the deck of cards used have have no associated Hebrew letters, one generally counts by five. This means that one starts with the significator (No. 1), one counts over three cards (2, 3, 4) and looks at the fifth card, which is the "second word" in our sentence. This fifth card now becomes No. 1; one counts over three cards and looks at the new fifth card, which will be the "third word" in our sentence, and so on, until the counting up or down the three rows of our spread brings us back to the starting point.

For example, when looking at the layout for the Italian Method, if the significator appears in the place of card 10 and one starts counting by fives toward the right, the next "word" card will be card 2, next card 6, then card 20, and then card 16. The next count brings us back to the beginning.

Our divinatory sentence will be formed thus of five "words" given by cards No. 10, 2, 6, 20, and 16 respectively. Should a final word be needed, one can use the left-over card. Additional information can also be obtained by looking at the cards surrounding the significator and interpreting the picture that emerges from the group.

The Twenty-one-Card Gypsy Method

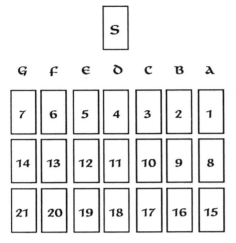

In another variation of the Seventh-Card Spread, three rows of seven are laid (starting top left) with the significator centered above them. The triads thus formed are read as follows (LeMieux, pp. 153ff.):

Column A (cards 1, 8, & 15):   Present psychological outlook;

Column B (cards 2, 9, & 16):   Present environment, home life;

Column C (cards 3, 10, & 17):   Hopes, wishes, desires;

Column D (cards 4, 11, & 18):   Positive influences, expectations;

Column E (cards 5, 12, & 19):   Potential dangers, the unexpected;

Column F (cards 6, 13, & 20):   Immediate future;

Column G (cards 7, 14, & 21):   Long-term outcome.

Within each triad, the top card is positive, the middle is negative, and the bottom card is neutralizing; in other words, they represent thesis, antithesis, and synthesis.

The Esoteric Gypsy Method

Here again are seven groups of three with the significator centered above, but the cards are laid in a different pattern (LeMieux, pp. 158ff.). The cards are then read in the developmental sequence shown on page 385.

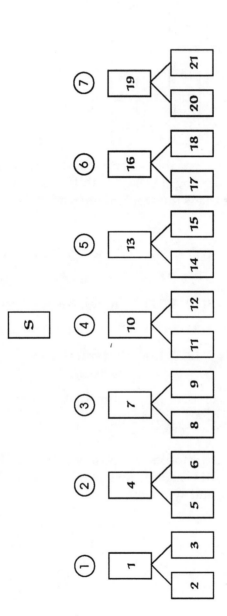

Card 1: The father (or some important early childhood male figure);
Card 2: The mother (or some important female figure from childhood);
Card 3: The questioner as a child (desires, experiences);
Card 4: Teachings and beliefs, formative experiences, general philosophy;

Card 5: Power and leadership, dealings with challenges, control issues;

Card 6: Taste and choices, what appeals to the artistic, sensual level;

Card 7: Movement and conflict, mental capabilities, attitude toward discoveries and discord;

Card 8: Home and possessions, family life in past, present, or future;

Card 9: Prudence and protection, wise counsel, caution;

Card 10: Well-being and security, contentment; reversed or negative cards are weak in this position;

Card 11: The law, justice and judgment, legal disputes;

Card 12: Hope, luck, imagination, wishes likely to come true. In this position also, bad cards are weakened and no card is considered reversed;

Card 13: Sacrifice and discipline, something one is willing to fight for, ethical courage;

Card 14: Disaster; only Temperance or the World can neutralize this very negative position;

Card 15: Bondage, stifling situations, feeling stuck in material problems;

Card 16: Communication, talents, and means of optimal expression;

Card 17: Changes that will occur, attitude, and opposition to change;

Card 18: Fears and anxieties, relationships and situations that produce apprehension and stress;

Card 19: Hopes and aspirations, events that may take place, people that may be helpful;

Card 20: Fate, future influence, or situation that will definitely occur;

Card 21: Final outcome, may describe a person, a situation, or an attitude.

This spread is very demanding, takes from one to two hours to complete, and covers events from the past, the present, and the future. For a young person, all positions after card 7 pertain to the future; for an older person, only the last three cards are future oriented.

The Five-Pointed Star or The Prosperity Spread

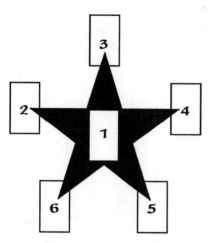

To clarify feelings about money (that is, what one likes and does not like about it, what one is afraid of, why one does or doesn't deserve it, etc.), the cards are shuffled, cut, and spread according to the following layout:

Card 1: What the universe can contribute to the questioner's needs;

Card 2: What can help the questioner relax and be at ease;

Card 3: What will bring prosperity and contentment;

Card 4: What will counterbalance the questioner's negative feelings;

Card 5: What can provide rewards, positive feedback, reinforcement;

Card 6: What prosperity could mean to the questioner.

The Double Five-Pointed Star or the Five-Year Fantasy

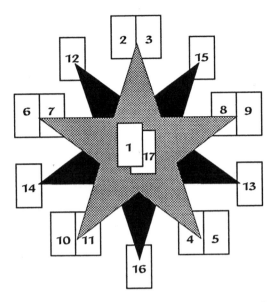

To acknowledge hopes and dreams for the future, to clarify options and bring one closer to one's goals, a card is chosen to represent the questioner creating the fantasy; after shuffling, ten cards are selected and spread around the significator.

Card 1:   How the questioner creates his or her goals;
Cards 2 & 3:   Recent major success;
Cards 4 & 5:   Work situation;
Cards 6 & 7:   Current source of excitement and stimulation;
Cards 8 & 9:   Talents and abilities;
Cards 10 & 11:   Home environment.

The remaining cards are reshuffled and six are dealt one-by-one, as indicated.

Card 12:   Intellect;
Card 13:   Creativity;
Card 14:   Love and sexuality;
Card 15:   Insight, intuition;
Card 16:   Money and power;
Card 17:   Ideal self.

This is a spread that invokes arcanum XVII, the Star, and its positive influence. Should this card appear in the spread, the prediction is favorable.

The Alchemist's Spread

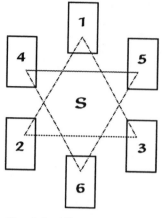

Reputed to have been devised by Nostradamus, this spread should not be repeated for the same question (that is, one must have respect for the answer received and not insist at the ego level on forcing another outcome). Using the pattern of The Six-Pointed Star, it purports to unite the personal with the universal, to place individual destiny in perspective. After selecting the significator, the cards are shuffled and spread as follows

Card 1:   Past;
Card 2:   Present;   } Universal forces,
Card 3:   Future;   context
Card 4:   Near-future events;
Card 5:   Future events (next few years);   } Personal level
Card 6:   Long-term future events.

This spread can also be used when a question refers to a relationship. In this case, the first three cards pertain to one of the partners and the next three cards indicate the role of the other. The significator represents the outcome of the interaction as it manifests in the present, should the attitude of the partners remain unchanged. The relationship under examination may involve the inner masculine and feminine qualities of the questioner. If so:

Card 1:   The ideal masculine;

Cards 2 & 4:   The way the questioner interacts in a positive situation;

Cards 3 & 5:   The way the questioner interacts in a negative situation;

Card 6:   The ideal feminine.

It may also clarify what qualities the cards that form the feminine triangle have in common and what qualities are common to those forming the masculine triangle.

The Six-Pointed Star

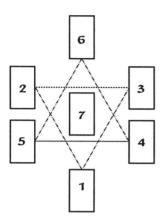

This variation of the Alchemist's Spread indicates a clear line of development. The positions of the cards are as shown; their meanings are as follows.

Card 1: Root, cause, origin of the present situation;

Card 2: Present unfavorable circumstances evolving from that situation;

Card 3: Present favorable circumstances evolving from that situation;

Card 4: Recent events that contributed to the favorable outcome;

Card 5: Recent events that contributed to the unfavorable outcome;

Card 6: Presaged future development taking all these influences into consideration.

A seventh card can be selected by reduction of the first six (see explanation on p. 353); it elucidates the questioner's relation to the entire situation. For additional information, four cards can be drawn from the remaining reshuffled deck.

The Magic Seven Spread

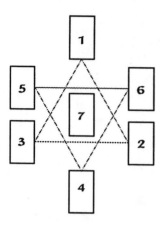

Another variation of the Six-Pointed Star uses the accompanying layout in which the cards have the following meanings:

Card 1:   The history of the matter at hand;

Card 2:   The present evolving from that past;

Card 3:   Immediate future, brought about by past and present;

Card 4:   Favorable influences or state of mind;

Card 5:   Surrounding environment;

Card 6:   Obstacles;

Card 7:   Result.

The Seal of Solomon

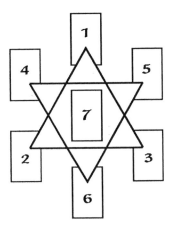

Here also a seventh card is selected by reduction of the first six. Laid as for The Alchemist's Spread, the cards are interpreted individually by focusing on the following triangles.

Cards 1, 4, & 5:   The question;

Cards 2, 3, & 6:   The questioner;

Cards 1, 2, & 3:   Psychic resources;

Cards 4, 5, & 6:   Material circumstances;

Cards 2 & 4:   What is behind;

Cards 3 & 5:   What is ahead;

Cards 1, 6, & 7:   The final outcome.

The upward-pointing triangle is the creative *yang*; its left card indicates matter; its right, spirit. The downward-pointing triangle is the receptive *yin*; its left card is passive; its right, active. The cards at the upward and downward points of these triangles represent the synthesis.

The Star Spread

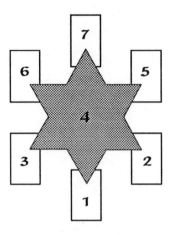

Here, all seven cards are incorporated in one single layout and interpreted as follows:

Card 1: The root of the matter; present situation;

Card 2: Feelings; relationships;

Card 3: Thoughts; profession;

Card 4: The heart of the matter;

Card 5: Shortly-to-be-revealed events;

Card 6: Desires and expectations;

Card 7: Outcome.

The Ten-Card Layout

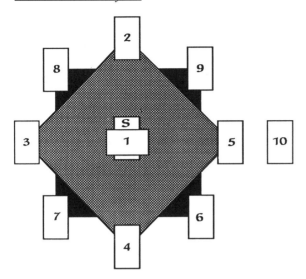

A significator is preselected, and the deck is shuffled and cut three times with the left hand. Ten cards are placed one-by-one around the significator as shown.

Card 1: Covering card, that which touches directly the problem at hand;

Card 2: Opposition card;

Card 3: Present or initial situation;

Card 4: Roots, past, foundation from which the situation arose;

Card 5: Near-future outlook;

Card 6: Development, synthesis of cards uncovered so far;

Card 7: Inner strength, inner depth, unconscious factors;

Card 8: Hopes or fears;

Card 9: Outside influences;

Card 10: Unknown factor, the power that is already at work upon which one must focus because it will become very important for the outcome.

The Mother Peace Eleven-Card Spread

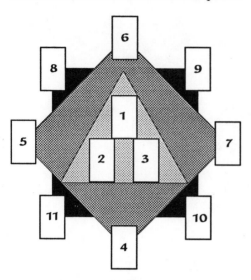

For this layout, a significator can be preselected or not; after shuffling, the cards are spread in the following pattern (Noble, 1983, pp. 232-233).

Card 1:   Significator or questioner;

Card 2:   Context and general atmosphere of the question;

Card 3:   Obstacles and challenges;

Card 4:   Unconscious attitude; foundation; bodily reactions;

Card 5:   Recent past;

Card 6:   Conscious position; thoughts and ideals;

Card 7:   Near future; direction in which things seem to be moving;

Card 8:   Self-concept; self-image;

Card 9:   Hopes and fears; projections;

Card 10:   Home; inner space;

Card 11:   Outcome.

The Druid's Star Spread

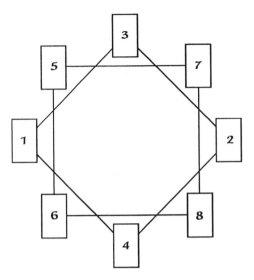

This variation of the previous layout uses only the eight cards in the outer circle. In this case, the first four cards represent the solar mode and the second four, the lunar mode of action. Less than a divination spread, it is used predominantly for in-depth analysis of personality components and their interaction with the present position and situation in life. After shuffling, the cards are cut three times and spread face down. Cards 1 through 4 are turned up first.

Card 1:   The fire element of character—active, enterprising;

Card 2:   The water element—emotive, expressive;

Card 3:   The air element—intellectual, imaginative;

Card 4:   The earth element—practical, materialistic.

Cards 5 through 8 are turned up next.

Card 5 (aligned with card 1):   Health problems or hidden weaknesses;

Card 6 (aligned with card 4):   Inherited traits, good or bad;

Card 7 (aligned with card 3):   Inner or outer polarities;

Card 8 (aligned with card 2):   Hidden fears, level of emotional reactivity.

The Magic Circle or Magic Wheel

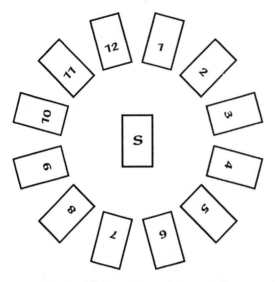

Tradition requires that this spread not be learned from books; it can be passed on by a master, or one can develop one's own technique (Golowin, p. 238). Therefore, the following are only directives for further experimentation. After preselecting the significator, the cards are shuffled and dealt face down in a circle. To answer the question at hand, a card is intuitively chosen and turned over; counting clockwise, every third card is turned until four cards face up.

Card 1: Desires.   Card 3: What supports them.

Card 2: What opposes them.   Card 4: Probable outcome.

Two more questions can be asked; all the cards will then have been turned over.

The Clock of Time

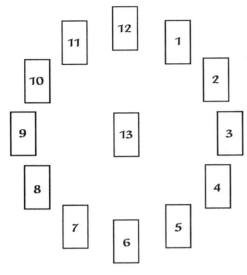

Similar to The Magic Circle, this spread can be used when one is concerned about a specific event—past or future. Twelve cards are selected and placed face down in the order of the hours on the face of a clock. A thirteenth card is then chosen and placed face up in the center of the spread. Depending on the event concerned, the questioner begins with the card placed at its hour (the hour of birth, of a tragedy, of an anticipated interview, etc.). Moving clockwise from that card, the cards are turned face up in an order based on the value of the thirteenth card (elemental, planetary, zodiacal; see p. 353).

The Circular Spread

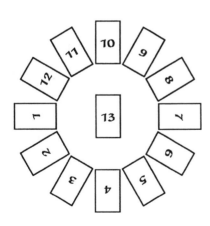

This variation of The Clock of Time is used to give a general forecast of the year ahead. After shuffling, the cards are dealt face up from the top of the deck and placed in astrological-chart sequence. A thirteenth card is placed in the middle. It gives the overall tone of the year to come and must be read first. The twelve remaining cards refer to events in the twelve months ahead, reaction to these events, etc.

The Horoscope Spreads

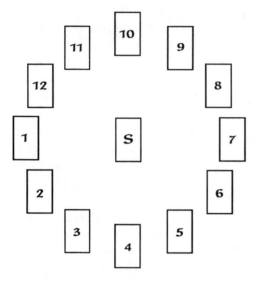

Whenever one needs to locate the source of confusion in one's life, this spread can be used. Identifying the zodiacal house in which obstacles or problems appear can locate the source of distress. After the cards are shuffled and cut, they are dealt counterclockwise beginning with the ascendant. A thirteenth card is then placed in the middle of the circle. Each card is interpreted according to the meaning of its house position; the houses in which cards with a negative connotation appear are the areas in which something needs to be resolved. Positive cards may suggest solutions, qualities that most need focusing and activation in order to see them manifest in one's present life. If the natal chart is well known, these cards can be placed around one's own horoscope. It is important to note the problem and the break-through cards as they relate to what's happening in the chart.

The interpretation of any of the horoscope spreads can be enriched by information from the transits in one's chart at the time of the reading. The planet transiting a particular house can be connected with and compared to the card placed there in the layout.

It has been proposed by some tarot readers that a significator be selected and replaced in the deck before shuffling. Twelve cards are placed face down in a circle, following the order of the astrological houses. The reading is affected by the tonality of the house in which the significator is found. Should it remain in the deck, its absence from the spread is considered a negative answer to the question.

In another variation of the Horoscope Layout, the cards are dealt in a circle after having been shuffled and cut. They are interpreted as follows:

Card 1: Complex of psychological patterns that relates the inner to the outer worlds; individual self-expression; the way one sees and wants others to see oneself; appearance.

Card 2: Money and movable property; things one values and to which one is attached.

Card 3: Capacity to deal with everyday situations and activities in a routine manner; communications; short trips; siblings as people one deals with automatically and easily, but this can become "conscious" if need be.

Card 4: Inward, personal, emotional life; support, foundation, sense of belonging; the parent as provider of nurturing and caring in early life; tradition, collective unconscious.

Card 5: Self-expression, play, love, children, creativity; energies within the self that want to be released for their own sake.

Card 6: Efficiency, service, servants, work, purpose one chooses; benefits from work of others; health problems.

Card 7: Marriage, partnership, conflict with primary relationships.

Card 8: Death, inheritance; transformation, resurrection; freedom from attachments; deep inner experience, occult and psychic.

Card 9: Philosophy, religion, capacity to deal with the exceptional; long-distance journeys; synthetic perceptions; exposure to the unfamiliar as expansion of consciousness.

Card 10: Career, profession; dealing with the outside world, concern about social status, honor, reputation; work as expression of one's identity; goals toward which one aspires in life but has not yet attained.

Card 11: Friends, hopes, wishes, ambition, socialized self-expression; ability to integrate and get along in groups; social attachments.

Card 12: Karma, secrets, confinements; psychic ability.

The Four Trines Horoscope Spread

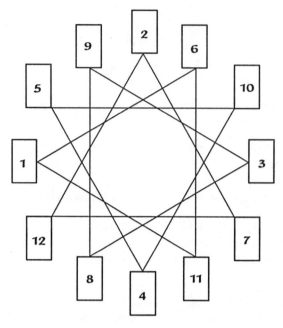

The cards are shuffled, cut three times, and dealt as shown. Although they are not laid out in the order of the houses of the horoscope, the interpretation reveals what might be expected in the life area ruled by the house in which the card is found.

Trine of Life

Card 1:   Personal life; health (first house);

Card 6:   Mental life; philosophy, travel, publications (ninth house);

Card 11:   Children; love affairs, pleasures (fifth house).

Trine of Power

Card 2:   Authority; business, credit; reputation (tenth house);

Card 7:   Labor; sickness; inferiors (sixth house);

Card 12:   Personal possessions, wealth (second house).

Trine of Social Interaction

Card 3:   Marital partner; enemies, lawsuits (seventh house);

Card 8:   Siblings; studies, writings; short trips (third house);

Card 9:   Friends, well-wishers (eleventh house).

Trine of Secret Things

Card 4:   Home, real estate; end of life (fourth house);

Card 10: Legacies; debts; transformation in depth (eighth house);

Card 5:   Restrictions, limitations; unknown enemies (twelfth house).

An additional clarification may be obtained by considering the astrological dimension of the card. If it is one of the zodiacal cards, it indicates a process; if it is one of the planetary cards, it represents a mode of behavior (for zodiac and planetary cards see p. 353). The elementary qualities may uncover feeling tonalities (water) or focus on ideas (air), passion (fire), or stability and nurturance (earth).

The Horoscope Spread (II)

In this variation of the Four Trines Horoscope (Doane and Keyes, pp. 104-105), the cards are dealt exactly in the sequence of the Trines Layout (page 402), but they are read in horoscope fashion from card 1 counterclockwise to card 5, the meaning of each card being given by the significance of the house position it occupies.

Table 19. Signs of the Zodiac and the Major Arcana.

Signs	European School	Paul F. Case	Dolores Ashcroft-Nowicki	Oswald Wirth	Eden Gray	Irene Gad
Aries	High Priest	Emperor	Star(s)	High Priest	Sun	Fool
Taurus	Lover(s)	High Priest	High Priest	Magician	High Priest	Lover(s)
Gemini	Chariot	Lover(s)	Lover(s)	Sun	Lover(s)	Hanged Man
Cancer	Justice	Chariot	Chariot	Moon	Temperance	Temperance
Leo	Hermit	Strength	Strength	Strength	Strength	Strength
Virgo	Wheel of Fortune	Hermit	Hermit	Empress	Hermit	Wheel of Fortune
Libra	Hanged Man	Justice	Justice	Justice	Justice	Justice
Scorpio	Temperance	Death	Death	Tower of Destruction	Judgement	Hermit
Sagittarius	Devil	Temperance	Temperance	Lover(s)	Chariot	Chariot
Capricorn	Tower of Destruction	Devil	Devil	Wheel of Fortune	Devil	Death
Aquarius	Moon	Star(s)	Emperor	Temperance	Star(s)	Star(s)
Pisces	Sun	Moon	Moon	Star(s)	Moon	World

The Life Reading Horoscope Spread

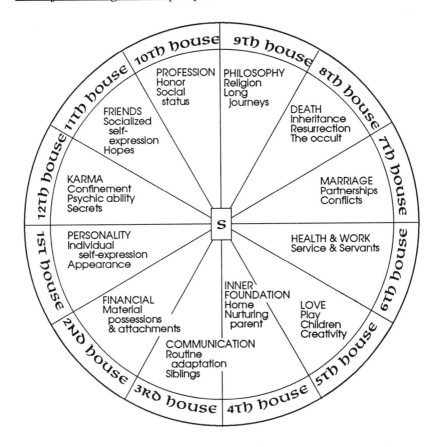

This method (Gray, pp. 103ff.) yields information about character traits and personality rather than answering a specific question. It is similar to reading a natal chart, on which it is based, as it correlates the major arcana cards and the astrological houses in which they fall. A significator representing the questioner is preselected; the cards are then shuffled and cut. The first card (on top of the deck) is placed face up in the position of the first house; the second card is similarly placed on the second house; and so on until twelve cards, representing the twelve houses, have been laid around the significator. For the sign/Major Arcana correlations, see Table 19. For the solar house/Zodiacal sign correlations, see Table 20, p. 410. In addition, Gray (p. 104) recommends that one attempt to correlate the meaning of the card with the solar-chart zodiacal sign corresponding to that house.

The Solar-Chart Method

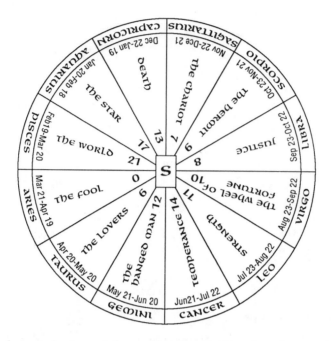

Here also, each sign of the zodiac is correlated with a card of the major arcana. The method is proposed by Gray (pp. 113ff.), who also presents her own personal zodiac/tarot correlations, which correspond at times (e.g., Strength/Leo, Justice/Libra) with Wirth's attributions and at other times with those of Case (High Priest/Taurus, Lover(s)/Gemini, Hermit/Virgo, Devil/Capricorn, Stars/Aquarius, Moon/Pisces; see Table 19 (page 404).

Step 1: Whatever the zodiac/trump pairing chosen, twelve trump cards are removed from the deck and spread on a table in a large circle beginning with the sun-sign card in the position of the first sign, Aries (the first house in the solar chart). The remaining eleven cards in the circle follow the solar chart sequence of signs (see Table 20, p. 410).

Step 2: The questioner identifies the birth sign, placing it over the first house. This is easily done if two circles are constructed: a larger one on which the astrological houses and their meanings are marked at the periphery, and a smaller one that fits inside the larger and shows the tarot/zodiacal correlations (Table 19). When the smaller is superimposed on the larger, they can be made to revolve around a pin through their centers so that the birth sign and the first house/tarot card are aligned (see page 456.)

Step 3: Each card is read, beginning with the one over the first house; its significance is interpreted in conjunction with the meanings associated with that house.

Step 4: The ten remaining cards are shuffled, cut, and placed around the circle, giving priority to the houses that are more meaningful or more problematic. This second group of cards describes personality characteristics, which combine with the general traits to give a fuller picture of the questioner. Thus the reading integrates the meanings of the astrological houses with the general traits of the questioner (as shown by the birth sign) and the personality characteristics.

As an alternative, one can use the four aces in addition to the major arcana cards. This will provide 12 cards for step 4, covering all the astrological houses and two left over cards for additional clarification, if needed. For the meaning of the four aces see p. 425.

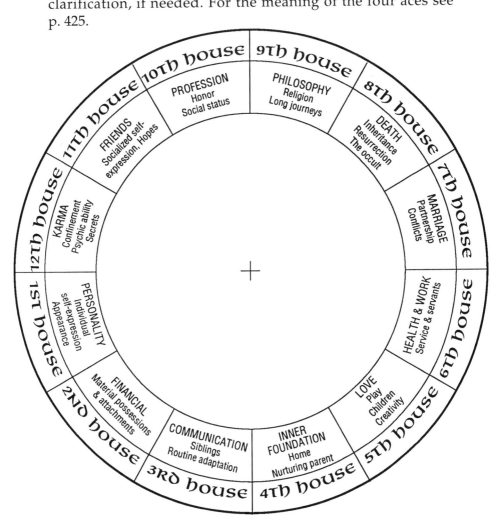

The Astrological Spread

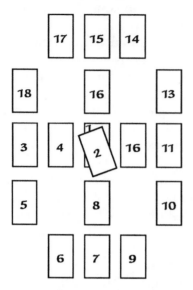

For Mann (pp. 148ff.), this is the most important and useful spread because it may be used to answer questions and can be applied to any period of time. Using eighteen cards in its structure, it expands the Celtic Cross and places an astrological wheel around it. A significator is preselected; the cards are shuffled, cut, and laid as shown.

Card 1:   Significator;

Card 2:   Addition to or modification of card 1;

Card 3:   First house—personality;

Card 4:   Essence of personality;

Card 5:   Second house—financial issues;

Card 6:   Third house—self-expression and siblings;

Card 7:   Fourth house—family, deep emotions, home;

Card 8:   Essence of the unconscious;

Card 9:   Fifth house—love, creativity, beauty;

Card 10: Sixth house—work, health, dependents, daily tasks;

Card 11: Seventh house—partnerships, marriage, contracts, enemies;

Card 12: Essence of relationships;

Card 13: Eighth house—depth, death and transformation, the occult;

Card 14: Ninth house—the higher mind, spiritual aspirations, long journeys;

Card 15: Tenth house—professional achievement, fame, wealth, standing;

Card 16: Essence of ego consciousness;

Card 17: Eleventh house—friends, groups, hopes, desires, altruistic interests;

Card 18: Twelfth house—secrets, seclusion, limitations, sacrifice.

Cards 4 and 12, and 16 and 8 are placed at important astrological points on the horizontal and vertical axes. At the top, point 16 designates the midheaven (MC, *medium coeli*), the essence of ego consciousness; point 8, its opposite, is at the nadir (IC, *immum coeli*) and indicates the depth of the unconscious; to the left, point 4 marks the ascendent (ASC), representing the personality in its inner-world aspect; and at the far right, point 12, the descendent (DSC), signifies the outer world and/or one's partner.

TABLE 20. ASTROLOGICAL SIGNS AND MEANINGS.

Solar House	Ruler	Meaning in Divination
1	Aries	Rules all beginnings; it is assigned to physical appearance and characteristics, temperament and personality, one's outlook on the world, and future potential.
2	Taurus	Conserves and builds; it concerns financial affairs, earning power, and tangible assets.
3	Gemini	Is assigned to relatives, especially siblings; it also refers to communications, writings, and short journeys.
4	Cancer	Governs the first home environment; it is also assigned to old age, old people, the father.
5	Leo	Is concerned with love affairs, children, things that cause excitement (e.g., theater, gambling, speculation), and creative ability.
6	Virgo	Rules work and employees, as well as general health, food, and hygiene.
7	Libra	Is assigned both to marriage and to business partners, as well as to dealings with the public, lawsuits, and open enemies.
8	Scorpio	Governs death, legacies, and occult experiences.
9	Sagittarius	Is concerned with law, philosophy, ideals, and religion; also dreams, intuition, education, and long journeys.
10	Capricorn	Rules public life, profession, fame, and social status. The mother is suggested here. (Sometimes this is reversed, with the mother occupying the fourth house and the father the tenth.)
11	Aquarius	Concerns friends, groups, hopes, wishes, and aspirations.
12	Pisces	Governs hidden limitations that restrict the power of expression; also secret desires, secret enemies, self-undoing; institutions and places that restrict or confine.

Astrological Spread Amplified

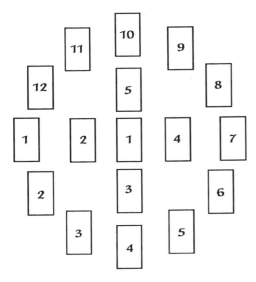

An amplification of the astrological spread is presented by Denning and Phillips (pp. 204ff.). Cards 2 through 5 are placed at the cardinal points around the significator.

Card 1: Significator;

Card 2: Beginning, birth;

Card 3: Development, growth;

Card 4: Maturity;

Card 5: Decline; long-term forecasts.

Twelve cards are then placed as shown. They follow the sequence of the astrological houses, and their meanings are derived narrowly from the meanings of the houses of the zodiac. The cards occupying house positions 2, 5, 8, and 11 represent important key assessments of the status of the subject of inquiry.

The Tree of Life or Tree of the Cabala

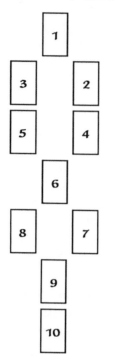

After shuffling and cutting, the cards are selected one-by-one and placed in the form of the sephirotic tree, following the established sequence of the Lightning Flash. The reading begins at *Malkuth* (card 10), and proceeds slowly upward to the triangle *Yesod—Hod—Netzah* (cards 9, 8, and 7), then to the triangle *Tipheret—Geburah—Hesed* (cards 6, 5, and 4), and finally to the supernal triangle *Binah—Hochmah—Kether* (cards 3, 2, and 1). As we know, each triangle contains two opposing concepts plus a third, which reconciles them. The tarot cards on the sephirotic tree should be read the same way.

Card 1: The questioner's highest spiritual awareness at the time;

Card 2: Spiritual creative potential, personal initiative, wisdom;

Card 3: Creative potential in the material world, understanding;

Card 4: Qualities of generosity, prosperity, abundance, expansion, mercy, financial success;

Card 5: Severity, competitiveness, self-defense, anger, self-rightousness, revenge, power;

Card 6: Receptivity to life force, the"heart," essential self;

Card 7: Participation in the natural world, passion, expressiveness, instinctive basis of creativity;

Card 8: Communication, intelligence, choice;

Card 9: Sensitivity, psychic receptivity, emergence of individuality;

Card 10: The totality of forces in the material world, instinctual physical appetites, purely material basis from which the slow climb begins.

Each card in this spread must be interpreted in the order in which it was set out, and by relating its meaning to the cards before and after it. The cards also have a vertical association. That is, the three pillars formed can be interpreted to reveal the father or masculine influence (right pillar), the mother or feminine influence (left pillar), and the questioner's inner development and its reaction to the masculine and feminine influences (center pillar, moving downward). Some readers interpret the cards in the right pillar as having a favorable influence; those in the left, an unfavorable effect; and the central cards as the outcome. Additionally, cards 1 through 3 represent spiritual qualities; cards 4 through 6, mental life; cards 7 through 9, emotional life; and card 10, the whole person, including the physical body. If important points remain obscure, one can take four cards from the remaining deck and place them face up, one-by-one, on top of the aspect to be clarified. Alternatively, one may interpret as follows:

Card 1: Key factor—spirituality;

Card 2: Long-term outcome—responsibility;

Card 3: Immediate outcome, short-term results—difficulties;

Card 4: What the questioner feels—helpful matters;

Card 5: What the questioner thinks—opposing matters;

Card 6: Current situations—achievements;

Card 7: Effects of people and environment—emotional relationships;

Card 8: Effects of inner guidance—communication—career;

Card 9: Values and beliefs—unconscious foundation;

Card 10: Current self-assessment—home and family.

After reading the cards from bottom to top (The Path of the Serpent), it is recommended that they be read from top to bottom (The Lightning Flash). The diagonals (cards 5, 6, 7, and 4, 6, 8) should also be examined along with the pillars, especially the central pillar, for indications of transformation. After the cards have been interpreted, one of the unused cards is selected to represent the invisible sephira *Daat*, which indicates hidden potential and higher-self aspirations; the portent of this card is never to be used in the service of the ego.

The Chakra Spread

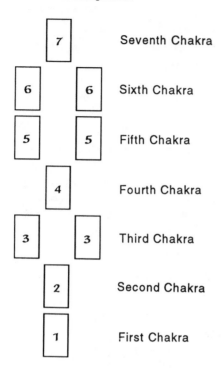

Seventh Chakra

Sixth Chakra

Fifth Chakra

Fourth Chakra

Third Chakra

Second Chakra

First Chakra

An arrangement similar to The Tree of Life has been used by Greer, (1984, pp. 160ff.) to ask the psychological source of bodily ailments. She envisions this spread as combining the Eastern concept of the seven energy centers with the Western vision of the Tree of Life and its application to the human body. After the cards are shuffled, cut into three piles, and the deck restored, ten cards are selected and placed as shown.

Chakra 1: The root, or *Muladhara chakra*, is concerned with basic survival instinct, vigor, vitality, the general life-energy level.

Chakra 2: The second, or *Svadhistana chakra*, governs sexuality and emotions.

Chakra 3: The navel, solar plexus, or *Manipura chakra*, shows how one expresses vital energies; the left represents ego and will; the right, emotional connections. (Two cards are drawn here.)

Chakra 4: The heart, or *Anahata chakra*, is the center of universal love and shows ability to experience compassion.

Chakra 5: The throat, or *Vishudda chakra*, shows self-expression, communication. If this is blocked, something that needs to be expressed is held back; the right card indicates outer-directedness, and the left card, inner-directedness contributing to this problem. (Two cards.)

Chakra 6: The third eye, or *Ajna chakra*, is the seat of inner vision; it contributes to the capacity to make thoughts reality. (Two cards.)

Chakra 7: The crown, or *Sahasrara chakra*, represents connectedness to the source of spiritual energy; the highest aspirations and knowledge of eternal truth are located here.

The card representing the heart chakra is the key card in this "health" reading.

The Cabala Spread

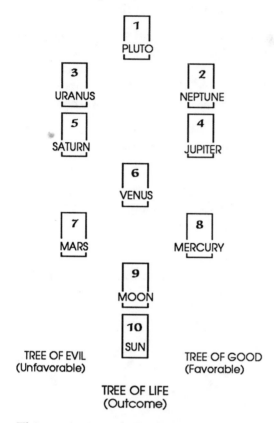

This variation of The Tree of Life is used by Doane and Keyes (pp. 67ff.) to elucidate the favorable and unfavorable influences leading to the outcome of the situation in question. The cards of the right pillar, or Tree of Good, indicate favorable forces or events; those of the left pillar, or Tree of Evil, represent unfavorable forces and events; and the cards of the central pillar constitute the outcome. Doane and Keyes interpret individual positions on this Tree of Life by correlating the meaning with the astrological correspondence of each place on the Tree.

Card 1: Pluto—spiritual orientation;

Card 2: Neptune—original wisdom;

Card 3: Uranus—background intelligence;

Card 4: Jupiter—influence of mercy;

Card 5:   Saturn—desire for justice;

Card 6:   Venus—love of beauty and life;

Card 7:   Mars—desire for victory;

Card 8:   Mercury—outgoing splendor and show;

Card 9:   Moon—home conditions;

Card 10:   Sun—physical power and material results.

The 3-Card Wish Spread

The questioner should concentrate on the wish while shuffling and utter it mentally while the cards are cut. The top three cards are selected and set in a horizontal row; they assess and comment on the wish. If additional information is needed, they can be reduced (see p. 353) and the card thus determined will provide the needed clarification.

The 15-Card Wish Spread

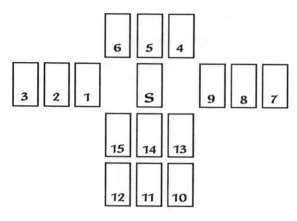

A more expanded Wish Spread uses fifteen cards. A significator representing the questioner or the wish is chosen. The cards are shuffled, and fifteen are drawn at random from the deck, intuitively. They are laid face down according to the following pattern.

Cards 1-3:   The immediate environment;

Cards 4-6:   Elements of the wish;

Cards 7-9:   Components blocking or opposing it;

Cards 10-12: What needs attention;

Cards 13-15: What will become clear.

The 18-Card Wish Spread

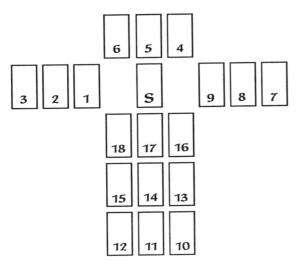

If cards 13 through 15 do not give a satisfactory solution, Roberts (p. 72) suggests drawing three more cards for clarification. If, after the significator is selected, it is reintroduced into the deck before shuffling, it will contribute to the interpretation of the outcome as follows. If it appears in the spread (except in the group 7 through 9), the wish will be realized (the closer it appears in numerical sequence to card 1, the sooner this will happen); should it appear in the 7 through 9 sequence, the probability of its fulfillment is low and the cards will explain why; should the significator not appear at all, the answer will be given by the general meaning of the spread.

The Name Spread

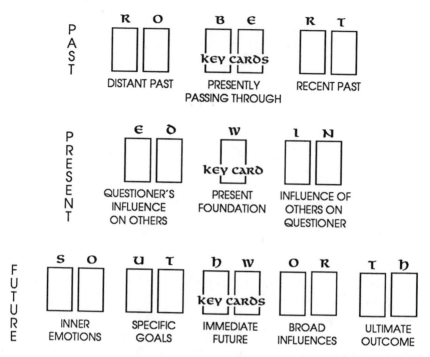

The cards are laid from left to right in three rows such that the top, middle, and bottom rows each contain as many cards as there are letters in the first, middle, or last name, respectively. Should the questioner have no middle name, the number of cards in the first name is repeated in the middle row. If the first or middle names contains fewer than three letters, it is assigned three cards. If the last name contains fewer than five letters, that row is allocated five cards. The center card in each row (or the two middle cards) are important key cards. The top row (the past), shows what was given or bestowed at birth. Cards to the left of key indicate broad background influences, whereas those to the right of it describe relatively recent ones. The middle row (the present), shows how the questioner influences others (left of key) and how others influence her/him (right of key). The bottom row relates to future prospects and to the outcome, with expectations and goals to the left of key and a progression of near-future events to ultimate outcome described to the right. If reversed, this last card can depict obstacles to be met and overcome. The Name Spread also provides identification of the "age card," which is very important, as it indicates past, present, and future elements that interact with the personality of the questioner. To find it, the cards are counted starting top left and going through the spread as often as necessary until the card corresponding to the age of the questioner is reached.

The Yoni Yantra

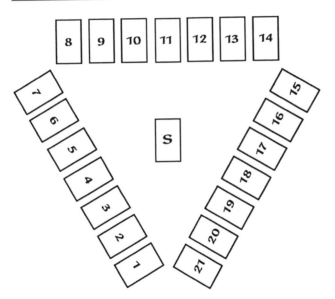

Traditionally incorporating the entire deck, a short form uses only the trumps in three groups of seven cards. A significator is pres-elected, and the remaining cards are shuffled and cut. Beginning bottom center, the cards are laid one-by-one in a triangular pattern as shown. The top row represents the present; the right side, the future; and the left, the past. The number 21 is sacred (Walker, p. 48) and is associated with the magic numbers 3 and 7 (its only factors), which are related to the Triple Goddess and her Seven priestesses, the seven sisters, the Pleiades. Each side of the Yoni Yantra can represent seven months or seven years, depending on the age of the questioner or the dimensions of the question.

The Infinity Layout

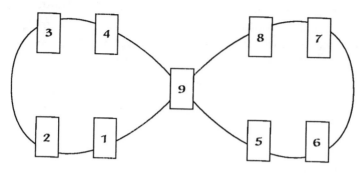

The numinous qualities of the infinity symbol have inspired Steiner-Geringer to use its shape as the basis of her spread (pp. 220–224). She felt that nine is the most appropriate number of cards to use for this layout because numerologically nine symbolizes completion, perfection, truth. Nine stands for enrichment and expansion of consciousness by contact with the unconscious through introverted descent into one's inner world. Nine is the treble triad embracing all numbers; it is connected with motherhood and fertility, death and rebirth, wisdom and occult powers. This spread is used whenever contradictory elements in a situation or within a person demands resolution and integration.

After the cards are shuffled and cut, they are picked out of the deck one by one and placed face up, according to the illustration. The cards on the left side (counterclockwise) represent unconscious factors, hidden elements in the situation, the difficulties, the obstacles. The cards on the right side (clockwise) represent conscious factors, well-known elements that have to be taken into consideration, the opportunities, the favorable aspects. The cards are first interpreted one at a time. In the next step, the cards of the counterclockwise and clockwise side are paired as follows: cards 1 and 8; cards 2 and 7; cards 3 and 6; cards 4 and 5; and then card 9. Whenever two alternatives are presented, cards 1 through 4 can offer information regarding one option and cards 5 through 8 provide information for the other. Card 9 suggests the solution, the outcome, or the integration of the conflicting elements. For this reason, it can sometimes be selected by reduction of all the other card numbers (rather than being drawn from the deck.) If one allows intuition to connect to the cards, the answer comes. The example reading has been included to show how this works.

EXAMPLE READING: A 50-year-old professional woman is in an intimate relationship with a married man who has repeatedly attempted to separate from his wife but had never succeeded in doing so. Consulting the cards regarding the relationship's future, she draws the cards shown in the diagram.

Interpretation: 1) The Empress, reversed: the nurturing and protecting expected from the relationship is not forthcoming; confusion and complexity create a climate of anxious concern. 2) The Lovers: there is passion and promise of fulfillment; a true partnership may develop. 3) The Hanged Man: there must be a voluntary accepted change in perspective for both partners; sentimental daydreams and unrealistic projects must be avoided; time is needed to consolidate and deepen the feelings that do exist. 4) The Magician, reversed: doubt, uncertainty, and changing moods interfere with the vitality needed to overcome opposition. The partners have to see each other and accept each other as they really are and must avoid projecting onto the other their own dissatisfaction with themselves. 5) The Chariot, reversed: moments of paralysis alternate with bursts of reckless activity; there is danger of hasty decisions. 6) The Hermit: meditation and introspection are needed to sustain this type of relationship. A well-centered personality enables concentration of the positive aspects and discretely avoids emphasizing the missing elements. 7) Death, reversed: despite intensely painful experiences, redemption and resurrection are at hand; there is hope for an important and beneficial transformation. 8) The Emperor: there is real potential for the future development of the relationship, provided the qualities of mercy, acceptance, and mutual understanding can be activated. There is expansive potential and generosity but also a lack of discipline. 9) The High Priest: the outcome is based on a strong sense of values. The frictions of a life shared under difficult circumstances provide an opportunity to expand integrity and self-knowledge.

Next, the cards are interpreted in pairs. Card 1 & 8: The Empress, reversed, and The Emperor: this could have shown an ideal relationship had the Empress card not been reversed. As it stands, it seems to indicate that a certain lack of nurturance may curtail the capacity to endure. Card 2 & 7: The Lovers and Death reversed: there seems to be a real feeling connection between the partners; however, death and transformation will play a major role in the final decision. Card 3 & 6: The Hanged Man and The Hermit: a change in perspective so total as to feel oneself hanging upside down may counterbalance the effect of the pair that follows. Card 4 & 5: The Magician and The Chariot, both reversed: both are powerful but ill-aspected in this layout; neither The Magician's vision nor The Charioteer's enthusiasm is available to help sustain the relationship.

In the 9th position, the outcome is represented by a card (The High Priest) that stands for lawful acceptance of the values and the rules of orderly behavior. Given the nature of the relationship for which the reading was requested, it is doubtful that this relationship will fulfill the real promises it does show. For the present it can go either way, but in order to succeed, much work needs to be done. (The reading of the outcome may have been different, if for example, the same cards had been selected by an artist, because the person, age, character, and general situation of the questioner play an essential role in any interpretation.

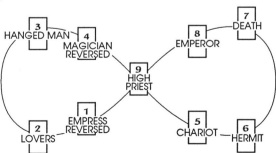

The Jungian Spread

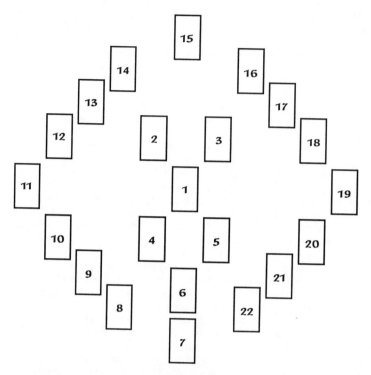

To provide an in-depth life reading, the twenty-two cards of the major arcana are shuffled, cut, and laid one-by-one face down according to the illustration (from Roberts, pp. 230-231). Card 1, the "Unnamed Namer," the unmanifest, the spiritual essence, the creative matrix, is not turned over. The next four cards, called "the heritage cards" because they represent the father and mother (cards 2 and 3) and the *animus* and *anima* (cards 4 and 5), are interpreted first. Card 6, signifying the individual means by which the inner world of the questioner relates to the outer world, is turned over next and interpreted in relation to the preceding four. Indeed, card 6 is the bridge between the inner and the outer worlds, symbolized by the outer circle of cards that stands for the wheel of mundane experience. They are interpreted as follows:

Card 7:   Heritage at the moment of birth;

Cards 8 and 9:   Early development;

Card 10:   Intellectual birth;

Cards 11 through 13: Growing inward—beginning the descent to the nadir;

Card 14: The nadir of life, point of reversal;

Cards 15 through 17: The search for what is lacking—inner transformation;

Cards 18 through 22: The later part of life, its challenges and its high points.

The entire spread describes the Hero's Journey, card 14 representing the deepest point of The Night Sea Journey.

THE TEN-THRONES LAYOUT

With few exceptions, most of the foregoing spreads can be used not only with the major arcana as described, but also with the entire tarot deck. However, I have chosen not to work with full-deck layouts, preferring to limit myself to those that utilize only the twenty-two trumps. There is, nevertheless, a particular spread that uses the aces with the trumps; it is called the *Sephirot* Spread, or the Ten-Thrones Layout (Doane & Keyes, pp. 45ff.) and is included here because the four aces complete the alchemical "quintessence," sometimes equated with the fifth suit, the trumps, the major arcana (Walker, p. 29).

The accompanying figure graphically illustrates the relationships between the major arcana and the four suits. The multifaceted tarot is shown to synthesize the world of the spirit (the triangle, representing God, the Trinity), the physical world (the square), and human consciousness (the center point). The four suits are represented along the sides of the square, and the major arcana form the sides of the triangle within (Kaplan, *Encyclopedia of Tarot*, Vol. I, p. 14). The aces have important connections to archetypal quaternities: these are the four seasons, the four cardinal points, the four elements, the four ages of the human being, the four temperaments, the four psychological functions, the four cabalistic worlds. Hoeller (p. 7), among others, suggests the following relationships:

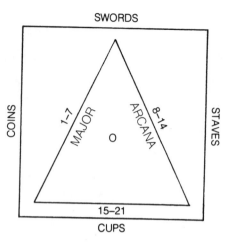

Suits	Elements	Functions
Coins	Earth	Sensation
Cups	Water	Feeling
Swords	Fire	Thinking
Wands	Air	Intuition

While the associations coins/earth/sensation and cups/water/feeling are consistent, some authors (e.g., Halevi, *Tree of Life/Introduction to the Cabala*, p. 102) associate swords with air and wands with fire, and make the following correspondences:

Suits	Elements	Worlds
Coins	Earth	*Assiah*
Cups	Water	*Yetzirah*
Swords	Air	*Beriah*
Wands	Fire	*Aziluth*

or match swords with earth and coins with fire (Thierens, pp.17-26).

The Ten-Thrones Spread

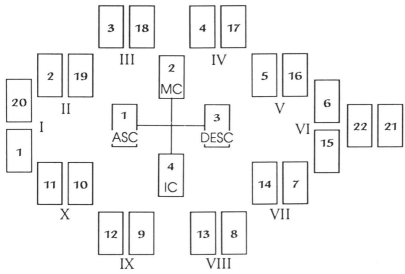

In addition to the twenty-two major arcana, the Ten-Throne Spread uses the four aces which are shuffled and cut separately and dealt face down in the inner circle of the spread. Called astral keys, they mark the four stations corresponding to the four angles of a horoscope: ascendant (ASC), midheaven (MC), descendant (DSC), and nadir (IC). The first station pertains to life; the second, to business; the third, to love or war; and the fourth, to hidden things or outcomes. The suit of the ace at each station determines the meaning of the astral kingdom in that reading. See Table 21 on page 428.

The reading begins with the ace indicated by the question asked (i.e., if it relates to life, one starts with the ascendant; if it pertains to business, one starts with midheaven, and so forth). Use Table 21 (page 428) to understand the various symbology connected to the aces.

The major arcana are then shuffled and dealt facedown in the outer circle according to the illustration of the spread. The first ten cards are placed in the positions of thrones I through X, and the rest are dealt back from thrones X to I. The two leftover cards are placed to the right of the layout and serve as a final clarification if the reading seems ambiguous. In interpreting the spread, the four cards in the position of thrones of the MC and IC are of equal importance; in position of thrones ASC and DSC, the two center cards (I or VI) indicate the most important factors; the other four (II and X or V and VII) show modifying influences.

The ace associated with the question asked is located (Table 22) and turned up, followed by the throne cards of that astral key ace. These indicate the reason for the condition described by the astral key. The opposite ace (turned over next) depicts the quality of that opposition, and its throne cards explain it. The key that follows the ace (clockwise) that represents the question is read next; this key, its ace, and its thrones show the progress expected. The end of the matter is described by the ace opposing the progress, which—along with its throne cards—gives the significance of the conclusion of the reading.

TABLE 21. ACES AND KEY STATIONS.

Aces	Ascendant (Life)	Midheaven (Business)	Descendant (Love and War)	Nadir (Hidden Things) (Outcome)
Cups	Love, pleasure, may deplete vitality	Hedonistic pursuit, negative influences	Joy, happiness	Pleasant results
Coins	Strength, vigor, vitality	Effort, favorable influences	Abundance of strength	Difficulties, even possible failure
Swords	Illness, unfavorable influences	Failure	Dispute	Favorable outcome
Wands	Intuition, originality, favorable influences	Power	Difficulties with status and position	Struggles

TABLE 22. THE READING SEQUENCE

Subject Matter	Question	Opposition	Progress	End
Body, self-interest, personality	ASC	DSC	MC	IC
Love, marriage, partnership, enemies	DSC	ASC	IC	MC
Business, profession, reputation	MC	IC	DSC	ASC
Psychic matters, hidden secrets	IC	MC	ASC	DSC

NONDIVINATION SPREADS

No tarot book can cover all the possibilities of the meanings of the cards. What the tarot can be made to reveal is limited only by the capacity of insight of the person using it. In astrology knowing the planets, the signs, and the houses is only the beginning; as one becomes more knowledgeable the aspects and the patterns the planets form increases with experience. To become a good reader of the tarot one must similarly go beyond individual cards and find out the many ways they can change as they interact with each other. The cards will start to "speak," and any interpretation one gives them will go beyond the usual, accepted meaning. The nondivination spreads help reveal the deeper meanings and connections of the cards. Starting on page 435 a brief compilation is given of the most frequently encountered key meanings used for divination purposes for each of the 22 cards.

The Paths to Salvation

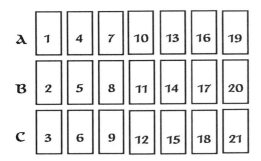

Golowin (pp. 224-226) proposed a form of the Twenty-one Card Gypsy Method to enhance our understanding of the cards. However, instead of shuffling and selecting the cards at random, he begins at the upper left with the Magician (I), and places the High Priestess (II), followed by the Empress (III), below. The Emperor (IV) heads the next column of three, and the spread proceeds until it ends with the World (XXI) at the lower right. The Fool (0) is then placed bottom center. For Golowin, the three rows, read right to left, represent three paths to higher consciousness. See Table 23 on page 430.

TABLE 23. THREE PATHS TO HIGHER CONSCIOUSNESS

The Way of The Magician	XIX: XVI: XIII: X: VII: IV: I:	The light of realization; Destruction; Death; Fortune; Conscious action; Ability to rule one's own world; The goal is represented by the Magician no longer bewildered by the confusions of the game of life.
The Way of The High Priestess	XX: XVII: XIV: XI: VIII: V: II:	Divine creation; Divine source of cosmic energy; Capacity to keep natural energies in balance; Strength resulting from mastery; and Discrimination in service to Cosmic energies; The ultimate goal is represented by the High Priestess and the model she sets.
The Way of The Empress	XXI: XVIII: XV: XII: IX: VI: III:	The World, leading to an encounter with The forces of the night; and The forces of darkness; Rigorous tests follow, resulting in Wisdom; Finally one is able to come to terms with oneself and the world with care and compassion. This is a path of increased experience.

THE WHEELS OF BECOMING

This spread uses the very powerful symbol of the lemniscate, a mystical-world symbol of two serpents swallowing each other's tail, the symbol of infinity, the figure eight traced on the ground during holy ritual dances: the clockwise circle followed by the counterclockwise. The layout presents us with these same joined circles. Clockwise—the Apollonian, the world of outer appearances, followed by the counterclockwise—the lunar, the world of inner meanings.

The lemniscate appears twice in the major arcana: first as the hat brim of The Magician (I), a figure leading the first decade, the solar-circle cards. The second appearance is in the hat brim of Strength (XI), which leads the second decade, the lunar-circle cards (Walker, pp. 35ff.).

The Wheels of Becoming

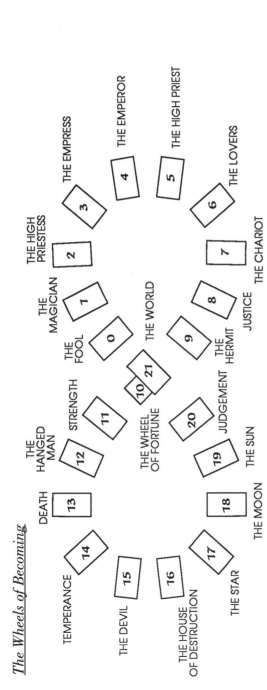

When the trumps are laid out in the shape of the infinity sign, each card in the first circle corresponds to a card in the second; the numbers of the paired cards add up to 20, the finger-and-toes number sacred in both Indo-European and Mayan numerology. The only exception to this total are the two cards at the junction of the circles: the Wheel of Fortune (X), indicating the midpoint of life when attention turns inward, and the final card, the World (XXI), signalling a new beginning. This layout reveals the hidden correlations between cards V and XV, between cards II and XVIII, and between cards VII and XIII. These hidden correlations were dangerously heretical in the 14th century (for example the Pope, Card V, and the Devil, card XV correlation). Today, however, they are very helpful in revealing the shadow aspect behind the most "positive" cards (for example Death, card XIII, lurking in the shadow of the Charioteer in card VII).

The Three Hexagrams

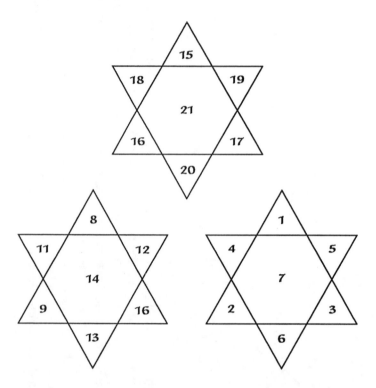

Rather than divination, this spread provides a sense of the profound meaning and inter-relatedness of the cards. These three star-shaped hexagrams, sometimes seen as the creator, the destroyer, and the savior (or the Hindu "bringer of joy") are usually spread with the first hexagram on the left, the second on the right, and the third in the middle. The essence of the three aspects is represented by the seventh card (in the center). On the downward-pointing triangle of each hexagram, the card on the right represents the spirit; that on the left, the material or visible world, and the card at the tip, the synthesis of the two, containing both aspects in balance. In the upward-pointing triangles, the card to the right represents the passive, introverted stance; the card to the left, the active, extroverted stance; the central card is once again a synthesis of the two. The first hexagram can be seen as the macrocosmic elements and the second, the microcosmic, personal elements interacting in our lives. The third hexagram symbolizes the road to integration and wholeness (see Golowin, pp. 226ff. and Wirth 1990, pp. 41-42).

The Three Dancing Wheels.

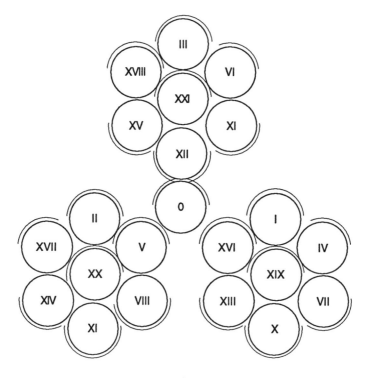

Similar to the Three Hexagrams this spread can be used to understand the themes of action, reaction, and integration underlying the major arcana (Greer, 1984, p. 112). Three wheels of cards are created by placing the Magician at 12 o'clock on the first wheel (right), the High Priestess at 12 o'clock on the second wheel (left), and the Empress at 12 o'clock on the third wheel (above). The rest of the trumps are arranged clockwise, as indicated in the illustration; the last three cards are placed in the hub of each wheel, while the Fool provides the fulcrum of the entire spread. In each wheel the juxtaposed cards reduce to the same digit (for example in wheel one $4 + 7 = 11 = 2$; $16 + 13 = 29 = 11 = 2$) and the final card reduces to the number of the first (for example in the first wheel $1 + 9 = 10 = 1$), thus revealing their interconnectedness.

The Magic Dance

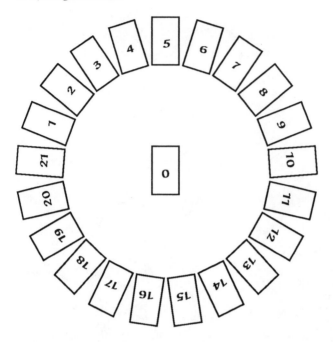

This layout also reveals the rhythmic energy among the cards, which are spread in a circle around the Fool. This image can be envisioned as a dance of the trumps with The Fool at its center, and one can speculate on the dynamic interplay between him and each individual card of the major arcana.

DIVINATORY MEANINGS

CARD I (THE MAGICIAN)

LE BATELEUR

On the spiritual level, the Magician may be interpreted as wholeness of the personality, as disciplined search for knowledge, as the capacity and power to deal with events, to use and change the world. He signifies thought that becomes action, choice of appropriate means, dedication, active will, sacrifice, magic, ritual.*

On the tangible level, this card indicates reflection before starting a project, self-knowledge, self-reflection, self-awareness, initiative, calculated risk taking; the capacity to discriminate and to judge, to be goal oriented; the ability to defend oneself, to enter into the details of a problem, the facility to put things together; vitality, diplomacy, eloquence, rapid reaction of thought, lack of prejudice, fantasy, helpfulness, body/mind integration. He represents the person asking for the consultation.

Card I warns against presumption and bragging, deviousness and lying, charlatans and con men, exploitation and lack of scruples; against social strivings, vain pursuits, usurpation, agitation, and provocation; against inattention even in small things, scattering of strength, careless checking of foundations, unlucky enterprise, neurasthenia, obsession, isolation in daydreams, conflicts that can degenerate into violence, the danger of remaining stuck at the concrete level or of being lured away from reality by inflation.

---

* The cards used in this section are from the *Tarot Rhenan* deck.

CARD II (THE HIGH PRIESTESS)

The High Priestess represents intuition, inspiration, the unity of power, the sea of origin, retrograde motion. She is divine wisdom, strength, faith, religious and philosophic knowledge, inductive thinking, readiness for sacrifice. She depicts trust in God, providence; she helps comprehension of what is hidden, interpretation of omens; she is seer and transmitter of ritual. She is silence, inner composure, tranquillity, withdrawal. She symbolizes human personality as receptacle of the divine. The joy and tragedy of each creative birth belong to her, as do letting go, and victory over fate. Experiencing the fruit of interiority as purity of primordial nature, the unity of conscious light and of the unconscious essence, and influx of the powers of truth in the form of ideas are her domain.

On the spiritual level, this card mediates new understanding, but solves no problem. It can facilitate helpful hints from the unconscious for deciphering problems in the realm of nature.

On the tangible level it indicates reserve, perseverance, patience, compassion, fame, victory over evil, and tenacity. She represents the stores of the collective unconscious, memory, meditation, recognition of the hidden.

Card II warns against inactivity, daydreaming, wishful thinking, distortion, deception, hidden intentions, damage due to lack of knowledge or insufficient reflection. She warns against grudges and vengefulness, fantasies and unrealistic plans, self-torment and extravagance, indiscretion, fanaticism, and intolerance. She warns against confining dogmatism and against the dangers that a study under duress brings with it, against fatalism, erroneous intuitions, lateness, remaining at a standstill, painful realizations, morbid scrupulosity, loss of zest for life, despair, suicide, and coldness of heart.

Cards I and II represent the divine couple, the elected, the incarnation of the spark from eternal energy, the birth of the new individual, being and living, light and power, love and will, father and mother, warm and cold light.

CARD III (THE EMPRESS)

On the spiritual level, the Empress represents love, fertility, creative imagination, the influence of form on ideas, the bridge between intuition and logical thinking, the link between power and knowledge, and the realm of wishes, formed and unformed.

On the tangible level, this card denotes the love of the concrete, openness, culture, knowledge through study, perseverance, the readiness to exertion. She represents observations, precision, circumspection, softness, kindness, conviviality, richness, generosity, pertinent appraisal of practical possibilities, appropriate utilization of materials, psychic balance, situations changing for the better, fertility. For women she means all that pertains to marriage, the joys and the tragedies of giving birth. For men she means all that pertains to expansion, to travel. For both she refers to support from friends and family.

Card III warns against ostentation, dissipation, grandiosity, frivolity, phoniness, seduction. She warns against false evaluation of a situation and bad timing, against ambivalence toward goal-setting and unwise vacillation of decisions, against stubbornness that adheres too long to a personal opinion or that opposes decisions already made. She warns against not paying heed to dangers, temerity, absence of judgment, superficiality and precipitation, discussion on all levels at once, confusion, postponement of an unavoidable event. She warns against catastrophes of nature.

Cards I, II, and III represent the unity of being that can unfold in the multiplicity of existence; just as in dreams the dreamer is at the same time himself and all the other dream figures, multiplicity can manifest as possibility without disrupting the basic unity of the essence of existence.

CARD IV (THE EMPEROR)

On the spiritual level, the Emperor represents the objective world, law, providence, expansiveness, clemency, goodness, love of one's fellow human, active willingness to serve, forebearance, good memory, the world of ideas (the amplitude and depth of which has been gauged), stabilizing force, stagnation, rigidity, the masculine strength of the woman, the feminine *yang*.

On the tangible level, this card denotes authority, energy, power, right, perseverance, rigor, firmness, consequence, precision, pertinent definition as the basis of certainty, possibilities that facilitate the execution of a project, favorable circumstances, pertinent work, peace, union, harmony of feelings, goodness, pity, signing of contracts, fusion of commercial enterprises, corporations, good health, an influential protector.

Card IV warns against arbitrariness, injustice, despotism, brutality, flattery, despoiling of inheritance; against lack of self-control and giving in through weakness, lack of discernment, impossibility to foresee, tenacious adversaries, lateness in intention and execution. It warns against unexpected unfavorable results and losses; against political opportunism and corrupt officials; against storms, floods, shipwrecks, and natural catastrophes; against devastation of the world by profiteering, hardness of heart, compulsive determination to hang onto fading youth; against polemical debate instead of political realism; against war.

CARD V (THE HIGH PRIEST)

On the spiritual level, the High Priest (or Pope) represents striving for redemption, sublimation, understanding faith, submission to the will of God, *credo ut intelligam* (to believe is to understand). It shows inner certainty, oral transmission, religious and philosophical wisdom. It is the sphere of activity of intelligence, the opposition of contraries, the organization and exchange of spiritual forces. It depicts the material structure of rituals, conservation, strengthening, constraint. It designates the pentagon as symbol of materialization, foundation. It is the power of lawfulness.

On the tangible level, this card indicates religious instruction and appropriate practical advice, heartfelt piety, meditation, prayer, veneration, goodness. It represents respect for decorum and the accepted forms.

Card V warns against theoretical and practical impatience, dogmatic behavior or lack of direction, dissembling and being bombastic; against unrealistic advice, vindictiveness and utilization of acquired capacities to harm others. It warns against inactivity, indolence in fulfilling tasks, and idleness. It cautions against repressive aspects of rigid orthodoxy and against black magic.

CARD VI (THE LOVER[S])

On the spiritual level, the Lover(s) indicates inner struggle between higher will, wisdom, stability, and passion. The courage to break away from inherited models and preexistent sentimental ties creates the possibility for new life. The Lover(s) also connotes love of beauty, exploration of the domain of feeling in all its breadth and depth, idealism.

On the tangible level, this card indicates attraction, inclination, spiritual and sensual love, freedom of will, choice, sincerity, responsibility, caring for others, marriage, sexual intercourse, the fire of passion and the water of spirituality, flowing forms, and erotic friendships.

Card VI warns against degrading desires, weakness, too much self-indulgence, falling prey to fascination, replacing one dependency with another, addictive habits that become chains. It warns against doubts, oscillations, hesitation and dispersion, but also against precipitation and hasty decisions. It warns against aggression, constraint and violent imposition of one's own will; against marital conflict, perplexity, embarrassment, divorce; against frigidity, impotence, venereal disease; against deterioration of health due to excess or neglect.

CARD VII (THE CHARIOT)

On the spiritual level, the Chariot indicates that the earthly must be mastered through reconciliation and transcendence of the opposites in order to reach higher levels of development; it also denotes the spiritual background of activity; riddle and revelation; the road to uncertainty; wish, will, accomplishment, doubt, confusion, illusion, spiritual victory.

On the tangible level, this card means balance between thinking and feeling, the capacity to mold and shape, receptivity to art and philosophy, creation of an inner and outer harmony of life forms, reliability, determination, emotional tolerance and endurance, tactfulness, politeness, being conciliatory insofar as circumstances warrant. It also denotes outward success due to far-sighted planning as well as speed and precision of execution and organization; reaching a position of command but also a higher spiritual level; spiritual maturity that enables one to take an individual stance, independent of the collective; it means monetary gain through trading and planning; surprising news, unexpected occurrence; verbal skill, the ability to persuade; it means spending or earning, buying or selling, conquest.

Card VII warns against lack of life-planning, of stability or purposiveness, of daring; it warns against lack of constancy of will under increasing difficulties, against negligence, absent-mindedness in execution; against lack of talent, incapacity to react to the unexpected, propaganda, slander. It warns against hanging on rigidly to the habitual and the resulting lack of flexibility in unexpected circumstances; against intolerance, incompetence, quarrelsomeness, bearing grudges, tactless behavior, arrogance, and bragging. Card VII discloses accidents, quarrels, enemies, destruction, and rebellion.

CARD VIII (JUSTICE)

On the spiritual level, Justice represents the order and harmony of things, the link between cause and effect, lawfulness of consequences, original harmony, balance. Sentence is passed without favor or disfavor; the decision may create new goals.

On the tangible level this card denotes understanding of the weight of individual experience, personal justice, authority, impartiality of sentence, lawfulness, method, inexorability of consequences, integrity, incorruptibility. It indicates precise discrimination of the appropriate means to be used, sureness of judgment, capacity for decision making, useful ideas, moderation of judgment, memory, logic, method, observation, precision, caution. It means attraction and repulsion, reward and punishment. It means judge, administrator, executive director, the cunning lawyer who makes the appropriate remark at the right moment, conservative opinion, fear of personal initiative, observation of needful amenities in everyday life and in social interactions, economy.

Card VIII warns against failure to fulfill commitments, overestimation of personal influence, ignorance, incomplete information, unilateral evaluation of a situation, prejudice or identification, injustice, indecision, fickleness. It warns against conventionality and blind faith in authority or routine; against excess; against chicanery, arguments, litigation; against unjust taxation or honoraria, limitation of freedom of movement, hospitals, hypochondria, prison; against going beyond the limits of acceptable behavior.

CARD IX (THE HERMIT)

On the spiritual level, The Hermit represents immanent justice; the germ that contains the intimation of future development; the spiritual master who directs strivings toward a higher goal; meditation in stillness and solitude; the wise old man, the searcher, the introverted; distancing from everyday occurrences; attempts to listen in stillness to the oscillations of energy, being conscious of responsibility.

On the tangible level, this card denotes self-reflection, self-clarification, self-confidence, self-discipline, self-determination; courage, solitude, meditation, silence; insight into the solution of a problem; discovery of a secret; tradition; secret knowledge, study, wisdom, prudence, circumspection, experience, trust in fate; hope, shared joy and shared pain; discretion, reserve, purity, renunciation, counseling dependents or students. He is physician, psychoanalyst, obstetrician.

Card IX warns against misanthropy, taciturnity, exaggeration, isolation, self-contemplation, giving up on oneself, fatalism. It warns against escape into the imaginary, moodiness; against death, loss of all kinds, secret intrigue, fraud, defamation, cupidity, sloth. It warns against litigation, against inappropriate behavior, and against inadequate appreciation of a situation and of the effort needed to remedy it.

CARD X (THE WHEEL OF FORTUNE)

On the spiritual level, The Wheel of Fortune represents the eternal return, impartiality, victory over the ups and downs of existence through serenity. Awareness of fullness and emptiness allows judicious utilization of one's own strengths. It means seed and root, germ and fertilization. It evokes the riddle of inner images and metaphors, external or internal change, new insight due to spontaneous perception. It recalls the decisive instant, fate, good and bad luck.

On the tangible level, this card denotes prudence, determination, necessity. It shows that correct work can be done due to knowledge, will power, courage, discretion, openness toward new approaches, going with changing times, foresight prevailing over materialism and egotism. It indicates that the fleeting quality of life can be mastered through equanimity, relativizing luck, whether deserved or undeserved. It suggests the presence of Spirit, the acuteness that enables one to seize the opportunity at the right moment and profit from the chance given. It stands for confidence, talent of invention and calculation, practical and mechanical gifts, advantages stemming from discoveries, research taking time and place into account, concentration, the capacity to find helping forces, consistency, just decisions. It may express activation of feelings and charm.

Card X warns against overestimation of the intellect or of gain, ignorance of existential necessity; against arrested ego, bragging, presumption, boasting, or faint-hearted despondency; against inconsistency of fate, of the situation; against negligence, insufficient preparation for the task at hand, accepting responsibilities for which one does not measure up; against inadequate undertakings, play with serious matters, plans based on contingency or speculation, lack of decision and precaution; against adventures and time-consuming changes. It warns generally against everything that can adversely influence social and marital relationships, opening of the spirit, and the capacity to experience life fully. It warns against fatal entanglements and effects of heredity, especially the burden of the maternal heritage creating compulsive dependency on the mother in later years.

CARD XI (STRENGTH)

On the spiritual level, Strength represents shining energy, victory of spiritual impulses through recognition and discipline. It means strength of purpose and prudence; when the nature of these powers is not recognized and admitted, they act and develop autonomously. Knowledge confers power without violence—natural authority. It means harmony with nature and with all animals, sexual energy.

On the tangible level, this card stands for vitality, knowledge about power. It emphasizes the importance of psychic and instinctual impulses discovered through analytical work, acceptance or taming by moral courage, force, tranquillity, intrepidity, endurance, and virtue. It depicts an energetic human being who can master inner and outer difficulties. It shows victory of intelligence over brutality and over blind natural forces, a way of relating not only with a partner but also with oneself. It indicates the integration of antagonistic tendencies into a whole. It suggests that a woman must defend her individuality against attack without denying her partner's rights; it shows a woman entrusted with organizational tasks not only as a wife and mother but also as an equal partner. It may mean scientific and industrial success through the application and respect of universal laws.

Card XI warns against wrath, fury, hate, impatience, hesitation; against thoughtlessness and overestimation of one's strength, bragging, sterile revolt against fate. It warns against missing the right moment; against brutality, rudeness, coarseness, cruelty; against pettiness, quarrelsomeness; against repression of sexuality or unbridled liberation, seduction; against perversions. It warns against surgery, against fire, against injustice and the misuse of power. It suggests that badly applied force is destructive.

CARD XII (THE HANGED MAN)

On the spiritual level, the Hanged Man represents the transformation of evil, deliverance through sacrifice. Spiritual powers can be influenced through mediation of sacrificed material demands; however, one should never sacrifice bodily needs because that would result in repression. The Hanged Man represents liberation from instinctive egotism; spiritual recognition; willingness to examine the opposite point of view and to allow resolutions to come to fruition in stillness; giving up worldly success and distractions, habits and attitudes, security and reminiscences.

On the tangible level, this card indicates change, trial, abnegation, renunciation, devotion, sacrifice, dedication to the task without allowing it to dominate us, discipline, mastery of the situation through personal power. It depicts the visionary in us. It represents healing through concentration, strength through remembering. Recognizing that illness has meaning helps one to endure it. It represents knowledge of healing methods and willingness to adopt them.

Card XII warns against escape into ecstasy or numbness, against unrealistic daydreams, utopian plans and desires, illusions, false enthusiasms, unhappy love, overestimating one's own capacities; against indecision, remaining stuck in a theory or satisfied by good intentions alone; against letting time go unutilized, premature resignation, or unwise enthusiasm for the untested; against doubtful projects that can be realized only with outside help; against betrayals and humiliations; against despair, unkept promises, exploitation by and of others; against loss of emotional balance; against material losses, endangered position, monetary uncertainty, social problems, fateful interventions of destiny.

CARD XIII (DEATH)

On the spiritual level, Death means endless evolution, transformation, rebirth. It shows incessant motion that opposes any inactivity. It signifies the Holy Spirit of the Gnostics, the Comforter. It means unselfishness, self-reflection, trial, separation.

On the tangible level this card means destiny, blow of fate, a failure for which we are not responsible. It means sacrifice, turning point, disillusion, loss of affection or hope, renunciation. It indicates liberation through recognition of an unavoidable necessity, mastering a situation through personal power or skill. It denotes broader understanding, selflessness, sacrificial spirit, detachment, liberation from suffering. Death shows uncompromising clarity of judgment, the capacity to renew a deteriorating environment. It means a new area of work, initiation, mastery, heredity.

Card XIII warns against melancholy, inactivity, mourning, senility, alteration, dissolution, separation, self-pity, the incomprehensible. It warns against corruption, immobilizing illness, hospital, prison, or demise; it warns against death or suicide.

CARD XIV (TEMPERANCE)

On the spiritual level, Temperance indicates all-encompassing life revolving in multiple forms, miraculous healing through redirecting vital forces, transformation, new pathways and developments, translating images into ideas, intuition and discipline.

On the tangible level, this card indicates moderation, frugality, abstinence, equanimity, parsimony, cheerfulness, transcendence of human suffering, adaptation, flexibility, health, favorable conditions for prolonging life, leisure, hospitality, the capacity for cooperation.

Card XIV warns against prodigality, indifference, neglect of everyday tasks, unreliability, frivolity, laziness, passivity, choosing the easy way out and letting things go, living only for oneself, overtaxing one's strength, disproportionate demands.

CARD XV (THE DEVIL)

On the spiritual level, the Devil shows the substantial reality of evil, the pull of instincts, cosmic forms as a container of both unfolding and limitation of the breath of life. It depicts the daily routine, the devilish circle of self-defeating unconscious patterns.

On the tangible level, this card connotes vulnerability to demogogic eloquence, suggestibility, dubious endeavors, false assumptions, erroneous information, injustice, and intrigue, revolution, overthrowing governments. It also represents the capacity to bring lower instincts into the service of the good.

Card XV warns against illness, insanity, hysteria; against misguided or precipitated action; against panic, cupidity, perversions, passion, disorder, intemperance in any form; against thirst for vengeance, actions that avoid the light of day, perfidy, gruesome or chaotic impulses, unbridled emotionality, lack of self-knowledge; against blindly adopted moral concepts, partiality, naivete. It warns against compulsive instinctuality and obsessions; against false spiritual pretending, despair, murder, witch-hunts, epidemics, environmental pollution, collective guilt; against temporary success, nervous instability, health problems, repression instead of integration of incompatible psychic contents. This card cancels out or weakens the meaning of other cards. Its reverse position has a more positive meaning than when it occurs upright.

CARD XVI (THE TOWER OF DESTRUCTION)

On the spiritual level, the Tower of Destruction shows that we should not attempt projects that go beyond our powers, but also that we should not be discouraged by failures and tribulations. We must pay attention to plans that cannot be actualized; they may have consequences that cannot be estimated. It is the finger of God raised in warning, to be received in humility, lest it destroy us.

On the tangible level this card means presumptuous pride, shattered hopes, unfortunate results of an endeavor, loss of goods illicitly obtained. It means renewal through destruction, dissolution of solidified structures, of patriarchial powers that have become obsolete.

Card XVI warns against grandiosity, false ambition, lack of faith, intolerance, illness, accident, unexpected difficulties, overtaxing bodily strengths, stress. It warns against theorizing, confusion, mental illness; against unnecessary accumulation of goods, pursuit of success, decadence; against uncleanliness of body and spirit, avidity and exploitation; against presumption; against unacceptable manipulation of organic processes; against revolt as a consequence of difficult life conditions; against sectarianism and religious intolerance. It warns against burdening children with parents' ambitions, driving them one-sidedly to perform, spoiling or neglecting them. It warns against anxiety, self-pity, revolt against fate; against punishment, imprisonment, prison, higher authority.

CARD XVII (THE STAR[S])

On the spiritual level the Star represents immortality, destiny, predetermination, rebirth, beauty, aesthetic ideals, poetry, differentiation between deceptive appearance and true being, creative energy, calm radiation of the living thing, gift instead of sacrifice, hopes, dreams come true, inspiration, eloquence.

On the tangible level, this card signifies artistic gifts, intuition, premonition, astrological prediction, charm, zest for life that maintains the balance between tension and relaxation or between difficulties and pleasures, hope for improvement, anticipation of forthcoming change, confidence, trust, faith in destiny, sensitivity, improvement, tenderness, hedonism, dreams, understanding nature.

Card XVII warns against destruction of existing harmony, frivolity, lack of modesty, constraint, unrealistic romantic ideas, disregard for daily tasks, lack of foresight, leaving warnings unheeded, lack of understanding of the meaning of symbols. It warns against ignorance, busyness and running on empty, lack of inner calm, credulity, instability, negligence. It warns against curiosity, disappointment, resignation; against life limited by materialism; against rash promises; against both levity and pessimism.

CARD XVIII (THE MOON)

On the spiritual level, the Moon represents Maya, the illusions of appearances, the nebulous threshold between the material and the spiritual; also, the uncertainty of human understanding. It shows that emotional or spiritual negative powers can be mastered through intuition or reflection.

On the tangible level, this card indicates the capacity to recognize emotions and to learn to sort them out. It advises that times of rest should be savored. It evokes tests that lead to understanding, examination of conscience, conversion, clairvoyance, imagination, insights. It may mean bodily pain, passion, unrest, sea voyages, wide-ranging detours.

Card XVIII warns against imaginings, moodiness, chaos, superstitions, gullibility, false certainties, slander, laziness of thought processes. It warns against ambiguous situations and material dependency, calculated flattery; against being ambushed, misled, and betrayed; against vain threats, deformation of truth, loss of identity, mental cruelty. It warns against fickleness, using feminine wiles to gain power, against mother fixation. It warns against denial of or falling victim to instinctual forces; against ambiguous formulations, despair, misanthropy, drug addiction, mythologizing technology.

This card may also indicate having reached the lowest point, whether by our own fault or not; appropriate behavior, suggested by the cards that follow, will bring about the upward return.

CARD XIX (THE SUN)

On the spiritual level, the Sun is the primordial light that organizes chaos; it means illumination, enlightenment, the spiritual clarity that dissipates the obscurity of ignorance. The sunlight has healing power, just as love frees from anxiety.

On the tangible level this card symbolizes art, poetry, peace, generosity of heart, friendship, fraternity, harmony. It connotes the clear and penetrating judgment that foresees hidden dangers, the readiness to test and accept new ideas, to respect the individuality of the partner. It means personal radiance, protection, acceptance of the demands of the moment, success in the chosen area of activity, celebrity, but also the unrecognized artist whose concepts are ahead of his or her time. It signifies sincerity, mastery of the body and of its developmental needs, recently renewed courage, marriage, lasting happiness.

Card XIX warns against intellectual arrogance, spiritual sterility, imprecise discrimination, self-centeredness, the incapacity to relate to or too much dependence on the partner, giving up on oneself, vanity, pretention, susceptibility, irascibility. It warns against impracticality and negligence, overlooking or not being able to recognize favorable opportunities; against conflict, blows of fate, bluffing, trying too hard, and unnecessary spending; against false pretenses, overestimating technical discoveries and utilitarian practical thinking; against destruction of the quality of life, and destruction by fire.

CARD XX (JUDGEMENT)

On the spiritual level, Judgment means ultimate reckoning, initiation, inspiration that leads to illumination; the triad body-life-being become conscious; spiritualization of matter, intimacy, courage, readiness; judging one's actions and omissions truthfully, conquering death; alchemical sublimation. The aura of the living is activated during states of meditation. Learned skills are utilized joyfully.

On the tangible level, this card means final achievement, prophetic sight, awakening of higher senses, prediction of the future, recall of past life; it means recognized artistic talent, enthusiasm, piety, healing, liberation, surprise, just judgment, reparation of suffered injustice; it means preacher.

Card XX warns against artificial exaltation, useless chatting, and projects that serve only personal aggrandizement; against self-delusion and false estimation of values; against extravagance, oversolicitation of one's strength, overexcitement, drugs; against lack of decision and delays.

CARD XXI (THE WORLD)

On the spiritual level the World represents fulfillment, initiation, totality, reintegration, rapture, completion, perfection of the universe, mastery of intellectual and psychic forces, as well as mastery of the body. It means compensation for the conscious standpoint, freedom from desire and anxiety, fulfillment of experience and recollection.

On the tangible level, this card signifies completion, success, the happy end of a cycle, favorable environmental conditions, perfection and general validity of knowledge, altruism, love of humankind, inspiration, readiness to sacrifice, contemplation, ecstasy, incorruptible honesty, simplicity, trust, enthusiasm.

Card XXI warns against failure in planning or realization, disregard for intuitions and premonitions, lack of purpose, feeling ambushed or scattered, loss of fortune, putting others down, self-derogation and self-degradation, coming down the social ladder. It warns against external uncontrollable obstacles and high-placed enemies; against extravagance, stubbornness, and blindness.

CARD 0 (THE FOOL)

On the spiritual level the Fool means the eternal, all-encompassing void, equanimity, dissipation of delusion, detachment, love without judging, intuition instead of knowledge, responsibility without power, trust.

On the tangible level, this card means receptivity, giving up resistance and ego-centered willfulness, serenity, cheerfulness, silencing unrest, innocence, mediumistic quality. Only those whose understanding is not limited to the intellectual can comprehend the totality of the meaning of this card.

Card 0 warns against confusing objects with functions, things with phenomena; against madness, mental alienation, misunderstanding, loss of judgment in submitting to the will of others or to occult powers, being easily swayed; against lack of attention, of sensitivity, apathy, moodiness, giving in to crazy ideas, the inability to see and acknowledge one's mistakes; against being stubborn, opinionated, and prejudiced; refusing to and being incapable of understanding. It warns against uncontrolled and unnecessary self-reproach, against a spiritual wasteland and materialism, temptations, adventures, being led astray, aggressive attacks; against psychosomatic complaints; against destruction and unwarranted self-sacrifice.

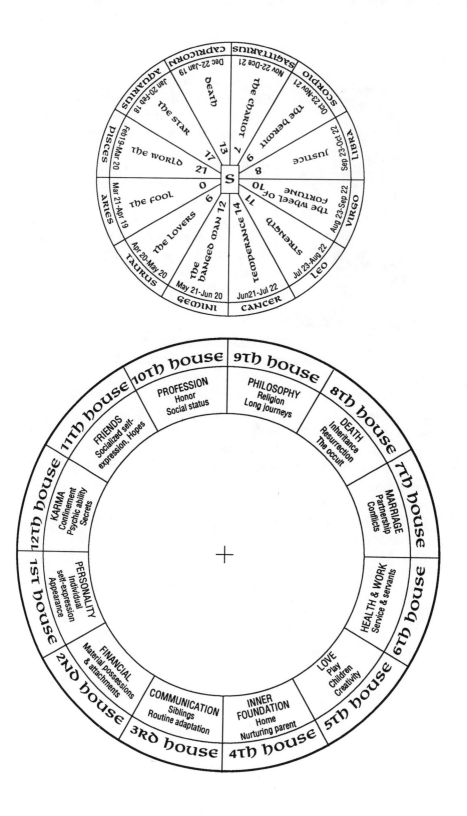

BIBLIOGRAPHY

Anonymous. *The Cloud of Unknowing*. Edited by Evelyn Underhill from the British Museum Ms. Harl. 674. London, John M. Watkins, 1912.

Anonymous. *Meditations on the Tarot: A Journey into Christian Hermeticism*. Amity, NY: Amity House, 1985.

Arroyo, Stephen, *Astrology, Psychology, and the Four Elements*. Sebastapol, CA: CRCS, 1975.

———. *Astrology, Karma, and Transformation*. Sebastapol, CA: CRCS, 1978.

Ashcroft-Novicki, Dolores. *The Shining Paths: An Experimental Journey Through the Tree of Life*. London: Aquarian Press, 1983.

Belmonte, Thomas. "The Trickster and the Sacred Clown," *C. G. Jung and the Humanities*, ed. Karin Barnaby and Pellegrino D'Acierno. Princeton, NJ: Princeton University Press, 1990, pp. 45-66.

Berg, Philip. *Kabbalah for the Laymen*, Vol. 1. Jamaica, NY: Research Centre for Kabbalah, 1986.

Bernoulli, Rudolf. "Zur Symbolik Geometrischer Figuren und Zahlen," *Ostwestliche Symbolik und Seelenführung*. 1934 Eranos Jahrbuch, pp. 369-415. Zürick: Rhein Verlag, 1935.

———. "Spiritual Development as Reflected in Alchemy and Related Disciplines," *Spiritual Disciplines*. Papers from the Eranos Yearbooks, Bollingen Series XXX/4, pp. 305-340. Princeton NJ: Princeton University Press, 1970.

Bias, Clifford. *The Way Back: A New Age Approach to the Western Mystery Tradition*. York Beach, ME: Samuel Weiser, 1985.

Boehme, Jacob. *The Key*, trans. William Law. Grand Rapids, MI: Phanes Press, 1991.

Burt, Kathleen. *Archetypes of the Zodiac*. St. Paul, MN: Llewellyn Publications, 1988.,

Butler, Bill. *The Definitive Tarot*. London: Rider & Co. 1975.

Campbell, Joseph. *The Mythic Image*. Bollingen Series C. Princeton, NJ: Princeton University Press, 1974.

Campbell, Joseph and Bill Moyers. *The Power of Myth*. New York: Doubleday, 1988.

Campbell, Joseph and Richard Roberts. *Tarot Revelations*. San Anselmo, CA: Vernal Equinox Press, 1979.

Case, Paul Foster. *The Book of Tokens: Tarot Meditations*. Los Angeles: Builders of the Adytum Press, 1968.

———. *The Tarot: A Key to the Wisdom of the Ages*. Richmond, VA: Macoy Publications, 1975.

Cavendish, Richard. *The Tarot*. New York: Crescent Books, 1986.

Cook, Roger. *The Tree of Life: Image for the Cosmos*. New York: Thames & Hudson, 1974.

Crowley, Aleister. *Tarot Divination*. York Beach, ME: Samuel Weiser, 1976.

Denning, Melita and Osborne Phillips. *The Magick of the Tarot: How to Read and Shape Your Future*. St. Paul, MN: Llewellyn Publications. 1973.

Doane, Doris Chase and King Keyes. *How to Read Tarot Cards*. New York: Barnes & Noble, 1979.

Douglas, Alfred. *The Tarot: The Origins, Meaning, and Uses of the Cards*. New York: Penguin Books, 1983.

Dummett, Michael. *The Visconti-Sforza Tarot Cards*. New York: Braziller, 1986.

Edinger, Edward. *Ego and Archetype*. New York: Penguin Books, 1980.

———. *Anatomy of the Psyche: Alchemical Symbolism in Psychotherapy*. La Salle, IL: Open Court, 1985.

Eliot, T. S. *Four Quartets*. New York: Harcourt Brace, 1943.

Epstein, Perle. *Kabbalah: The Way of the Jewish Mystic*. Boston: Shambhala, 1988.

Fairfield, Gail. *Choice-Centered Tarot*. Seattle, WA: Choices, 1984.

Fortune, Dion. *The Mystical Qabalah*. York Beach, ME: Samuel Weiser, 1988.

von Franz, Marie-Louise. *Aurora Consurgens: A Document Attributed to Thomas Aquinas on the Problem of Opposites in Alchemy*. New York: Bollingen, 1966.

———. *Alchemy: An Introduction to the Symbolism and the Psychology*. Toronto: Inner City Books, 1980.

Garin, Eugenio. *Astrology in the Renaissance: The Zodiac of Life*. London: Routledge & Kegan Paul, 1983.

Gettings, Fred. *The Book of Tarot*. London: Triune Books, 1973.

Godwin, Malcom. *Angels: An Endangered Species*. London: Labyrinth; and New York: Simon & Schuster, 1990.

Golowin, Sergius. *The World of the Tarot: The Gypsy Method of Reading the Tarot*. York Beach, ME: Samuel Weiser, 1988.

Gray, Eden. *Mastering the Tarot: Basic Lessons in an Ancient Mystic Art*. New York: Crown, 1971.

Greene, Liz. *The Outer Planets and Their Cycles: The Astrology of the Collective*. Sebastapol, CA: CRCS, 1983.

———. *The Astrology of Fate*. York Beach, ME: Samuel Weiser, 1984.

Greer, Mary. *Tarot for Your Self*. North Hollywood, CA: Newcastle, 1984.

Greer, Mary and Rachel Pollack, eds. *New Thoughts on Tarot: Transcripts from the First International Newcastle Tarot Symposium*. North Hollywood, CA: Newcastle, 1989.

Grossinger, Richard, ed. *The Alchemical Tradition in the Late Twentieth Century*. Berkeley, CA: North Atlantic Books, 1983.

Guggenbühl-Craig, Adolf. *Power in the Helping Professions*. Dallas, TX: Spring Publications, 1982.

Haich, Elizabeth. *Tarot: Die Zweiundzwanzig Bewusstseinsstufen des Menschen*. München und Engleberg: Drei Eichen Verlag, 1972; Also published as *Wisdom of the Tarot*. Santa Fe, NM: Aurora Press, 1983.

Halevi, Z'ev ben Shimon.*Tree of Life: An Introduction to the Kabbalah*. London: Rider, 1972. Available in the United States as *Introduction to the Cabala*, published by Samuel Weiser; available as *Tree of Life* from Gateways, Bath, England.

———. *The Work of the Kabbalist*. York Beach, ME: Samuel Weiser, 1985; and Bath, England: Gateways, 1984.

———. *Kabbalah: Tradition of Hidden Knowledge*. London: Thames & Hudson, 1985. Written as Warren Kenton.

———. *The Way of Kabbalah*. York Beach, ME: Samuel Weiser, 1991; and Bath, England: Gateways, 1991.

Hand, Robert. *Horoscope Symbols*. Atglen, PA: Whitford Press, 1981.

Harding, M. Esther. "A Short Review of Dr. Jung's Article: Redemption Ideas in Alchemy," Lecture. The Analytical Psychology Club of New York: October, 1937.

———. *Woman's Mysteries: Ancient and Modern*. Boston: Shambhala, 1990.

Harrison, Jane. *Themis*. London: Merlin Press, 1977.

Hasbrouck, Muriel Bruce. *Tarot and Astrology: The Pursuit of Destiny*. Rochester, VT: Destiny Books, 1989.

Hillman, James. "The Therapeutic Value of Chemical Language," *Method of Treatment in Analytic Psychology*, ed. Jan Baker. Stuttgart: Bonz Verlag, 1980, pp. 118-126.

———. "Salt: A Chapter in Alchemical Psychology," *Images of the Untouched*, ed. Joanne Stroud and Gail Thomas. Dallas, TX: Spring, 1982, pp. 111-137.

Hinton, Ladson W. "Fools, Foolishness, and Feeling Foolish," *Psychological Perspectives*, Vol. 12, No. 2, 1981, pp. 43-51.

Hoeller, Stephan. *The Royal Road: A Manual of Kabbalistic Meditations on the Tarot*. Wheaton, IL: Quest Publications, 1980.

Hurwitz, Siegmund. "Psychological Aspects in Early Hasidic Literature," *Timeless Documents of the Soul*. Evanston, IL: Northwestern University, 1968, pp. 151-239.

Innes, Brian. *The Tarot: How to Use and Interpret the Cards*. New York: Crescent Books, 1987.

Johnson, Robert A. *Owning Your Own Shadow: Understanding the Dark Side of the Psyche*. San Francisco: Harper Collins, 1991.

Jung, Carl Gustav. *The Collected Works*, Vol. I-XX, trans. R. F. C. Hull, ed. H. Read, M. Fordham, G. Adler, and Wm. McGuire. Bollingen Series XX, Princeton, NJ: Princeton University Press, 1953-1979.

———. *C. G. Jung Speaks*. Edited by William McGuire & R. F. C. Hull. Princeton, NJ: Princeton University Press, 1977.

———. *Letters*, Vol. I and II, ed. Gerhard Adler and Aniela Jaffé. Princeton, NJ: Princeton University Press, 1975.

———. *Memories, Dreams, Reflections*, ed. Aniela Jaffé. New York: Random House, 1989.

Kaplan, Aryeh. *Sefer Yetzirah: In Theory and Practice*. York Beach, ME: Samuel Weiser, 1990.

Kaplan, Stuart. *Tarot Classic*. Stamford, CT: U. S. Games Systems, 1972, also available in England as *The Classical Tarot* by Aquarian Press, 1980.

———. *The Encyclopedia of Tarot*, Vol. I-III. Stamford, CT: U. S. Game Systems, 1988.

Kast, Verena. *The Dynamics of Symbols: Fundamentals of Jungian Psychotherapy*. New York: From International, 1992.

Kenton, Warren. *Astrology: The Celestial Mirror*. London & New York: Thames & Hudson, 1974.

Klossowski de Rola, Stanislas. *Alchemy: The Secret Art*. London and New York: Thames & Hudson, 1973.

Knapp, Bettina. "Nachman: The Master of Prayer," *The Jungian Approach to Literature*. Evansville, IL: Southern Illinois Press, 1984, pp. 188-226.

Knight, Gareth. *A Practical Guide to Qabalistic Symbolism*. York Beach, ME: Samuel Weiser, 1988.

Lamney, Wm. C. *Karmic Tarot: A New System for Finding and Following Your Life Path*. North Hollywood, CA: Newcastle, 1988.

LeMieux, David. *Forbidden Images: The Secrets of the Tarot*. New York: Barnes & Noble, 1985.

MacMonnies-Hazard, Berthe. "The Tarot and the Accomplishment of the Great Work." *Spring*, 1942, pp. 31-41.

Mann, A. T. *The Mandala Astrological Tarot*. San Francisco: HarperCollins, 1987.

Marks, Tracy. *The Astrology of Self-Discovery*. Sebastapol, CA: CRCS, 1985.

McLean, Adam. *The Alchemical Mandala: A Survey of the Mandala in the Western Esoteric Traditions*. Grand Rapids, MI: Phanes, 1989.

———. *A Commentary on the Mutus Liber*. Grand Rapids, MI: Phanes Press, 1991.

Montalban, Madeline. *The Prediction Book of the Tarot*. London: Blandford Press, 1983.

Moon, Sheila: *Dreams of a Woman*. Boston: Sigo Press, 1983.

Mouni, Sadhu. *The Tarot: A Contemporary Course of the Quintessence of Hermetic Occultism*. London: Allen and Unwin, 1968.

Neumann, Erich. "On the Moon and Matriarchal Consciousness." *Spring*, 1954, pp. 83-100.

———. *The Great Mother*. Bollingen Series XLVII, Princeton, NJ: Princeton University Press, 1955.

———. *The Origins and History of Consciousness*. Bollingen Series XLII, Princeton, NJ: Princeton University Press, 1973.

Newman, Kenneth. *The Tarot: A Myth of Male Initiation.*. New York: Quadrant Monograph, C. G. Jung Foundation, 1983. (Distributed to the trade by Samuel Weiser, Box 612, York Beach, ME 03910.)

Nichols, Sallie. *Jung and the Tarot: An Archetypal Journey*, York Beach, ME: Samuel Weiser, 1980.

Noble, Vicky. *Motherpeace: A Way to the Goddess through Myth, Art, and Tarot*. San Francisco: HarperCollins, 1983.

Ouspensky, P. D. *The Symbolism of the Tarot: Philosophy of Occultism in Pictures and Numbers*. New York: Dover, 1976.

Papus. *The Tarot of the Bohemians*. New York: Samuel Weiser, 1971; Reprint: Los Angeles: Wilshire Publications, 1978.

Paterson, Helena and Courtney Davis. *The Celtic Tarot*. London: Aquarian Press, 1990.

Peach, Emily. *The Tarot Workbook*. London: Aquarian, 1984.

Pennick, Nigel. *Magical Alphabets: The Secret and Significance of Ancient Scripts*. York Beach, ME: Samuel Weiser, 1992.

Perera, Sylvia. *Descent to the Goddess: A Way of Initiation for Women*. Toronto: Inner City Books, 1981.

Poncé, Charles. *The Game of Wizards: Psyche, Science, and Symbol in the Occult*. London: Penguin Books, 1975.

———. *Kabbalah: An Introduction and Illumination for the World of Today*. Wheaton, IL: Quest Books, 1986.

———. *Working the Soul*. Berkeley, CA: North Atlantic Books, 1988.

Quispel, Gilles. "Gnosis and Culture," *C. G. Jung and the Humanities*, ed. Karin Barnaby and Pellegrino D'Acierno. Princeton, NJ: Princeton University Press, 1990, pp. 24-35.

Rilke, Rainer Maria. *Selected Poems*, trans. C. F. MacIntyre. Berkeley, CA: University of California Press, 1956.

———. *Selected Poems*, trans. Robert Bly. New York: HarperCollins, 1981.

———. *The Sonnets to Orpheus*, trans. Leslie Norris and Alan Keele. Columbia, SC: Camden House, 1989.

Roberts, Richard. *The Original Tarot and You*. San Anselmo, CA: Vernal Equinox Press, 1971.

Scholem, Gershom. "Kabbalah und Mythus," *Der Mensch und die Mythische Welt*. 1949 Eranos Jahrbuch, Vol. XVII, pp. 287-344. Zürich: Rhein Verlag, 1950.

———. *Kabbalah*. Jerusalem, Israel: Keter, 1974; and New York: Random House, 1978.

Schwartz-Salant, Nathan. *The Borderline Personality: Vision and Healing*. Wilmette, IL: Chiron, 1988.

Settle, Mary Lee. *Charley Bland*. New York: Farrar, Straus & Giroux, 1989.

Sharman-Burke, Juliet. *The Complete Book of Tarot*. New York: St. Martin's, 1986.

Sharman-Burke, Juliet and Liz Greene. *The Mythic Tarot: A New Approach to the Tarot Cards*. New York: Simon & Schuster, 1986.

Silberer, Herbert. *Hidden Symbolism of Alchemy and the Occult Arts*. New York: Dover, 1971.

Simon, Sylvie. *The Tarot: In Art, Mysticism, and Divination*. New York: Crescent Books, 1991.

Spector, Richard. "Strategic Tarot." *Networker*, 1986, pp. 36-37, 68-69.

Steiner-Geringer, Mary. *Tarot als Selbsterfahrung*. Köln: Diedrich, 1985.

Stuart, Micheline. *The Tarot: Path to Self-Development*. Boston: Shambhala, 1977.

Suarès, Carlo. *The Cabala Trilogy*. Boston: Shambhala, 1985.

Sucher, Willi. "The Zodiac of Constellations," *Star Rhythms*, ed. William Lonsdale. Richmond, CA: North Atlantic, 1982.

Thierens, A. E. *Astrology and the Tarot*. North Hollywood, CA: Newcastle, 1975.

Thompson, C. J. S. *The Lure and the Romance of Alchemy: A History of the Secret Link Between Magic and Science*. New York: Bell, 1990.

Tillich, Paul. *The Courage to Be*. New Haven, CT: Yale University Press, 1952.

Trismosin, Solomon. *Splendor Solis*, trans. Joscelyn Godwin. Grand Rapids, MI: Phanes Press, 1991.

Valentinus, Basilus. "The Triumphal Chariot of Antimony," *The Alchemical Tradition in the Late Twentieth Century*, ed. Richard Grossinger. Berkeley, CA: North Atlantic, 1983, pp. 34-47.

Waite, Arthur Edward. *The Hermetic Museum*. York Beach, ME: Samuel Weiser Reprint, 1973, 1991.

———. *The Secret Tradition in Alchemy: Its Development and Records*. New York: Knopf, 1926.

———. *The Pictorial Key to the Tarot*. York Beach, ME: Samuel Weiser, 1975.

Walker, Barbara. *The Secrets of the Tarot: Origins, History, and Symbolism*. San Francisco: HarperCollins, 1984.

Wang, Robert. *An Introduction to the Golden Dawn Tarot*. York Beach, ME: Samuel Weiser, 1978.

———. *The Qabalistic Tarot: A Textbook of Mystical Philosophy*. York Beach, ME: Samuel Weiser, 1983.

———. *Tarot Psychology*. Neuhausen, Switzerland: Urania Verlag, 1988.

Whitney, Elizabeth. "Tarok, Tarot, or Taroc." *Spring*, 1942, pp. 13-40.

Wilhelm, Richard (trans.). *The I Ching* or *Book of Changes*. London: Routledge & Kegan Paul, 1978.

Wirth, Oswald. *Introduction à l'étude du Tarot*. Paris: Le Symbolisme, 1931. Also published in English as *Introduction to the Study of the Tarot*, York Beach, ME: Samuel Weiser, 1980.

———. *The Tarot of the Magicians: A Guide to the Symbolism and Applications of the Wirth Tarot Deck by Its Designer*. York Beach, ME: Samuel Weiser, 1990.

Wolff, Toni. *Structural Forms of the Feminine Psyche*. Zürich: C. G. Jung Institute Students Association (private printing), 1958.

Zabriskie, Beverly. "The Feminine: Pre- and Post-Jungian," C. G. *Jung and the Humanities*, ed. Karin Barnaby and Pellegrino D'Acierno. Princeton, NJ: Princeton University Press, 1990, pp. 267-278.

Zohar. Tr. Maurice Simon & Paul Levertoff. New York: Soncino Press, 1934.

INDEX

Dr. Irene Gad received her M.D. from the Medical
School in Bucharest, Romania, and her Master of Arts in
Psychology from Denver University. She has taught
experimental psychology and human sexuality at the
university level and has published numerous articles
in her field. In 1980 she started analytic training in
Zurich, Switzerland at the C. G. Jung Institute. She is
currently a certified Jungian psychoanalyst in private
practice in the Washington, D.C. area.